MARKETING AND DISTRIBUTION

The Authors

RALPH E. MASON is chairman of the Department of Business-Distributive Education and Office Administration at Indiana State University. Dr. Mason began his career in business and distributive education in 1940 in the public schools of Illinois. He worked in several school systems, first as a coordinator of secondary distributive education, then as a director of adult education, and finally as a director of vocational education. He later joined the staff of the University of Illinois as one of the state's first teacher educators in distributive education. Dr. Mason is former president of the Council for Distributive Teacher Education. He has contributed much to the growth of marketing and distributive education through his writings, which include several popular professional books.

PATRICIA MINK RATH is currently a marketing and career education consultant to schools and businesses in Winnetka, Illinois. She also serves on the board of several state and local educational organizations. Mrs. Rath was formerly a high school teacher-coordinator and an instructor for adult- and teacher-education programs in distributive education. She has also been a state supervisor of business and distributive education and president of the National Association of State Supervisors of Distributive Education. Mrs. Rath has been a retailing executive and is the author of several widely used instructional materials.

HERBERT L. ROSS is a professor of business and distributive education at Indiana State University. In this capacity, he serves as a teacher educator in distributive education and a teacher of marketing. Dr. Ross has had extensive experience as a high school teacher-coordinator of distributive education. He also has had experience in several types of marketing businesses and is presently a director of a corporation that owns and franchises motels. Dr. Ross is a former president of the Illinois Business Education Association and is active in many professional organizations, including the American Marketing Association, the National Business Education Association, and the Council for Distributive Teacher Education.

The Consultants

MARY V. MARKS is program specialist for teacher and leadership education in the Curriculum Development Branch of the Center for Occupational and Adult Education, Office of Education, U.S. Department of Health, Education and Welfare. She has been employed in the retailing field and has held a variety of positions in distributive education, including high school teacher-coordinator, head of the Distributive Education Department at Richmond Professional Institute (now Virginia Commonwealth University), and most recently, program specialist for distributive education in the Office of Education. Miss Marks has made many contributions to her field both as a consultant and as an author.

PETER G. HAINES is a professor of secondary education and curriculum at Michigan State University. His assignments include teaching and conducting research in vocational education and serving as program leader for business and distributive education. He was formerly director of the Research and Development Program in Vocational-Technical Education. Dr. Haines has had extensive experience as a teacher of distributive education and marketing. He has been president of the Michigan Business Education Association and the Council for Distributive Teacher Education. He is a frequent contributor to professional publications and has appeared at teacher workshops, seminars, and conferences throughout the United States.

marketing and distribution
second edition

Ralph E. Mason
Patricia Mink Rath
Herbert L. Ross

Consultants

Mary V. Marks and Peter G. Haines

Gregg and Community College Division
McGraw-Hill Book Company
New York • St. Louis • Dallas • San Francisco • Düsseldorf • Johannesburg
Kuala Lumpur • London • Mexico • Montreal • New Delhi • Panama • Paris
Rio de Janeiro • São Paulo • Singapore • Sydney • Tokyo • Toronto

Sponsoring Editor	William K. Fallon
Editing Manager	Toby Uger
Editing Supervisors	Carole Chatfield and Joretta Wright
Production Supervisor	Richard Jacobson
Art Supervisor	Charles A. Carson
Designer	Kay Wanous
Illustrator	Ari Haas/*Flex, Inc.*

Illustrations on Unit Opening Pages

Pages X-1, courtesy *National Petroleum News.* Pages 46-47, Editorial Photocolor Archives, Inc. Pages 98-99, courtesy Fruehauf Div., Fruehauf Corp. Pages 120-121, courtesy International Harvester. Pages 160-161, courtesy Backroads Touring Co., Inc. Pages 234-235, courtesy Food Fair Stores, Inc. Pages 268-269, courtesy J. C. Penney. Pages 318-319, photograph by Guy Gillette. Pages 436-437, courtesy American Express Card Division. Pages 458-459, courtesy The Service Bureau Corp. Pages 514-515, courtesy DECA—Distributive Education Clubs of America.

Library of Congress Cataloging in Publication Data
Mason, Ralph E.
    Marketing and distribution.
    1. Marketing. I. Rath, Patricia Mink, joint author. II. Ross, Herbert L., date.   joint author. III. Title.
HF5415.M3324   1974   658.8   73-2826
ISBN 0-07-040690-1

Marketing and Distribution, Second Edition

Copyright © 1974, 1968 by McGraw-Hill, Inc. All Rights Reserved. Printed in the United States of America. No part of this publication may be reproduced, stored in a retrieval system, or transmitted, in any form or by any means, electronic, mechanical, photocopying, recording, or otherwise, without the prior written permission of the publisher.

 23456789 KPKP 7 3 2 1 0 9 8 7 6 5 4

Preface

One of the major goals of career education is to give every student a salable skill upon exit from school. This is and always has been one of the primary objectives of distributive education. In fact, there are few established areas of study in which so many of the goals of career education are embodied as firmly as they are in DE.

Today the training of people who are planning to enter the marketing field is more important than ever. The problems and interests of the American consumer are receiving long-overdue attention in the form of government legislation and consumer education. The consumer of the '70s is asking questions about the quality of products, the nutritional value of foods, and the reasons for pricing policies. The marketer must be able to answer such questions intelligently and honestly.

In addition, the shift of emphasis from a production orientation to a marketing orientation continues in American business. Instead of making a product and then trying to sell it, the modern manufacturer first finds out what the consumer wants and then produces it. Thus, the world of marketing has become more complex and therefore more challenging and more interesting.

OBJECTIVES

Marketing and Distribution, Second Edition, is a basic text for distributive education programs that prepare people to meet the challenges of modern marketing. In an age when professionalism in this field is required increasingly, the need for qualified people with marketing skills, judgment, and communicative abilities is quite apparent. This text is designed to teach the students about the world of marketing logically and systematically while motivating them to develop the abilities necessary to enter the field and move ahead in it.

The book presents all areas of marketing and discusses various marketing jobs without overemphasizing any single activity. Students in cooperative programs will find many specific applications in the book to make their work and career objectives more meaningful. They will also find many practical problems and projects to increase their general understanding and make them more aware of available jobs.

ORGANIZATION

The book is divided into 12 units, which are subdivided into 45 parts. Each part is a self-contained learning experience complete with performance goals and correlated activities to help students use the book to its full advantage.

Unit One establishes the marketing course in an economic setting. The examples and illustrations firmly tie in the theory of marketing with a familiar home, school, and community environment. Units Two, Three, and Four advance the students' understanding of different markets. The students are first introduced to the consumer market and then to the industrial, farm, and international markets.

Unit Five introduces the students to marketing channels. Retail merchandising is highlighted, but not to the exclusion of other kinds of marketing middlemen. Units Six through Eleven cover the steps in the marketing process, from marketing research, product planning, and physical distribution to promotion, customer services, and marketing management. Unit Twelve, the concluding unit, helps the students set their sights for the jobs they want and for more specialized study in marketing.

Each of the 45 parts of the textbook concludes with a complete set of student activities. First, the students are asked to define key marketing terms italicized in the text. Next comes a series of discussion questions. Finally, there are two marketing problems and a project. Thus, the book contains a total of 90 problems and 45 projects, each closely correlated with the subject matter and performance goals of the part. The key marketing terms highlighted throughout the text are also listed in a handy glossary at the end of the book.

SUPPORTING MATERIALS

The *Project Activity Guide for Marketing and Distribution, Second Edition*, enriches and extends the learning experience. Each part opens with a marketing vocabulary builder and a series of quick-check questions. Following these are two problems and a project with accompanying forms. Finally, there is a unique problem that combines human relations with marketing and asks the students to make an important decision.

The *Teacher's Manual and Key for Marketing and Distribution, Second Edition*, contains solutions to the student activities in both the textbook and the guide. It also contains a wealth of helpful suggestions for organizing the course and teaching it most effectively. Also included is a complete set of objective tests with answers.

ACKNOWLEDGMENTS

The authors are grateful to the many teachers and businessmen who have given them endorsement, encouragement, and helpful suggestions. Special appreciation is due to The American Association of Advertising Agencies, The American Marketing Association, Levi Strauss & Company, and The Ford Motor Company for their assistance in the preparation of this book.

Ralph E. Mason
Patricia Mink Rath
Herbert L. Ross

Contents

UNIT 1 / The World of Marketing

1	Marketing Is All Around You	2
2	Marketing Is Jobs	10
3	The Economic Climate of Marketing	23
4	The Benefits of Marketing	36

UNIT 2 / The Consumer Market

5	The Changing Consumer Market	48
6	Market Segmentation	60
7	Customer Buying Behavior	72
8	Customer Buying Patterns	85

UNIT 3 / The Industrial Market

9	Industrial Goods and Markets	100
10	Marketing Industrial Goods	109

UNIT 4 / Special Markets

11	Marketing Farm Products	122
12	International Marketing	135
13	The Marketing of Services	149

UNIT 5 / Marketing Channels

14	Channels of Distribution	162
15	The Retailing Business	170
16	Types of Retail Stores	179
17	Problems and Opportunities for the Retailer	194
18	The Wholesaling Business	206
19	Selecting Channels of Distribution	217

UNIT 6 / Marketing Research

20	The Importance of Marketing Research	236
21	Collecting and Analyzing Data	245
22	Preparing the Research Report	257

UNIT 7 / The Product

23	Product Planning	270
24	Brand Names and Trademarks	284
25	Packaging and Labeling	297
26	Pricing the Product	308

UNIT 8 / Physical Distribution

27	Transporting the Goods	320
28	Warehousing the Goods	331

UNIT 9 / Promotion and Selling

29	The Elements of Promotion	342
30	The World of Advertising	352

UNIT 9 / Promotion and Selling (Continued)

31	Advertising Media	365
32	Sales Promotion and Visual Merchandising	377
33	Publicity and Public Relations	388
34	The Importance of Personal Selling	399
35	Principles of Effective Selling	409
36	Planning the Promotion Campaign	423

UNIT 10 / Customer Services

37	Credit as a Customer Service	438
38	Other Customer Services	449

UNIT 11 / Marketing Management

39	Organization for Marketing	460
40	Financing a Marketing Business	469
41	Reducing Marketing Risks	481
42	Financial Management	491
43	Systems and Uses of Data Processing	503

UNIT 12 / Your Career in Marketing

44	Getting a Job	516
45	Working at Your Job	529

GLOSSARY 540

INDEX 554

The World of Marketing

UNIT 1

Marketing Is All Around You

YOUR GOALS

1. Given a list of businesses, such as a part of the Yellow Pages, distinguish between those that market goods and those that market services. Indicate also those businesses that provide both goods and services.
2. On a field trip through your local business community, identify and classify the marketing activities that you find.

Marketing is all around you. You are surrounded by stores and other businesses that carry products or offer services. "Products" are goods grown or manufactured and available for sale. "Services" are benefits or satisfactions that improve the user's personal appearance, health, or comfort or give him peace of mind. Getting these products from farms and factories to the retail establishments where people can buy them involves many activities, such as selling, advertising, marketing research, transportation, and product planning. These activities make up the world of marketing—a world of people, products, action, and ideas.

To prove the statement "Marketing is all around you," you need only take a quick imaginary tour of the community you live in.

2 / Unit 1 / The World of Marketing

MARKETING IS STORES AND OTHER BUSINESSES

Your first glimpse of marketing on your imaginary tour may be a store that sells food. It could be a small grocery store on the corner of your block, or it could be a large supermarket. Of course, these are not the only places that sell food. There are also meat markets, bakeries, delicatessens, and, if you live in the country, roadside fruit stands. Some stores feature one special kind of food, such as health foods, cheeses, or barbecued chicken.

As you continue your tour, you are sure to see many stores that deal in home furnishings, for example, lamp shops, furniture stores, antique shops, appliance stores, fabric stores, china shops, radio and television centers, and carpeting and floor-covering establishments.

Other stores you are likely to see are at least one department store and stores specializing in articles such as shoes, jewelry, sporting goods, auto supplies, stationery, flowers, books, luggage, toys, phonograph records, gifts, and clothing.

You may also see establishments that sell both products and services. Service stations, for example, sell not only gasoline, oil, and other products

People may choose from a variety of businesses to satisfy their needs and wants.

but also lubrication and repair services. And you will surely come across restaurants and snack bars that provide food and food service.

As your tour progresses, you may notice places that sell mainly services. These include banks, car-rental agencies, shoe-repair shops, upholstery shops, travel agencies, beauty salons, barbershops, hotels, dry cleaners, movie theaters, bowling alleys, skating rinks, amusement parks, laundries, and parking lots.

So far we have noted some of the establishments that are engaged in marketing. But marketing consists of more than just stores and other places of business; it is activities. Marketing is advertising, promotion, selling, delivery service, customer services—all the activities that take place to put the goods and services you want and need in your hands.

MARKETING IS ADVERTISING

As you continue touring your community, the billboards on highways or streets may encourage you to "Fly the friendly skies of United" or ask, "Wouldn't you really rather have a Buick?" Large neon signs will flash above stores, and attractive displays in store windows will invite you to stop. Splashed across supermarket fronts will be huge posters proclaiming the specials of the day. If you turn on your car radio, you are sure to hear the announcer tell you why you should buy a certain product or service. Step inside a large air terminal and you are likely to see a display of a new car, revolving under a spotlight that shows its features to best advantage. Drive back to town and you may see a new car-wash business, with a huge sign "Grand Opening Today—Half Price," and many cars lined up to take advantage of the bargain. All kinds of advertising and promotion are an essential part of marketing.

MARKETING IS SERVICES

Other examples of marketing you will probably see on your tour are trucks delivering products such as new clothes dryers, bedroom furniture, and lawn mowers to the homes of buyers. Other trucks may be parked near retail stores, unloading carpets, hardware equipment, television sets, and skis. Still others, displaying signs such as "Vienna Pastry Shop," "Marco Brothers TV," "Berger Florists," and "Lon's Cantonese Kitchen," may be delivering merchandise to various homes.

No doubt you will see many parking lots on your tour. Some charge a fee for their services. Parking space provided by retail stores, however, is usually free to customers. At some stores, you may see employees helping customers load their cars with the merchandise they have just purchased. These are only a few examples of the services that are a part of marketing.

MARKETING IS PEOPLE

People are involved in marketing in many ways. They may be salespeople in department stores, cashier-checkers in supermarkets, countermen in lumberyards, ticket sellers in movie theaters, or service-station attendants. These people are directly involved in marketing. Many others whom you may not see are also a part of marketing. This group includes receiving clerks in a large store, designers of window displays, artists preparing posters, copywriters preparing newspaper advertisements, and so on.

MARKETING IS MANY THINGS

As you go on with your tour, you will see some businesses that sell goods mainly to other firms. These include steel mills, refineries, foundries, manufacturing and processing plants, and the sales offices of companies such as Control Data Corporation (CDC) and International Harvester (IH). Almost every town has one or more businesses specializing in providing services for other companies. Such businesses include advertising agencies, warehouses, transportation companies (such as Railway Express and United Parcel), accounting firms, and even management consulting companies.

What else can you see on your tour that is related to marketing? You might see one or more of the following:

- Three children ordering sodas at a lunch counter.
- A family looking at used cars.
- A man cashing a check at a bank.
- Two women looking at a travel poster.
- A bookstore owner changing a window display.
- Two women modeling coats for a fashion photographer.
- A truck driver carrying cases of soft drinks into a supermarket.
- A salesman demonstrating a photocopier to a real estate agent.
- A pharmacist ordering medical supplies from a salesman.

Yes, marketing is all around you. Marketing exists wherever goods or services are sold. On your imaginary tour you saw many marketing activities— selling, advertising, delivery, and services. These are the marketing activities that everyone sees. But you will learn that these activities represent only the

Courtesy N.Y. Convention & Visitors Bureau

Window-shopping is a popular pastime. How is it related to marketing?

later stages of marketing. Marketing begins long before any merchandise can be sold and delivered. In later units you will learn about the other activities that make up this exciting field.

MARKETING DEFINED

Leafing through the Yellow Pages of your home telephone directory will give you an idea of the vastness of marketing in the United States. Nearly every person or firm listed is engaged in marketing. Multiply the hundreds or perhaps thousands of listings by the thousands of communities throughout the country and you will realize the vastness of the marketing field.

But your picture of marketing would be incomplete if you thought that marketing consists only of businesses serving local communities. A very important part of marketing is made up of large firms, such as automobile manufacturers, whose goods and services are sold nationwide.

Now let us try to define marketing. Although marketing is sometimes called distribution, the terms actually have different meanings. *Marketing* is the sum total of the planning, pricing, promotion, and distribution activities that take place in order to get goods or services from the producer to the consumer. *Distribution* is the total process of moving, handling, and storing goods on the way from the producer to the consumer.

YOU ARE A PART OF MARKETING

When you go to one of the stores in your community to buy something—a can of soup, a ball-point pen, a phonograph needle, or a magazine—you have taken the last step in a vast and complicated marketing process. Business has done a great deal of planning and has spent huge sums of money to get you to take that important step. There is hardly anything you do that does not put you in touch with marketing or influence marketing activities. You participate in marketing when you get a haircut, ride a bus, or cash a check. You influence marketing when you phone a friend, buy a record, or order a hamburger.

Every business that has a product or service to sell considers you and other consumers the center of its world. A *consumer* is anyone who uses products or services. Consumers may be individuals like you or institutions, such as schools, businesses, and governments. A *customer* is anyone who buys products or services. Often the customer and the consumer are the same. If you purchased the pencils and paper you are using, you are both customer and consumer. Sometimes, however, the customer and the consumer are separate persons. When a mother buys baby food and infants' clothing, she is the customer, but her children are the consumers.

Both the customer and the consumer are important in marketing. In fact, business has both in mind from the time a product is designed to the time it is sold. For example, a great deal of automobile advertising is directed to women. Although most actual car buying is done by men, wives often help select the car. Thus business must know what consumers as well as customers want, for even when consumers do not do the buying, they influence it.

As a potential worker in marketing, and also as a consumer and customer, you have a most important role to play. Never have the opportunities been so plentiful for those who want to work in marketing, and never has the field been more dynamic. "Dynamic" means energetic, active, forceful, changing — and there is no better term to describe marketing!

The customer and the consumer seem pleased with this product. Satisfying both is important in marketing.

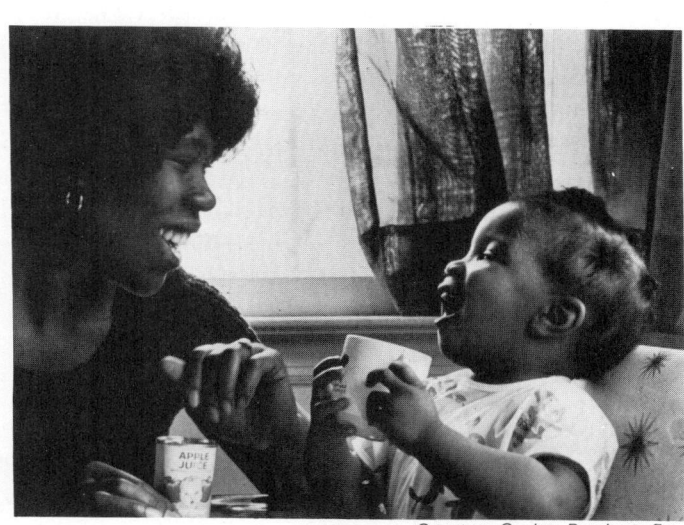

Courtesy Gerber Products Co.

Part 1 / Marketing Is All Around You / 7

YOUR MARKETING VOCABULARY

On a separate sheet of paper define each of the following marketing terms; then use each term in a sentence.

Consumer   Distribution
Customer   Marketing

FOR REVIEW AND DISCUSSION

1. What does the saying "Marketing is all around you" mean?
2. Marketing consists of stores and various activities. Name the activities.
3. What kinds of people are directly engaged in marketing?
4. What kinds of businesses sell goods mainly to other businesses?
5. What kinds of businesses sell services to other businesses?
6. Name five marketing activities that you might see on a trip through your own town.
7. What is the difference between marketing and distribution?
8. What role does the consumer play in the marketing process?
9. Describe the field of marketing.
10. What is the job situation in marketing?

ANALYZING MARKETING CONCEPTS

1. Marketing is all around you and involves many activities. On a separate sheet of paper, prepare a form like the one below and list the following activities in the left-hand column: (a) a person preparing a newspaper advertisement, (b) an artist painting a picture, (c) a worker pouring steel in a steel mill, (d) a man delivering a new TV set, (e) a farmer plowing his field, (f) a door-to-door salesman selling household goods, (g) a salesperson selling a dress, (h) a man applying for a loan at a bank, (i) a woman purchasing an airline ticket from a travel agency.

    Place a check mark in the appropriate column to indicate whether the activity is a marketing or a nonmarketing activity.

Activity	Marketing	Nonmarketing
Example: A United Parcel Service truck making a delivery.	✔	

2. Marketing activities involve the distribution of products and services. On a separate sheet of paper, prepare a form like the following one, listing these activities in the left-hand column: (a) a group of people waiting to enter a theater, (b) a teen-ager buying a tennis racket, (c) a businessman

boarding an airplane, (d) a family staying at a hotel, (e) a woman selecting a skirt from a display rack, (f) a young man ordering a hamburger, (g) a salesperson wrapping a customer's purchase.

Place a check mark in the appropriate column to indicate whether the activity involves the distribution of a product or a service.

Activity	Product	Service
Example: A young woman entering a beauty salon.		✔

Note to Student: A project is an organized learning activity that requires research or observation on your part. As you complete each project in this book, you will be acquiring skills and knowledge that will help you achieve your career objective.

Whenever you begin a project, prepare a form like the one below. Give the completed form to your teacher along with your finished project.

Project Number _____

Name_____ Date Assigned_____

Career Objective_____ Date Completed_____

Value of the Project to You_____

▣ MARKETING PROJECT 1
Distinguishing Between Marketing Businesses

Project Goal: Given a list of businesses, such as a part of the Yellow Pages, distinguish between those businesses that market goods and those that market services.

Action: Turn to the Yellow Pages of your telephone directory and select ten businesses. On a separate sheet of paper, prepare a form like the one below. In the left-hand column, list the names of the businesses you have selected. Check the appropriate column for each business to indicate whether it is engaged primarily in marketing goods or services.

Name of Marketing Business	Goods	Services
Example: Allegheny Airlines		✔

Marketing Is Jobs

YOUR GOALS

1. Given a list of job descriptions, identify those jobs that are in marketing.
2. Given a group of marketing job descriptions, list several jobs in which you believe you have ability and interest, and state why.

There are about 80 million people in the total work force of the United States today. One of every four of these people works in some phase of marketing. Most work for someone else, but one of every seven is self-employed or working in a family business.

Many people in your community work at marketing products: food, farm equipment, clothing, sporting goods, flowers, stationery, books, appliances, phonograph records, baby carriages, and shrubbery, to name a few. Some of your other neighbors are engaged in marketing services: insurance, apartment rentals, lawn care, tailoring, house painting, banking, transportation, hair styling, and amusements. Wherever products or services are bought or sold, there is marketing. Real estate agents, furniture movers, route salesmen, telephone and telegraph workers, used-car dealers, appliance repairmen, and florists all help to make up the world of marketing because they provide goods or services or both.

TYPICAL MARKETING JOBS

If you work part time in a store, you are engaged in marketing, whether your job is opening crates of merchandise, stamping prices on articles and putting them on the shelves, checking customers' purchases and receiving the money for them, helping customers select the articles they want, weighing vegetables, putting up window displays, packing groceries, or wrapping meat.

The restaurant worker is engaged in marketing, whether he is a waiter, a cashier, or a dining-room host. Each of these persons assists in providing people with food, and the increasing habit of dining out makes the restaurant worker an indispensable part of marketing.

Motels and hotels provide a much-needed service to people on the go. Not only do motels and hotels offer the traveler a comfortable room, but they also make available food, swimming pools, magazines, and various other goods and services. Many large motels and hotels serve as headquarters for conventions and meetings, providing guest accommodations, dining facilities, and meeting rooms. There are many types of marketing jobs in this, the hospitality industry.

Amusement parks, miniature golf courses, movie theaters, bowling alleys, skating rinks, and stock-car racetracks all provide entertainment to help satisfy the growing demand for recreation. These and many other organizations that cater to the leisure-time activities are growing in number and need many workers of various talents.

In what way is the work of these auto mechanics a part of marketing?

University Films/McGraw-Hill

Even those who serve customers in banks, loan offices, and insurance companies are engaged in marketing. Individuals and businesses must have a safe place in which to keep their money, important papers, and other valuables; they want the convenience of a checking account and of a place to buy traveler's checks and other money substitutes. People also often need to borrow money to finance a car, to open or expand a business, or to buy a home or a building. Many individuals want and need life and health insurance in addition to insurance on their possessions. Businesses need insurance to protect them against the risk of losing their assets. Most Americans share the belief that having insurance is important. This means many marketing jobs to be filled by people who can explain insurance programs, sell policies, and service the policies after they are sold.

These are only a few examples of marketing jobs and areas of marketing where jobs exist. Some of the major fields of employment in marketing are discussed in this part. These fields include selling, promotion, buying, receiving, stockkeeping, credit, delivery, and accommodation services.

JOBS IN SELLING

One of the greatest needs in the field of marketing is for people who can sell. Although some 5 million people are employed in sales jobs now, another million will be needed within the next 10 years. This will mean important opportunities for those young men and women who want a career in selling.

Basically there are three types of selling jobs: retail, wholesale, and industrial. Each of these jobs requires different abilities and skills.

Retail Selling

The retail salesman performs the final step in the process of moving goods and services to the consumer. One great advantage of retail selling is that the salesman usually has the merchandise to show to the customer. Furthermore, most retail salesmen do not have to find customers for their products; the customers come to them. Other types of salesmen, however, must constantly seek prospects (potential buyers). The three types of retail salesmen discussed here are in-store salesmen, specialty salesmen, and route salesmen. (In this book, the term "salesman" refers to both men and women.)

In-Store Salesmen. Those who sell inside a store are known as *in-store salesmen*. The main duties of the in-store salesmen include serving customers, writing up the sale or ringing it up on a cash register, wrapping merchandise, making change, arranging and replenishing stock, keeping stock clean, and handling customer problems. Some in-store salespeople may spend part of their time calling on prospects in their homes or places of business. Appliance stores, furniture stores, and automobile dealers often sell in this manner.

Some people think that in-store salespeople are becoming less important because of the trend toward self-service stores, in which people select their purchases usually without the help of a salesman. Although the self-service idea has changed the jobs of some salespeople, in-store salesmen are still needed in large numbers to assist customers in selecting merchandise, to demonstrate the use of merchandise, and to write up sales.

A good in-store salesman is courteous and helpful and tries to understand his customers. He learns all he can about his line of merchandise so that he can demonstrate its uses effectively and answer customers' questions. Once a customer has decided to buy, the salesman remembers to suggest additional merchandise in which the customer might be interested. In this way, the salesman not only increases business for the store, but also adds to his potential for promotion.

Specialty Salesmen. Individuals who sell a particular product or line of products to the customer in his home or place of business are called *specialty salesmen*. Many specialty salesmen sell door to door, dealing in products such as cosmetics, magazines, vacuum cleaners, brushes, silverware, and storm windows. Specialty salesmen also sell real estate and insurance.

The specialty salesman's biggest challenge is finding prospects for his product or service. He compiles a list of names from various sources, such as newspapers, tax lists, replies to advertising, and recommendations of others. Then he calls on as many of these prospects as possible each day—perhaps twenty or more. In order to be successful, the specialty salesman must be hardworking, ambitious, energetic, and persuasive. Some specialty salesmen earn very high incomes.

Route Salesmen. Sometimes called driver salesmen, *route salesmen* are individuals who travel a regular route, selling products such as baked goods, milk, heating oil, newspapers, and soft drinks. Many salesmen find route selling interesting and challenging, and they enjoy the open air and the close contact with the families they serve. One of the responsibilities of the route salesman is to constantly increase the number of his customers. He is therefore always on the lookout for families that have just moved into his territory as well as for customers who are no longer satisfied with a competitor's product or service.

Other Retail Salesmen. Although they may not be called salesmen, those who work at airline ticket counters, in travel agencies, at drugstore fountains, in restaurants, and in similar establishments offering primarily services are also

A dissatisfied customer of one route salesman is a good prospect for another.

engaged in selling. The manner in which these employees greet and serve customers has a direct bearing on the sales volume of the business by which they are employed.

Wholesale Selling

The wholesaler is the link between the manufacturer and the retail store or industry. While some manufacturers sell direct to the retailer and to the industrial user, many use wholesalers to distribute their products. In some cases, manufacturers use wholesalers in addition to their own sales efforts.

The wholesaler is essentially a distributor. He employs *wholesale salesmen,* individuals who sell the products of a manufacturer to retailers, business firms, and organizations. Wholesale salesmen may represent several manufacturers and carry a number of products that are noncompetitive. The typical wholesale salesman works with a group of regular customers and calls on them periodically. Products often handled by wholesale salesmen include pharmaceuticals, food and food products, automotive equipment, farm and garden supplies, appliances, and apparel.

Industrial Selling

Manufacturers often employ *industrial salesmen,* individuals who specialize in selling products or services to industry. Some industrial salesmen handle products such as grain, lumber, cotton, leather, cloth, and office stationery. Other industrial salesmen are sales engineers who must have a high degree of knowledge of the complex technical products they handle. Sales engineers sell products such as computer and data processing systems, refinery equipment, and heavy machinery.

A familiar type of industrial salesman is the service salesman. He sells, installs, and services his product, which may be heating and air-conditioning equipment, typewriters, printing presses, or small motors. The service salesman must have good mechanical aptitude and a thorough knowledge of how his product works.

Certain industrial salesmen concentrate on marketing new products in new territories. The new product salesman, or pioneer salesman, must be dynamic and creative and have the ability to communicate his ideas readily. After the pioneer salesman has established a new product in a particular area, his company will then turn the account over to another industrial salesman, who is expected to maintain a constant flow of reorders. The pioneer salesman then moves on to introduce the product in another area.

JOBS IN RETAIL PROMOTION

Retail salespeople take care of customers once they have entered a store. But what is it that brings in the customers? An attractive, well-balanced window display will often catch the attention of both shoppers and browsers. Advertisements in local newspapers, particularly ads that announce sales, are also effective. The people who produce these displays and ads work in the field of retail promotion.

While people who work "out front" in a retail store are concerned with the display of the merchandise they sell, certain people are responsible for creating these displays—the display specialists. Their job is to construct and arrange attractive and inviting window and interior displays. This job calls for artistic ability; a knowledge of color, balance, and design; and good merchandising sense. Display specialists work very closely with the department managers in a store. Display is used not only in department and specialty stores, but also in banks, real estate offices, airline offices, travel agencies, and restaurants.

Many stores, especially large department stores, spend a great deal of money advertising in local newspapers. The larger stores usually have an advertising department where advertising copy is written, illustrations are

Attractive displays such as this one are created by display specialists.

Reprinted with permission of Architectural Record

prepared, and layouts are made. This work calls for illustration artists, copywriters, and layout technicians. A knowledge of industrial printing methods is often important in these jobs.

In smaller retail establishments, the owner or manager may have to prepare his own advertising because he cannot afford a full-time specialist. He therefore welcomes employees who have talent in advertising and can assist in this work in addition to their other duties.

OTHER JOBS IN RETAIL STORES

Many of the key people in retail selling have little or no direct contact with customers. The manager of a large store and his top assistant, for example, work in their offices for much of the day because their jobs involve making the decisions that keep the store operating smoothly. Buyers and assistant buyers are responsible for acquiring from manufacturers and wholesalers products that will sell. Other people work in the receiving department or as stockkeepers. Still others are concerned with store security. Thus, the large retail store offers many employment opportunities besides those in selling and promotion. Some of these opportunities are described here.

Buying

Buying for resale is one of the most important jobs in retailing. It is important to distinguish between buying for resale and buying for business use. Those who buy for business use are usually called *purchasing agents* or industrial buyers; those who buy for resale are called *buyers*. The buyer is a very important person in any retail store because the success of the business often depends on his ability to buy intelligently. He decides what, when, and how much to buy; what price to pay; from whom to buy; and so on. Only those who have had considerable merchandising experience can qualify for the job of buyer; it is one of the best-paying jobs in retailing.

Receiving

When goods are received at the retail store, they must be unpacked, counted for correctness of quantity, checked for quality, price-ticketed, and stored in stockrooms or sent to selling areas. In small stores the job of receiving and marking may be done by salespeople. In larger stores, however, people are employed especially to do this work. The young person who seeks a career in retailing frequently begins in the receiving department and later moves on to more challenging positions. The receiving department offers him an excellent opportunity to learn about merchandise.

Stockkeeping

The job of keeping goods on the shelves in the right quantity and variety, so that customers may make their selection easily, is called *stockkeeping*. In a supermarket, stockkeepers are needed to bring boxes of canned goods and other packaged products into the store. They then stamp the prices on the merchandise and arrange it on the shelves. In a department store, stockkeepers see that goods are protected from dust, are attractively displayed, and are in plentiful supply. While salespeople in all stores have some responsibility for stockkeeping, larger stores employ stockkeepers who do only this kind of work.

Delivery

Some retail stores—such as drugstores, department stores, appliance stores, and small grocery stores—provide delivery service. Those who work in the delivery department are in direct contact with the customer and, in a sense, can be considered salesmen. The extent to which they are courteous, helpful, and prompt in carrying out their duties will reflect the dependability of the store to the customer. Jobs in delivery services include drivers, rate clerks, shipping clerks, weighers, dispatchers, route delivery clerks, traffic clerks, and checkers.

Credit

Credit privileges are offered by most retail stores. Businessmen have found that people buy more and are more loyal customers when they have charge accounts. Many activities are connected with credit. The applicant's credit rating must be determined, records must be kept of his purchases, and reminders must be sent of amounts due.

Credit workers are an important part of the marketing process. They must exercise sound judgment in deciding whether to grant credit. At the same time, they must offer courteous service, which can increase business substantially. Jobs involving credit are also found in credit-rating bureaus, savings and loan offices, and banks.

Accommodation Services

In large retail stores, shoppers are offered many accommodation services. These services include parking, personal shopping (in which merchandise is selected for customers and sent to them), telephone ordering, interior decorating, gift wrapping, restaurants, nurseries, and fur storage. Retail stores need many people to provide all these services, and this means many employment opportunities for young men and women.

JOBS IN SERVICE ENTERPRISES

There are also many jobs in service enterprises for young people in marketing. Many people in the amusement and recreation field, for example, perform marketing tasks, and the job opportunities increase year by year. There are job opportunities for managers, cashiers, ushers, and attendants in movie theaters, bowling alleys, skating rinks, swimming pools, and amusement parks.

Many jobs in hotels, motels, and other lodging places are essentially marketing jobs, and due to the growing number of such establishments, this job market is expanding rapidly. There are many year-round and seasonal hotels and motels, tourist camps, trailer parks, sports camps, and private clubs. Some of the jobs in such places are manager, desk clerk, bellman, information clerk, social director, and service attendant.

Advertising

Advertisements in newspapers, magazines, and various other media encourage people to buy. Workers in advertising agencies create and bring these advertisements before the public. These workers include executives, who plan and coordinate advertising policy and campaigns; artists, copywriters, and layout specialists, who prepare the artwork, text, and finished design of the advertisement; production people, who turn the artwork into print or film; media personnel, who decide where the advertisement should be shown and buy the needed newspaper space or TV time; and research people, who collect information for planning future advertising. In small agencies a few people do all this work; in the larger ones each function employs several people.

Opportunities are abundant in advertising, and people with many different abilities are needed. There are jobs for people who can work well with others, jobs for people who can write advertising copy, and jobs for people who have a talent for art and design.

Insurance

Insurance protects people against financial losses. Types of insurance widely sold are life insurance, property insurance, and liability insurance. Insurance policies are sold by insurance agents and brokers. These agents and brokers may offer their customers various other services, including advice on types of protection, assistance in planning financial protection, and help in settling claims. Insurance agents and brokers also develop insurance programs and prepare reports; however, their main job is selling. They want to win and keep the confidence of customers. To do this they must have a thorough, up-to-date knowledge of their service and the principles of selling.

Courtesy Occidental Life Insurance Co. of California

The insurance agent gives his customers advice about financial protection and helps them plan for the future.

Real Estate

Real estate salesmen and brokers play a role in most property transactions. They can represent either customers seeking property or property owners who want to sell or rent homes or commercial properties. Real estate salesmen may show and sell residential real estate, or they may specialize in business properties. People in real estate also make appraisals (determine the worth of property), help arrange for loans to finance purchases, and develop new building projects. To do their jobs well, real estate people must know about property values, community facilities, and laws and taxes affecting property owners. In the United States each state has certain standards that applicants must meet to deal in real estate as salesmen or brokers.

Personal and Business Services

Jobs in personal services include those in commercial and self-service laundries, linen supply companies, dye plants, photographic studios, beauty shops, barbershops, shoe repair shops, fur repair and storage establishments, and clothing rental firms.

Many organizations provide services mainly to other business firms. Such organizations include accounting firms, outdoor advertising services, collection agencies, office services (duplicating, mailing, addressing), blueprinting and photocopying firms, and telephone answering services. The jobs within these organizations are varied. Most of them require specific skills, but these can be learned quickly on the job.

OTHER JOB OPPORTUNITIES

Long-term employment trends show that there will be a shift from jobs in manufacturing to jobs in sales and service. Over the next 10 years the number of people employed will increase 20 percent, while jobs in trade (retailing and wholesaling) will rise more than 30 percent—a rate well above average. Jobs in finance, real estate, and insurance also will increase at an above-average rate.

In all these job areas there is a great need for managers. Although the number of small-business owners and proprietors may be decreasing, the number of large businesses, such as chain stores, is increasing. This growth creates a need for salaried managers in many areas of marketing.

Only a few of the vast number of employment possibilities and marketing jobs have been mentioned in this part. You can probably name several other growing marketing businesses, some perhaps that are located in your own neighborhood.

YOUR MARKETING VOCABULARY

On a separate sheet of paper, define each of the following marketing terms; then use each term in a sentence.

Buyers
Industrial salesmen
In-store salesmen
Purchasing agents
Route salesmen
Specialty salesmen
Stockkeeping
Wholesale salesmen

FOR REVIEW AND DISCUSSION

1. Name seven jobs in marketing.
2. Identify three types of retail salesmen and describe the job of each.
3. Describe the job of a wholesale salesman.
4. What kinds of goods do industrial salesmen handle?
5. What kinds of ability and knowledge are needed by a person who creates window displays?
6. What abilities are needed by people employed in advertising?
7. Why is the buyer such an important person in a retail store?
8. Who receives and marks goods in small stores? in larger stores?
9. In what way can people employed in a delivery department be considered salesmen?
10. What kinds of marketing opportunities are found in amusement and recreation businesses?

ANALYZING MARKETING CONCEPTS

1. Retail salespeople may be classified as in-store, specialty, and route salesmen. Prepare a form like the one below. Write the following types of products in the left-hand column: (a) furniture, (b) records, (c) insurance, (d) newspapers, (e) cameras, (f) dairy products, (g) cooking utensils, (h) cosmetics, (i) household supplies, (j) magazines.

    Place a check mark in the appropriate column or columns to identify the type of retail salesperson who would most likely sell each product.

Product	In-Store Salesman	Specialty Salesman	Route Salesman
Example: Silverware	✔	✔	

2. The large retail store offers a variety of job opportunities. Prepare a form like the one near the top of the next page. In the left-hand column, write the following activities: (a) deciding on new items to sell, (b) storing goods, (c) price-marketing items, (d) gift wrapping, (e) unpacking

new goods, (f) supervising customer lounges, (g) recording charge purchases, (h) shipping goods to customers, (i) arranging goods on shelves, (j) recording payments on accounts.

Place a check mark in the appropriate column to identify the type of activity listed.

Activity	Buying	Receiving	Stock-keeping	Delivering	Credit	Service
Example: Parking						✔

◻ MARKETING PROJECT 2
Identifying Marketing Jobs

Project Goal: Given a group of marketing job descriptions, list several jobs in which you believe you have ability and interest, and state why.

Action: Locate a copy of the *Dictionary of Occupational Titles* or the *Encyclopedia of Careers and Vocational Guidance*. Prepare a form like the one below. From your reference, select four marketing jobs. In the left-hand column, list the title of each job. In the center column, write a brief description of the job. In the right-hand column, state the abilities you have for the job and why it interests you.

Job Title	Description	Your Ability and Interest
Example: Travel agent	Assists people taking trips by planning itineraries, making reservations, and obtaining tickets.	I do detail work well and enjoy helping people with travel plans.

The Economic Climate of Marketing

YOUR GOALS

1. Given the marketing concept, list three businesses in your community and indicate how they apply this concept.
2. Given the four forms of business ownership, state the advantages and disadvantages of each.

There was a time when a family could provide for most of its own needs. Family members could grow their own food and make their own clothes, and parents could teach their children the skills they would need when they grew up. Now life is not so simple. We want things that we cannot produce ourselves: telephones, television sets, washing machines, automobiles, a variety of food products, and services such as specialized medical care and higher education. To satisfy these needs, we turn to business.

WHAT IS BUSINESS?

To understand marketing and its functions, we must first understand what business is. Business may be defined as all the activities of an individual or group of individuals involved in producing goods or services and distributing them to consumers—that is, to the people, firms, or institutions who will use them. In other words, business involves three elements; namely, production, marketing, and consumption.

Production

The process of creating or improving goods or services that will satisfy human wants is called *production.* Production creates useful products and services for business firms and individual consumers.

Production is so important that we measure the health of our entire economy by the amount of goods and services produced each year. The total value of the production of goods and services over a specified period is called the *gross national product,* often referred to as GNP. GNP is expressed in dollars. In 1970 the GNP of the United States topped one trillion dollars.

Closely tied to the GNP is the standard of living. "Standard of living" refers to how well a nation of people lives. This standard is measured by the number and kinds of goods and services the people have. The more goods and services a nation produces in proportion to population, the higher its standard of living.

Production is also important in our relationships with other countries. Our ability to maintain a favorable balance of trade, a situation in which our exports exceed our imports, depends on our ability to supply other nations with goods such as food products and machinery. Our ability as a supplier, in turn, depends on our maintaining a high and efficient rate of production.

America's high production rate can be traced to its natural resources, diversified population, and technical expertise.

Natural Resources. Natural resources might be called nature's gifts. Water, fertile soil, useful minerals, fuels such as oil and coal, and favorable climate are all natural resources.

Natural resources are vital to the well-being of a country. Water must be available for power, transportation, and drinking; rich soil is needed for raising grain, fruits, and vegetables; and oil is needed for operating and lubricating machinery.

The United States is fortunate to have abundant natural resources. The temperate weather favors agriculture, the lakes and rivers provide an ample supply of water, and the rich oil fields are the source of fuel that keeps homes warm and factories running. Without adequate natural resources it would be impossible to produce goods in large quantities.

However, even this country's vast resources are limited and must be conserved. Through ecology, the study of man's relationship to his physical environment, we are learning how to preserve our natural resources. Some of

Natural resources, such as rivers and forests, are important to production. The United States is fortunate to have an abundance of such resources.

the means used by various businesses to conserve natural resources include controlling the dumping of industrial waste products into lakes and rivers, marketing low-lead gasoline to combat air pollution from automobile exhausts, and designing and improving packaging materials so that they can be reused or disposed of easily.

Diversified Population. The United States has always been fortunate in having a diversified population. There are Americans whose ancestors lived here long before Columbus's time. There are Americans whose forefathers immigrated to this country as free men and Americans whose forefathers came as slaves or indentured servants. There are Americans who are themselves immigrants. All these groups contribute to the growth and development of the nation.

Unfortunately, as a result of discrimination, the contributions of many groups have not been fully recognized. These groups—particularly blacks, Indians, Asians, Mexicans, Puerto Ricans, and women—form a huge human resource. As the barriers of discrimination are removed, these people will be able to make even greater contributions to the nation's economic growth.

Businesses are showing their concern about using our valuable human resources. They are giving various types of assistance to corporations that provide training for employment and promotion, give advice to small businesses, and provide social services. For example, private businesses support financially the Chicago Economic Development Corporation (CEDC), which is involved in community affairs and helps businessmen who work with minorities living in deprived areas. The Peoples Involvement Corporation (PIC) in Washington, D.C., is concerned with social service, housing rehabilitation, and economic development in the inner city. PIC receives technical aid from private companies. Similar projects exist in many other cities.

Technical Expertise. The United States is one of the world's foremost producers of manufactured goods, as well as one of the leading agricultural nations. An important factor in this success is the use of machines that make possible the efficient production of many goods.

Although the Industrial Revolution, the period in which machines were introduced to accomplish work formerly done by people, began in England in 1760, it did not have a great effect on the United States until after the Civil War, or roughly a hundred years ago. Until that time, American farmers raised their own food and sold their surplus at local stores. Clothing was made at home. The little manufacturing that existed was done through hand operations or through the use of crude machines. Gradually, as manufacturing machinery was imported from England and inventions were developed here, the crafts that were formerly done at home moved into factories. Farmers were able to cultivate more land and increase farm production through the use of mechanized equipment. Constant improvement in basic machinery over the years finally led to "mass production," the efficient and rapid production of large quantities of standardized goods through the use of machinery.

Marketing

After goods or services have been produced, they must be made accessible to the people who will use them. To distribute goods effectively, people involved in marketing must consider both the product and the consumer. So modern firms are asking themselves: What do our customers really need that we can supply? This consumer-oriented attitude, the viewpoint that the purpose of business is to fulfill the needs of consumers, is called the *marketing concept*.

In practice, a business that applies the marketing concept has distinctive characteristics. It centers all company planning, policies, and operations on consumer needs. Instead of trying to sell to everybody, the firm selects the most likely potential customers for its products. In addition, management realizes that its primary function is marketing rather than production.

Consumption

The process of using goods and services is called "consumption," and anyone who uses goods and services is a consumer. Individuals, governments, institutions, and business firms are all consumers. In our economy what consumers want and buy determines to a large extent what businesses will produce and how much they will produce. A business will succeed if it can produce what consumers want and if it can market its products effectively. Conversely, a business will fail if it does not produce products that will satisfy consumers. It is therefore important for businesses to know which goods and services will be in demand.

WHAT IS AN ECONOMIC SYSTEM?

The way in which a nation uses its natural and man-made resources to produce various commodities and to distribute them to its people is called an economic system, or economy.

Resources are means used to accomplish a goal, and each nation has a variety of resources that it can use. Wages and salaries are resources because they are a means of buying goods and services. Productive resources are means of producing goods and services. They include natural resources, the labor force, and the man-made items used in production, such as tools, machinery, and buildings. Another important productive resource is capital, which is money that can be used to finance production.

The Basic Problem

Any nation's productive resources have limits. Each country has only a certain amount of land, a certain number of people, and a certain amount of capital. Therefore, the amount of goods and services that any nation can produce is limited. But human wants are endless. Whenever some of our wants are satisfied, others take their place. Even the richest nations do not have enough resources to supply everything their people want. Therefore, they have to decide how to secure the greatest benefit from their available resources. Every country, however large or small, must make this decision, and how it deals with this problem determines the form of its economic system.

The Basic Decisions

Any economic system must cope with the following problems: what goods and services should be produced, how they should be produced, and how they should be distributed. A *planned economy* (also called a controlled economy) is one in which the government makes all the decisions. Free enterprise is a system in which the people—as consumers, business owners, or workers—make the decisions. *Modified free enterprise,* in practice in the United States, is a system in which the people make most of the decisions, but some decisions are controlled or modified by the government.

In a modified free-enterprise system, the government may modify or control some decisions made by businessmen.

What Should Be Produced? Should productive resources be used to produce movie cameras, barbecue grills, automatic dishwashers, rockets, parks, or schools? In a planned economy the government decides which goods and services should be produced. In free enterprise the choices of the people, as consumers, determine the goods and services to be produced. In modified free enterprise, however, the people's choices are restricted to some extent. Certain products, such as some narcotics, cannot be legally produced. Also, certain resources are set aside for specific purposes; for example, some land is saved to be used for parks.

How Should It Be Produced? An economic system must determine how to produce its products most efficiently by making the best use of its resources. A method of production that uses only a little of one resource might use too much of another. For example, a procedure might require a great deal of hand labor but only a little capital. If the hand laborers were replaced by machines, there would be a savings in one resource (labor) but increased spending of another resource (the capital required to buy the machines).

In a planned economy the government either owns the means of production or dictates who shall own them. Moreover, it decides how best to use its resources. In free enterprise the businessman decides which resources would be most efficient to employ. In modified free enterprise the businessman is not totally free to make such a decision. Safety laws, for example, might prevent him from using less expensive but more hazardous equipment.

How Should It Be Distributed? Who will get the movie cameras, barbecue grills, and automatic dishwashers? If there are not enough to go around, who will be left out? What will business owners get in comparison to workers? Division of available goods and services is important to a sound and rational economy. In a planned economy the government decides how and to whom distribution is made. In free enterprise, goods and services are distributed according to personal income. The more you earn, the more you can accumulate or use. In modified free enterprise, goods and services are redistributed to some extent by means of taxes and through such programs as welfare and social security.

ENVIRONMENT OF A MODIFIED FREE-ENTERPRISE SYSTEM

A marketer who establishes his business in a modified free-enterprise environment knows that he will enjoy certain privileges, run certain risks, and be subject to some government control. He will enjoy the freedom of ownership, but with some restrictions. In striving to make his business profitable, he will have to face competition and take economic risks. His success will be measured mainly by his net earnings, or profit. These elements—regulated freedom of ownership, competition, risk, and profit—are the characteristics of a modified free-enterprise business.

Freedom of Ownership

In some countries, personal belongings such as clothes, books, and toothbrushes are all that people are allowed to own. Everything else—forests, factories, machinery—is owned by the government. Because the government owns all the productive resources of the country, it can easily control what is produced.

However, in a modified free-enterprise system such as ours, individuals may own land and other natural resources as well as buildings, tools, and equipment. There are, however, some restrictions on the use of property. For example, a law may prohibit the building of factories on land reserved for private housing. In general, however, people are free to let their property stand idle, lease it, sell it, or give it away. Or they may decide to put it to work to earn an income; that is, they may start a business. These property rights are preserved by law.

Competition

The struggle of each business to obtain a share of the market is known as *competition.* It is an essential ingredient in the modified free-enterprise system. Because any person can start his own business, many people may choose to operate the same kind of business. For example, in many communities there are at least a half-dozen places where a person can buy a pair of sneakers, go bowling, get a haircut, have his shoes repaired, or buy a chocolate malt.

Competition serves the public in many ways. To prove this statement, suppose there were only one place in your community where you could buy a pair of shoes. Unless you were willing to go to the trouble and expense of traveling to stores in other communities, you would have to be satisfied with the selection this one store had to offer, whether you liked it or not. You would also be forced to pay whatever price the store asked, and you might have to settle for a pair of shoes that did not fit properly. Without competition, businesses could offer you a minimum of service. They could refuse to sell on credit, to make an exchange, or even to show you their complete line. Knowing that there are other shoe stores nearby, however, the shoe-store owner is more likely to offer you a wide selection, courteous service, and a fair price.

Competition is keen among oil companies.

Courtesy National Petroleum News

30 / Unit 1 / The World of Marketing

Risk

Every day in the United States more than 1,000 new businesses are started. Some are quite small, such as a lunch wagon; others are huge, such as a discount store occupying several acres. Each involves risk, because no one can be absolutely sure when he opens a business that it will succeed. About one of every three new businesses fails in the first year of operation; only one in five lasts as long as 10 years.

One of the important reasons for business failure is lack of ability to manage effectively. Every business—even an established one—must manage wisely and stay alert to changing conditions. Few people realize the risks a businessman assumes; the possibilities of failure are always present. The difference between success or failure may rest on one decision—whether to take on a new line, to build a new building, to lower prices, to give easier credit terms, or to expand facilities.

Thus, every day the businessman is faced with risks. If his expenses are high, he must reduce some of his operating costs, eliminate some services, or increase prices. But any of these actions may result in a loss of business to his competitors. The business owner's need to reduce risks may help to explain why he may not always pay salaries as high as employees think they deserve, why he is careful about expenses, and why he expects his employees to work hard. (Risk is discussed more fully in Part 41.)

Profit

If the risk of going into business is so great, why are people so anxious to start a new business or invest their money in an existing one? The answer is that people hope to earn a profit. *Profit* is the amount left from sales income after all expenses have been deducted. It may be thought of as the "take-home pay" of any business or the reward of business risk. It is what motivates people to invest their savings in businesses.

Of course, any businessman knows that he cannot earn a profit if he has no customers. And customers will not buy from a businessman who does not give them what they want at a reasonable price. Thus, the businessman cannot afford to think only in terms of profit; if he does, his business will quickly fail. The businessman who wants to stay in business knows that he can do so only by giving people what they want. Thus, for him, realizing a profit and satisfying the needs of customers are two very important related goals.

FORMS OF BUSINESS OWNERSHIP

A characteristic of the modified free-enterprise system is that businesses are owned by individuals instead of by the government. But this does not mean that each business has only one owner. In the United States there are four fundamental forms of business ownership: sole proprietorship, partnership, corporation, and cooperative. Each of these forms of business ownership has its own risks and rewards.

Sole Proprietorship

A business owned by one person is called a *sole proprietorship*. Most businesses fall into this category. In a sole proprietorship the owner invests his money, makes all decisions, and gets all profits. He also has freedom of operation and the opportunity to profit from his own initiative.

The owner in a sole proprietorship may, however, have no one to help him with financing; as a result, he is often forced to operate on inadequate capital. Moreover, he is personally liable for his debts if his business fails. This is a big drawback of the sole proprietorship. In addition, most sole proprietors work long hours. They may do all buying, advertising and promotion, hiring and supervising of employees, budgeting, and financial recordkeeping.

Partnership

A business owned by two or more people is called a *partnership*. The partners share the responsibility for financing, operating, and managing the enterprise. They also share the profits. There are several ways of sharing the profits, but usually they are divided in proportion to the amount of money that each partner has invested in the business.

One advantage of a partnership over a sole proprietorship is that the risks

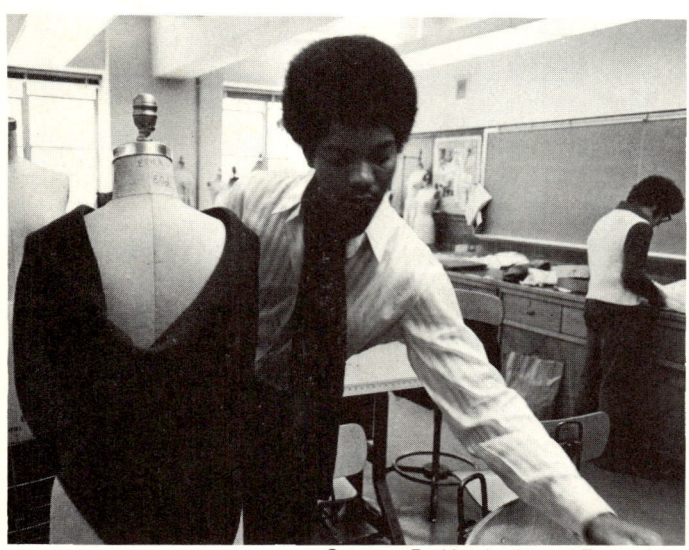

Fashion designers may combine their talents to form a partnership.

Courtesy Fashion Institute of Technology

and management are shared by two or more people. Also, it is usually easier for two or three people to raise money for a business than it is for one; thus a partnership usually has more funds to draw on. The big drawback of a partnership is that each partner is responsible for the actions of the others. One partner may make foolish decisions, shirk his duties, or even cheat his partners by taking more than his rightful share of the profits.

Partnerships are built on mutual trust. But, even though the partnership agreement is usually in the form of a written contract, there is no assurance that one partner will not bankrupt the business. However, as you look around your community, you will find many thriving partnerships in which the partners are working together effectively and realizing a profit.

Corporation

A corporation is owned by many persons, often as many as several thousand. These owners hold stock, or shares, in the corporation and are called stockholders, or shareholders. In most corporations, a stockholder is entitled to one vote on business and management affairs for each share of stock he owns. Thus the more shares an owner has, the greater will be his influence in the corporation.

The stockholders of a corporation periodically elect a board of directors to manage the corporation. The directors, however, are not personally responsible for the debts of the corporation; that is, they could not be forced to give up their personal belongings to pay the corporation's debts.

A corporation operates under a charter granted by a state or the federal government. A charter is a legal document that sets forth regulations for the operation of a business, such as the legal name of the business and the number of shares of stock that may be issued.

A *corporation,* then, is a business organization that has many owners and operates under a charter granted by a state or the federal government. Large department stores, automobile agencies, and furniture stores are examples of retail businesses often organized as corporations. Most of the familiar names in television commercials and other advertising—General Motors, Coca-Cola, and McDonald's—are corporations.

Cooperative

A business that is owned and operated by its customers is a *cooperative.* A cooperative is somewhat like a corporation in that it is financed by the sale of stock and managed by a board of directors. Usually cooperatives are made up of people with similar interests. Independent food retailers sometimes form a cooperative to buy in larger quantities and to compete with supermarkets. Growers of fruit and other agricultural products often organize cooperatives to give their individual, comparatively small production the importance and advantages of large-scale distribution. Consumers' cooperatives are fast becoming a favorite form of business ownership in inner cities, and there may be one or more in your community.

The purpose of a cooperative is not to make a profit for itself, but to improve the income of its members. It may do this by saving money for its members or by getting higher prices for its members' products.

YOUR MARKETING VOCABULARY

On a separate sheet of paper define each of the following marketing terms; then use each term in a sentence.

Competition
Cooperative
Corporation
Gross national product
Marketing concept
Modified free enterprise
Partnership
Planned economy
Production
Profit
Sole proprietorship

FOR REVIEW AND DISCUSSION

1. What are the three basic elements of business?
2. Explain the phrase "standard of living."
3. To what three factors can the high production rate of American farmers and manufacturers be traced?
4. Describe three ways various businesses are trying to conserve resources.
5. Explain how business is joining the effort to improve the quality of life.
6. Why is it important for businesses to know which goods and services are in demand?
7. What do modern firms now realize about the true purpose of business?
8. What are resources? productive resources?
9. Why is there a limit to any nation's productive resources?
10. What problems must a nation cope with through its economic system?
11. Name four basic characteristics of business under the modified free-enterprise system.
12. List four basic types of business ownership. Give the advantages and disadvantages of each.

ANALYZING MARKETING CONCEPTS

1. Competition is essential in the modified free-enterprise system. Prepare a form like the following one, listing these products in the left-hand column: (a) automobile, (b) ball-point pen, (c) cereal, (d) deodorant,

(e) radio, (f) shampoo, (g) toothpaste, (h) wristwatch. List in the right-hand column the names of at least five manufacturers of each product.

Product	Names of Manufacturers
Example: TV set	Zenith, RCA, Philco, Sony, G.E.

2. Competition encourages better service to the consumer. Prepare a form like the one below. List the following products in the left-hand column: (a) apples, (b) books, (c) candy, (d) coffee, (e) gloves, (f) hammers, (g) ice cream, (h) nails, (i) neckties, (j) overcoats, (k) picture postcards, (l) radios, (m) shampoo, (n) sweaters, (o) toothpaste, (p) toys, (q) vitamins. Assume that a shopping center includes the following stores: (1) food store, (2) department store, (3) drugstore, (4) clothing store, (5) hardware store, (6) small department store. In the right-hand column, place the number of each type of store that would be likely to sell the item listed.

Item	Type of Store
Example: Screwdriver	1, 2, 3, 5, 6

◊ MARKETING PROJECT 3
Comparing Forms of Business Ownership

Project Goal: Given the four forms of business ownership, state the advantages and disadvantages of each.

Action: Prepare a form like the one below. In the left-hand column, list the various forms of business ownership. Talk with several businessmen to learn their views of the advantages and disadvantages of each form of ownership. Then write your findings in the appropriate columns.

Form of Ownership	Advantages	Disadvantages
Example: Sole proprietorship	Owner makes all the decisions and receives all the profits.	Owner invests his money and is personally liable if business fails.

part 4

The Benefits of Marketing

YOUR GOALS

1. Given a product in a retail store, determine the utilities added to the product as it moves from the factory to the retailer.
2. Given the same product, list and explain the value added by marketing.

Through its productive capacity and modified free-enterprise system, the United States is able to produce a wealth of clothing, food, and other products. This outstanding production rate has important meaning for those who choose marketing as a career. If we are able to produce goods in greater and greater quantities, we must also find ways of marketing these goods with greater and greater efficiency. The marketer's goals, then, are to make customers aware of the goods and services available and to find the most efficient means of getting these goods and services to the customers.

HOW MARKETING SERVES US

Both production and marketing processes add utility to products and services. In marketing, *utility* means usefulness to consumers. The production processes add *form utility,* which is the increased usefulness of a product to a consumer because of a change in the basic material of the product. For example, by changing the shape, size, and texture of steel to produce a car, the production process makes the final product more useful to the consumer than was the basic material.

Marketing processes add three other utilities to products. They are time utility, place utility, and possession utility.

Time Utility

Months before the Christmas season begins, marketing people are busy getting ready to bring us the merchandise we expect to see—toys, greeting cards, jewelry, decorations, books, gifts and gift wrappings, and tree ornaments. Soon after Thanksgiving these and hundreds of other signs of Christmas begin to appear in stores all over the country.

Other events that take place during the year, such as Mother's Day, Father's Day, Halloween, and Valentine's Day, are similarly planned months in advance, so that we will have the things we want when we want them. In late summer stores begin to feature back-to-school clothing, school supplies, and luggage for college students who are going to schools away from home. In August sporting-goods stores are ready with a full array of football equipment; in late November they feature basketball, bowling, and other winter-sports gear. With the first signs of spring, baseball gear occupies the spotlight, and a little later, tennis, water skiing, and camping equipment are featured.

Not only does marketing provide goods at the time of year we want them, but also at the time of day most convenient for us to shop. Many stores are open six nights a week, so that a person who works all day can shop after working hours. The increased usefulness that a marketer gives to a product by making the product available to the customer at the appropriate and most convenient time is called *time utility*.

Place Utility

For most Americans, just a short car or bus ride will take them to a nearby store or shopping center, where many of their wants and needs can be satisfied. The modern shopping center is a concentration of retail stores and service establishments with generous parking space, usually located in a suburban area. You can walk just a few steps from where you bought a suit and pick up your clothes at the dry cleaner. Nearby you can also get your hair cut, a picture framed, and your dog shampooed. Marketing activities have added place utility to the goods and services. *Place utility* is the increased usefulness of goods and services to a customer that results because they have been located where it is convenient to buy them.

Marketers strive for the ultimate in place utility.

Possession Utility

Even if goods were brought to a place convenient for you at a time when you wanted them, they would be of no use if they were not available for sale. If they remained in a warehouse, you could not buy them until they were placed on display in your local store. Or if goods displayed in store windows were not available for sale, no possession utility would be added to them because you could not take them home with you. *Possession utility,* then, means the increased usefulness of goods to a customer that results from helping him to obtain them.

If a customer is short of cash, a store adds possession utility to its merchandise by offering credit, which enables the customer to possess the goods immediately.

Other Benefits of Marketing

In addition to time, place, and possession utility, marketing provides other benefits to society. People enjoy more conveniences and luxuries because marketing has made them possible. Through advertising and promotion, marketing makes us aware of new goods and services. By creating a demand for goods, marketing encourages greater production; and when goods are manufactured in large quantities, the costs of producing them are lowered. The resulting decrease in the selling price puts the goods within financial reach of more people. The introduction of color television provides a typical example.

When color TV was first introduced, the sets were very expensive and only a few people could afford them. By constantly reminding people how much more enjoyable TV is in color than in black and white, marketers succeeded in creating demand for color TV. Once the demand was created, it was possible for manufacturers to produce sets in larger quantities and thus lower the cost to the point where thousands of families now feel that they can afford to buy them. In fact, for a time the demand for color TV sets was greater than the manufacturers' ability to produce them!

Marketing encourages people to spend more on things that make life easier and more pleasant. The housewife who thinks she can get along without a clothes dryer is suddenly attracted by advertisements that tell her she need not wait for a sunny day to do her wash. She can avoid the chore of carrying heavy, wet clothes to the backyard and hanging them on a line. If she buys a clothes dryer, she will have more time to spend with her family, more time to entertain her friends, to pursue a hobby, to read, or to work as a volunteer in community organizations.

THE ACTIVITIES OF MARKETING

Marketing activities are many and varied and are by no means restricted to the buying and selling of goods. The activities of marketing can be divided into three main groups: exchange activities, physical distribution activities, and facilitating activities. Each group plays a vital role in getting goods from the producer to the consumer.

Exchange Activities

Exchange activities are basically buying and selling. Before a marketer can buy goods either for resale to the customer or for use by his company, he must determine his needs through careful research. He must find the supplier who can best satisfy his needs, and he must arrive at an agreeable price. He must also arrange for shipping dates of the merchandise.

Selling activities require the marketer to find customers, meet competition, set prices that will attract customers, and use other selling tactics to persuade prospective customers to buy his goods.

The storage of goods in warehouses is an important physical distribution activity. These two young warehouse workers are filling orders for customers.

Courtesy Electrical Wholesaling

Physical Distribution Activities

Physical distribution activities involve the actual movement of goods from producer to consumer. Two physical distribution activities are transportation and storage. Transportation is important in marketing because many products must be moved long distances from the producer to the actual market. The marketer must not only find the best way to ship a product; he must also know time schedules and costs involved.

On their way to market, goods must often be stored in warehouses. This is necessary when goods are produced far in advance of the time they will be needed, or when goods shipped in large quantities must be broken down into smaller shipments before being marketed. Transportation thus gets goods to the right place, and storage allows marketers to get goods to the right place at the right time.

Facilitating Activities

Many activities support the basic buying, selling, storage, and transportation activities. These supporting activities are known as facilitating activities. They are concerned with creating a demand for new products, seeking ways to improve products, and providing financial assistance in the operation of a business. Financing, risk taking, market research, advertising and other sales promotion, product planning, branding, packaging, standardizing, and grading are all facilitating activities.

THE COST OF MARKETING

Marketing costs represent about half the selling price of a typical article. Thus, a ball-point pen selling for $1 may cost 50 cents to produce; the other 50 cents is the cost of marketing. Let us try to find out whether these costs can be fully justified.

When the ball-point pen comes off the production line, it must be packaged. Perhaps it will be encased in a plastic bubble and attached to a card imprinted with the manufacturer's name and instructions for using the pen and obtaining refills. The pens must be packed into cartons and loaded on a delivery truck. The destination of the truck is a large wholesaler of stationery supplies, who sells notebooks, pencils, erasers, pens, greeting cards, and art materials to stationery stores. The wholesaler must provide a storage place for the cartons of pens until they are sold. His salesmen must call on retail-store owners to interest them in stocking the pens in their stores, and the resulting orders must be shipped from the wholesaler to the various retailers buying the pens.

All along the line from the pen factory to the retail store, there have been advertising operations. The pen manufacturer has advertised in wholesale trade journals and perhaps in national consumer magazines. The wholesaler has promoted the pen in retail trade papers. In turn, the retail-store owner has advertised in local newspapers and perhaps on local and regional radio and television to bring the pen (and his other products) to the attention of the consumer.

Each of these activities—the printing, design, and making of the package; the packing operation; the loading, shipping, and storing; the selling; and the advertising—is a marketing cost. Each one is a necessary step in the pen's long journey from the end of the production line to the consumer's pocket. In addition, every person or business that performs these various marketing functions must earn a profit for the effort involved—and this profit adds to the cost of marketing.

Another factor contributing to marketing costs is the consumer's desire for more convenience and more elaborate services. These cost money. Consider corn on the cob, for example. Thirty years ago corn on the cob was shipped "as is" to the grocer or wholesaler. When a shopper bought fresh corn on the cob, she bought it by the ear. The produce man put husks and all into a paper bag, and the shopper finished processing the corn at home. She husked it, trimmed it, washed it, cooked it, and cleaned her working area when the process was completed.

Today's shopper can still buy fresh corn on the cob in the supermarket, but often it is already husked and packaged. Or, she can head for the frozen-food department, where she can buy corn on the cob that is husked, trimmed, cleaned, boxed, and frozen. If she chooses the frozen corn, she can have her choice of whole kernel cut from the cob, in butter sauce, creamed, or with lima beans in succotash. The additional processing required to provide these conveniences increases the cost of the corn, and marketing costs also rise. For example, now the corn must be husked and cut, put into a carton, and sealed. It must be stored in commercial freezers. It must be shipped in special low-temperature railroad cars or refrigerated trucks. The supermarket must provide a freezer for displaying the corn and other frozen vegetables. The necessary packaging, labeling, transportation, and storage facilities add to the marketing costs.

Marketing costs are receiving increasing consumer attention. Critics claim that marketing is inefficient compared with production. Although the cost of producing an article gets lower and lower because of mechanization and automation, marketing costs seem to get higher and higher. But there is a good reason why it is easier to control the costs of production than it is to control the costs of marketing. Production deals primarily with machines and systems, which can be automated; marketing deals mainly with people, who cannot be. Production planners spend much of their time devising ways to make machines do more, and these machines can be made to do as they are directed. Marketers spend most of their time studying people, and certainly no one has discovered how to control—or predict with any certainty—the habits and behavior of human beings.

THE VALUE ADDED BY MARKETING

Marketing services, since they often cannot be seen and do not change the form of the manufactured product, are often unappreciated by the consumer. As a result some consumers resent marketing costs because they increase the selling prices of products. Modern marketers feel that this resentment of marketing costs is not justified and are attempting to make consumers realize the contributions made by marketing in meeting their demands for goods and services. To shift the emphasis from marketing costs to a more accurate picture of marketing's role, the term "value added" has been introduced to describe the advantages that marketing provides for the consumer. The "value added" idea emphasizes what the consumer receives in return for the costs involved in bringing the product to market.

An illustration of the "value added" concept is provided by the story of Our-Sound Company, a record-player manufacturer.

Our-Sound makes a portable record player in the medium-price range. The basic parts of the record player—turntable, tone arm, receiver, and speaker—are worth $20 in their unassembled condition. In the factory, skilled workers put the parts together, make minor adjustments, and give the record

Carrying cases for photographic equipment provide convenience as well as protection and are typical examples of the value added by marketing.

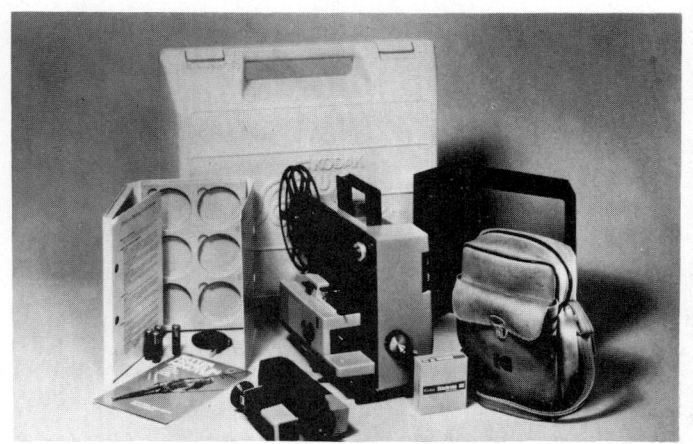

Courtesy Eastman Kodak

player a thorough inspection. It is easy to see how the manufacturer has added value to the original assemblage of parts through the work on the assembly line. At this point the record player is worth $40.

But the record player cannot be sold as it is. The customer wants his record player in an attractive, decorative case to protect and carry it. So the design department creates a streamlined case to contain the player and several records too. After the record player is completed, marketing activities begin to add still more value to it. When the record player has been placed in its carrying case, packagers slip the case into a cardboard box to protect against damage in shipment. Although this packaging does not change the basic form or function of the record player, the added protection assures the customer that he will be able to enjoy a damage-free record player.

Marketing enters the picture again when the manufacturer is ready to send a shipment of record players to music-store suppliers throughout the country. Each supplier must temporarily store the shipment in a warehouse, while he divides the shipment into smaller quantities for delivery to music stores in the area that he serves.

When the retailer receives his shipment of Our-Sound record players, he places an ad in the local paper listing the outstanding features of the machine, guaranteeing it for one year, and offering it for sale at $79.95. All the services involved in making the record player available to the consumer—the packaging, the transporting, the storing, the advertising, and the retailer's selling and repair service—have added additional value to the record player. Without many of these services, customers in the area might not be able to buy an Our-Sound record player.

The "value added" approach to marketing explains to the consumer the contribution made by marketing in bringing goods to the marketplace.

YOUR MARKETING VOCABULARY

On a separate sheet of paper define each of the following marketing terms; then use each term in a sentence.

Form utility
Place utility
Possession utility
Time utility
Utility

FOR REVIEW AND DISCUSSION

1. What are the marketer's goals?
2. Why are time utility, place utility, and possession utility important in marketing?
3. Give an example of how a store could add possession utility to its merchandise.
4. In addition to time, place, and possession utility, what other benefits does marketing provide to society?
5. What are three main groups of marketing activities? Describe each of these groups.
6. Cite four marketing costs that add to the final price of an item such as a ball-point pen.
7. In buying items such as corn on the cob, what kinds of services are customers demanding that add to marketing costs?
8. Why is it easier to control the costs of production than it is to control the costs of marketing?
9. What does the "value added" idea mean? Why was it introduced?
10. What marketing services add value to a product such as the Our-Sound record player? Why is this added value important?

ANALYZING MARKETING CONCEPTS

1. Marketing activities can be classified as exchange, physical distribution, or facilitating activities. Prepare a form like the one below. List the following marketing activities in the left-hand column: (a) advertising, (b) buying, (c) storing, (d) creating demand for new products, (e) selling, (f) grading, (g) transporting, (h) setting prices.

    Place a check mark in the appropriate column to indicate the classification of each type of activity listed.

Activity	Exchange	Physical Distribution	Facilitating
Example: Financing			✓

44 / Unit 1 / The World of Marketing

2. Consumers want more conveniences and more elaborate services. These increase the value of the product or service and its marketing costs. Prepare a form like the one below. List the following products in the left-hand column: (a) instant coffee, (b) electric toothbrush, (c) instant mashed potatoes, (d) automatic can opener, (e) electric shaver. In the right-hand column give a reason for the increase in value and increase in marketing cost for each product.

Product	Reason for Increase in Value and in Marketing Cost
Example: Frozen corn on the cob	Cleaned, trimmed, boxed, frozen, ready to eat.

◨ MARKETING PROJECT 4
Determining Utilities Added to Products

Project Goal: Given a product in a retail store, determine the utilities added to the product as it moves from the factory to the retailer.

Action: Select a product that is sold in one of your local retail stores. After preparing a form like the one below, list and explain the utilities added to the product as it moves from the factory to the retailer.

Product Name	Utility Added
Example: Ice cream bars	Form utility—Production creates ice cream from basic materials.

The Consumer Market

UNIT 2

NATURAL & ORGANIC
MANNA
FOOD
BREAD
NO PRESERVATIVES
SEVEN GRAIN 69¢
SPROUTED WHEAT 69¢
RASIN HONEY 69¢
BANANA 69¢
(SOY + WHEAT) 59¢
SALT FREE 59¢
Whole Grain Wheat 47¢
SOLD HERE
BAKED BY
MANNA FOOD CORP.
202 8TH ST.
JERSEY CITY, NJ

part 5

The Changing Consumer Market

YOUR GOALS

1. Given the annual income for a family of four, show how the family might budget this income for disposable and discretionary expenditures.
2. Given a set of data, identify five potential marketing uses for the data in determining customer expenditures.

What is a market? We speak of a supermarket or a stock market, and when we want to buy something, we sometimes say we are "in the market" for it. Thus, the word "market" has several meanings. In a more specialized sense, however, a *market* is all the potential customers for a product or service, or group of products or services.

There are two types of markets: the consumer market, which is discussed in this part, and the industrial market, which is discussed in Part 9. The *consumer market* is all the potential customers for goods and services sold for personal use. The consumer market includes people like you and your family, people who buy clothes, wristwatches, food, notebook paper, and televisions, among other items, for their own use and enjoyment. These are *consumer goods,* products intended to satisfy the needs and wants of the individual consumer. When you buy automobile insurance or the services of a repairman to fix your car, you are buying consumer services, services intended to satisfy the needs and wants of the individual consumer.

The consumer market in this country is tremendous. There are more than 200 million people in the United States, and the population is growing. The consumer market is also constantly changing. Every year thousands of young people get married and start their own households. Every year people obtain jobs for the first time and earn their own money. Every year new consumer products and services are introduced. Every year thousands of individuals and families move to different parts of the country. Every year the average earnings of the average person increases. Every year thousands of people retire and completely change the patterns of their lives.

All these changes affect marketing. The more people there are, the greater the demand for goods and services. The higher the average income, the more money people can afford to spend on those goods and services. The changes in the consumer market that most affect marketers are in three areas: the size and characteristics of the population, the amount of money people have available to spend, and the way people spend their money.

POPULATION

It is expected that by 1980 more than 230 million people will be living in this country. They will form a larger consumer market than the one we have today. By 1980 the characteristics of the population also will have changed. Various groups within the population will increase in proportion to other groups, while others will decrease. This change in the characteristics of the consumer market will present marketers with new challenges and new opportunities.

Size

At present, there are 3.5 billion people in the world, and more than 200 million of them live in the United States. The chart on page 50 gives the estimated size of the United States population from 1960 to 1970 and indicates the projected changes in its size through 1985.

Births will account for the largest part of the increase. Even though the birth rate has gone down, the actual number of babies born has been about the same for the past few years.

Increased life expectancy also will play a part. According to statistics, people live longer today and will have even longer life expectancies in the years to come. This means that the average person will be a part of both the population and the consumer market for a steadily increasing span of time.

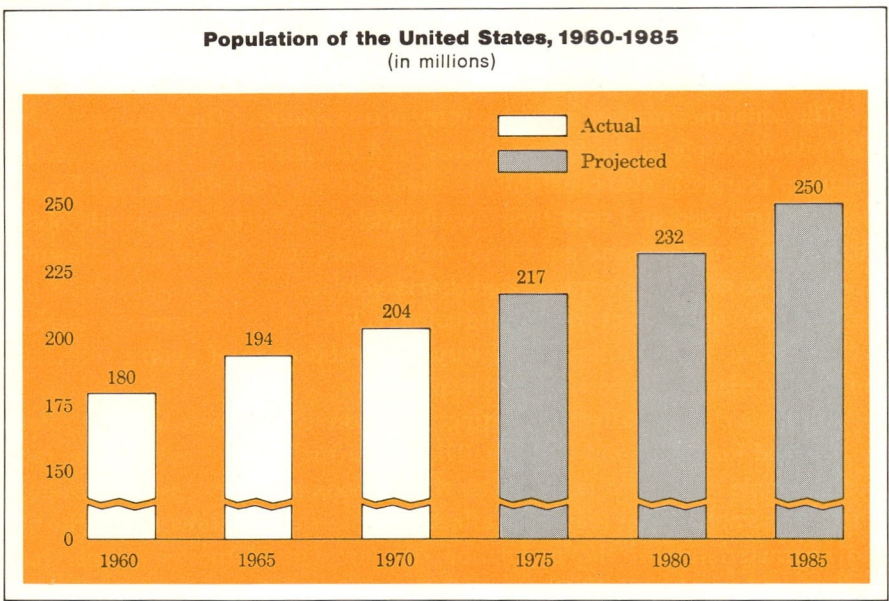

Population of the United States, 1960-1985
(in millions)

Year	Population	Type
1960	180	Actual
1965	194	Actual
1970	204	Actual
1975	217	Projected
1980	232	Projected
1985	250	Projected

Source: Bureau of the Census.

Characteristics

Think about your own neighborhood for a minute. If you have lived there for a number of years, you have probably noticed some changes. Perhaps it used to be made up mainly of young couples and their children. Now the couples are older, their children are almost grown, and many of the apartments or houses have new occupants. Perhaps new apartment buildings or houses have been built in the neighborhood, or perhaps old ones have been torn down.

Such changes in the characteristics of the population are occurring throughout the nation. The changes in population characteristics that will probably most affect marketers in the next decade involve the number of households within the population, the sizes of the various age groups, and the geographic distribution of the population.

Households. The number of households in this country is increasing even more rapidly than the size of the population. A household is a social unit that consists of one or more people living in the same dwelling place. (A family, another important population measurement, consists of two or more related people living together. Two unrelated people sharing a dwelling form a household, not a family.) The following chart gives the estimated number of households in the United States from 1960 to 1970 and the projected increases through 1985.

Number of Households in the United States, 1960-1985
(in millions)

Year	Households
1960	52.8
1965	57.3
1970	62.9
1975	68
1980	74
1985	81

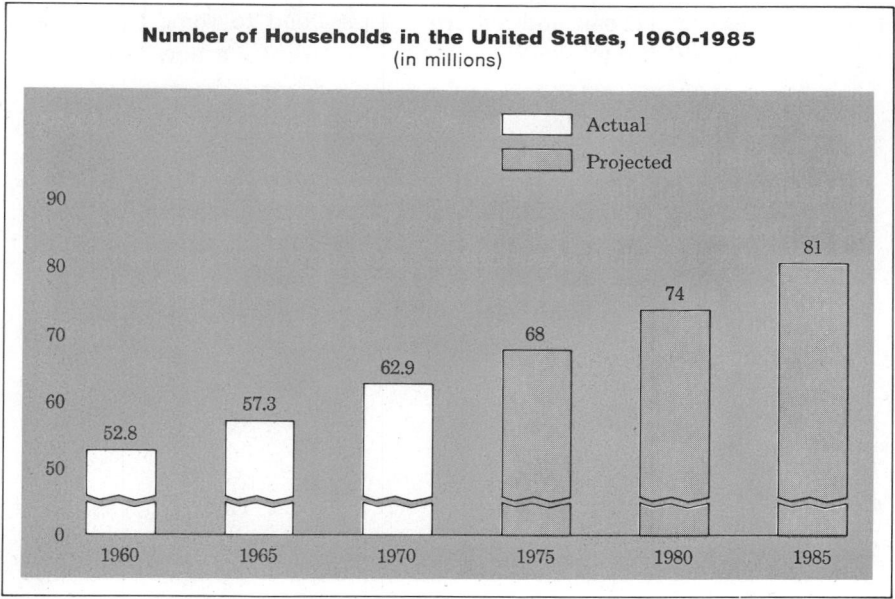

(1960–1970 Actual; 1975–1985 Projected)

Source: Bureau of the Census.

Keeping informed of the growth in households in the United States is important for marketers because the market for consumer goods and services —such as home furnishings, electrical appliances, heating and air-conditioning systems—is more closely related to the number of households in the country than to the number of people. An increase in the number of households means an increase in sales opportunities.

Age Groups. The fastest-growing age group is that of young adults between 20 and 34 years old. Today, one in five persons is in that age bracket. By 1980, probably one in four persons will be between 20 and 34. The result of this group's growth is a rapidly expanding market for housing, insurance, recreation, clothing, furniture, and other goods and services for young adults.

The second most rapidly growing age group is that of people aged 65 and older. Even though they always have been and will continue to be the smallest of the age groups, by 1980 they will make up a larger proportion of the total population than ever before. This means another important opportunity for marketers. The importance of age groups as a market factor is discussed further in Part 6.

Geographic Distribution. Americans move often and in great numbers, and this mobility is expected to continue. In general, the population is moving away from the central part of the country and toward the coasts, away from rural areas and into urban and suburban areas, and to some extent away from urban areas and into suburban areas. There is also a flow from east to west, and another flow from north to south. The three regions that are expected to grow most rapidly in the next years are the Pacific region, the Mountain region, and the South Atlantic region.

Mobility—the ability of people to move from place to place—has significance to marketers. It means good business for moving companies and storage companies. It means a loss of customers for rural retailers and an increase in customers for suburban retailers. And it may mean an increase in sales opportunities for those marketers whose goods have particular appeal in specific geographic regions.

INCOME

To be a customer, a person must have money to spend. This money is usually referred to as *income,* which is money received or earned. In marketing, income is divided into four types: national, personal, disposable, and discretionary.

- *National income* is the money measurement of the annual flow of goods and services in a nation. National income consists of income such as employee earnings and corporate profits.
- *Personal income* is the amount of money that a person earns or receives before any taxes are deducted.
- *Disposable income* is the amount of money that a person has for spending and saving. It is the money he has left after paying taxes.
- *Discretionary income* is the amount of money that a person has left to spend as he chooses after he has paid for the basic costs of living. Thus, discretionary income is disposable income minus the money spent for such necessities as food, shelter, clothing, transportation, and medical expenses. The word "discretion" means freedom to decide; so discretionary income is that part of a person's income that he may spend on anything he wants.

In analyzing income, marketers must find answers to the following questions: How much income do consumers have available to spend? Where is that income located geographically? How is that income distributed among the population?

Amount of Available Income

Marketers are interested in trends in disposable income and discretionary income. These incomes determine how much money the consumer has available to spend on goods and services (although, of course, he may put some of his income into savings or investments).

A person may spend his discretionary income as he wishes.

The marketers who supply the necessities of life—food, housing, and clothing—are interested in disposable income. The success of their business depends upon how much disposable income consumers use to buy the goods or services that will satisfy their basic needs. Marketers, then, want to know how much disposable income consumers have and whether that amount is increasing.

The average person has more disposable income than ever before. Disposable income on a per capita basis (amount of money divided by number of people) rose from slightly less than $2,000 in 1960 to more than $3,000 in 1970, and it is still rising.

Nearly every type of marketer is interested in the trends in discretionary income. Discretionary income is spent on luxuries rather than necessities. Therefore, marketers who make and sell so-called luxury goods are especially interested in this type of income.

Although discretionary income is increasing, it did not increase as rapidly between 1960 and 1970 as did disposable income. It increased less rapidly during that period because prices rose and people had to pay more for basic necessities. In addition, a few products and services that had been considered luxuries were added to the necessities list. However, people do have more discretionary income now and will continue to have more. Undoubtedly this will mean more business for all types of marketers.

Location of Income

Information on income level in various geographical areas helps a marketer determine whether to try to sell in a particular area and what kind of marketing effort to use. Income levels can be figured for a large region such as the West Coast, for a city, or even for a neighborhood.

At present, the highest levels of income in the United States are found along the Atlantic Coast and in the Great Lakes region. However, the greatest growth in income level is occurring on the West Coast because of the growth in population, industry, and business.

In general, how can marketers use this information? A distributor of fine jewelry might decide to reserve his best and most expensive pieces for his East Coast customers, or a manufacturer of home furnishings might decide to start promoting a higher-price line in his West Coast outlets.

Distribution of Income

Although poverty is and will continue to be a serious problem as long as a single person lacks enough money for necessities, more people in this country have more money than ever before. More families are earning incomes that place them in the middle- and upper-income brackets, and fewer families find themselves in the lower-income bracket.

This trend means that the increasing amount of money in the country is not going to just one group of people. Nearly everyone is getting a share. Almost every income group has more money to spend on consumer goods and services than it did 10 years ago.

Income is usually measured in terms of the family unit. In 1960 nearly one of every four families in the United States had an income of less than $3,000. In 1970 this proportion had decreased to only one of every nine or ten families. In 1960 one of three families earned $7,000 or more. In 1970 this proportion had increased to two of three families.

To marketers this increase means that sales opportunities exist at every income level. To some marketers it offers the possibility of encouraging customers to buy better-quality goods and services. For example, the couple that took a two-week vacation in the Pocono Mountains last year may be ready for a three-week tour of Europe this year. To other marketers the increase in family income offers the possibility of selling more goods or services.

EXPENDITURES

Once a marketer knows the approximate size of the market he wants to serve and the amount of money the customers in that market have, the final question he needs to answer is, "How are customers likely to spend their money?" An amount spent is an expenditure. The different ways in which groups of people spend their money are called *expenditure patterns.* Marketers get information on expenditure patterns from a number of sources: magazine and newspaper surveys, advertising company surveys, research organizations, and—perhaps most important—the federal government. The federal government collects enormous amounts of statistical data, analyzes them, and makes the results of the analyses available to anyone who wants them.

Marketers find two kinds of expenditure-pattern reports particularly useful. One examines expenditures according to income levels and shows the different ways in which people with different incomes spend their money. The other examines expenditures over a period of time and traces the way in which some products gradually get more of the customer's dollar and others gradually get less.

Patterns in Spending by Income Level

The federal government uses an imaginary family to explain consumer expenditure data. The family lives in an urban (in contrast to a rural) area. It consists of a 38-year-old man, his wife, a son 13 years old, and a daughter 8. The husband is a full-time skilled worker. The wife is not employed. The couple have been married for 15 years.

The government provides data about how the family spends its income. The data are worked out for three different income levels; the lowest income level is well above the poverty level, and the highest is in the upper-middle class. Thus the government's figures show the variations in spending that are typical of the largest part of the population, those consumers in the middle-income groups.

In 1970 the lowest budget for the imaginary family was set at $6,960; the intermediate budget, at $10,664; and the highest budget, at $15,511. The table on the next page shows how each of these budgets is spent during that year by the family.

These patterns have little meaning to the owner of a small store, but they are useful to large retailers and manufacturers. A large chain organization can use the patterns to help determine the probable sales volume when opening a unit in a new area. A national manufacturer can use them to help determine how a shift in national income level is going to influence the general market demand for his type of products.

Typical Budgets for a Family of Four

Item	Lower Budget	Intermediate Budget	Higher Budget
Food	$1,905	$2,452	$3,092
Housing	1,429	2,501	3,772
Transportation	505	912	1,183
Clothing and personal care	807	1,137	1,655
Medical care	562	564	588
Taxes	1,064	1,920	3,262
Other costs	688	1,178	1,959
Total budget	$6,960	$10,664	$15,511

Source: Bureau of Labor Statistics.

Note some of the expenditure patterns at different income levels:

■ The proportion of the budget spent for food decreases as the amount of income increases.

■ The proportion of the budget spent for housing increases as income increases.

■ The proportion of the budget spent for clothing and personal care increases slightly at the intermediate- and higher-income levels.

Changes in Product Demand

How people divide their expenditures among the various consumer-products categories changes from year to year. Every general category of consumer products and services has shown increased sales, but the rates of increase have been different. Between 1960 and 1969, total consumer spending in the United States rose approximately 45 percent. The amounts spent on housing and clothing showed about the same increase. The amounts spent on recreation and on cars, however, showed larger percentage increases, while the amounts spent on food showed smaller percentage increases.

If you look at the individual groups of products that make up each of these categories, you will find that the following were among the products receiving the greatest share of the consumer's dollar:

■ Radio, television, etc. (recreation)
■ Health and beauty aids (health care)
■ Sporting goods (recreation)
■ Foreign travel (recreation)
■ Auto parts and auto care (transportation)
■ Medicines and supplies (health care)
■ Jewelry and watches (clothing and accessories)

The increase in family recreation is an important factor contributing to the growth of the sporting-goods market.

If the patterns continue in this way and there is no leveling off in demand, they will mean important opportunities for marketers. They will mean good news to travel agencies, auto-supply stores, and department stores.

The patterns may also affect the future of supermarkets. Many supermarkets have found that adding products to meet changes in customer demand can pay off in increased sales. Food sales have not increased as rapidly as sales of many other categories of products, but supermarkets and grocery stores have acquired considerable nonfood business. If you have ever done the weekly food shopping, you know the many products besides food that you now can find in supermarkets. These markets have carried paper products for a long time, but the number and variety of paper products available have increased tremendously. There are all kinds of medicines and beauty aids, ranging from headache pills to hairsetting lotions. Pet products are not limited to food but include leashes, medication, and toys. Baby products include diapers, pants, and bottles as well as food. There usually is a variety of hardware products, and some supermarkets even sell clothes. The American consumer has shown a preference for one-stop shopping, and supermarkets have catered to that demand by expanding into a number of nonfood lines. By so doing, they have added to their sales.

These are the essential reasons why marketers watch changes in the consumer market so carefully. Those marketers who can best adapt their operations to meet changes in consumer demand win the major share of the consumer market.

◊ YOUR MARKETING VOCABULARY

On a separate sheet of paper define each of the following marketing terms; then use each term in a sentence.

Consumer goods
Consumer market
Discretionary income
Disposable income
Expenditure patterns
Income
Market
National income
Personal income

◊ FOR REVIEW AND DISCUSSION

1. Describe two types of markets.
2. What are consumer services?
3. What characteristics of the population will have changed by 1980?
4. Give three changes in population characteristics that will probably most affect marketers in the next decade.
5. What do the marketers who supply the necessities of life—food, housing, and clothing—want to know about disposable income?
6. Which marketers are most interested in the trends in discretionary income?
7. Give two reasons why discretionary income increased less rapidly than disposable income between 1960 and 1970.
8. From what sources do marketers get information on expenditure patterns?
9. Name five products that received the greatest share of the consumer's dollar between 1960 and 1969.
10. How have supermarkets shown that adding products to meet changes in customer demand can pay off in increased sales?

◊ ANALYZING MARKETING CONCEPTS

1. Discretionary income is spent on luxuries rather than necessities, and the purchase of one luxury item often leads to desire for related items. Prepare a form like the following one, and list these activities in the left-hand column: (a) boating, (b) cycling, (c) traveling, (d) playing tennis, (e) painting, (f) skiing. In the right-hand column, list several products that a consumer might want because of his interest in each of these activities.

Activity	Related Products
Example: Swimming	Swimsuit, fins, goggles, snorkel, scuba gear

2. The consumer market is constantly changing and the changes create increased demand for products. Prepare a form like the one below. In the left-hand column, list the following activities that a family might begin doing or do more often after moving from a city apartment to a suburban home: (a) outdoor cooking, (b) household repairs, (c) outdoor recreation, (d) gardening. In the right-hand column, list at least five products or services that the family would need because of these activities.

Family Activity	Demand for Products
Example: Weekend driving trips	A second car, more gas and oil, more frequent car service, extra snow tires.

◊ MARKETING PROJECT 5
Determining a Budget for a Typical Family of Four

Project Goal: Given the annual income for a family of four, show how the family might budget this income for disposable and discretionary expenditures.

Action: According to the Bureau of Labor Statistics, in 1970 a typical family of four needed an annual income of approximately $10,664 to live on a moderate budget. Determine the dollar amounts such a family would have budgeted for the following expenditures: food, housing, transportation, clothing and personal care, medical care, entertainment, taxes, and miscellaneous services and materials.

Prepare a form like the one below. In the two left-hand columns, write the expenditures listed in the preceding paragraph and the dollar amounts you would budget for each expenditure. Then place a check mark in the appropriate right-hand column to indicate whether the expenditure is disposable or discretionary. (Note that an expenditure may be part disposable and part discretionary.)

Expenditure	Budgeted Amount	Disposable	Discretionary
Example: Contributions	$50		✓

part 6

Market Segmentation

YOUR GOALS

1. Given a list of several types of market segments, identify the characteristics of each type.
2. Select ten specific products and identify the market segment or segments to which each product would appeal.

When Henry Ford made his first successful automobile, the Model T, he may have had plenty of problems, but marketing was not one of them. Customers were ready and waiting for their "horseless carriages," and the demand for them was far greater than the supply. The Model T was produced in one model and in one color (black); if a customer wanted a car at all, that was what he got.

However, as competition increased, Ford had to pay more attention to what the customer wanted. By studying the market, he realized that the customer wanted not only a car that would "get him there," but also one that suited his individual needs and tastes. A family man did not want the same type of car a young college student wanted. Likewise, a company president and a traveling salesman probably were not interested in exactly the same type of car. The market for cars was not simply a big mass of people, all with the same needs and the same characteristics. Instead, it was made up of a number of different groups, each with different needs and different characteristics.

So Ford and the other car makers began to give customers a wider selection. Before long, the sedan was identified with the family man, and the coupe, with its rumble seat, became the favorite car of the college crowd. Today the Ford Motor Company and other automobile manufacturers make many models in a great variety of colors and with a large choice of optional equipment and accessories, so that almost everyone can find exactly what he wants.

The automobile industry has grown to its present size and diversity because car manufacturers recognize and try to meet the needs of the many different groups, or segments, within the total market. The division of a total market into groups according to customer needs and characteristics is called *market segmentation.*

Thinking in terms of market segmentation helps the marketer do a much more effective job of selling. Only when he identifies and understands the different groups of potential customers can he tailor his offerings to meet the exact needs of one of or all these groups.

For example, instead of aiming at the total market for blue jeans, a manufacturer could divide the market into several segments and then plan his

Market segmentation helps the marketer identify the most likely customers for his product.

production to meet the needs of one or more of those segments. He could divide the market according to sex, age level, or intended use of the product. If he wanted to make something for several segments, he could offer heavy-duty jeans for work, slacks-styled jeans as sportswear for both men and women, and brightly colored jeans for children's wear.

This kind of thinking should continue throughout the pricing, promotion, and distribution of a product. Market segmentation is just as important to wholesalers and retailers as it is to manufacturers. For example, a department store and a discount store may offer the same television set, but their ways of pricing, promoting, and distributing that set may be extremely different because they are tailoring their marketing efforts to two distinct segments of the consumer market.

A market may be divided according the certain characteristics, including age, education, geographical location, and ethnic background. The marketer chooses the division that is most useful to him.

AGE

Persons within a specific age group have many buying needs and wants in common. Thus the group as a whole creates a specific market demand. For example, all babies need diapers and special foods; people over age 65 tend to use more medicine and other health-care products than do younger people.

Marketers generally divide the consumer market into five age groups: (1) children, (2) teen-agers, (3) young adults, (4) the middle-aged, and (5) the over-65s. Segmentation by age group is probably the most important method of market segmentation used today. Manufacturers and retailers alike spend considerable time planning and choosing products for their appeal to a specific age group. The promotion for these products often includes a direct reference to a specific age level: "For the young—and the young at heart," or "For those who are mature enough to appreciate the best."

Some manufacturers concentrate their entire production on a single age group. Most children's clothing, for example, is made by firms that make only children's clothing. Some retailers set up their entire store to serve a single age level. Others, including most big department stores, set aside departments within the store to serve various age levels. The popular teen shop is a good example of such a department.

The Children's Market

At one time, marketers considered the children's market to be made up of youngsters aged 12 and under. Today, however, marketers consider it to be made up of those aged 10 and younger. The drop from age 12 to 10 is due to the tendency of 11- and 12-year-olds to mimic the behavior and attitudes of teen-agers rather than children.

Even before a child enters school, he gains some independence and begins to form tastes and preferences of his own. Although he has no income, he influences the purchasing decisions of others. Breakfast cereals compete with each other in their colorful design and packaging in order to reach the youngster. The brand of cereal is often secondary to the comic-strip figures that cover the package and the premiums and toys that are promised to the lucky purchaser. The market for toys and games is guided by children's preferences, and children's television programs carry the advertisements of toy manufacturers who know that promotion aimed right at the child will influence how the parent's dollar is spent.

Children do have some money to spend as they wish. This is why a chewing-gum manufacturer tries to attract a preschooler's interest by offering candy-coated balls of bubble gum in eye-catching colors. For the older child the manufacturer sparks interest by offering regular bubble gum in a wrapper printed with a comic strip.

Perhaps the most important consumers within the children's age group are babies. Parents willingly spend money on their babies. They are seldom interested in bargains because they are afraid of sacrificing quality for economy. Instead, they buy from those marketers who have proven that they can supply their customers with the goods and services that keep babies healthy and happy.

The Teen-Age Market

The idea of a teen-age market apart from a children's market or an adult market is relatively new. In the late 1950s and early 1960s, teen-agers with considerable amounts of money to spend began to appear in the marketplace in large numbers. It did not take marketers long to realize that this age group has specific tastes and attitudes. The typical teen-ager is interested in the "new"—new fashions, new music, new cars, new foods, new hair styles, and new ideas. He wants to buy a new record every week, see "action" movies, and go bowling, skating, or dancing as often as possible. The teen-age market thus resulted from the special tastes, attitudes, and outlook of the teen-ager and from the fact that the teen-ager of today has more of his own money to spend.

The "youth quake" that made this market so important is also affecting other segments of the consumer market. Family purchases of automobiles, furniture, and even homes are influenced by teen-agers. Furthermore, many buying trends originate with high school students. Teen-age girls are very clothes-conscious, and their clothing choices sometimes have far-reaching effects on adult fashions. Many cars are designed with the tastes of the 17- or 18-year-old boy in mind. While he rarely buys a car himself, he influences his parents' choice.

Marketers know that buying habits formed by the young are likely to continue beyond the teen years. In catering to the young person as a customer, the manufacturer hopes to build loyalty to his product and the retailer hopes to build loyalty to his store—the kind of loyalty that will persist when the teen-ager is an adult, with an adult's buying power.

The Young-Adult Market

As mentioned in Part 5, the fastest-growing age group in this decade is that of young adults, those from 20 to 34 years of age. This age group is important not only because it is growing, but also because of its purchasing potential. People in this age group have their first jobs, get married, establish their own homes, and start families. Thus they are a vital market segment for marketers of automobiles and automobile accessories, clothing, housing, home furnishings, and babies' and children's products.

Young adults make up a large part of the market for home furnishings.

Courtesy Two Guys Department Store, a subsidiary of Vornado, Inc.

64 / Unit 2 / The Consumer Market

To reach the young-adult market, a manufacturer may place ads for his line of modern furniture in magazines that are read by young adults. An automobile dealer may put a commercial in a spot right before a television program that is popular with this age group. Or an airline promoting off-season vacations may mail brochures to a list of young adults. Marketers know that this group has major needs and wants, the money to satisfy those needs and wants, and a willingness to spend.

The Middle-Aged Market

The middle-aged group—people between 35 and 64 years old—numbers about 65 million. It is this group that has the most buying power and that buys the largest amount of consumer goods and services.

In spite of their importance, however, the middle-aged are sometimes called "the forgotten consumers." One reason for this is that most of them have established homes and grown children. Thus, they are no longer major buyers of houses, home furnishings, and babies' and children's products. Although the middle-aged often pay the bills for goods and services designed for other age groups, marketers of those products generally aim their promotion at the age groups who will use them.

Some marketers, however, have always paid attention to the middle-aged group. They include marketers of cars, insurance, and the more expensive kinds of sporting goods, such as golf clubs, boats, and swimming pools. Other marketers are beginning to realize that they cannot take this group's business for granted forever. If they do, they run the risk of losing that business to more attentive and energetic competitors.

The Over-65 Market

Many marketers direct their efforts at the people in our society aged 65 and older. All these people are, of course, consumers of the basic necessities. Most have some discretionary income, and a good number have a considerable amount. Most of these people have considerable leisure time that they want to fill. In addition, many of them have physical problems that require special attention.

Marketers of housing have planned apartment colonies exclusively for those who have retired. These colonies usually feature easy-to-maintain apartments, neighborhood social centers, nearby shopping areas whose stores cater to the over-65 group, nearby recreational facilities, and the availability of medical care. In some areas, retirement neighborhoods spring up independently. This often occurs where older people are attracted by a comfortable climate and a reasonable cost of living. The marketers of the area do their

Recreational facilities are one of the features that marketers of housing include in retirement communities.

A. Devaney, Inc., N.Y.

share to make it attractive to older residents by tailoring their offerings to the residents' needs as follows:

- Cafeterias and restaurants serve good, plain food at inexpensive prices and often do a booming business.
- Supermarkets sell a surprising amount of baby food to older people. Baby food is gentle, ready-to-eat nourishment for those with digestive problems.
- Handicraft classes and bridge classes are given in areas where people have leisure time to fill.
- "Par-3" golf courses are popular. Shorter and easier to play than the average course, they also cost less.
- Gardeners, painters, repairmen, cleaners, tailors, and seamstresses all find themselves very busy doing the jobs that the over-65s either no longer can do or no longer want to do themselves.
- Travel agencies offer group trips and tours geared to the more leisurely pace of the older person. While an agency advertising a tour of Europe may not say "for older people," everything about the tour will appeal to

this group. All reservations are made for them, ample free time for rest is scheduled, and visas and passports are provided. Everything is taken care of by the travel agency.

Marketers have been exploring this growing market for more than a decade, and yet they find that they are still able to discover many new and different opportunities to serve it.

EDUCATION

In 1920 only 2 people of each 100 in the work force were college graduates. Today, 33 of 100 have attended college, and the percentage is increasing. There are several reasons for this increase. One reason is that there are more schools of higher education, and many of them are located near the homes of their students. This means that more people can go to college and live at home, which makes it less expensive to get an education. Another reason is that people have more money today to spend on education. Also, students realize they are living in a rapidly changing world where jobs are becoming more specialized and more education is required. In fact, for most people, education is becoming a lifelong process.

To the marketer this increased interest in education means that more people may develop interest in a larger variety of products and services, such as books, photographic equipment, power boats, foreign travel, and summer homes. It also means that many people, because they are better educated, will be able to earn more money to spend on these goods.

And, marketers know that "education" does not mean just college. For example, most insurance companies give high school students who have taken a driver's education course a lower automobile insurance rate because such courses produce safer drivers.

GEOGRAPHICAL LOCATION

The consumer market may be divided geographically, that is, by regions or sections of the country. In the 1930s the Eastern and Great Lakes states contained 75 percent of the population. A marketer in those days probably located his offices in New York, Boston, Cleveland, or Chicago. Times have changed. While the East and the Great Lakes areas are still growing, their rates of growth have slowed down in comparison with the growth in the Southeast and Southwest.

Every change in the geographical location of the population produces at least one change in the consumer market. If you moved from the Northeast to the West Coast, there would be one less consumer in the Northeast and one more consumer in the West. And because people in the Northeast buy more overcoats and rainwear than people in the West (it is generally colder and wetter in the Northeast), your moving away would mean a slight decrease in the size of the potential market demand for outerwear. On the other hand, people on the West Coast tend to buy more barbecue equipment, so your move would mean a slight rise in the size of the potential market demand for barbecue equipment.

ETHNIC BACKGROUND

Markets for goods and services can be segmented according to ethnic groups. An *ethnic group* is all the people who have certain characteristics in common, such as language, social customs, or physical traits.

There are many ethnic groups in our country. Various ethnic groups want or need goods that help them preserve or conform to their cultural traditions. Thus these people form individual markets within the general consumer market.

Among the ethnic groups that have formed important individual markets for years are the Chinese (on the East Coast and the West Coast), the Japanese (on both coasts), the Germans (in the Northeast and Midwest), the Scandina-

Rona Beame/DPI

Meat markets often specialize in products that appeal to local ethnic groups.

68 / Unit 2 / The Consumer Market

vians (in the Midwest), and the Irish (in the Northeast). When members of these groups first arrived in America, they settled near other members of their group and formed ethnic neighborhoods. Soon local restaurants, grocery stores, and other marketing outlets offered products and services to suit the tastes and preferences of each group.

Among the ethnic groups rapidly growing in importance are black Americans. The black population in the United States is 23 million, or 11 percent of the total population. The income of black people is rising. Although the gap between the incomes of black people and white people has not yet been closed, progress has been made.

This progress in the income of black Americans has had two important effects on the consumer market: (1) Black Americans are becoming an increasingly important buying force, and marketers are appealing to them. Thus ads and commercials often feature black fashion models, entertainers, or athletes. (2) Because of the black people's renewed pride in their cultural heritage, there has been an increase in the demand for specialized products among black consumers. Such products include beauty aids, clothing, and fabrics based on African traditions and styles.

LIMITATIONS OF MARKET SEGMENTATION

Market segmentation is very useful and important to marketers, but it results in measurements that are likelihoods, not laws. The lines between all market segments are fuzzy, as are the lines between social classes. Many assumptions about the consumer market can be made. But because consumers are people and people are never completely predictable, none of the assumptions can be considered infallible and unchanging.

◘ YOUR MARKETING VOCABULARY

On a separate sheet of paper define each of the following marketing terms; then use each term in a sentence.
Ethnic group
Market segmentation

◘ FOR REVIEW AND DISCUSSION

1. How does market segmentation help the marketer do a more effective job of selling?
2. A market may be divided according to several characteristics. Name four such characteristics.
3. Why is market segmentation by age important?

4. What methods does the chewing gum manufacturer use to appeal to the children's market?
5. What is the fastest-growing age group in this decade? Why is this group important to marketers? What are some ways in which businessmen reach the market formed by this group?
6. Why are people in the middle-aged market sometimes called "the forgotten consumers"?
7. Why do marketers frequently direct their efforts at people aged 65 and older?
8. Name three products that would be marketed in Alaska that would not be marketed in a location that has a tropical climate, such as southern Florida.
9. For the marketer, what is the importance of a general increase in education?
10. What are some of the limitations of market segmentation?

◊ ANALYZING MARKETING CONCEPTS

1. Certain variations in products appeal to particular market segments. Prepare a form like the one below. In the left-hand column, list the following products: (a) stereo system, (b) tape recorder, (c) shampoo, (d) ballpoint pen, (e) coat, (f) magazine, (g) aspirin. In the center column, give a variation of the product that would appeal to a particular market segment. In the right-hand column, identify the market segment to which the product variation might appeal.

Product	Variation	Market Segment
Example: Wristwatch	Ballerina on dial	Girls, ages 6–10

2. Marketers use many activities to appeal to a particular market segment. Prepare a form like the one below, and list the following types of businesses in the left-hand column: (a) record shop, (b) shoe store, (c) bank, (d) drive-in restaurant, (e) insurance company, (f) travel agency, (g) real estate company, (h) drugstore, (i) men's clothing store. In the right-hand column, describe one marketing activity that each business might use to appeal to a market segment.

Type of Business	Marketing Activity
Example: Department store	A free fashion show for teen-age girls.

◊ MARKETING PROJECT 6
Identifying Market Segments for Products

Project Goal: Select ten specific products and identify the market segment or segments to which each product would appeal.

Action: Obtain copies of several current magazines and select ten products advertised in the publications. Prepare a form like the one below. In the left-hand column, list the products you have selected. In the right-hand column, name the market segment or segments to which each product would appeal.

Product	Market Segment
Example: Portable color TV set	Teen-agers, college students living away from home, people with a summer home.

part 7

Customer Buying Behavior

YOUR GOALS

1. Given a specific product, name several buying motives to which the advertisers of the product might appeal.
2. Given a specific product, show how a marketer might appeal to six different motivation groups.

To do an effective job of selling its products, a company must pay close attention to the attitudes, intentions, and desires that influence customers to buy the type of product it offers. For example, a customer buys a car basically as a means of transportation. But all brands of cars provide transportation. What makes a customer prefer one brand to another? How can an automobile marketer produce the right kind of car for the customer he wants to attract? To answer these questions, the alert marketer has to understand how people make their buying decisions.

Marketers can easily gather a great deal of information about the marketplace. By examining a particular geographic area, a marketer can learn how many people live in that area, how many of them were graduated from high school, how much money the families of the area earn, and how many families own two or more cars. Marketers also have at their fingertips a great deal of information about the buying process, and about where people buy and who does the buying. What marketers know little about is how people buy and why they act as they do in a particular buying situation.

Some people say that consumers are helpless in the marketplace and that they are totally under the control of marketers. If this were so, then quantity information, such as the size of incomes and the number of households, would be all that marketers would need. As income and population grew, so would sales.

But consumers are not puppets manipulated by marketers. Rather, they react in their own ways based on their own needs and wants. Even when incomes and earning power are high, people may decide to stop spending for a while, no matter what marketers do.

Thus, to market goods and services successfully, quantity information is not enough. The amount of people's incomes, the extent of their education, and the size of their families do not completely explain the differences in their buying behavior.

To understand buying behavior, it is necessary to understand the fundamentals of all human behavior. The way a person acts and reacts is his behavior. The way a person acts and reacts in the marketplace is his *buying behavior*.

Marketers have learned that buying behavior follows a pattern, just as all human behavior does. In addition, while every customer buys for reasons slightly different or vastly different from the reasons motivating other customers, there are definite types of buying behavior that can be identified by marketers.

Marketers do not want to manipulate the customer. Rather, they want to offer him the right product at the right price at the right time and place. Learning about customer buying behavior helps them to do this.

STIMULUS AND RESPONSE

The pattern of all behavior consists of a stimulus and a response. The stimulus prompts the response. You are cold: That is the stimulus. You put on a sweater: That is the response. You are happy about some good news you have received and want to share it: That is the stimulus. You telephone a friend: That is the response.

A stimulus gives a person a desire or a motive to do something. "Stimulus" and "response" are words used mainly in psychology. "Motive" is a word used commonly by people in the field of marketing. A motive is an urge that prompts a person to do something. A *buying motive* is an urge that prompts a person to buy something.

The pattern of all behavior, including buying behavior, involves both a stimulus and a response. Here the response follows the stimulus quickly.

Buying behavior follows the same pattern as all other behavior. A stimulus makes a person aware of a need or want. This need or want gives the person a buying motive, or an urge to change his present condition. The person's response is the action he takes to satisfy that need or want.

The pattern of behavior can be diagrammed as follows:

Stimulus	Motive	Response
Need or want ▶	Desire or urge to change conditions ▶	Action

For example, a consumer realizes that she needs groceries for the weekend. A stimulus, the need for groceries, has given her a buying motive. Her response, or action, is to take a trip to her favorite supermarket, where she will be able to satisfy her need.

74 / Unit 2 / The Consumer Market

BUYING MOTIVATION

People buy goods and services because of needs and wants. There are numerous kinds of needs and wants and therefore numerous kinds of buying motives.

Very few purchases, if any, are made on the basis of a single buying motive. In the simplest buying situation, there may be one major buying motive and a few minor motives. In more complicated buying situations, there may be a number of buying motives, each influencing the final purchase.

Over the years experts in motivation research have developed a number of ways to classify buying motives. These include classifying buying motives as physical or psychological, rational or emotional, and product or patronage. Each classification helps explain buying behavior in certain situations.

Physical and Psychological Motives

Physical motives are, of course, based on physical needs, whereas psychological motives are based on psychological needs. Man's physical needs are fairly obvious: the needs to satisfy hunger and thirst and to avoid danger.

Psychological needs are less obvious. They can be divided into the following three main groups:

1. *Need for love.* Man needs to have and keep warm and harmonious relationships with others.
2. *Need for ego-support.* Man needs to think well of himself, to achieve, and to gain prestige.
3. *Need for ego-defense.* Man needs to protect himself against any unfavorable opinions that others might develop about him, to avoid loss of prestige when possible, and to obtain relief from anxieties.

Physical needs are satisfied by buying goods that range from candy bars and soft drinks to houses and apartments. People buy an even greater variety of goods and services to satisfy psychological needs. To satisfy their need for love, people may buy greeting cards and gifts for their friends and relatives. To satisfy ego-support needs, they may buy the newest styles in apparel, a barbecue grill just like one the neighbors have, or membership in various clubs and social organizations. To satisfy ego-defense needs, they may buy wigs or cosmetics to enhance their appearance, or insurance to relieve themselves of anxiety about possibly losing their possessions.

Rational and Emotional Motives

Rational buying motives are based on reason, whereas emotional ones are based on instinct and emotion. Examples of rational motives are efficiency and dependability. Emotional motives include adventure and romance.

Any buying decision, remember, usually involves more than one buying motive. It may even involve a combination of opposite types of motives; that is, the decision may be part emotional and part rational.

A way of measuring motivation in terms of these two motives is to think of a kind of bar scale. Emotional motives are at one end of the scale and rational motives are at the other end, as shown below.

Emotional	Rational

The motivation for any single buying decision is measured by putting a pointer somewhere along the bar scale. The exact position of the pointer depends on the amount of influence each motive has on the buying decision. For example, if a buying decision is primarily rational and emotional motives play a very small part, the pointer would be placed at the rational end of the scale:

Emotional	▲ Rational

On the other hand, if a buying decision is primarily emotional and rational motives play a very small part, the pointer would be placed at the emotional end of the scale:

Emotional ▲	Rational

Product and Patronage Motives

Product motives are based on the customer's choice of a particular product. Patronage motives are based on the customer's choice of a particular distributor or store. Product motives often result from advertising of the product itself. Patronage motives are generally the result of a favorable image of the distributor or store.

Consider a customer who wants to buy a particular brand of washing machine because two of her friends recommended it. She compares the prices of the machine at two local department stores and a discount store. Finding that the discount store sells the machine at the lowest price, she buys it there. Her motive is a product motive.

Another customer in need of a washing machine might visit her favorite department store and ask a salesman in the appliance department to recommend a brand. She likes the store and the service she has received there in the past, and she trusts the salesman's judgment. Her motive is a patronage motive.

It is not unusual for a customer to make a buying decision on the basis of both a product motive and a patronage motive. Suppose, for example, that you want to buy a pair of shoes and you prefer a certain brand. You know that a number of local stores carry the brand, but you prefer shopping at a certain department store. Your motive for selecting the brand of shoes is a product motive, but your motive for selecting the particular store in which to purchase them is a patronage motive.

THE RESPONSE: ACTION

When buying needs are realized and buying motives appear, action follows. The action starts as a mental process and ends when the purchase is made and the need is satisfied.

The mental processes—perceiving, remembering, thinking, and judging—are called *cognitive activities.* The conscious decision-making process that people go through when buying goods and services involves these processes.

For example, Mrs. Schultz wants to buy a sewing machine. She "perceives" the one she wants by trying out various models and by choosing one that seems to be the most efficient and that feels the most comfortable. She "remembers" that the brand has a well-known and respected reputation. She "thinks" about the features of the machine, evaluating whether the machine will do everything she wants it to do. Finally, she "judges" that the machine will satisfy her needs. She then makes her purchase.

How large a part these mental processes play in a buying decision varies according to the sales situation. When a person buys a product that is important or expensive, such as a car, a house, or a boat, he spends considerable time on the mental processes before he reaches his final decision. On the other hand, when making a routine purchase, such as buying toothpaste or shaving cream, a person will spend a minimum of time "thinking" about the product before buying it.

Cues

A stimulus that, in certain situations, leads the individual to respond to a need is called a *cue.* Marketers have found the idea of cues to be very useful, particularly in introducing new products. Man is especially receptive to cues that will help him determine how to satisfy his needs. If he finds that his needs are satisfied by a product or service, he is likely to adopt a loyalty for that particular brand of product or service and buy it again.

For example, suppose a consumer needs some laundry detergent. She decides to try a new brand after seeing a TV commercial (cue) and noticing a sale on that brand at the supermarket (cue). *Response* is an action that the person takes after being exposed to cues. The consumer's response is to buy the detergent. *Reinforcement* is an action that tends to confirm a previous response and lead the customer to make the same response again. In the above examples the reinforcement is the satisfactory condition of the finished wash. If the laundry detergent does a satisfactory job, then the experience of buying it becomes a rewarding one, and the consumer will buy the same brand the next time she needs detergent. However, if the detergent was not satisfactory, she will not repeat the pattern and will look for another brand instead.

People and Surroundings

In addition to cues, other outside influences affect buying decisions. These outside influences include both people—those in the potential customer's family or circle of friends and acquaintances—and the surroundings in which the potential customer moves.

The effect of a person's family on his buying behavior can readily be seen when you look at shoppers in various buying situations. Each family member plays a part. Family members may influence buying decisions even when they are not present when the purchase is made. In the supermarket, for example, a woman chooses a beef rather than a pork roast because her husband prefers beef, and she chooses a particular kind of cereal because her children like it.

What outside influences might cause this customer to buy health foods?

Editorial Photocolor Archives, Inc.

78 / Unit 2 / The Consumer Market

Friends, too, both as individuals and as groups or organizations, influence buying behavior. A girl may buy a certain pair of shoes because she admires the pair her friend bought. Boys in a baseball group may all buy the same brand of glove.

Influences on buying behavior also come from the customer's surroundings: the school, the job, the neighborhood, the climate, and the weather conditions on a particular day. A student may buy a particular notebook because it is a school requirement. A young man who works in a smoggy city may buy dark-colored suits instead of light-colored ones so that he will look well-groomed on the job without having to have his suits cleaned often. A woman caught in a rainstorm while shopping may buy a rain hat.

CUSTOMER BEHAVIOR PATTERNS

Each person has his own buying motives and acts on them in his own way. Many people can identify the motives for their buying behavior, but others cannot.

The buying motives that influence a person can change. What has long been a strong buying motive for someone can cease to be one. Changes in normal life, such as changes in age or income or responsibilities, can bring about changes in buying behavior. For example, a young married couple may buy a small sports car because to them it represents fun, pleasure, and good times. Several years later, when they have children, they may buy a station wagon because their buying motives now are comfort and convenience for the whole family.

In spite of the fact that buying motives change, it is important for marketers to try to divide the market according to people's buying motives and buying behavior. Only when a marketer can get a general idea of how and why his customers buy—regardless of all the exceptions that exist—can he organize his marketing effort to appeal to those customers.

Awareness of Motives

It is possible to divide customers into three groups according to their awareness of their own buying motives: those who know why they buy, those who know why they buy but will not admit why, and those who do not know why they buy.

Customers in the first group—those who know why they buy—understand their motives and thus can explain them clearly to any marketer who seeks the information.

The second group—those who are aware of their buying motives but will not admit them to someone else—make it difficult for a marketer to do any kind of accurate research. A man who buys a sports car because its powerful engine makes him feel like a more powerful person may say that the car's excellent handling is what convinced him to make the purchase. He has, in effect, given the marketer misleading information. Thus marketers who want to obtain information on buying behavior from this group must handle their research carefully if it is to produce useful and accurate data.

The third group—those who do not know the real reasons why they buy—may act impulsively or hide their real reason for buying. They do this so successfully that often they fool even themselves. For example, a boy may say he is going to a football game because he enjoys watching football. He really believes this is his basic reason. However, his basic reason may be his desire to be with his friends. It is difficult for a marketer to find the real buying motives of this group.

To find out the motives of those people who will not reveal them or who do not know what they are, marketers may apply the techniques of *motivation research,* a form of market research that studies factors influencing buying behavior. Working generally with small groups, motivation researchers concentrate on the deepest reasons why people buy. By using in-depth interviews and other techniques, motivation researchers sometimes can discover buying motives that people may not admit to themselves or may not realize they have.

Editorial Photocolor Archives, Inc.

This student may have several motives for buying a record. Can you name some of them?

80 / Unit 2 / The Consumer Market

Marketers of perfume often use glamorous images to appeal to customers.

Courtesy Chanel, Inc.

Motivation Groups

The buying behavior patterns of customers can be classified into several basic groups. No marketer can say for sure that any one customer belongs in a particular group. However, he can make a rough estimate of the groups into which customers fall. These groups are (1) the habit-determined group, (2) the cognitive group, (3) the price-cognitive group, (4) the impulse group, (5) the emotional group, and (6) the group of new customers.[1]

The habit-determined group tends to be loyal to particular brands and products. This loyalty is based on satisfaction with the brand or product bought previously. When a customer of this group is stimulated by a need, he usually responds by buying whatever satisfied him the last time he had the same need. He does not care what the toothpaste ads say. He has used a particular brand for a number of years, has found it satisfactory, and continues to buy that brand.

The cognitive group, on the other hand, is very responsive to rational

[1] Walter A. Woods, "Psychological Dimensions of Consumer Decision," *Journal of Marketing,* Vol. 24, p. 17, January, 1960.

appeals in ads. This is the group at which the "fact ads" are aimed. The customer is likely to read, compare, and examine before he makes his purchase. He may do this even in the case of a relatively simple and routine product. It often takes time and care to make a sale to this customer. But the marketer who does not take the time and care may lose him to a competitor who does.

The price-cognitive group decides what to buy primarily on the basis of price or economy. This does not mean that the customer is unable to judge quality. He knows the specific quality he wants, and he chooses the most economical brand or product with that quality. This customer is the one who is stimulated by price-reduction sales.

The impulse group usually ends up spending more than planned. The customer starts out with a few definite needs to satisfy and ends up buying twice as much as he expected. He responds quickly to special offers and displays. He can be a marketer's delight because he accounts for a number of plus sales; but he can also be a marketer's frustration if he later regrets his purchases and returns them to the store.

The emotional group is strongly swayed by product symbols and images. The customer in this group likes status merchandise, regardless of cost. Depending on which symbols and images sway him, his need for an automobile may be satisfied by buying a Cadillac or a Volkswagen. To make a sale to this customer, the marketer must find out the symbols and images the customer lives by and then offer products that fit them.

The group of new customers are those who have not yet established their buying patterns. They may be spending their own money for the first time, or they may have changed their way of living and are now developing a new spending pattern. All a marketer can do about these customers is wait. Much of their buying behavior will eventually fit into one of the recognized patterns.

◊ YOUR MARKETING VOCABULARY

On a separate sheet of paper define each of the following marketing terms; then use each term in a sentence.

Buying behavior
Buying motive
Cognitive activities
Cue

Motivation research
Reinforcement
Response

◊ FOR REVIEW AND DISCUSSION

1. What have marketers learned about buying behavior?
2. What does the pattern of human behavior consist of?
3. Name three ways of classifying buying motives.

4. Give examples of four kinds of goods people buy to satisfy psychological needs.
5. When a person is buying an important or expensive product, what does he do before he reaches his final decision?
6. When in particular have marketers found the idea of cues very useful? Explain.
7. In addition to cues, give two other outside influences that affect buying decisions.
8. Cite three changes in normal life that can bring about changes in buying behavior.
9. List the three groups into which customers may be divided according to their awareness of their own buying motives.
10. List the six motivation groups and describe their buying behavior.

◊ ANALYZING MARKETING CONCEPTS

1. Most buying decisions involve several motives, but one of these motives may be the most important. Prepare a form like the one below. List the following items in the left-hand column: (a) bread, (b) tires, (c) dictionary, (d) vitamins, (e) ring, (f) chair, (g) set of wrenches, (h) blanket. In the center column, list several possible buying motives for each item. Circle the one motive that you feel is the most important. In the right-hand column, explain briefly why you think this motive is the most important.

Item	Buying Motives	Why Circled Motive Is Most Important
Example: Jogging shoes	(Comfort,) bargain, attractiveness	A comfortable pair of shoes is necessary to enjoy jogging.

2. A marketer knows that a specific product may be bought by different customers for different reasons. Prepare a form like the one below. List the following products in the left-hand column: (a) gloves, (b) electric can opener, (c) magazine, (d) comic book, (e) record, (f) shirt, (g) dress shoes, (h) doll, (i) picture. For each product listed, identify in the center column one type of customer who might buy that product. In the right-hand column, list the customer's main motive for buying the product.

Product	Type of Customer	Main Buying Motive
Example: Pants	Teen-ager	Social approval

◊ MARKETING PROJECT 7
Appealing to Buying Motives

Project Goal: Given a specific product, show how a marketer might appeal to six different motivation groups.

Action: Select a product advertised in a newspaper or magazine. Study the advertisement to determine its marketing appeals. Prepare a form like the one below. In the appropriate columns, write the name of your product, the six motivation groups discussed in this part, and the marketing appeal of your product to each group.

Product Name	Motivation Group	Marketing Appeal
Example: Chrysler station wagon	Habit-determined	Members have owned Chrysler cars that performed well.

part 8

Customer Buying Patterns

YOUR GOALS

1. Given three stores in your community, rate them according to their effectiveness in selling to customers.
2. Given an assortment of consumer goods, show how the buying patterns for these goods vary among different customers. Explain why the customers buy and when and where they buy.

Every successful marketer knows that his business depends on pleasing his customers. Cash registers keep ringing only when the customer gets the service he expects, the conveniences he demands, and most important, the merchandise he wants at the price he is ready to pay. To keep his customers satisfied and to attract new ones, a marketer must ask himself the following questions:

- What are the tastes and attitudes of my customers?
- Which member of the family is making the buying decision?
- Who else influences the buying decision?
- Where and when do my customers choose to shop?
- What additional services will encourage them to buy my products or shop in my store?

HOW PEOPLE BUY

People's tastes and attitudes profoundly influence how they buy. However, over a period of time and under certain circumstances, their tastes and attitudes can change (as described in Part 7). And when tastes and attitudes change, buying patterns also change. To serve customers effectively, then, alert marketers must keep up with changes in buying patterns. Marketers have identified many buying patterns that are common today. They have discovered that people are doing a great deal of unplanned, or impulse, buying; that people are placing a value on time; and that people are seeking convenience.

Buying on Impulse

Buying with little or no advance planning is called *impulse buying.* For example, a customer goes into a hardware store to buy flashlight batteries. While there he also selects light bulbs from one display and a ball of twine from another. He then sees some special glue he has heard about and buys it. All these items except the batteries were bought on impulse.

Items that a customer wants when he sees them although he had not set out to buy them are called *impulse goods.* Goods frequently purchased on impulse include candy bars, chewing gum, razor blades, pens, pencils, note pads, hand cream, and goods that are popular at certain seasons of the year, such as antifreeze in winter and fishing lures or insect spray in summer.

University Films/McGraw-Hill

Marketers encourage impulse buying by placing goods close to where customers pay for their merchandise.

Impulse goods are generally displayed where they can easily be seen, for example, near a cash register or along a busy aisle.

Many people consider impulse buying a sensible way to shop, since self-service and open merchandise displays encourage them to wait until they are in the store to make buying decisions. Retailers encourage impulse buying by placing eye-catching displays of impulse goods around the store. Manufacturers try to encourage impulse buying by packaging their goods attractively.

Placing a Value on Time

"If I had the time, I could rotate the tires myself," says a busy executive. "With more time, I could have my own boat," says a hardworking young businessman. "I just don't have time to wash stacks of picnic dishes," protests a busy mother. In today's world, time is of increasing value. The new importance of time, combined with higher incomes, is taking away some of the glamor of owning certain goods. Many people now prefer to buy services; that is, they prefer to rent an item rather than buy it and have to spend time maintaining or repairing it. People are beginning to ask themselves why they should take time to clip the dog when dog-grooming services are available. They wonder why they should maintain their own boat or trailer when they can avoid trouble by renting one. This increased interest in saving time will mean greater business opportunities in the markets for services as well as for rented and disposable goods.

Seeking Buying Convenience

Many people are seeking goods and services that provide ease and comfort. Marketers are responding to this demand by offering a wide variety of conveniences. They offer conveniences in the product and in the store. In addition, many marketers offer the convenience of credit.

The Product. People want products in forms that are easy to use, and marketers are trying to provide such products. Clothing manufacturers use fabrics that are stain-resistant and permanently pressed. Food processors offer a variety of canned and frozen foods. Manufacturers wrap items such as soap and paper towels in packages of two or four for easy handling and storage. Manufacturers also add convenience by providing packages that are easy to open and use.

The Store. People want to shop in locations that are convenient to them, and retailers recognize this fact. Department stores were established in the center of the city when that was the most convenient place for many people to shop.

These stores have kept pace with their customers by following them to the suburbs. Supermarkets and discount stores have made shopping convenient by offering self-service. Retail stores have added evening hours, making shopping convenient for working people. A new kind of store—the convenience store—has been developed to offer food and household items during hours when most supermarkets are closed. Vending machines, which now can even give change for bills, offer goods and services at times and in places convenient to customers.

Credit. One of the most important buying conveniences that marketers are offering is credit. Today many kinds of businesses offer credit. These businesses include banks, oil companies, hotels, supermarkets, and drugstores. Lots of businesses offer a choice of credit plans. Many people believe that credit enables them to enjoy goods and services while they are paying for them, and this attitude encourages marketers to continue offering their customers a variety of credit plans.

WHO BUYS?

To a marketer the term "buyer" can refer to several people. There is the person who decides to buy the product or service and the person who actually uses it. All the members of a family may participate in making a buying decision when an item is important to them. For example, an entire family may select an automobile, a home, or camping equipment.

Teen-agers are a growing influence in family buying because, increasingly, they have their own money to spend. Young children are also increasingly influencing family buying because of their exposure to radio and television advertising.

Young married couples usually decide together how to furnish their homes, what kind of insurance to buy, or where to spend their vacations. When the decision to buy is shared, a company's marketing program is directed at each participant. Advertisements for hiking and camping equipment appear in boys' magazines as well as in adult sports magazines. Automobile salesmen talk about color and styling in order to appeal to women, as well as about engine specifications and gasoline mileage in order to appeal to men.

Marketers design their advertising, merchandise displays, and even store appearance and layout to appeal to the tastes and attitudes of their customers. *Store layout* refers to the interior arrangement of a store for both selling and nonselling activities. Since women do most of the food buying, every successful

Editorial Photocolor Archives, Inc.
Couples usually decide together how to spend their vacations.

supermarket manager is aware of the importance of maintaining a clean and attractive store. He will see that shopping carts have seats for small children, since many of his customers bring their youngsters along when they shop.

As mentioned earlier in this part, people who use a product can also be thought of as buyers and thus can influence a firm's marketing policies. If the users are children—as is often the case with dry cereal, bubble gum, or ice cream specialties—the manufacturer may include a football card, plastic toy, or other premium in the package. Some manufacturers need to consider a combination of buyers. For example, manufacturers of children's wear must offer practical but attractive clothing which will appeal to the children who wear it and to the mothers who buy it.

WHERE PEOPLE BUY

People rarely have just one reason, or motive, for buying in a particular store. A retailer must understand all possible motives if he hopes to get his fair share of the business for any particular product. The sum of all the reasons why a person decides to buy from a certain retailer is known as his *patronage motives*. The following are some patronage motives that affect a customer's decision to shop in a particular store.

- *Reputation of the store.* The customer knows the store and knows that it is honest and fair in all respects.

- *Location of the store.* A customer with a car will prefer a store that offers ample parking space. A customer without a car may prefer a store located near public transportation or one near enough to walk to.
- *Customer services.* Customer services, although they may seem insignificant, can add up to a favorable impression that will keep the customer coming back to the store. Customer services vary with the type of business. Commonly they include gift wrapping, delivery, return privileges, credit plans, and repair services.
- *Price.* Some stores cater to a fashionable clientele, and the store projects an "image" of distinction and quality. In such stores, price is not a major factor. Other stores, such as discount houses, build their reputations on products offered at low prices.
- *Assortment.* If the customer knows the product he wants but not the exact brand, he will seek a store that has an assortment, that is, a variety of price, quality, and styling choices. Thus if a customer wants to buy a wristwatch but does not know exactly which one he wants, he is likely to go to the department or jewelry store that carries the widest assortment.
- *Treatment by the salespeople.* When a customer is shopping for an inexpensive product, such as toothpaste, he wants to be able to make the purchase fast. He will probably prefer self-service selling. But when he is seeking an important item, such as a record player, he will probably want help from a salesperson. He wants the salesperson to wait on him without delay and to offer his advice. He does not want pressure or rude treatment. The salesperson often plays a key role in helping a customer feel comfortable about his purchase.
- *Grouping of stores.* When various stores and other businesses are grouped together, a customer may be able to buy a gift, stop at the bank, get a haircut, have a snack, and shop for an item in two or more stores all during one parking stop.
- *Provision for cars.* We live in a mobile society, and today's customer wants the marketer to provide for his car. Some marketing businesses have failed not because of their location, prices, or choice of merchandise, but simply because they overlooked cars in their efforts to please. As you drive down a street, notice how certain businesses almost beckon the customer to drive in. Their signs are large and easy to read, and you can see plenty of available parking space.
- *Concern for shopping enjoyment.* The marketer knows he must provide a pleasant atmosphere for his customers. The marketer wants the customer to enjoy his shopping, so that he will shop often. This is why a shopping center may have covered malls, piped-in music, colorful special events, and modern, colorful displays and showcases.

WHEN PEOPLE BUY

Timing is important to the marketer, just as it is to the athlete, the actor, and the storyteller. To market his goods at the time they are in demand, a businessman must know certain facts about when people buy. Most marketing businesses are interested in the season, the day of the week, and the time of the day when customers are most likely to buy.

The Season

Some marketing businesses are particularly concerned about the season or time of year when their goods are purchased. These businesses include manufacturers and distributors of toys, sportswear, home furnishings, sporting goods, and building materials. Toy manufacturers, for example, know that 90 percent of retail toy sales are made in the months of November and December. This knowledge is of great value to the toy manufacturers in planning their production, advertising, and sales promotion.

Marketers of certain kinds of products always keep the season in mind.

The Day

Other marketing businesses, such as supermarkets, must know the day or days of the week when customers prefer to shop. This knowledge aids them in ordering goods, planning promotions, and scheduling the work of part-time employees. Many customers choose to shop for groceries on weekends, so food stores run their major ads on Thursday and Friday. Often weekend newspapers will feature food sections that contain articles on menu planning, recipes, and shopping values, along with the food-store advertisements.

The Time of Day

Some marketing businesses, such as retail shopping centers, began a trend toward night openings when they determined that many of their customers preferred evening shopping. This trend later was followed by the established downtown stores. Restaurants need to know whether the noon or evening crowd will be larger. Knowing the time of day for peak business aids the marketer in buying, storing, and promoting his goods and services.

THE BUYING DECISION

To market its products effectively, a company must keep in mind where the decision to buy is made. Sometimes the decision to buy is made at home. Families decide at home to buy insurance or home improvements, such as room additions and remodeling. At other times the decision to buy is made where the actual buying takes place. For example, a young man looking at fishing gear in a sporting-goods store may see a display of golf balls and, recalling that his supply is low, decide to buy some. A father may set off to buy a birthday present for his four-year-old son but wait until he is in the store before deciding on a toy dump truck or fire engine.

    A business should therefore put most of the strength of its promotional activities at the place where the buyer makes his buying decision. If the buyer makes the decision at home, most of the promotion should be in the form of newspaper, magazine, and TV advertising, and personal calls by salesmen. If the buyer makes his decision in the store, promotional emphasis should be placed on packaging, displays, and arrangements of the company's products on store shelves.

    Where the buying decision is made also influences how the manufacturer distributes his product. When a customer views the colorfully wrapped packages of gum on display in the store, he decides on impulse to buy a pack. The decision to buy was unplanned. The marketing of impulse goods requires that manufacturers not only create attractive packaging and displays, but also bring the goods within easy reach of the customer. Therefore, manufacturers seek widespread distribution of these goods, and try to place the goods in as many outlets as possible.

TYPES OF CONSUMER GOODS

Marketers often divide consumer products into three basic groups: convenience goods, shopping goods, and specialty goods. (Impulse goods, which were mentioned earlier, can be any of these, but they are generally convenience goods.) Each type requires different marketing methods, because the consumer has different attitudes about making purchases of products from each of the different groups.

Convenience Goods

Goods that the customer buys often and without shopping around for the best buy are known as *convenience goods.* Convenience goods include magazines, records, light bulbs, and toothpaste.

A manufacturer of convenience goods knows that the customer spends little time shopping for a jar of sweet pickles, for example. The customer is usually more interested in getting the jar of pickles quickly than in getting a particular brand of pickles. Even if he has a brand in mind, he will quickly substitute another brand should he have trouble locating the preferred brand.

This means that the pickle marketer must see to it that many stores carry his pickles, because the customer will quickly choose a substitute. The pickle marketer must also arrange to have attractive store displays to call customers' attention to his product.

Shopping Goods

Items that the customer usually compares with other similar items before deciding to buy them are called *shopping goods.* Shopping goods include wristwatches, shoes, furniture, and small appliances. The customer's comparisons will include price, style, and general suitability. The customer does not find shopping goods at just any store. He buys them seldom and pays a substantial amount for his purchases. He considers shopping goods important items and expects to use them quite a while.

A manufacturer of shopping goods knows that the customer plans to shop around and compare values. Therefore, he must carefully choose the stores that are to carry his product. If he manufactures shoes, for example, he must try to sell them in an area where there are a number of shoe stores. Once he is established in a store, he must display his shoes, his brand name

Even though a customer may have been presold on a specialty good, she is likely to want to hear the salesman describe its features.

Courtesy The Maytag Company

(particularly if he uses newspapers or magazines to advertise his brand), and his price. In this way the customer can see the manufacturer's shoes and compare them with other brands in the store or in neighboring shoe stores.

Specialty Goods

Definite brands of products that the customer will go out of his way to obtain are called *specialty goods*. The customer may have been presold on the brand by national advertising, and he will make great effort to find the one store that carries the preferred brand rather than accept a substitute. Specialty goods include luggage, cars, major appliances, and higher-priced apparel.

A manufacturer of specialty goods depends heavily on his dealers to represent him. He must also spend a considerable sum on national advertising and maintain his good reputation.

◇ YOUR MARKETING VOCABULARY

On a separate sheet of paper define each of the following marketing terms; then use each term in a sentence.

Convenience goods   *Shopping goods*
Impulse buying   *Specialty goods*
Impulse goods   *Store layout*
Patronage motives

FOR REVIEW AND DISCUSSION

1. Identify three important buying patterns that are common today.
2. Why are many people finding impulse buying a sensible way to shop?
3. What is the new importance of time, combined with higher incomes, doing to the glamor of owning certain goods?
4. In what ways do the product, the store, and the availability of credit add buying convenience?
5. To a marketer the term "buyer" can refer to several people. Identify them.
6. When the decision to buy is shared, at whom does a company direct its marketing program?
7. To market his products effectively, what two elements does a marketer keep in mind about where people buy?
8. List six patronage motives for shopping in a particular store.
9. In marketing its goods and services, where does a company put most of the strength of its promotional activities?
10. List the three basic groups of consumer products.

ANALYZING MARKETING CONCEPTS

1. People may have several reasons for shopping at a particular retail establishment. Prepare a form like the one below, and list the following retail establishments in the left-hand column: (a) service station, (b) department store, (c) restaurant, (d) drugstore, (e) clothing store, (f) supermarket, (g) music shop, (h) shoe store, (i) jewelry store. In the right-hand column, write one patronage motive that a person might have for shopping at each establishment listed. Give a different patronage motive for each.

Business	Patronage Motive
Example: Pet shop	Clean, comfortable environment for pets.

2. A marketer classifies his consumer products as convenience, shopping, or specialty goods. Prepare a form like the one below, and write the following products in the left-hand column: (a) candy bar, (b) tennis racket, (c) portable radio, (d) slacks, (e) luggage, (f) toothpaste, (g) sweater, (h) school-letter jacket. Place a check mark in the appropriate column to indicate whether the product is a convenience, shopping, or specialty good.

Product	Convenience Good	Shopping Good	Specialty Good
Example: Newspaper	✔		

◇ **MARKETING PROJECT 8**
Studying Retailers' Effectiveness in Selling

Project Goal: Given three stores in your community, rate them according to their effectiveness in selling to customers.

Action: Prepare a form like the one below. In the left-hand column, list three stores of the same type that you know well or that you can observe for this project. In the center column, list those factors that make a store appealing to shoppers. Think about each of the stores you have listed and decide how many of the factors apply to each store. Then rate the three stores in order of their effectiveness in selling.

Store	Factors That Make the Store Appealing	Rating

◇ **CASE STUDY**
Expanding Into a New Market

Spring Foods Company is a relatively small but very successful food producer. The company's main product lines are whole grain cereals, canned meats, and canned prepared dishes. Three large supermarket chains buy Spring Foods products and share exclusive rights to distribute them in a 200-square-mile area that surrounds the company. The customers of the supermarkets gladly pay a few cents more for the products, because they know that the Spring Foods label means top quality.

The company has done well enough to believe it could profit by investing in expansion, but in what direction? An article in the December 1971 issue of *Fortune* magazine made Pete Marconi, the marketing director, begin to think seriously about one possible additional market. The article began: "One of the fastest-growing and perhaps most profitable food products of the Seventies is some stuff that most people won't eat. Luckily for the food manufacturers, the product isn't meant for people—it's for their dogs and cats."

"I think that's for us," Pete told Leon Hamil, executive vice president of the company. "Look at those figures. People are spending over a billion dollars a year on prepared pet food—that's more than they spend on two staple food items, cereals and baby foods, combined. And we've already got the production facilities that can turn out pet food."

"Yes," said Leon. "We've got the materials and the plant to make it—if the market is really there. You know, this pet food business has grown so rapidly that it could be just a fad; it could die just as rapidly."

"The prediction is that the national market is going to keep on growing. My next step is to find out what the market looks like in our area," said Pete.

First, Pete collected industry-wide information about the pet-food market. Then, with the help of the supermarket chains, he did a survey of the marketing area in which Spring Foods products are sold. His survey revealed the following significant information:

- Nationwide, approximately one-half of all households have pets. In the Spring Foods area, almost two-thirds of the households have pets.
- Dogs tend to be owned by people living in houses; the cat population is owned by people living in either houses or apartments.
- Nationwide, nearly one-half of the dogs and one-third of the cats eat prepared food (the industry considers the remainder an exciting untapped market). In the Spring Foods marketing area, slightly more than one-half of the dogs and nearly two-thirds of the cats eat prepared foods.
- The fastest-growing kinds of pet foods are quality brands (for example, those that feature meat rather than meat by-products), the most popular of which are made by major food producers.
- In the Spring Foods marketing area, new housing is planned at a somewhat higher-than-average rate, with most of the increase expected in suburban one-family houses.
- Sociologists see people's attitudes toward their pets as another aspect of the increased interest in ecology. More and more people see themselves as just one part of the whole natural world, and pets are considered another part of that natural world.

Questions

Pete took his idea to the company's management committee. After listening to his report, some members of the committee were still not convinced about the advisability of trying to win a portion of the pet-food market. Below is a list of their objections. What was the reason for each objection, and how might Pete have answered each?

1. "In our marketing area, more dogs and considerably more cats are already being fed prepared foods than in the rest of the country. That means the untapped market in our area isn't so impressive."
2. "Six big companies already have nearly three-fourths of the pet-food market. What chance do we have to break in?"
3. "Wouldn't it hurt the reputation of our foods if people began seeing our label on pet foods?"
4. "According to the figures, people are spending nearly $100 a year on the average to feed their pets. Why, that could buy almost a ton of food for hungry people. Don't you think people are going to wake up to that?"

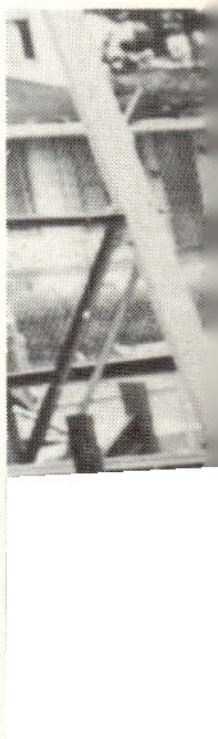

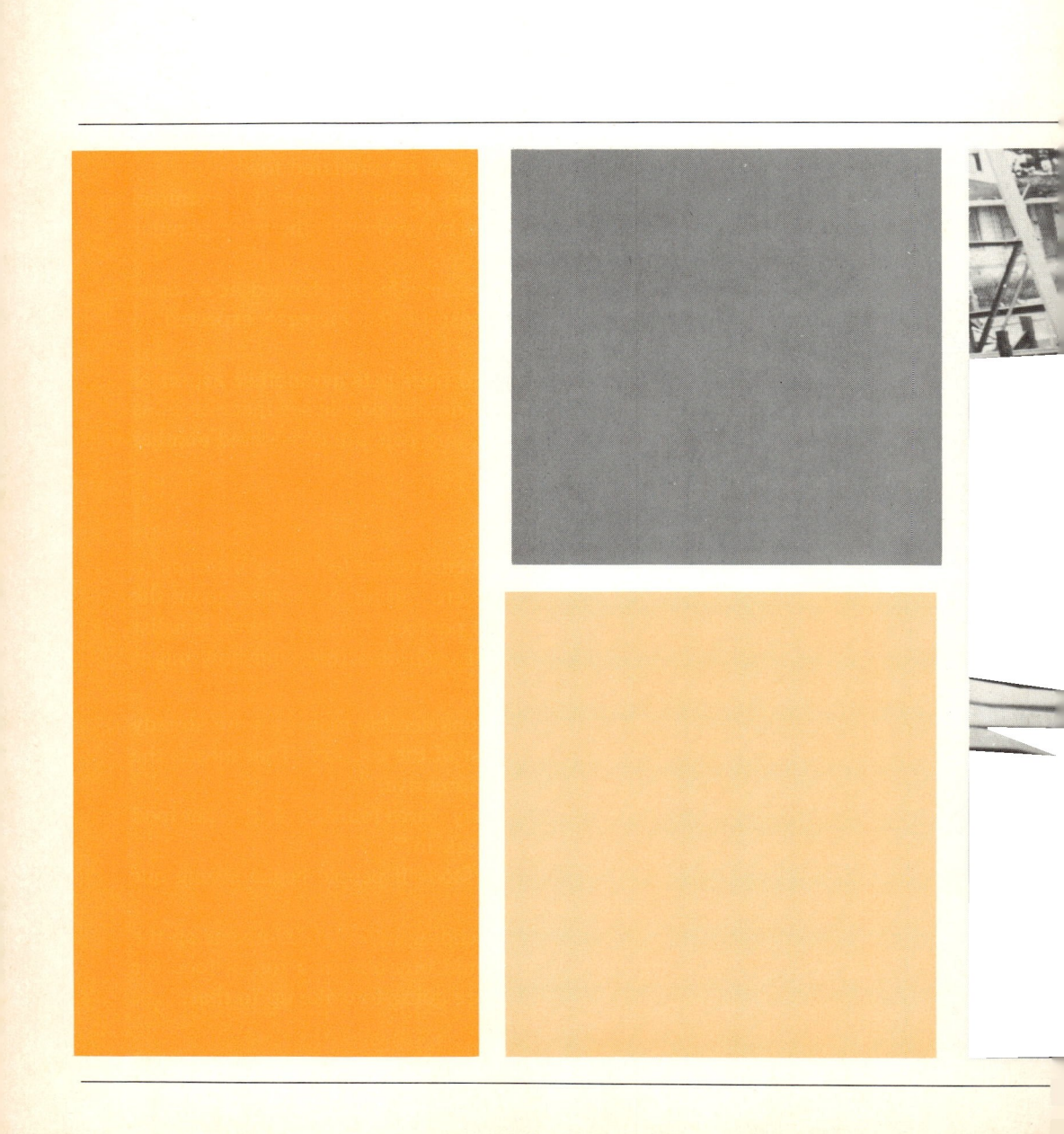

The Industrial Market

UNIT 3

part 9

Industrial Goods and Markets

YOUR GOALS

1. Given several types of business organizations, select six that are in the industrial market.
2. Given the four types of industrial goods, classify certain goods according to type.

The customers within our economy can be divided into two basic markets: the consumer market (which was discussed in Part 5) and the industrial market. The *industrial market* is all the potential customers for industrial goods and services. These customers are businesses. You, as an individual, are part of the consumer market. If you have a job, the company you work for is part of the industrial market. The company is a customer for industrial goods and services.

Businesses buy raw materials, equipment, furniture, and stationery, among many other items. These are *industrial goods,* products intended to satisfy the needs and wants of businesses. Many businesses also buy insurance, transportation for employees who must take business trips, and consulting services. These are *industrial services,* services intended to satisfy the needs and wants of businesses.

Note that some products and services can be either industrial products and services or consumer products and services, depending on who buys them. If a company buys furniture for an office, that furniture is being sold to the industrial market. If you buy furniture for your home, that furniture is being sold to the consumer market.

Every consumer product was once a part of the industrial market. For example, consider that pair of ice skates in the sporting-goods store window. The steel in them had to be smelted from iron ore and then shaped into runners. The leather had to be tanned, dyed, and fashioned into shoes. The laces had to be woven from fibers. Then all these components had to be put together. By the time that pair of skates was displayed in the store window, it already had been involved in considerable industrial market activity.

There are several types of organizations that make up the industrial market. These include suppliers of basic materials, manufacturers, service organizations, and industrial customers. Each of these organizations produces or uses industrial goods or services.

THE INDUSTRIAL MARKET

The industrial market can be divided into five groups: (1) extractors, (2) manufacturers, (3) service organizations, (4) institutions, and (5) national, state, and local governments. Some authorities include retailers as a sixth group in the industrial market.

Extractors are those companies involved in mining ores, in drilling for oil, and in taking seafood from the rivers and oceans. Farmers are technically extractors, because they "extract" food from the earth. However, this group forms such a special kind of market segment that it is discussed in detail in Part 11. Extractors are usually more important to the industrial market as suppliers of goods than as customers.

Manufacturers are those companies engaged in processing materials (turning crude oil into gasoline, for example) and in making products for use by the consumer or by other businesses. There are more than 300,000 manufacturing firms in the United States. They process such materials as hides, food, rubber, and ores. They make such products as machinery, furniture, musical instruments, and transportation equipment. Manufacturing firms employ more people than any other single type of business.

Service organizations include airlines, banks, insurance companies, movie theaters, restaurants, hotels and motels, and consulting firms. To conduct their business, they need equipment, supplies, and services themselves. A movie theater needs film projectors, carpeting, and rest-room equipment. A hotel buys laundry service, furniture, television sets, and stationery.

The industrial marketer sells to different types of customers.

Institutions, such as hospitals and schools, also purchase equipment and supplies. Like hotels, hospitals need laundry service and furniture. Of course, they also need medicines, food, and surgical supplies. Schools are a significant market for textbooks, school furniture, and laboratory equipment.

The federal government is the largest single customer in the industrial market. Its various departments and agencies buy airplanes, automobiles, furniture, electronic equipment, uniforms, construction materials, cleaning services, and hundreds of other products and services. State and local governments buy products such as highway construction materials, adding machines, park benches, and snowplows.

INDUSTRIAL GOODS

The goods that are bought and sold in the industrial market can be divided into four types: materials, installations, accessory equipment, and operating supplies. Of the four types, materials become a permanent part of the finished product. Installations, accessory equipment, and operating supplies are necessary to manufacture the product, but they do not become a permanent part of it.

Materials

Just as you build a model airplane from plastics or light woods and glue, a manufacturer constructs his finished products from several basic materials. These materials can be either raw materials or fabricating materials.

Raw materials are goods that are more or less in their original form. Examples of raw materials include wheat from the field, sand from the quarry, trees from the forest, and fish from the sea. Raw materials need additional processing before they can become useful.

Fabricating materials are goods that have already been changed from the state in which they are found in nature. Some fabricating materials are so changed in the manufacturing process that their original form cannot be detected. For example, the animal fats used as an ingredient in soap are not recognizable in the smooth, fresh-smelling bars you buy at the store.

Other fabricating materials keep their original appearance throughout the manufacturing process. For instance, a car manufacturer buys fabricating materials such as tires, spark plugs, batteries, radios, and steering wheels. These materials are easily recognizable in the final product—the automobile.

Courtesy Weyerhaeuser Company

Trees provide a basic raw material for the industrial market.

Part 9 / Industrial Goods and Markets / 103

Installations

There are two types of *installations:* (1) machines used to process raw materials or manufacture products from fabricating materials, and (2) equipment used to conduct a service business. The number and size of the installations have a direct bearing on the amount of goods or services that can be produced.

In manufacturing or processing plants, installations are the machinery used to produce the finished product. Blast furnaces are installations in a steel mill, for example. In a service organization, installations are the equipment required to produce the service, and they are directly involved in that service. For example, airplanes are installations in an airline, beds are installations in a hospital, and desks and chairs are installations in an educational institution.

Accessory Equipment

Equipment that is needed to operate a business but which is not used in manufacturing a product or providing the service for which the company was organized is called *accessory equipment.* Examples of accessory equipment include forklift trucks, hand tools, typewriters, adding machines, and desks.

Operating Supplies

Items necessary for the operation of a business are known as *operating supplies.* Such supplies are usually low in cost. They are used up rapidly and must constantly be replaced. Operating supplies in a hotel, for example, include furniture polish, scouring powder, rug-cleaning solutions, and floor wax. Office stationery, paper towels, ink, and typewriter erasers are examples of operating supplies that are used by businesses and organizations of all types.

INDUSTRIAL GOODS ILLUSTRATED

The Four Star Baking Company specializes in several varieties of doughnuts —cinnamon, chocolate, glazed, frosted, jelly, cream-filled, apple, and spiced. The doughnuts are packed 12 to a carton, and the carton has a clear plastic top, so that the customer can easily choose the doughnuts he likes best.

In manufacturing these doughnuts, Four Star uses all four types of industrial goods: materials, installations, accessory equipment, and operating supplies. Let us take a look around the plant to see how these goods are used.

Just arriving at the plant's loading station are enormous bags of flour. As we move inside the building, we see large supplies of yeast, sugar, baking powder, and salt, and smaller supplies of cinnamon, nutmeg, allspice, and baking chocolate. There is a large refrigerator tank of milk. These are the baker's fabricating materials. Each of these materials has already been processed to some degree by another manufacturer and is now ready to be used as an ingredient in the doughnut-making process.

As we move on into the production room, we see giant mixing vats, in which huge quantities of dough are being blended automatically. In other huge vats, a yeast dough has been set to rise. Near the middle of the room are the doughnut-cutting machines, which turn out identical circles of dough, each with a hole in its center. Then on to the frying area, where the doughnuts are automatically placed in baskets, which are then lowered into square wells of hot, bubbling vegetable oil. After a few minutes, the baskets are lifted out of the oil, and the doughnuts are placed on racks for draining and cooling. After the doughnuts have been frosted or sugared, they are moved into the packaging department, where they are put into cartons of a dozen doughnuts each. All the machines needed to mix the dough, fry the doughnuts, and complete the packaging operation are installations.

After the doughnuts have been packaged, they are put into huge boxes and moved by small forklift trucks to the loading platform. There they are put on delivery trucks to be taken to retail stores. Both kinds of trucks—plus such items as typewriters, adding machines, time clocks, air-conditioning equipment, and electric fans—are accessory equipment. They do not become part of the finished product or help in its manufacture, but they are moderately expensive items that support the manufacturing process.

We pass an open-shelf cabinet on the way out. Its shelves are loaded with machine oil, paper towels, employees' coveralls, floor wax, paper, pencils, and light bulbs. These are the operating supplies needed to run the business; they are consumed and have to be replaced from time to time.

INDUSTRIAL SERVICES

Just as a number of different types of services are sold to the consumer market, a number of different types of services are sold to the industrial market. Among the more common ones are consulting services, protection services, and maintenance services.

Often a business would like the advice or help of an expert, but does not want to pay the cost of adding such an expert to its staff as a permanent employee. In such a case the firm usually goes to a consultant. For a fee the consultant agrees to do a certain amount of work for the firm, perhaps to solve a particular problem. For example, the firm may want the consultant to determine how a new wing could be added to a processing plant, or even how to set up a Christmas display in a window. The consultant does the job, collects his fee, and moves on to his next client.

The Pinkerton Security Service specializes in providing guards for various businesses.

Courtesy Pinkerton's Inc.

Many businesses find it necessary to provide some protection for their factory, office, or store. A guard on duty at the door of a department store may be a full-time member of the store's staff, but he also may be someone hired by a service organization that supplies trained security personnel to stores.

At one time most businesses hired their own maintenance personnel, but an increasing number of businesses now use professional maintenance services. The maintenance company agrees to clean a specific building, floor, or other area regularly for a set fee. The maintenance company supplies both the equipment to do the cleaning and the people to operate the equipment. A machine breakdown or a vacationing employee does not keep the job from being done; the service organization simply substitutes a different machine or rearranges its work schedules so that another person is sent to do the job.

Services have become increasingly important to industry over the past few years, and more industrial services are being purchased each year.

◆ YOUR MARKETING VOCABULARY

On a separate sheet of paper define each of the following marketing terms; then use each term in a sentence.

Accessory equipment *Industrial services*
Fabricating materials *Installations*
Industrial goods *Operating supplies*
Industrial market *Raw materials*

FOR REVIEW AND DISCUSSION

1. What is the difference between consumer goods and industrial goods?
2. List five groups of organizations into which the industrial market can be divided.
3. How do manufacturers use industrial goods?
4. What kinds of industrial goods are purchased by service organizations?
5. What kinds of industrial goods are bought by institutions?
6. Who is the largest single customer of industrial marketers? What does this customer buy?
7. What are four types of goods which are bought and sold in the industrial market?
8. Distinguish between raw materials and fabricating materials.
9. What are two types of installations?
10. List three types of services that are sold to the industrial market. Give an example of each.

ANALYZING MARKETING CONCEPTS

1. Some products can be either consumer goods or industrial goods, depending on how they are used. Prepare a form like the one below. List the following consumer products in the left-hand column: (a) automobile tire, (b) bicycle, (c) camera, (d) comb, (e) hammer, (f) record player, (g) radio, (h) typewriter, (i) tape recorder. In the right-hand column, describe a situation in which each product listed would be an industrial good.

Consumer Good	Industrial Good
Example: Loaf of bread	To make sandwiches to be sold in a restaurant.

2. Industrial goods are divided into four types: materials (M), installations (I), accessory equipment (AE), and operating supplies (OS). Prepare a form like the one on the next page, listing these items at the left: (a) typewriter in office, (b) paper in office, (c) waxed paper in bakery, (d) tires for car manufacturer, (e) wheat for a flour mill, (f) beds in a hospital, (g) light bulbs in a school, (h) telephone in a store, (i) fish for a restaurant, (j) desks in a school, (k) pencils in an office, (l) movie screen in a theater, (m) coin wrappers in a bank, (n) iron ore in a steel mill, (o) time clock in a factory, (p) pumps in a service station, (q) floor wax in a motel, (r) forklift truck in a warehouse.

   Place a check mark in the appropriate column to indicate the type of industrial good listed.

Industrial Good	Type			
	M	I	AE	OS
Example: Cash register in a store			✔	

◆ MARKETING PROJECT 9
Classifying Industrial Goods

Project Goal: Given the four types of industrial goods, classify certain goods according to type.

Action: Using the Yellow Pages of your telephone directory, select four industrial goods, one for each of the four types that make up the industrial market. Prepare a form like the one below. In the appropriate columns, list each good, its type, the name of the business marketing the good, and the use of the good.

Industrial Good	Type of Good	Name of Business	Use of Good
Example: Display fixtures	Accessory equipment	Advance Fixture Company	Marketer's merchandise display

108 / Unit 3 / The Industrial Market

part 10

Marketing Industrial Goods

YOUR GOALS

1. Given a specific industrial good, determine four effective ways to promote and sell it to an industrial buyer.
2. Given a specific industrial good, determine at least five buying motives on which the industrial buyer might base his decision to purchase that product.

"Marketing is marketing," said the experienced sales manager of a large company. "If I can sell one thing, I can sell another." He was probably correct in his assumption. But if he were to switch from consumer goods to industrial goods, he would have to do some homework first. Marketing industrial goods differs from marketing consumer goods in two important ways: the methods used by sellers (often called suppliers) to promote and sell industrial goods, and the buying motives and procedures of industrial buyers.

PROMOTING AND SELLING

Promoting and selling to the industrial market differs from promoting and selling to the consumer market in four ways: the number of industrial buyers is smaller, industrial purchases are larger on the average than consumer purchases, the responsibility for buying industrial goods is frequently shared by several people, and the demand for an industrial product is sometimes derived from the demand for another product.

Number of Buyers

Nearly 5 million businesses in the United States buy industrial goods. If this number seems large, compare it with the more than 200 million people in the consumer market and you will get some idea of the relatively small size of the industrial market in terms of numbers of buyers.

The limited number of buyers in the industrial market calls for sales promotion methods that differ from those used in the consumer market. To reach as many consumers as possible, a national manufacturer sponsors a popular television show, places advertisements in *Newsweek* and other consumer magazines, purchases newspaper space and radio time in thousands of communities throughout the country, and uses outdoor and transportation advertising extensively.

The industrial marketer, on the other hand, has far fewer customers to reach—in some cases, just a few hundred. He is more likely to spend his advertising money on direct mail, on advertisements in trade magazines, and on exhibits at trade shows and conventions. He is also more likely to select his salesmen on the basis of their education and experience, to train them carefully, and to pay them high salaries plus commissions.

Size of Purchases

Although the number of industrial buyers is only a fraction of the number of consumers, sales to the industrial market total almost as much as those to the consumer market. The reason is that purchases are made for an entire company rather than for personal use. As stated in Part 2, a person who purchases those goods used in the operation of a business is called an industrial buyer or purchasing agent. His average purchase is, of course, much larger than the average consumer purchase.

Because an industrial buyer or purchasing agent often buys in huge quantities, a salesman may spend months trying to sell to one buyer. He may carefully research the buyer's problems and needs and ask the scientists and engineers in his own company to help him solve the buyer's problems. The salesman makes it his business to call on the buyer frequently and to provide him with technical know-how. A salesman who sells goods in the industrial market is called an industrial salesman. Some industrial salesmen make regular calls on only two or three large accounts, or customers, because the volume of business they obtain from those accounts can support this kind of personal attention.

Responsibility for Buying

In a small industrial firm, buying is usually done by the owner or manager. The operation is so small that the owner or manager can easily watch his inventory, keep up with price changes, and talk to industrial salesmen. In larger firms, however, the buying of industrial goods is done by the industrial buyer. Often he has several assistants. Sometimes the industrial buyer shares the responsibility for buying with other people in the company. For some types of large, expensive equipment, engineers, foremen, industrial buyers, and department managers—perhaps even the company president—may participate in making the buying decision.

The industrial salesman must reach all the people who share in making the buying decision. Thus he tries to see as many key people as possible when he calls on the firm. He may reach those whom he cannot see in the following ways: by sending direct mail (perhaps letters from his firm's director of marketing), by exhibiting his company's products at trade shows where the buyers are likely to be in attendance, by mailing product catalogs, and by placing advertisements in various trade magazines and trade newspapers.

Courtesy American Machinist

In purchasing some types of large industrial equipment, several people may participate in making the buying decision.

Part 10 / Marketing Industrial Goods / 111

Demand for Goods

The demand for industrial goods depends on the demand for consumer goods produced by using the industrial goods. When demand for a consumer product drops, the industry's demand for the raw or fabricating materials used to make that product also drops. Thus we call the demand for industrial goods *derived demand,* because the need for industrial goods exists only when they are needed to make consumer goods. For example, Briggs and Stratton manufactures engines for power lawn mowers. The engines themselves are not sold to consumers but are attached to the power mowers made by other companies. In this case the demand for a Briggs and Stratton engine is derived from the sale of the lawn mower of which it is a part.

Briggs and Stratton concentrates its promotion on all companies that assemble and sell power lawn mowers. To encourage these manufacturers to use its engines in their mowers, Briggs and Stratton also advertises in consumer magazines, hoping to persuade readers to purchase only power mowers with engines made by Briggs and Stratton.

Many women look for the label "Made of Dacron" when shopping for clothing. Du Pont, which manufactures Dacron, not only promotes it to the textile mills but to consumers as well. Thus Du Pont helps to stimulate a derived demand for its product.

BUYING MOTIVES

An industrial buyer bases his buying decisions on his company's need to make a profit. Emotional appeals that affect a consumer have only a slight influence on the industrial buyer. He uses his powers of reason and logic to obtain the most suitable materials from a reliable company at the lowest possible price. Factors that the industrial buyer considers before making a purchase for his company are (1) quality, (2) reputation of the supplier, (3) production efficiency, (4) customer service, and (5) price.

Quality

The industrial buyer does not always buy the best possible grade of an industrial product. He bases his quality requirement on the intended use of the product. A buyer for a manufacturer of men's shirts looks for inexpensive but durable cotton cloth if the shirts must sell for $4.98 each. If the shirts are to sell for $10.95 each, the buyer will still want durability but will also expect to be shown fine cottons, Dacron and cotton blends, and high-fashion colors. For shirts that will sell for $20 or $25 each, he is likely to choose very expensive fabrics, such as pure silk or imported materials in a variety of unusual weaves and colors.

The buyer for a fruit processor buys several grades of peaches. For canned peach halves or frozen slices, he must buy the highest grade possible, because both the appearance and taste of the peaches must be excellent. For peach jam and jellies, however, he buys lower-grade peaches. He does not need perfect fruit for this purpose, since all imperfections will be cut off the fruit before it is made into jam or jelly.

Thus in the industrial market, the quality required of a product is based on its intended use. An industrial buyer will not pay the price for high quality that he does not need, nor will he accept a product that does not meet his minimum standard of quality even though the price is low.

Reputation of the Supplier

A buyer bases part of his buying decision on the reputation of the seller. Although the seller's reputation cannot be seen or determined from advertisements or product catalogs, an alert industrial buyer can find out about a seller's integrity. If his company has had previous dealings with the seller, the buyer will ask certain questions: Was the quality of the product satisfactory? How do our engineers and production people rate the product? Did the company meet its delivery schedules?

A supplier builds his reputation on a number of factors.

The buyer is interested in the reputation of the supplier because he will probably need to reorder certain equipment, spare parts, and supplies from that same company. He wants to make sure that the firm is well established and is not likely to be "here today and gone tomorrow." He wants a continuous source of supply, and he can be assured of this only by dealing with a reputable supplier.

Two additional elements enter into the buyer's consideration of the reputation of the supplier. One element is the buyer's faith in the supplier. He has faith in a supplier who has always delivered what was promised—even under trying circumstances. The other element is the buyer's personal friendship for the salesmen and others who represent the supplier. These elements of faith and friendship are rooted deeply in how the buyer feels about a supplier. This attitude is based partly on cold, hard reason and partly on emotion.

Production Efficiency

One of the best ways for a manufacturer to meet market demand is to increase productivity. This means purchasing installations and accessory equipment that provide maximum efficiency. In buying machinery, for example, the buyer must ask certain questions: Will it make as many products in less time? Will it decrease "downtime" (time needed for repairs)? Does it require fewer people to operate it? Will it give longer service?

Customer Service

The variety of customer services offered by firms selling industrial goods is often an important addition to effective marketing. When several companies offer approximately the same product, an industrial buyer is likely to choose the supplier who offers the most valuable services.

An important type of customer service in the industrial market is technical assistance. Industrial salesmen are sometimes graduate engineers, who can give their customers advice concerning the solution of production or engineering problems. Some companies make technical information available through bulletins or by providing a consulting service.

Another kind of customer service in the industrial market is reliable repair and maintenance work. The industrial buyer expects the supplier to provide fast, efficient repair service when it is needed. The buyer also expects that essential parts and materials will be available whenever he needs them.

An industrial firm will sometimes give sales and advertising assistance to its customers. Frequently, a supplier will give his industrial customers important market information or a list of potential customers. These services are valuable to manufacturers because they provide a head start in marketing the finished product.

Often a firm that supplies materials to manufacturing firms will advertise in consumer magazines in order to promote sales of the finished product. For example, when a textile manufacturer (supplier) such as Klopman Mills advertises fashions made of Klopman fabrics and lists stores in which the clothes are available, this is really a service to the clothing manufacturers producing garments made of Klopman fabrics. Those clothing manufacturers benefit because retailers are more willing to stock products made with a widely advertised fabric, and the retailers' customers are more willing to buy them. As a result, suppliers often sponsor advertising programs aimed at the consumer in an attempt to attract the interest of industrial buyers.

Price

It seems almost too obvious to say that industrial buyers are interested in buying materials, equipment, and supplies at the lowest possible prices. If two firms offer products of identical grade, backed up by similar service, delivery guarantees, and reputation, the decision will nearly always be in favor of the company that offers the lower price. Price is an important factor in industrial buying decisions, but the factors of quality, reputation, service, and efficiency may outweigh price in the buyer's mind. In fact, the industrial buyer may consider price only after he has satisfied himself that the other factors meet his standards.

INDUSTRIAL BUYING

Once an industrial buyer has decided what he wants to buy, he faces the problem of finding the best source of supply. Locating the best sources for materials, equipment, and operating supplies often calls for a good deal of research. Once the industrial buyer establishes his basic sources of supply, he purchases his materials in three ways: direct from manufacturers, from catalogs or from printouts of manufacturers' data processing systems, and from distributors.

Buying Direct From Manufacturers

The industrial buyer may place his order with the manufacturer's salesmen, he may telephone or wire his order, or he may mail his order. He prefers direct buying when the manufacturer maintains sufficient stock and adequate shipping facilities to enable the buyer to receive prompt service.

Direct buying is also preferred when the buyer knows exactly what products he wants and therefore needs little assistance in making selections. Some buyers, uncertain about styles, models, and specifications, want help before they place their orders. In such cases, they may prefer buying from catalogs that offer detailed descriptions of the products. Frequently such catalogs also contain helpful illustrations.

Buying From Catalogs

Just as Sears, Roebuck and Montgomery Ward provide customers with catalogs of their consumer merchandise, manufacturers of industrial goods provide industrial buyers with catalogs of their products. Catalogs range from short lists to huge books and contain illustrations and detailed descriptions of the items offered, their prices, and order forms.

Some companies also buy space in catalogs published by commercial publishers. Such catalogs are indexed by type of product, very much like the listings in the Yellow Pages of the telephone directory. If a manufacturer of kitchen equipment wants to buy stainless steel, for example, he checks the listing under the general heading "Metals." Under the subheading "Steel and Iron," he finds advertisements placed by the suppliers of stainless steel. Each supplier gives detailed information about his product and lists the locations of the company's offices.

Today, many manufacturers computerize the data on their industrial goods so that automatic or semiautomatic ordering can take place. (Ordering through data processing by computers is discussed in Part 43.)

Industrial catalogs provide a convenient means of buying goods direct from the manufacturer.

Courtesy Shaw-Walker

Buying From Distributors

Rather than buy direct from manufacturers or from catalogs, many businesses buy from distributors. A *distributor* is an independent middleman who stocks the industrial products of various manufacturers and sells them to industrial users. Four advantages in buying from a distributor are as follows:

1. A distributor often handles many lines of industrial goods. If a buyer purchases the goods of several manufacturers who use the same distributor, his paperwork is simplified because he need place only one order with the distributor, and the distributor does the rest of the order processing.
2. Because there are many more distributors of a product than there are manufacturers of it, a distributor is likely to be located close to the industrial user. This means that the distributor can offer the buyer quick delivery service.
3. The distributor, being a local businessman, makes it a point to know the buyer's needs. He can offer the buyer a wide assortment of products tailored to the special requirements of the buyer's business.
4. A distributor provides service in locating hard-to-find equipment and supplies, thus saving the time and effort of the industrial buyer. This service is usually provided at no extra charge.

Of course, the industrial buyer cannot always choose between buying direct from the manufacturer or from a distributor. Some manufacturers have a policy of distributing their products only by a direct channel to the buyer. Other manufacturers, seeking to avoid the costs of warehousing and shipping, have a policy of using distributors exclusively and will not sell direct. Still others use both methods in distributing their products.

◳ YOUR MARKETING VOCABULARY

On a separate sheet of paper define each of the following marketing terms; then use each term in a sentence.
Derived demand
Distributor

◳ FOR REVIEW AND DISCUSSION

1. In what two important ways does marketing industrial goods differ from marketing consumer goods?
2. In what four ways do promoting and selling to the industrial market differ from promoting and selling to the consumer market?
3. Although the number of industrial buyers is only a fraction of the number of consumers, sales to the industrial market total almost as much as those to consumers. Why?

4. How does the industrial salesman reach all the people who may share in making the buying decision?
5. List five factors that the industrial buyer considers before making a purchase for his company.
6. Does the industrial buyer always buy the best possible grade of an industrial product? Explain.
7. What does the reputation of the supplier mean to an industrial buyer?
8. Is price necessarily the most important factor in industrial buying decisions? Explain.
9. In what three ways can an industrial buyer purchase his products?
10. What are the advantages of buying from a distributor?

ANALYZING MARKETING CONCEPTS

1. The demand for industrial goods is derived from the demand for consumer goods. Prepare a form like the one below and list the following industrial goods in the left-hand column: (a) paint, (b) polyester material, (c) leather, (d) plastic, (e) lumber. For each industrial good, list in the right-hand column at least three consumer goods in which the industrial good is used.

Industrial Good	Consumer Good
Example: Steel	Car, table knife, washing machine

2. Prepare a form like the one below and list the following industrial goods in the left-hand column: (a) paint, (b) gasoline engine, (c) textiles, (d) light bulb, (e) typewriter, (f) paper, (g) oil, (h) tires. For each good, write in the right-hand column one question that an industrial buyer might ask the supplier about it.

Industrial Good	Question
Example: Zipper	Will this zipper last as long as the garment it will be a part of?

MARKETING PROJECT 10
Determining Industrial Buying Motives

Project Goal: Given a specific industrial good, determine at least five buying motives on which the industrial buyer might base his decision to purchase that product.

Action: Consult the advertisements in an issue of *Business Week, Newsweek,* or *Fortune* magazine. Prepare a form like the one below. In the left-hand column, list five industrial goods that are advertised in the magazine you selected. In the center column, write the words or phrases the ad used to indicate why the particular good should be bought. For each word or phrase, list a buying motive that corresponds to it in the right-hand column.

Industrial Good	Why Product Should Be Bought	Buying Motive
Example: Briggs and Stratton engine	1. Precision parts 2. Leading name in the field 3. Starts easily 4. Technical assistance 5. No comparable engine sold at this price	1. Quality 2. Reputation of supplier 3. Production efficiency 4. Customer service 5. Price

Special Markets

UNIT 4

part 11

Marketing Farm Products

YOUR GOALS

1. Given a knowledge of changes in farm production and marketing during the past 40 years, indicate the effects that these changes have had on employment in farm production and employment in marketing occupations connected with farm products.
2. Given one leading soil crop and one leading livestock product produced in your state, chart the path of each product from the farmer to the consumer, and indicate the marketing services performed at each step.

Farm products are familiar to everyone. You probably buy meat, eggs, and milk at your local store. You may buy fresh tomatoes, apples, or sweet corn at a roadside stand. Products such as these, which reach the consumer without undergoing any major changes in form, are called *consumer farm products.* For example, although a head of lettuce is cleaned, trimmed, graded, and packed, it is still physically the same head of lettuce that came from the farm. About 20 percent of all farm products reach the consumer without undergoing a major change in form.

Products that reach the consumer after having undergone a major change in form during a manufacturing process are called *industrial farm products.*

The consumer rarely sees them in their original form. They become a part of another food (such as the tomatoes that make up the basic part of spaghetti sauce, for example). Or they become food for farm livestock or part of your clothing (such as the wool yarn that is used to make a pair of socks). About 80 percent of all farm products are industrial farm products.

FARMS AND FARM POPULATION

For many years the amount of land used for farming in the United States has remained steady at about one billion acres. Yet the country has tripled its output of many farm products by making farmland more productive and the raising of livestock more efficient. This increase in output has been accomplished with the help of better fertilizers and farm equipment, more productive feed and seed, and the efficient use of insecticides and herbicides.

In 1950 the billion acres of American farmland held almost 6 million farms. Today the same amount of land holds about 3 million farms. In other words, the average farm is larger and the number of farms is smaller.

In 1790, 95 percent of the American people were farmers; today, only about 5 percent are. The typical farmer now enjoys most of the conveniences of the city dweller. He has free mail delivery, electricity, modern roads, and one or more cars. He enjoys central heating, modern plumbing, radios, TVs, washing machines, and the latest kitchen appliances. His farm equipment is mechanized. In short, few American farmers are isolated from the rest of the world, either geographically or in the way they live.

CLASSIFICATION OF FARM PRODUCTS

Modern farming is market-oriented; that is, most farmers are producing products for sale rather than for home use. Their products come from two major sources, namely, crops and livestock. *Crops* are products obtained from the soil, and *livestock products* are those items obtained from animals. Both sources provide us with food and clothing.

Products Obtained From the Soil

In 1969, crops, or soil products, had annual sales of nearly $19 billion. They accounted for almost 40 percent of total farm sales.

Farm marketers find it helpful to classify the basic kinds of products obtained from the soil because each type requires a different marketing method. These types of products are grain, fruits and vegetables, cotton and flax, and other edible and nonedible soil products.

The modern farmer harvests his grain crops mechanically. Grain crops are important in the consumer market and are also used extensively to feed livestock.

Courtesy International Harvester

Grain. Grain is the most abundant type of crop produced in the United States. Grain includes corn, wheat, sorghum, rye, alfalfa, barley, and soybeans. Corn is the most abundant grain crop, but only a portion of it reaches the consumer market. A great deal of the corn grown in this country is used to feed livestock. Wheat, although not the most abundant grain crop, is the most profitable one.

Fruits and Vegetables. Fruits and vegetables make up the second most abundant type of crop produced in the United States. Faster transportation and improved refrigeration have increased the efficiency of the marketing process, so that it is now possible to enjoy many fruits and vegetables all year rather than just during the local harvest season. Fruits and vegetables can be grown in Florida and California in seasons when areas in other states are not productive. The Florida and California crops can then be transported to various parts of the country for consumer use.

Cotton and Flax. Cotton and flax are grown to produce wearing apparel. Cotton is a major crop in much of the South. Cotton supplies more than one-third of the world's textile needs and is also a major source of oil for margarine. In addition, cotton is used to make rope and cord.

The flax industry is much smaller than the cotton industry. Flax is used almost entirely to make linen, which is made into clothes and many household accessories, such as sheets, tablecloths, and towels.

Other Edible and Nonedible Soil Products. Specialized products are also grown on farms. They include cane and beets for sugar production as well as oil-bearing crops, such as soybeans and peanuts. Although most of the oil that comes from soybeans and peanuts is used in the manufacture of foods, some of it is put to various industrial uses. For example, soybean and peanut oils are used in the production of varnishes, inks, linoleum, pharmaceuticals, and cosmetics.

Products Obtained From Animals

In 1969 livestock products, or products obtained from animals, had annual sales of more than $28 billion and accounted for more than 60 percent of total farm sales. Livestock products fall into several groups. The sales of each group and the percent of total farm products that each group represents are shown in the following table.

Sales of Livestock Products in 1969

Livestock Products	In Millions of Dollars	Percent of Total Farm Products
Calves and cattle	$12,644	26.8
Chickens	1,634	3.4
Dairy products	6,172	13.1
Eggs	2,256	4.7
Hogs	4,667	9.8
Sheep and lambs	327	.7
Turkeys	533	1.4
Wool	72	.1
Other livestock products	134	.2
Total livestock products	$28,439	60.2

Source: U.S. Department of Agriculture, Economic Research Service, *The Farm Income Situation,* 1969.

MARKETING METHODS FOR FARM PRODUCTS

The marketing and distribution of farm products are more complex than the marketing and distribution of other types of goods. An important reason is that many farm products are perishable and thus require special storage and distribution methods. Because the farmer is not able to properly store and distribute his goods, he must use the services of middlemen.

The marketing of farm products is further complicated by the fact that a comparatively large number of farms (3 million) produce products for both the consumer and the industrial markets. These markets are composed of a great number of customers. In general, when a large number of relatively small producers provide goods for a great number of customers, the producers need the help of middlemen. *Middlemen* are business organizations that perform buying and selling services which aid the flow of goods from the producer to the consumer. In farm marketing, certain middlemen assemble farm products in local markets and other middlemen assemble them in central markets.

Local Markets

The local market is the first assembly point for the farmer. He brings his crops or livestock to this market (perhaps a stockyard or a grain elevator located near his farm) and sells his products to the middleman who operates the market. Sometimes the process of grading is begun at the local market. *Grading* is the act of sorting goods into categories according to established specifications. Grain is graded according to its weight by the bushel, according to its moisture content, and according to the foreign matter it contains, such as cracked grains, dirt, or weed seeds.

Every farmer must be a marketer.

Central Markets

The middlemen in the local markets transport their products to the central market. The central market may buy the products, grade them, store them, and arrange for an orderly method of offering them for resale or for trading. Trading takes place in a *commodity exchange,* which is a center where buyers and sellers of agricultural goods transact business. The commodity exchange is operated for the benefit of both buyers and sellers, and certain rules for trading are established and maintained to save time and keep the trading process orderly and efficient.

MARKETING SERVICES FOR FARM PRODUCTS

Farm products are often more expensive to market than other industrial products. Whereas the cost of marketing a bus may be 30 percent of the selling price, the cost of marketing a head of lettuce may be as much as 70 percent of the selling price. The primary reason for the difference is the likelihood of deterioration of the lettuce during the marketing process. The bus has been assembled, painted, and finished so that it does not deteriorate during the marketing process, but the lettuce can wilt or spoil in a short time if not kept cool and moist.

The three main marketing services that are essential in handling farm products are transportation, storage, and grading. Each service not only adds to the final cost but also adds to the value of the product.

Transportation

Farm products pass through several intermediate steps on their way from the farmer to the consumer or the industrial user. Each step involves transportation. The farmer usually takes his products to the local market by truck. Later, the more perishable goods are assembled in quantity, and they may be shipped by a bulk carrier, such as rail freight or air freight. When the product is not highly perishable, water transportation may be used.

Storage

Most farm products are seasonal. In the days when transportation and storage facilities were poor, items such as peaches, strawberries, and grapefruit were luxuries to most people. Better processing and storage methods now make it possible for these products to be available all year. Many perishable food products are now frozen in concentrated form or by the dry-freeze method and then stored in commercial freezers for use throughout the year. Less perishable products, such as cotton or wheat, are stored in local or central warehouses until the market price is most favorable.

Grading

Industrial users, such as textile companies, must obtain a certain type or grade of product each time they make a purchase. Consider cotton, for example. There are approximately 1,500 varieties of cotton. Fortunately, the rules established to maintain consistency in the quality and type of cotton sold make it possible for the textile company to obtain the same type and texture of cotton in each purchase.

DETERMINING PRICES OF FARM PRODUCTS

Farm products are produced by many relatively small farms that cannot individually affect the price of the products. The federal government, therefore, attempts to assist the farmer by maintaining the prices of the products through subsidies (direct payments to the farmer) and other support activities. Farmers sometimes form marketing organizations to accomplish the same type of support for farm prices.

Nature of the Supply

The supply of any farm product depends on the season and varies with the amount of acreage planted, the number of young animals born, the availability of feed, the weather, and the amount of damage from insects. Most crops require a growing season of from two to five months. The raising of livestock may take several years. This means that the total supply is slow to react to the demand for the product. And if the supply does not satisfy the demand, prices are likely to be higher than usual.

Nature of the Demand

The total of farm products demanded by customers—particularly food and raw materials for clothing—is remarkably stable. People must have food and clothes regardless of the time of year or general business conditions. In bad times, families may postpone the purchase of a new car or a new house, but they still buy food and clothing. What will vary is the demand for a particular food product. A shopper who planned to buy pork chops may find that a sudden price increase forces him to buy chicken instead. Price, then, becomes the deciding factor in determining how much of a particular product will be in demand and will sell.

Courtesy International Harvester

These cattle are being fed by an automatic feeding machine hauled by a tractor. The raising of livestock must be done with care, and it may require a sizable investment of money over a period of several years.

    If the supply of a particular crop is abundant, the price is likely to be low. On the other hand, if the supply is limited, the price is likely to be high. Thus if a farmer has produced a crop that has been produced in large quantities by other farmers, he may make only a small profit on his crop. But the farmer who has produced a crop that is in short supply may charge higher prices than usual and have a very profitable season.

THE GOVERNMENT AND THE FARMER

The government must take an interest in the welfare of farmers in order to give the country a strong, productive, and profitable farm system. It must also recognize the political influence and power of the farm bloc. The *farm bloc* consists of a group of legislators who frequently vote the same way on agricultural issues.

    The table on pages 130 and 131 lists some of the more important federal agencies and laws which have been established by Congress in order to help the farmer.

Part 11 / Marketing Farm Products / **129**

Government Assistance to Farmers

Year	Agency or Law	Purpose
	U.S. Department of Agriculture	To make low-cost loans, to make crop insurance available, to promote the exporting of American farm products, and to encourage the formation of farmers' cooperative associations. It also sponsors agricultural research at various state colleges and at state and federal experiment stations.
1930	Federal Farm Board	To raise the price of farm products by buying, holding, or storing them until prices rise.
1933	Agricultural Adjustment Act	To reduce farm production by assigning acreage allotments by crop to farmers. In return for planting only the agreed acreage, farmers receive subsidies from the government.
1933	Commodity Credit Corporation	To administer the Agricultural Adjustment Act of 1933. It arranges acreage quotas, makes subsidy payments, and stores surplus products until their price rises.
1961	Agricultural Act of 1961	To retire productive farmland by paying farmers not to plant it. This land is put in the so-called "soil bank" for possible future use. Meanwhile, the reduced acreage should mean fewer surplus crops and higher prices for farmers.
1965	Agricultural Act of 1965	To provide direct payments to farmers who cooperate in limiting certain crops. It departs from artificial price supports (a system by which the government sets the minimum market price for a farm product) and follows a free-market condition. Consumers benefit by paying the lower free-market price, and farmers are protected against a loss due to a sudden drop in price.
1968	Agricultural Act of 1965 extended to December 31, 1968	To extend the provisions described above.

Year	Agency or Law	Purpose
	Government Assistance to Farmers *(Continued)*	
1972	Agricultural Act of 1965 extended to December 31, 1972, and modified	To drop Rural Environmental Assistance Program (REAP) and no longer pay farmers for soil conservation. The weather program was deleted. Corn allotment percentages were reduced from 45 percent to 25 percent.

No government program has entirely solved the farm problem; too many farmers still work too many inefficient, unproductive farms and as a result earn only a bare livelihood. However, the federal laws and agencies listed above have had the following positive effects:

- Better farming methods have been discovered and been made available to all farmers.
- The soil is being preserved and improved.
- The risks of farming have been reduced through loan programs and low-cost insurance.
- New international markets have been developed for certain kinds of products.

Critics of the government farm programs are opposed to retiring land in an effort to eliminate an oversupply of farm products. They argue that a farmer can reduce his crop acreage by 25 percent, but actually increase his total production by retiring only the poorest acres and using better fertilizers or more efficient farming techniques on the remaining acres. Thus, they argue, the government's program has no effect on total farm production.

FARM COOPERATIVES

An association of farmers organized for the purpose of processing and marketing their products is called a *farm cooperative*. A farm cooperative may replace the local market, or it may compete on a larger scale with the central markets. The primary purpose of the cooperative is to improve the income of its members. To accomplish this goal, a cooperative uses the following marketing techniques:

- *Markets at the proper time.* The cooperative may withhold a portion of each season's harvest and wait for the best time to sell the products.
- *Stimulates demand.* The cooperative advertises its members' products and may try to develop its own brand name.

- *Processes the product.* A cooperative may process farm products for its members. It may prepare cheese, for example, and then sell its own brand of the product to the consumer and industrial markets.
- *Uses bargaining power.* A single farmer has limited bargaining power. Often he must take the only price he is offered. The cooperative bargains with many buyers, because it has a staff to do this. It also has a greater quantity and variety of products to offer a buyer than any single farmer could have. Greater quantities and variety give the cooperative more bargaining power.
- *Improves grading and standardization.* People who buy farm products want to be assured of uniform quality. The consumer is more likely to purchase a certain type of canned peaches if he knows that he will get uniformly good peaches with every purchase. If he has one bad experience, he may switch to another brand. The cooperative helps assure the consumer of uniformity in quality through grading and standardization.

TRENDS IN FARMING

In the future, farmers are more likely to operate large farms. The farmer has to pay high prices for farmland, equipment, and supplies. He may need to borrow a huge sum of money in order to buy his farm and equipment. In order

Courtesy International Harvester
This is how an artist visualizes the harvesting and processing of hay in the 1980s. The upper machine harvests and chops hay and discharges it into a wagon. The lower one harvests and bales hay and loads it into a trailer.

to succeed, a farmer has to be both a good farmer and a good businessman, especially when he must repay a loan and earn a profit as well. According to research, there will be fewer people in farming in the future because of the increasing need for greater skills on the part of the farmer.

High schools and colleges are helping to provide future farmers with the skills they will need. Tomorrow's farmers are studying in thousands of high schools and colleges throughout the country, where they receive the latest information on farming methods. Through cooperative farm training programs, they have an opportunity to apply their knowledge and to develop the leadership qualities they will need. The Future Farmers of America, a youth group of vocational agriculture students, has done a great deal to develop leadership and technical know-how in high school students.

YOUR MARKETING VOCABULARY

On a separate sheet of paper define each of the following marketing terms; then use each term in a sentence.

Commodity exchange
Consumer farm products
Crops
Farm bloc
Farm cooperative
Grading
Industrial farm products
Livestock products
Middlemen

FOR REVIEW AND DISCUSSION

1. Why has the United States been able to triple its output of farm products?
2. What are the four major classifications of crops?
3. Why are middlemen essential in the marketing of farm products?
4. What are the activities of the local market?
5. Why are the marketing and distribution of farm products more complex than the marketing and distribution of other types of goods?
6. What three marketing services are essential in handling farm products?
7. Explain what is meant by the nature of (a) the supply of farm products and (b) the demand for farm products.
8. Although government programs have not solved the farm problem, they have had some good effects. Discuss this statement.
9. What kinds of services do farm cooperatives provide for their members?
10. How are high schools and colleges helping to prepare tomorrow's farmers?

ANALYZING MARKETING CONCEPTS

1. Prepare a form like the one near the top of the next page. List the following products in the left-hand column: (a) eggs, (b) tomatoes, (c) cabbage, (d) chickens, (e) sweet corn, (f) milk, (g) potatoes, (h) apples. Assume

that these products will be used as consumer farm products; that is, they will not undergo a major change in form before reaching the consumer. In the right-hand column, describe the activities that do take place to prepare each product for the consumer market.

Consumer Farm Product	Activities That Prepare Product for Consumer Market
Example: Head of lettuce	Cleaning, trimming, grading, packing

2. Prepare a form like the one below. List the following products in the left-hand column: (a) cucumbers, (b) apples, (c) wheat, (d) chickens, (e) sweet corn, (f) milk, (g) eggs, (h) pears, (i) soybeans, (j) potatoes. Assume that these products will be used as industrial farm products; that is, they will undergo a major change in form before reaching the consumer. In the center column, write the change in form that may occur as each product is processed. In the right-hand column, name the final consumer product.

Industrial Farm Product	Change in Form	Consumer Product
Example: Tomatoes	Tomatoes are cooked.	Spaghetti sauce

◊ MARKETING PROJECT 11
Charting the Marketing of Farm Products

Project Goal: Given one leading soil crop and one leading livestock product produced in your state, chart the path of each product from the farmer to the consumer, and indicate the marketing services performed at each step.

Action: Identify a soil crop and a livestock product grown in your state. For each product, talk with a representative of the business that markets the product to find out the steps followed in getting it from the producer to the consumer. The business may be a local grocer, central market, wholesaler, or retailer. Also, determine the marketing services performed at each step.

Based on the information you have obtained, list each product and chart its path from the producer to the consumer. Using the same information, list the marketing services performed at each step.

part 12

International Marketing

YOUR GOALS

1. Given a specific product, list and explain at least three difficulties that might be encountered in marketing it overseas.
2. Given a specific product, determine the most effective method for selling and distributing it in foreign markets.

Many American companies sell and distribute their goods and services in other countries. At the same time many foreign companies sell their products here. The buying and selling of goods among companies in different countries is called *international marketing.* International marketing enables Americans to buy a variety of foreign products, such as cars made in West Germany, watches made in Switzerland, transistor radios made in Japan, boots made in Brazil, wines made in France, cheeses made in the Netherlands, and baskets made in China.

Today, almost all the countries of the world are involved in international marketing. There are many opportunities in this field, and modern marketers are alert to the chances for profit that exist in *importing*, buying the products of other countries for resale, and *exporting*, marketing the products of one's own country in other countries.

THE INTERNATIONAL MARKET

American businesses are especially active in the international market. American goods are sold in most countries of the world, and many raw materials and manufactured goods from abroad are imported by American companies. Just as we enjoy imported tea, coffee, sugar, bananas, silk, olive oil, and spices, people in other countries enjoy textiles, machinery, automobiles, and grains exported by the United States.

In the years before World War II, manufacturers in the United States did comparatively little international marketing, mainly because money was scarce in many foreign nations. Nor did the United States import many foreign goods. To protect American businessmen from the possible loss of customers to foreign manufacturers whose products were lower-priced, the United States tended to discourage foreign producers from marketing their products here.

After World War II, however, the situation began to change. With the financial assistance of the Marshall Plan (a plan to help Europe economically), European businesses were able to rebuild industries that had been destroyed by the war. In Japan and other Asian countries, American financial aid enabled businessmen to rebuild their factories. And some countries that formerly were not technically advanced began building modern factories and using the latest and most efficient methods.

As foreign industry grew, jobs were created in these countries and standards of living rose sharply. The new buying power of foreign consumers caused American businessmen to look with interest at this expanding market. Today exporting is big business for American manufacturers. In 1940 American exports totaled $3 billion. In 1970 this figure was over $43 billion.

The following table shows the value of United States exports and imports in 1960, 1965, and 1971.

U.S. Exports and Imports of Merchandise by Areas: 1960, 1965, and 1971
(in millions of dollars)

Area	Exports 1960	Exports 1965	Exports 1971	Imports 1960	Imports 1965	Imports 1971
Africa	793	1,229	1,694	534	878	1,237
Asia	4,186	6,012	9,850	2,721	4,528	11,783
Australia and Oceania	514	956	1,169	266	453	895
Europe	7,399	9,364	14,574	4,628	6,292	12,846
North America	5,506	7,742	13,557	4,429	6,579	15,790
South America	2,177	2,175	3,293	2,435	2,624	3,011
Total	20,575	27,478	44,137	14,654	21,366	45,562

Source: *Statistical Abstract of the United States,* 1972.

It is also interesting to know what the United States exports and imports. The charts on pages 138 and 139 show the types of products that were exported and the types of products that were imported in 1971.

Balance of Trade

Every nation is eager to have its exports exceed its imports in order to maintain a favorable balance of trade. The *balance of trade* of a nation is the difference in value between the goods it exports and the goods it imports. When exports exceed imports, the balance of trade is favorable; when imports exceed exports, the balance of trade is unfavorable. The export of American goods to other countries results in an inflow of dollars to the United States. On the other hand, the import of foreign goods results in an outflow of dollars. In the first half of 1971 the United States suffered its first unfavorable trade balance since 1893, and government and business became concerned.

To help American products compete in world trade, the federal government took the following measures: It imposed a 10 percent surcharge (extra tax) on imports; devalued the dollar, thus making foreign products more expensive here and American products cheaper abroad; gave tax credits to businesses that agreed to buy American equipment; and attempted to control inflation and thus hold down the prices of American products.

Other countries deplored these trade restrictions, but the United States government felt they were necessary to protect American business.

Markets

The federal government takes an active part in helping American businesses make their products available to foreign consumers. For manufacturers who are interested in establishing markets in foreign countries, the government has set up trade centers in six major foreign cities: London, Frankfurt, Bangkok, Milan, Tokyo, and Stockholm. These trade centers provide space for American companies to display their products. They make it easier for American businessmen to meet and select a foreign sales agent. They are also a source of valuable market information.

In addition, the federal government, through its sponsorship of trade missions, helps marketers seek potential customers abroad. A *trade mission* is a group of businessmen who volunteer to go abroad to promote the foreign commerce of the United States. They investigate business prospects for American companies that are eager to find foreign markets. Any American firm interested in foreign commerce can prepare a business proposal for the trade mission. Such a proposal describes the company's product or service. The company can then ask the trade mission to make contacts in its assigned country, to locate a sales agent, or to talk with prospects about the proposal.

Types of Products Exported, 1971

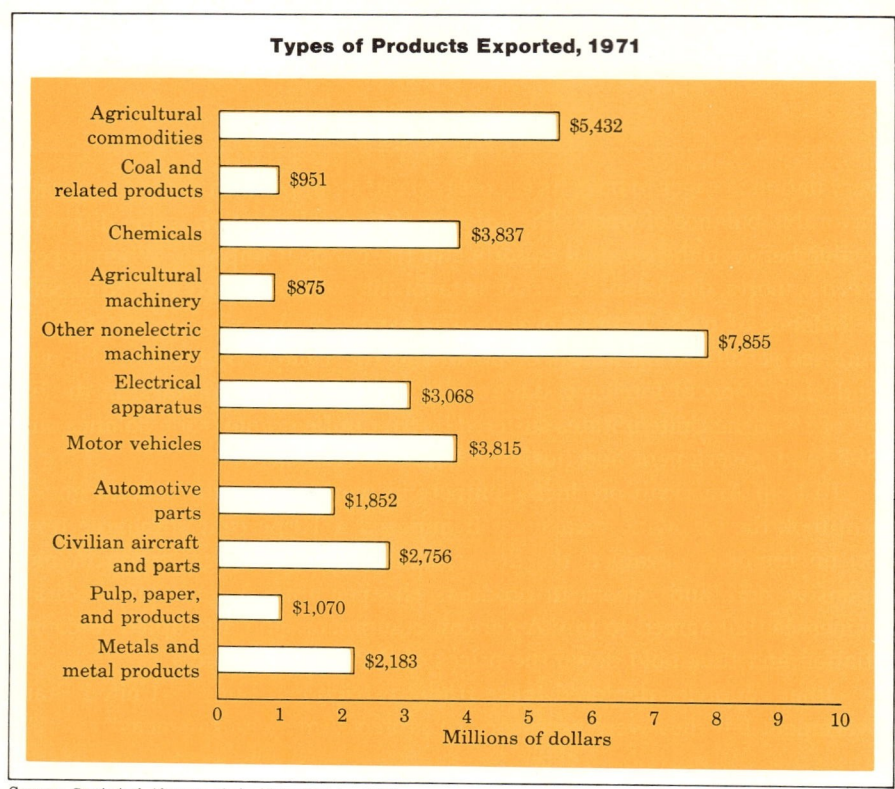

Product	Millions of dollars
Agricultural commodities	$5,432
Coal and related products	$951
Chemicals	$3,837
Agricultural machinery	$875
Other nonelectric machinery	$7,855
Electrical apparatus	$3,068
Motor vehicles	$3,815
Automotive parts	$1,852
Civilian aircraft and parts	$2,756
Pulp, paper, and products	$1,070
Metals and metal products	$2,183

Source: *Statistical Abstract of the United States*, 1972.

Since 1960 more than 25,000 business proposals from more than 5,000 American companies have been taken abroad by trade missions. The missions have brought back more than 40,000 trade and investment opportunities.

Financial Advice to Exporters. International marketers sometimes need advice on financing overseas businesses, and on tariff, tax, and currency regulations. Several agencies offer this type of advice. The Export-Import Bank (Eximbank) of the United States offers a counseling service to exporters and to banks and other financial institutions. The American Management Association holds conferences at which international authorities discuss financing problems. The Small Business Administration in Washington, D.C., and the United States Chamber of Commerce furnish advice about export trade to small businesses and assist them in solving financial problems.

Marketing Assistance to Exporters. Companies interested in international marketing may obtain information from several sources: the United States agencies discussed above, universities that teach international marketing,

Types of Products Imported, 1971

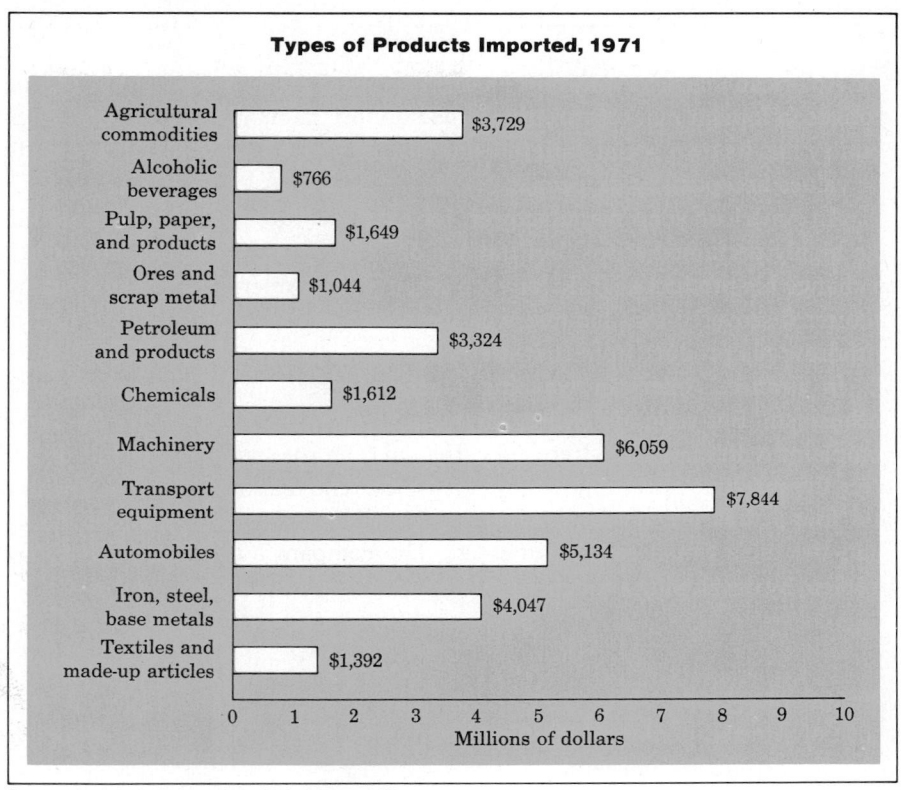

Product	Millions of dollars
Agricultural commodities	$3,729
Alcoholic beverages	$766
Pulp, paper, and products	$1,649
Ores and scrap metal	$1,044
Petroleum and products	$3,324
Chemicals	$1,612
Machinery	$6,059
Transport equipment	$7,844
Automobiles	$5,134
Iron, steel, base metals	$4,047
Textiles and made-up articles	$1,392

Source: *Statistical Abstract of the United States, 1972.*

foreign embassies or consulates, banks with international departments, and airlines serving foreign countries. The embassies are interested in helping because the trade relationship might benefit their own countries; the banks and airlines, because their businesses might profit. Airlines, for example, carry millions of tons of goods overseas. More international trade would mean more air freight and more passengers.

ANALYZING THE INTERNATIONAL MARKET

Before offering his products to foreign consumers, the international marketer must study the market carefully. His research tries to answer certain basic questions: Is there a need for my product? Who are my potential customers? What is their level of earnings? What are their buying habits? What are their buying motives?

Since each country has its own culture and customs, which influence its buying decisions, the marketer must conduct research in each country in which he hopes to sell his product.

Differences in Customs and Traditions

The American marketer may make a serious mistake if he assumes that buying motives in foreign markets are the same as those in American markets. Each country has its own social patterns, and buying choices are made according to the values accepted by its people.

An American soap manufacturer, for example, found that Swedes do not like highly perfumed soaps, but Italians do. Therefore, the manufacturer had to change his product slightly for each country. An American cake-mix manufacturer discovered that his mix was too sweet for British tastes and had to withdraw his product from that market.

In France, American washing machines were at first received with enthusiasm. But soon afterward, the manufacturer began to receive the same complaint with increasing frequency: the paint on the inside of the tub peeled after the machine had been used a few times. The manufacturer investigated and found that French housewives used extremely hot water, much hotter than the tub's finish could withstand. The company's engineers solved the problem by developing a tougher protective finish for the exported tubs.

Differences in Buying Habits

The shopping habits of foreign consumers are sometimes vastly different from those of American consumers. Consider, for example, this foreign shopper's morning trip to the marketplace:

Señora Leoncia Torres hurries to the marketplace just after dawn. She goes early in order to find the best selections of melons, lettuce, chicken, and fish. Each of these purchases may require several stops, because each stand is located in a separate part of the market area and because Señora Torres shops around before buying.

Señora Torres sometimes spends as much as 15 minutes bargaining with a vendor. She may leave abruptly if he stubbornly refuses to lower his prices. In a few minutes she may be heard bargaining with the next vendor. Once the price is decided, Señora Torres pays in coins—she has never used checks or charge accounts!

When her marketing is finished and her string bag is filled with the morning's purchases, Señora Torres heads for home. Walking up the path leading to her front door, she sees that the sun is high in the sky—she has been away from home all morning, just gathering the food for the day's meals.

The method of shopping used by Señora Torres has been taking place for as long as there has been recorded history, and it is still widely practiced in towns and villages throughout Europe, Latin America, and Asia.

Such piecemeal shopping is not the only way in which foreign buying habits differ from American ones. There are many local traditions, customs,

Shopping habits differ from country to country.

and cultural patterns to which the international marketer has to tailor his product, his advertising, and his selling methods.

In some countries the man of the family makes the buying decisions; in other countries, shopping is done by servants; elsewhere, the wife makes the buying decisions, but her husband does the actual shopping. Often in foreign countries, customers expect to question established prices.

International marketers must be careful in their use of brand names, because a name may have an unpleasant meaning in a foreign language. They must also take into account the established habits in a country. For example, Tetley Tea met with resistance when it tried to sell its tea bags in England. Tea is very popular in England. But because the custom has always been to use loose tea and to brew it in a teapot, the English scorned the tea bag. Tetley met the objection with an advertising campaign suggesting that Tetley's stringless tea bags be used in a teapot. Thus Tetley offered the convenience of tea bags and the full-bodied flavor of tea brewed in a pot. The idea took hold among the English and sales climbed.

In each foreign country the marketer must investigate which advertising and selling methods will work best for his products.

PROBLEMS OF INTERNATIONAL MARKETING

The marketer who exports or imports goods or services is faced with special marketing problems. He must reckon with tariffs. He must solve transportation problems. He must deal with people whose customs and language differ from his own. He must also consider the risks involved. All these concerns present a challenge to the international marketer.

Tariffs

The tax that an international marketer pays to a foreign country for the privilege of selling his product there is called a *tariff*. A tariff provides revenue for the country accepting imports, as well as protection for its own products, called domestic goods. *Domestic goods* are products produced within the country in which they are sold. When protected by a tariff, domestic goods are likely to sell at lower prices than imported goods. The imported goods are at a disadvantage because they must be priced high enough to cover the tariff and still bring in a profit. This price difference between domestic goods and imported goods often makes domestic goods more attractive to the consumer, thus ensuring that a country's industries will not be hurt by imported goods. It was for this reason that the United States imposed a tariff on imported goods in 1971.

A businessman planning to sell a product in another country must take into consideration the tariff that he must pay to that country. If the tariff will force him to charge a price higher than that of competing domestic goods, he may decide not to export at all. Tariffs, then, often act as barriers to international marketing. Many countries feel that tariffs should be lowered or removed altogether in an effort to encourage trade.

Since the end of World War II, several attempts have been made to lower tariffs and, in some cases, to remove them altogether. In 1948 the General Agreement on Tariffs and Trade (GATT) became effective. Twenty-three countries participated in the making of this international agreement on rules for tariffs and trade. The purpose of GATT is to continually reduce tariffs and ease trade between countries.

In 1958 the European Economic Community (EEC), usually called the Common Market, was formed by Belgium, France, Italy, Luxembourg, the Netherlands, and West Germany. In 1972 Britain, Ireland, Norway, and Denmark joined the group. The aim of the Common Market is to lower tariffs and remove other trade restrictions among its members while imposing high tariffs on goods imported into the Common Market from nonmember countries. Citizens of Common Market countries also have the right to work anywhere in the community.

Ramp servicemen load cargo onto a plane bound for a foreign port. International marketers must package their products to withstand long, rigorous trips.

Courtesy Trans World Airlines, Inc.

A smaller group of countries—Sweden, Switzerland, Finland, and Austria—makes up the European Free Trade Association (EFTA). The aim of this group is also to eliminate tariffs on goods traded among the member nations and to establish free and unrestricted trade.

Shipping Requirements

The loading of a product on a ship or a plane bound for a foreign country is the beginning of a possibly hazardous trip. The normal transportation problems that face any marketer are multiplied when a product is shipped overseas. During its trip the product may be subject to extreme changes in temperature and humidity and to possible damage, and during the unloading process, to theft and rough handling.

The international marketer must design packaging that will survive uncertain shipping conditions. He must choose the method of shipping that is best suited to his product. He must keep in mind his product's weight, its perishability, its breakability, and its value. He must investigate insurance coverage, become familiar with the shipping schedules of various freight carriers, complete the many commercial and government shipping documents, and be familiar with the handling facilities for his products at the various destinations overseas.

Communications

Communication between businessmen speaking different languages is, of course, more difficult than communication between businessmen speaking the same language. In face-to-face situations the marketer who cannot speak the language of the nation with which he is dealing must often rely on an interpreter, and much of the effectiveness of his selling approach is lost when it is delivered secondhand.

To overcome this disadvantage, the international marketer often learns the language of his customers. The use of their language creates a feeling of goodwill among his customers, who regard it as a mark of respect for their country and their customs.

Risks

As population increases and as the needs and wants of people in developing nations become greater, international trade will continue to grow. However, it would be unwise to neglect the risk factor.

An American company operating abroad must be aware that changing local conditions might destroy its market—or the entire company. If a local government is overthrown, the manufacturing plants or marketing networks of the American firm may be destroyed or seized by the new government.

METHODS OF SELLING AND DISTRIBUTING TO FOREIGN MARKETS

After a company has decided that its prospects for selling to foreign markets are good, it must decide how its goods will be marketed. The international marketer may do his own shipping, distributing, and selling; he may use middlemen to get his product to the foreign customer; or he may set up manufacturing operations in the foreign countries themselves. The international marketer, then, may use three different methods of distribution. He may sell direct to the customer, he may sell through middlemen, or he may sell through foreign headquarters.

Selling Direct to the Customer

Sometimes a manufacturer employs salesmen to make personal calls on potential foreign customers. This is often done by manufacturers of industrial goods, because a small number of salesmen can easily contact all prospective buyers. Orders resulting from such contacts are relayed to the home office, where the orders are filled and shipped direct to the customer.

When a large number of customers are involved, a marketer may find it worthwhile to establish a sales office abroad. This field sales office provides a convenient base for the company's traveling salesmen and serves as an information center for customer inquiries. Sometimes the traveling salesmen are citizens of the country in which they work who have been trained by the marketing company. Marketers often find this employment of local salesmen a distinct advantage, since it simplifies the problem of communication between salesmen and customers.

A marketer will often sell direct to the customer in cases where aggressive personal selling is required, where the product must be backed up by service, or where customers must be trained in the use of the product.

Selling Through Middlemen

When a manufacturer does not wish to, or cannot afford to, set up branch offices in another country, he may employ middlemen as contacts between himself and his customers. The types of middlemen that he may use include exporters and importers, distributors, and manufacturers' agents. These middlemen act as sales representatives for the manufacturer and perform a variety of services.

Exporters and Importers. Exporters and importers handle all the details involved in the buying, selling, and transportation of goods from one country to another. They take care of tariff payments, shipping and government documents, transportation arrangements, and necessary correspondence. For their services as middlemen, exporters and importers are usually paid on a commission basis; that is, they are given an agreed-upon percentage of the total amount of the shipment.

Distributors. A distributor is an independent businessman who markets products that customers cannot buy anywhere else in the sales area. The distributor actually buys the imported product and resells it at a profit. He handles all selling, advertising, service, billing, and warehousing.

A distributor is usually a resident of the country in which he does business. Therefore, he knows the language, customs, and trade regulations of the country. Also, he is usually established in a business other than distributing the manufacturer's product. These factors make it easier for him to sell the product.

Manufacturers' Agents. A manufacturer's agent usually represents two or more noncompeting manufacturers in foreign markets. He is paid a commission by these manufacturers. Like the distributor, he markets American

Many large corporations have headquarters in foreign countries.

Courtesy IBM World Trade Corp.

products in foreign countries. Unlike the distributor, however, he does not actually buy or store the imported merchandise; instead, he relays customers' orders to the home offices of the manufacturers.

Selling Through Foreign Headquarters

The sales volume of American companies in international markets has grown so rapidly that many companies have found it profitable to set up headquarters in other countries. These international headquarters often operate independently of their parent companies in the United States. They may manufacture their own products, hire their own personnel, and conduct their own advertising campaigns.

Having foreign headquarters allows a company to reduce its shipping costs, to take advantage of lower wage scales, and to avoid tariffs, although some countries tax foreign-owned businesses at a higher rate than domestic businesses. Some American corporations that have set up foreign headquarters are International Business Machines (France), Celanese Corporation (Belgium), and American Express Company (England).

Wholly Owned Subsidiaries. The foreign headquarters described above are wholly owned subsidiaries. A "wholly owned subsidiary" is a company in which all the manufacturing and marketing facilities are owned by the parent firm. The parent firm thus has complete control over the operations of the subsidiary. However, some American companies involved in international marketing prefer other arrangements.

Joint Venture. A "joint venture" is a partnership arrangement in which the foreign manufacturing or marketing operation is owned in part by an American company and in part by a local company or local citizens. It is often advantageous for an American company to enter into a joint venture to avoid trade restrictions, tariffs, or political exclusion of foreign-owned companies.

Licensing. Some companies enter into "licensing," an arrangement by which the company authorizes foreign manufacturers to manufacture its products. Companies using this type of arrangement are free to concentrate their major efforts on manufacturing products for the domestic market. To distribute their foreign-produced output, the companies may rely on foreign middlemen, or they may establish their own sales branches or subsidiaries in major foreign markets.

◻ YOUR MARKETING VOCABULARY

On a separate sheet of paper define each of the following marketing terms; then use each term in a sentence.

Balance of trade
Domestic goods
Exporting
Importing
International marketing
Tariff
Trade mission

◻ FOR REVIEW AND DISCUSSION

1. When and how did international marketing have its start on a large scale?
2. What was the attitude of American manufacturers toward international marketing before World War II?
3. Why is the United States eager to have its exports exceed its imports?
4. When is the balance of trade favorable? unfavorable?
5. How does the United States government aid in the development of foreign markets?
6. What must the international marketer do before offering his products to foreign customers?
7. What are the advantages and disadvantages of tariffs?
8. Why must businessmen consider the tariff when planning to sell in a foreign country?
9. Identify and explain GATT, EEC, and EFTA.

10. If an American manufacturer does not wish to, or cannot afford to, set up branch offices in other countries, what can he do to market his goods there?
11. Explain the terms "wholly owned subsidiary," "joint venture," and "licensing."
12. Some American firms, such as Eastman Kodak and Ford, now have plants in foreign countries where they manufacture their products. Why do large companies establish such plants?

ANALYZING MARKETING CONCEPTS

1. Assume that you want to export a product that you manufacture. You know that international marketing can be profitable but risky. List five questions that must be answered before you decide to export your product.
2. Assume that you are an American automobile manufacturer and you want to market your cars in West Germany. You know that German car makers have a competitive advantage over you in that they speak the native language and are familiar with customer buying habits and motives. You must choose the marketing method that will help to establish your reputation with German customers as quickly as possible. You can (a) ship the cars from the United States to Germany and market them through middlemen, (b) establish a manufacturing plant in Germany, hire only American employees, and deal with customers through interpreters, or (c) establish a manufacturing plant in Germany, hire German workers, and require the American managers to learn German.

    Choose one of the marketing methods above and explain why you chose it. Discuss how that method will affect your company's image and selling activities.

MARKETING PROJECT 12
Selecting Methods for International Marketing

Project Goal: Given a specific product, determine the most effective method of selling and distributing it in foreign markets.

Action: Select a product that is exported from the United States. Consult the manufacturer to learn the best method of selling and distributing the product in foreign markets. Prepare a form like the one below and state your findings in the appropriate columns.

Exported Product	Best Method of Selling and Distributing the Product	Why That Method Is Best

part 13

The Marketing of Services

YOUR GOAL

Given a group of businesses in your community, identify five businesses that provide services to the consumer and five businesses that provide services to industry.

The American Marketing Association defines *services* as "activities, benefits, or satisfactions which are offered for sale, or are provided in connection with the sale of goods." This part is concerned with the services described in the first half of that definition: "activities, benefits, or satisfactions which are offered for sale." The marketing of these kinds of services usually does not include the sale of goods to the customer. However, if goods are involved, they are not considered a major part of the sale. For example, food consumed in a restaurant is considered a purchase of a service because the cost of preparing and serving the food is greater than the cost of the food itself.

When a customer buys a service, he buys the time, knowledge, skill, or resources of someone else. He receives the satisfaction or benefit of that person's activity. When a person has his television set repaired, he buys the time, knowledge, and skill of a repairman. The fee the customer is charged helps pay for the tools the repairman needs and pays in full for any parts needed to repair the set. When the repairman has completed his work, the customer has the benefit and satisfaction of having his set working properly.

As mentioned in earlier parts, the marketing of services has increased at a very rapid rate in recent years. Let us review the reasons.

- The trend toward work specialization is increasing. Many firms prefer to hire only those people who perform jobs that are directly related to the firm's activities. For other jobs that need to be done, they employ service organizations that specialize in those jobs. For example, a store that once hired maintenance workers now may use the services of a professional maintenance company.
- The jobs that both businesses and individual consumers need to have done have become increasingly complex. For example, a marketer with a modest operation used to be able to prepare his firm's tax reports. Today, even a small firm is likely to hire the services of an accountant.
- The individual consumer has more money to spend. This means he can afford to buy services he does not want to perform as well as services he is not able to perform.

The buying of certain services gives consumers more time for leisure.

150 / Unit 4 / Special Markets

GROWTH OF SERVICES

The marketing of services has shown great increases both in total dollars earned and in employment. An important factor in this growth is the increase in the number of services offered by retailers. This increase has placed a much greater variety of services at the disposal of the consumer.

Increase in Dollars and Employment

The growth of the marketing of services can be measured in a number of ways. One way is to compare the total dollars earned by services and the total dollars earned by goods over a period of time. The following table shows how the dollar value of the gross national product increased in the 20-year period from 1950 to 1970.

Gross National Product
(in billions of dollars)

	1950	1960	1970
Goods	$162.4	$259.6	$468.3
Services	87.0	187.3	410.3
Structures	35.4	56.8	95.5

Source: U.S. Bureau of Economic Analysis.

Note that during the 20-year period the increase in the gross national product for services was considerably larger than the increase for goods. In other words, the marketing of services grew at a much more rapid rate than the marketing of goods.

A second way of looking at the growth in services is to compare national income figures. The table below shows the national income figures for that same 20-year period.

National Income Originating in Distribution and Services Industries
(in millions of dollars)

	1950	1960	1970
Wholesale trade	$13,307	$23,126	$44,715
Retail trade	27,636	41,270	76,473
Services	21,768	44,480	102,661

Source: U.S. Bureau of Economic Analysis.

Note that the increase in income from services was much greater than the increase in income from either wholesale or retail trade.

The percent of people employed in services has also increased in the same 20-year period, as shown in the following table.

Where Employees Work			
	1950	1960	1970
In manufacturing	33.7%	31.0%	27.7%
In wholesale and retail trade	20.8	21.0	21.0
In services	11.9	13.7	16.2
In other fields	33.6	34.3	35.1

Source: U.S. Department of Commerce.

The table shows that there has been a gradual drop in the percent of people employed in manufacturing (automation is making it possible for manufacturing companies to increase productivity without increasing the number of employees). There has been only a slight increase in the percent of people employed in wholesale and retail trade. But there has been a large increase in the percent of people working in service industries.

Increase in Services Offered by Retailers

Services are marketed both by companies that sell services only and by companies that sell goods as well. During recent years there has been a tremendous increase in the number of companies that sell both goods and services. Manufacturers and wholesalers have increased their marketing of services to customers; however, the most significant change has probably taken place among retailers.

At one time most retailers considered the offering of services simply a matter of customer convenience. A retailer was in business to sell goods, and the service market was not his concern. In recent years, however, retailers have developed a new attitude.

Department stores are a good example. In the early 1900s very few services were marketed by department stores. A customer could most likely find department stores that offered food services, beauty-salon and barbershop services, and fur storage. But even these were not expected to be important profit centers.

Today, department stores sell more kinds of services and expect more from those sales. Most stores expect the services they offer to bring in customer traffic, and they also expect their services to earn their way in sales and profit. A larger department store may sell 20 or even 30 kinds of services. The following list shows some of the most popular services and places offering services:

Beauty salon	Food (restaurants and cafeterias)
Fur storage	Upholstering
Jewelry and watch repair	Auto service center
Photography studio	Rug cleaning
Gift wrapping (for a fee)	Travel bureau

CLASSIFICATION OF SERVICES

Services may be grouped according to the market to which they are offered—consumer or industrial—and according to type.

Although some types of services may be directed only at the industrial market or only at the consumer market, many types are offered to both markets. An insurance company, for example, may do business with both markets. However, the policies that the insurance company offers the consumer market are different from those it offers the industrial market. Also, the ways of soliciting business in each market differ.

Services Marketed to Consumers

Many types of services are marketed to the consumer. Some of the most important are food, personal care, automotive, entertainment, lodging, transportation, communication, and insurance.

Food Services. Today, more and more individuals and families are eating out, and it has been estimated that restaurants serve more than 55 million meals each day. Restaurants range from small eating places that offer simple and inexpensive meals to elaborate places where the food is elegant and expensive. But regardless of how the ever-growing number of these establishments are classified, they will be successful if the service they sell is wanted by the buying public.

People are not only eating out more, but they are also making more use of caterers. "Caterers" are firms that specialize in providing food and service for at-home dinners and parties. They also provide food and service at other places that do not have food facilities of their own.

Personal Care Services. Those services that help a person to be well groomed are called *personal care services*. Personal care services are offered by beauty salons and barber shops, laundries and dry cleaners, garment-repair shops,

A. Devaney, Inc., N. Y.
Beauty salons provide the valuable personal care services of skilled and highly trained professional hairdressers.

and shoe-repair shops. Personal care services continue to grow because people today not only have the money but also are quite willing to spend it on themselves.

Automotive Services. There are almost 100 million cars in the United States, and their owners are dependent upon automotive service firms. Oil companies have large networks of stations that sell both goods and services. In fact, service has become such an important part of these stations that what used to be known as a "gas station" is now often called a "service station." There are also a large number of garages or repair shops that specialize in automobile repairs and maintenance.

Entertainment Services. Because people have more money to spend and more leisure time, the entertainment industries are growing. Among the many types of entertainment offered as a service are movies, athletic competitions, amusement parks, and circuses. Model-car racing, billiards, and bowling are also popular forms of entertainment today. Many of the more than 11,000 billiard parlors in the United States are designed to appeal to all members of the family.

Lodging Services. Every night, at least 2 million people use the lodging services provided by hotels and motels in the United States. Because a great number of people travel long distances by car, motels are growing at a particularly rapid rate. More than 40,000 motels are available, and new ones are going up rapidly. The newest motels provide valet and laundry service, restaurants, beauty shops and barber shops, heated swimming pools, meeting rooms, baby-sitters, and transportation to and from nearby airports and business centers.

More and more people are going camping on weekends and vacations. Some use trailers; others use tents. Most set up camp in one of the state parks or in privately owned parks that offer lodging services for a small fee. The fee entitles the campers to their own camping space and to the use of whatever facilities the campsite offers.

Transportation Services. Bus companies, railroads, steamship companies, and airlines provide transportation services. Of these four, airline service has grown perhaps the fastest because planes offer speedy travel at prices now within the range of most people's budgets. The airlines offer a number of discount plans: tickets at lower prices are provided to persons under 21 or over 65, to persons making trips of specific lengths, or to persons traveling on less-busy days. In addition, on many flights, passengers can watch, generally for a modest fee, the latest movies or listen to music in stereo while they dine.

Communication Services. One of the most widely used communication services in our modern civilization is that provided by a telephone company.

Although in nearly all areas the telephone company is considered to be a *public utility*—that is, a business organization performing a public service and subject to special government regulation—all telephone companies are also marketers. They continually try to improve their offerings to the public, they promote the use of their services, and they try to keep their prices competitively low, even though they seldom have a competitor.

Insurance Services. A person who is employed or who owns a home or car knows the importance of insurance. *Insurance* is protection against risk. People buy insurance to protect themselves against losses resulting from property damage, theft, accidents, sickness, or even death. Also, insurance companies provide policies that enable people to save for their children's education or for their retirement years.

Services Marketed to Industry

A wide range of services is offered to the industrial, or business, market. Some of them are sold by manufacturers and wholesalers; others are sold by service firms.

Business firms, of course, also buy many of the same services that consumers buy. For example, they buy transportation for employees who take business trips. They buy communication services. They buy insurance to protect themselves against possible losses.

Business firms also purchase specialized services, such as financial services, advertising and sales promotion services, engineering services, and office services.

Financial Services. Banks, investment companies, and accounting firms supply other business firms with financial services. Banks make loans to businesses. Investment companies advise businesses about the purchase of stocks, bonds, and property. Accounting firms not only keep records for business firms but also prepare their various income tax reports and financial statements.

Advertising and Promotion Services. A large number of marketers rely on advertising agencies to prepare advertising and promotion that will sell their products. Typographers, commercial art firms, and other graphic arts specialists also provide useful advertising and promotion services. If a marketer does not have advertising and sales promotion specialists on his payroll, he can buy their services. In fact, the marketer can buy the services of many kinds of experts to accomplish the job of advertising his products or services.

Engineering Services. Businesses often employ the services of engineering firms to assist them in the planning, designing, or construction of buildings, machinery, or special equipment. An engineering firm sells the services of the professional engineers on its staff. Some of these firms also sell equipment to their customers, but the charges for the planning and designing phase of the job are usually considered separate from the charge for equipment sold to the customer.

Courtesy Pfizer Inc.
Professional engineers offer consulting services and technical assistance to industrial customers. These services include planning, design, and construction.

Office Services. A variety of office services are available to businesses. Some companies supply temporary office personnel, usually typists, file clerks, or stenographers. Other companies specialize in making duplicates of material in whatever number and of whatever size needed. Businesses whose employees wear uniforms or lab coats or some other form of regulation dress may use laundry service firms.

It is easy to see that regardless of the kind of service a business or an individual wants, someone is probably offering it for sale. And, considering the way the service business is growing, a service that is not available today will likely be available tomorrow.

◻ YOUR MARKETING VOCABULARY

On a separate sheet of paper define each of the following marketing terms; then use each term in a sentence.

Insurance
Personal care services
Public utility
Services

◆ FOR REVIEW AND DISCUSSION

1. What does a person actually buy when he buys a service?
2. What are the characteristics of services?
3. Why has the marketing of services increased at a very rapid rate in recent years?
4. Where has the most impressive change occurred in the selling of services?
5. What kinds of services are sold to both consumers and businesses?
6. How are services classified or grouped?
7. Make a list of the consumer services you have bought in the last month.
8. Describe the services offered by a department store or other retail store in your community.
9. What services are offered by banks?
10. What services do advertising companies sell to businesses?

◆ ANALYZING MARKETING CONCEPTS

1. The marketing of services is one of the fastest-growing areas of marketing and distribution. Prepare a form like the one below. In the left-hand column, list the following types of services: (a) personal care, (b) entertainment, (c) lodging, (d) transportation, (e) communication, (f) financial, (g) advertising. In the right-hand column, list three specific examples of each type of service.

Type of Service	Examples of Service
Example: Automotive	Automatic car wash, engine repair, replacement of smashed fender.

2. Assume that you are the manager of a department store and use the services of other businesses. Prepare a form like the one below. In the left-hand column, list the following service businesses: (a) Dart Advertising Agency, (b) Vigo Insurance Company, (c) Major Construction Company, (d) Crane Engineering Consultants, (e) Instant Office Help, Inc., (f) Trans-Truck System, (g) Right-Copy Printers. In the right-hand column, give your purpose for using a service provided by each of those businesses.

Service Business	Purpose for Using Service
Example: Merchants Bank	To borrow money to buy merchandise for Christmas sales.

◆ MARKETING PROJECT 13
Identifying Service Businesses

Project Goal: Given a group of businesses in your community, identify five businesses that provide services to the consumer and five businesses that provide services to industry.

Action: Visit several retail and wholesale businesses in your community. Observe the activities of these businesses and ask questions to determine the kinds of services they sell. Use your city directory or the Yellow Pages as a source of names of businesses.

Based on your findings, list five businesses that provide services to consumers and five businesses that provide services to industry. For each business, list the services that it provides.

Marketing Channels

UNIT 5

part 14

Channels of Distribution

YOUR GOALS

1. Select a consumer product and contrast the benefits of using direct and indirect channels of distribution for that product.
2. Identify five businesses in your community that may be classified as agent middlemen and five businesses that may be classified as merchant middlemen.

Manufacturers send their products to market in one of two ways: direct to the consumer or industrial user, or through middlemen. As stated in Part 11, middlemen are business organizations that perform buying and selling services that aid in the flow of goods from the producer to the consumer. They are properly called middlemen because they function between the producer and the user of a product. Some middlemen, such as wholesalers, sell to retail stores and industrial users; others, such as retailers, sell direct to consumers.

To market his finished product, every manufacturer must decide which middlemen, if any, he will use. Should he sell to a wholesale middleman who will resell to many retailing middlemen, who in turn will sell to many more individual customers? Or should he sell direct to the consumer? The manufacturer must choose a channel through which to distribute his products.

A channel of distribution is not concerned with the actual transportation of goods. Rather, a *channel of distribution* is the transfer of ownership or control of the goods as they pass from the manufacturer to the consumer or industrial user. Transportation companies and independent warehouses ship and store goods on their way to market, but do not own or control them; they are therefore not part of a channel of distribution. Those who are part of the channel of distribution, then, are the buyers and sellers through whom goods pass on their way from the producer to the consumer or industrial user. The producer is always at the beginning of a channel of distribution, and the user is always at the end.

USING CHANNELS OF DISTRIBUTION

Throughout its passage through the channel of distribution, a product is not changed in any way. A middleman may break down large shipments into smaller quantities for resale, but he does not change the basic product. When the product reaches a point where it is consumed or changed in form, the end of the channel of distribution has been reached. Many raw materials travel through several channels of distribution before they reach their final destination, the consumer.

The marketing of baked goods, for example, requires three channels of distribution before raw wheat can be converted into baked goods for the consumer. A farmer growing wheat begins one channel of distribution when he sells his crop to a grain-elevator company—a middleman that stores wheat for future sale. The grain elevator sells the wheat to a central market, another middleman, which assumes the responsibility of selling the wheat from many grain-elevator companies. The wheat is sold to milling companies, which process it into flour. Because the milling company is the last organization to receive the wheat in its natural state, the first channel of distribution ends at this location.

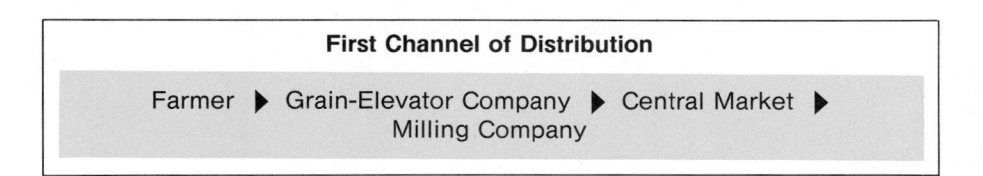

First Channel of Distribution

Farmer ▶ Grain-Elevator Company ▶ Central Market ▶ Milling Company

After the milling company has produced the flour, it is sold to a flour wholesaler; from the wholesaler it goes to commercial bakeries. Because the flour will be changed into baked goods at each of these bakeries, the second channel of distribution ends here.

Second Channel of Distribution

Milling Company ▶ Flour Wholesaler ▶ Baking Company

At one of the bakeries, production is started on huge quantities of cakes, rolls, pies, and pastries for sale to a large restaurant chain. The third and last distribution channel is begun when the bakery delivers its baked goods to the various restaurants in the chain. This distribution channel ends when the baked goods are sold to the consumer.

Third Channel of Distribution

Baking Company ▶ Restaurant Chain ▶ Consumer

DIRECT CHANNELS OF DISTRIBUTION

When a manufacturer markets his goods direct to the final user, he is using a *direct channel of distribution*. Many manufacturers market industrial and consumer goods direct to the final user. In the case of industrial goods, some manufacturers train their own sales force to sell the company's products direct to industrial users. Since the manufacturer's salesman is part of the company, the manufacturer uses a direct channel of distribution. The industrial user is at the end of this distribution channel, because he will either use the product in his own business or change it into another product. If the industrial user makes a new product, he will start a new channel of distribution when he sells it.

However, all industrial marketing cannot follow the direct channel. Sometimes wholesalers are needed to assemble the goods from several manufacturers and then sell them to industrial users.

In selling consumer goods, several types of direct channels can be used by the manufacturer. He can sell at the point of production, at his own retail store, door to door, or by mail.

Selling at the Point of Production

The simplest form of direct selling takes place when the producer makes his goods available to the consumer right where the goods are produced. Customers usually like buying at the point of production because they expect a bargain. There are no shipping charges or middlemen's costs involved in this form of selling, and therefore the price to the consumer can be kept low.

This marketer is making her products available to the consumer where they are produced.

A. Devaney, Inc., N.Y.

Almost everyone is familiar with the farmer's roadside stand. Although it is sometimes just a crude shed, it still attracts many customers with its displays of fresh eggs, fruits, and vegetables. To the farmer, the roadside stand means extra sales with very little selling cost, since members of his family often tend the stand.

Manufacturers, too, often set aside a room in their factories to sell goods direct to consumers. This is true chiefly in the clothing industry, where bargain-hunting customers will accept inconvenient facilities and lack of trained sales help.

Selling at the Producer's Retail Store

Many manufacturers operate stores to sell their products direct to the customer. Unlike the selling outlet at the factory or the farm, a producer's retail store may be located away from the production site and have all the advantages of the typical retail store: attractive merchandise displays, trained sales help, and various customer services.

Sometimes a producer will open a chain of retail stores for the distribution and sale of his product. For example, Fanny Farmer candy stores are a coast-to-coast chain that sells the Fanny Farmer brand of candy exclusively. The Singer Sewing Machine Company—which sells not only sewing machines but also the Singer brand of vacuum cleaners, transistor radios, and miniature television sets—has retail stores in almost every major city. And the Horn and Hardart retail shops, famous for their line of bakery products and prepared foods, produce and sell in their own outlets.

Selling Door to Door

Many products are sold to customers in their homes. Everyone is familiar with the Fuller Brush salesman, who sells household products door to door, and with the Avon representative and her selection of cosmetics. Many baking companies distribute their products through route salesmen, who sell and deliver door to door.

Selling Through the Mail

Some manufacturers encourage mail orders. In the last few pages of many magazines, space is devoted to numerous small advertisements that offer various products and services. A name-and-address coupon is often included in the advertisements, inviting the reader to order through the mail. Magazines often make a regular feature of such a mail-order section. For example, *House Beautiful* has a section called "Window Shopping"; *Seventeen,* a section called "Shop Wise"; *Better Homes and Gardens,* a "Shopping Editor's Choice"; and many Sunday-newspaper magazine supplements feature sections called "Shopping Mart."

Manufacturers and retail middlemen who specialize in mail-order selling often distribute catalogs to potential customers, inviting them to order through the mail. (Catalog retailing is discussed more fully in Part 16.)

INDIRECT CHANNELS OF DISTRIBUTION

When the manufacturer does not deal directly with the final user of his product but uses a middleman to act as a bridge between himself and the consumer or the industrial user, he is using an *indirect channel of distribution.* There are two types of middlemen that a producer may use to get his goods to market: agent middlemen and merchant middlemen. Depending on his specific needs, a producer may use either or both of these types of middlemen.

Agent Middlemen

Middlemen who perform buying and selling services for manufacturers or other middlemen are called *agent middlemen.* Agent middlemen do not become the owners of the goods they handle.

The job of some agent middlemen is to find buyers for firms that have goods to sell. The job of other agent middlemen is to find sources of supply for companies that want to buy certain merchandise. When an agent's efforts result in a satisfactory sale between a buyer and a seller, a commission is paid to the agent by the principal, the firm for which the agent has performed the marketing service. The agent's commission is usually a percent of the amount of the sale.

Agents work chiefly for wholesalers or manufacturers and sell their goods to other wholesalers or retailers. The few agents who sell direct to consumers are confined to the real estate and insurance fields and the stock market. Types of agents in the wholesaling field include brokers, commission men, selling agents, manufacturers' agents, and auctioneers. (The functions and business operations of some of these agents are further discussed in Part 18.)

Merchant Middlemen

Middlemen who actually buy goods and then resell them at a profit are known as *merchant middlemen*. They assume ownership of goods and thus become completely responsible for selling them. If the goods should go out of style and fail to sell, the merchant middlemen accept the loss. They also take the responsibility for finding customers for the goods they have purchased. Merchant middlemen work in both the wholesaling and retailing fields.

The auctioneer is an agent middleman who sells to the highest bidder.

◆ **YOUR MARKETING VOCABULARY**

On a separate sheet of paper define each of the following marketing terms; then use each term in a sentence.

Agent middlemen
Channel of distribution
Direct channel of distribution
Indirect channel of distribution
Merchant middlemen

◆ **FOR REVIEW AND DISCUSSION**

1. Name the two ways by which manufacturers can send their products to market?
2. Can transportation companies and independent warehouses be considered channels of distribution? Explain your answer.
3. Where does a channel of distribution begin and where does it end?
4. What channel of distribution might a farmer choose in order to market his wheat?
5. Give several examples of direct channels of distribution.
6. Describe how some manufacturers sell direct to consumers.
7. What are the duties of an agent middleman?
8. How is the amount that the agent middleman receives for his services usually determined?
9. In what fields are agents found who sell direct to consumers?
10. How does an agent middleman differ from a merchant middleman?

◆ **ANALYZING MARKETING CONCEPTS**

1. A channel of distribution is not concerned with the actual transportation of goods. Prepare a form like the one below. The following phrases describe either part of a channel of distribution or a method of transportation: (a) trucking company, (b) transfer of ownership, (c) series of buyers and sellers, (d) independent warehouse, (e) railroad route, (f) shipping goods, (g) ownership of goods, (h) responsibility for storing goods, (i) use of middleman. Identify each phrase by placing it in the appropriate column of your form.

Channel of Distribution	Method of Transportation

2. A manufacturer markets his goods by using a direct or an indirect channel of distribution. Prepare a form like the one following. Indicate whether each of these channels is direct or indirect by listing it in the appropriate

column: (a) door-to-door selling, (b) merchant middleman, (c) mail-order selling, (d) producer's retail store, (e) agent middleman, (f) point-of-production sale.

Direct Channel	Indirect Channel

◘ MARKETING PROJECT 14
Analyzing Types of Middlemen

Project Goal: Identify five businesses in your community that may be classified as agent middlemen and five businesses that may be classified as merchant middlemen.

Action: Using the Yellow Pages of your telephone directory, locate middlemen under such headings as manufacturer's agents, food brokers, insurance agents, warehouses, and so on.

Prepare a form like the one below. List the names of five agent middlemen and five merchant middlemen in the left-hand column. In the middle column, describe the nature of the business and the services that each middleman may provide for producers, customers, and other middlemen. Place a check mark in the appropriate column at the right to identify each middleman as an agent middleman or a merchant middleman.

Middleman	Nature of Business and Services	Type of Middleman	
		Agent	Merchant
Example: Office Supply Company	Sells office furniture, equipment, and supplies at retail and wholesale. Delivers supplies to local business firms free. Assists in design of office space and work flow.		✔

part 15

The Retailing Business

YOUR GOALS

1. Given a group of retail stores, classify each group by type of ownership.
2. Given a franchise business, determine the type of assistance provided by the franchisor to the franchisee.

The marketing institution with which people are most familiar is the retail store. A retail store sells direct to the consumer and is the last marketing institution in its channel of distribution. You probably visit retail stores often to buy food, clothing, furniture, sporting equipment, grooming aids, and many other products, as well as to use the services offered by these stores.

THE IMPORTANCE OF RETAILING

Retail stores perform a vital function for consumers. To satisfy customers' needs and wants, they bring together in convenient locations the products of the earth, forest, ocean, farm, and factory.

Retail stores are also important to most manufacturers and wholesalers of consumer products. Without retail stores these marketers would face the enormous task of getting their tremendous amount of products to consumers in all parts of the country. They would have to set up a network of stores and perform the selling activities themselves. As discussed in Part 14 and as will be discussed more fully later in this unit, some manufacturers operate their own retail stores; but in most cases, manufacturers and wholesalers prefer to concentrate on the problems of production and large-quantity distribution and leave the selling of consumer products in small quantities to retailers. Because retailers specialize in small-quantity distribution, they are generally far more efficient than manufacturers who try to handle both production and distribution.

Basically, the functions of the store retailer are as follows:

- He seeks out goods from buying sources in many locations.
- He provides a wide range of sizes, colors, types, and brands for his customers.
- He keeps merchandise in stock over weeks or months.
- He provides a pleasant place for customers to shop in.
- He offers customer services that make buying easier, such as credit, gift wrapping, and parking.
- He sells at competitive prices.

THE DEVELOPMENT OF RETAILING

Retailing as it is known today was made possible by three factors: the Industrial Revolution, which saw the development of machines to produce goods in large quantities; a steady increase in the movement of the population to cities, so that more and more people became dependent on stores to provide the goods they needed; and population growth, which provided more customers for larger outputs of goods. Retailing, then, developed as a major business activity because there were more goods to distribute and more people to use them. The distribution of a large variety of goods to large numbers of people is the main function of modern retail stores.

Since the end of the Civil War, retailing has developed into a tremendous industry. There are now more than 1,700,000 retail establishments in the United States. They employ more than 9,000,000 people. The number of retail establishments is decreasing slightly, but their total sales and the number of people they employ are increasing.

Certain kinds of retail stores—hardware stores, food stores, drugstores, and stores selling apparel and accessories—are fewer in number than they were 10 years ago. This has happened because in most communities such small stores are being combined to form large, modern units. Retail stores in general are thus fewer in number but larger in size.

Some small, independent stores specialize in a particular type of product.

THE OWNERSHIP OF RETAIL STORES

Retail stores may be classified according to the type of merchandise they handle (discussed in Part 16) or by their form of ownership. Forms of ownership include (1) independently owned and operated stores, (2) corporate chains, (3) voluntary chains, (4) franchise chains, (5) leased dealerships, and (6) manufacturer-owned stores.

Independent Stores

Stores that are operated and managed by the owner are called *independent stores*. Although some large department stores that handle a variety of merchandise are independent, the typical independent store usually offers only one type of merchandise—perhaps children's wear, yard goods, baked goods, or home furnishings—and employs only a few people.

Small independent stores generally have less money to spend than the large chains of stores that operate nationwide. The small stores therefore cannot buy large selections of merchandise or promote their products as effectively as the large chains. But they manage to survive because they offer their customers convenience of location, personal attention, and service. They may also cater to special-interest markets. For example, a small store may sell only tropical fish.

The small independent store provides an excellent opportunity for the beginning marketing worker to gain experience in all phases of business operation. The successful independent-store owner must be able to buy his own goods, control stock, plan displays, price merchandise, keep an eye on competition, and do an expert job of selling. Therefore, an alert, ambitious salesperson or clerk in such a store has the opportunity of working with a successful, small-business man and of learning firsthand the techniques that make a capable marketer.

Corporate Chains

A *corporate chain* is a number of similar stores owned and managed by a central corporate organization. A corporate chain may sell general merchandise, or it may specialize in one type of merchandise. The central headquarters sets standards for methods of operation, services, store layout, merchandise arrangement, and equipment. Usually, the headquarters is also responsible for buying the merchandise to be carried in the stores and for developing the advertising to be used in all the stores.

Corporate chains are large-scale retailing establishments and therefore may enjoy certain competitive advantages. They can benefit from lower costs because of favorable prices for quantity buying (although such discounts are to some extent limited by law). They may enjoy large-scale advertising and sales promotion.

On the other hand, corporate chains have certain disadvantages. For example, because most of the merchandise and services are standardized, an individual corporate chain store cannot freely adjust company policies or selling practices to suit the local community. As a result, the chain store is not always able to take advantage of local market conditions quickly. A small independent store, for example, may be able to stock fad items more quickly than a corporate chain store, which has to obtain permission from its headquarters before it can buy them.

There are national, regional, and local corporate chains. A *national chain* is one that has outlets in every state. Some national chains have stores in foreign countries as well. National general-merchandise chains, such as Sears, Roebuck and Company, Montgomery Ward, and J. C. Penney, are responsible for many billions of dollars in sales every year. These national retailers operate both retail stores and mail-order services. While the retail stores account for the larger amount of their business, the mail-order sales are also significant.

National chain stores such as this one account for a considerable amount of retail sales in the United States.

A *regional chain* is one that has outlets in a geographic area covering a few states. Examples of regional chains that offer general merchandise are Rhodes Western of Oakland, California, which operates stores in five western states; Top Dollar of Jasper, Alabama, which operates 68 stores in four southern states; and Carson Pirie Scott and Company of Chicago, which operates 24 stores in the Midwest.

A *local chain* is one that has outlets within a very small area, usually a city. Local general-merchandise chains include Columbia in Long Beach, which operates three stores in Long Beach, California; R. H. Stearn's Company, which operates two stores in Boston; and Yielding's, Incorporated, which operates three stores in Birmingham, Alabama.

Voluntary Chains

A group of independently owned stores that share some or all of their buying is called a *voluntary chain*. While each store retains its independence of ownership, the owner generally identifies himself as a member of the chain by adding the name of the chain to that of his own store.

One advantage of belonging to a voluntary chain is that the individual owner retains his ownership. At the same time, by combining his buying power with that of other retailers, the owner is able to buy merchandise at prices that are competitive with the prices paid by corporate chain stores.

An example of a voluntary chain in the food field is IGA (Independent Grocers Alliance).

Franchise Chains

A group of independently owned stores which are run under an agreement with a sponsoring manufacturer is known as a *franchise chain*. In such an agreement the manufacturer establishes the rules for the operation of the stores in return for the use of the chain name.

The sponsoring manufacturer, or franchisor, grants to each franchised store the exclusive right to sell his goods or services in a particular market. The franchisor usually provides the products for sale, the necessary equipment, and managerial services. The franchisee (the person who purchases the franchise) must agree to distribute the products in a manner established by the franchisor.

One of the great advantages of the franchise chain is the help the franchisee receives from the manufacturer in financing, management principles, recordkeeping, and sales promotion. Because he can rely on these services from the manufacturer, he faces less risk than someone who starts a business entirely on his own and who learns only by experience.

One of the disadvantages to the franchisee is that his own personal identity is lost to that of the franchisor. Moreover, the franchisor's control over the product and method of distribution may limit the initiative and creativity of the franchisee.

Franchise retailers include restaurants (Howard Johnson), ice cream stores (Baskin-Robbins), hamburger shops (McDonald's), and employment agencies (Kelly Girl).

Leased Dealerships

A business that is owned by a particular company but is leased to someone else to operate is called a *leased dealership*. The company owns and maintains the land, building, and major equipment; the operator owns his stock, small equipment, and tools. The most common form of leased dealership is the service station.

An advantage of a leased dealership is that the operator benefits from the company's national advertising. Also, the operator's initial investment is likely to be less than that of the independent retailer. The disadvantages are that the operator is responsible to the owner company for any material leased to him, and that he must deal exclusively in the products manufactured by the leasing company.

Courtesy McDonald's Corp.
Franchise chain restaurants such as McDonald's are familiar sights along America's highways. Name several other franchise chain stores in your community.

Manufacturer-Owned Stores

Stores that are owned by the manufacturer of a particular product are called *manufacturer-owned stores*. By owning his own retail outlets, the manufacturer controls the entire manufacturing and distribution process and bypasses the wholesale step in the channel of distribution. In other words, instead of selling to a retailer, he sells direct to the consumer. But he has the added responsibility of being involved in retailing as well as the manufacturing process. Many manufacturers prefer to concentrate on the production of their products and leave the selling to the retailers.

Manufacturer-owned stores include Fanny Farmer candy shops and the Horn & Hardart food stores.

YOUR MARKETING VOCABULARY

On a separate sheet of paper define each of the following marketing terms; then use each term in a sentence.

Corporate chain *Manufacturer-owned stores*
Franchise chain *National chain*
Independent stores *Regional chain*
Leased dealership *Voluntary chain*
Local chain

176 / Unit 5 / Marketing Channels

FOR REVIEW AND DISCUSSION

1. Why are retail stores a vital part of everyday living?
2. How did retailing as it is known today begin?
3. What are the functions performed by store retailers?
4. What is the employment trend in retailing?
5. What is the trend in sales in retailing?
6. Explain the opportunity available to an alert, ambitious salesperson in a small independently owned store.
7. List the responsibilities of the headquarters of a corporate chain.
8. What are the disadvantages of a corporate chain?
9. What are two advantages of voluntary chains?
10. What valuable aids are available to the owner of a franchise chain store?

ANALYZING MARKETING CONCEPTS

1. The operation and management of retail stores are influenced by the form of ownership. Prepare a form like the one below and list the following retail store characteristics in the left-hand column: (a) smaller store, (b) can spread business risks more easily, (c) less buying power, (d) lower costs through quantity buying, (e) owner is all-around businessman, (f) usually larger merchandise assortment, (g) less flexible in meeting local market conditions, (h) merchandising ideas from central headquarters, (i) can cater more easily to special-interest markets.

    Place a check mark in the appropriate column to indicate the form of ownership more likely to be involved.

Retail Store Characteristic	Independent Store	Corporate Chain
Example: Operated and managed by the owner.	✔	

2. One of the overall advantages of a franchise business is the assistance provided by the franchisor to the franchisee. Prepare a form like the one below. List the following types of franchise businesses in the left-hand column: (a) hamburger shop, (b) dance studio, (c) beauty salon, (d) printing-copying business. In the right-hand column describe the help you would expect from the franchisor if you were the franchisee.

Franchise Business	Assistance Expected from Franchisor
Example: Motel	Central reservation system for all motels in the chain.

◇ MARKETING PROJECT 15
Determining Franchisor Assistance

Project Goal: Given a franchise business, determine the type of assistance provided by the franchisor to the franchisee.

Action: Select a franchise business in your community that you would like to investigate. Obtain your teacher's approval for your selection.

Then prepare a form like the one below. In the left-hand column, list the following five areas of franchise assistance: (a) management, (b) financing, (c) recordkeeping, (d) promotion, (e) providing equipment and supplies. With your teacher's guidance, interview the manager of the franchise business concerning the specific assistance he receives from the franchisor in each of the five areas. Record the key points of the manager's comments in the right-hand column.

Under your form, list additional ideas the manager or you may have concerning possible franchisor assistance. Also, attach to your form any actual business materials you collected during your project. Be sure your form includes the name of the business and the name of the person you interviewed.

Area of Assistance	Assistance Received from Franchisor
Example: Management	The manager receives a weekly memo containing ideas on handling employees: how to motivate and criticize them, typical employee rules, and performance-appraisal ideas. One example of this memo is attached.

part 16

Types of Retail Stores

YOUR GOALS

1. Given the types of retail stores, compare the characteristics of two competitive types.
2. Given the name and description of a product, identify the specific types of retail stores most likely to carry that product.
3. Given the name and description of a product, describe how you could use methods of nonstore retailing to sell the product.

Retail stores can be classified not only by ownership but also by the type, quality, and variety of merchandise they carry as well as the services they offer. This classification is important to the producer, the wholesaler, the retailer, and the consumer. The producer and wholesaler must decide on the type of store that is best for distributing their products, so that they will realize the greatest profit. The retailer must determine the category in which his store belongs in order to join the appropriate merchant's association, read the appropriate literature, and in general, compare his practices with those of similar stores. The consumer must decide where he can get the kinds of merchandise he wants at the least cost, as well as the kind of service that he appreciates.

Based on the type, quality, and variety of merchandise carried or service offered, all retail businesses may be classified as one of the following: general-merchandise stores, limited-line stores, or nonstore retailers. In recent years the distinctions between these categories have narrowed because of the trend in many stores toward selling of goods that are unrelated to the particular retailer's main line of merchandise. However, the distinguishing characteristics of each type of store are still visible.

GENERAL-MERCHANDISE STORES

A retail establishment that offers a large variety of goods for sale under one roof is called a *general-merchandise store*. This category of retail businesses includes department stores, departmentized specialty stores, discount department stores, variety stores, and the formerly numerous old-fashioned country stores, or general stores.

Department Stores

According to the U.S. Census of Business, a *department store* is a retail establishment that employs 25 or more people and sells furniture; appliances; clothing for men, women, and children; and household linens and dry goods. Many department stores, of course, sell other items as well.

Department stores are organized into individual departments according to the type of merchandise sold. Each department is operated as a separate unit. The boys' clothing department, for example, has its own manager and buying and sales staff. Also, each department carries a full line of goods. The linen department might carry five or more types of towels in various price ranges, colors, and designs. The shoe department might sell three or four brands of shoes, with a full range of sizes and styles for each brand.

Department stores have many features designed to make shopping pleasant. The stores are usually furnished attractively and have colorful merchandise displays and cheerful lounges. Some stores offer additional attractions such as free parking, fashion shows, or special exhibits. Salespeople are trained to let the customer browse but to be ready to give help when it is needed. The customer who wants to postpone payment by charging his purchases may do so, and he often has a choice of payment plans. The customer can also have merchandise delivered to his home. If the merchandise that the store delivers is not satisfactory, the customer can exchange it or receive a price refund.

Prior to 1950, department stores were found mostly in the downtown shopping areas of large cities. Today, many established department stores have branch stores in the suburbs.

Department stores carry a wide variety of merchandise and offer many conveniences that attract shoppers.

A branch store carries all the merchandise lines available in the parent store and, like the parent store, is organized by departments. Usually, any item available in the parent store will also be available in the branch store. When a parent store advertises, it often stresses the fact that the merchandise advertised is "available in all branches." This tells the suburban customer that he need not travel to the parent store to buy the merchandise.

Branch stores are often huge, offer ample parking space, and provide the same customer services available in the parent store.

Discount Department Stores

A retail store that makes a policy of selling merchandise at reduced prices is known as a *discount store.* Discount stores first appeared in the 1930s but did not achieve major success until the early 1950s.

Early discount stores were distinguished from other stores by the low prices of their merchandise and by their policy of offering minimum customer services. Sales were strictly for cash, and stock was limited. Customers would often choose their goods from a floor sample or a catalog. In other cases, merchandise was displayed on large tables for easy examination. Therefore, only a few salespeople were needed.

Most of the early discount stores specialized in electrical appliances and kitchen equipment. But as they grew in popularity, many of them began to increase their range of merchandise and to organize the merchandise by departments. Thus they became discount department stores.

Many discount stores have increased their customer services and improved their decor by acquiring expensive buildings in high-rent areas. This has meant a compromise of their low-price goal. Although they still cut prices on national brands, in many cases they are unable to cut them low enough to withstand all competition. Therefore, in order to offer low-priced goods, many discount stores are now turning to the marketing of private brands.

Variety Stores

The variety store is a retail establishment that handles a wide assortment of goods in a low-price range. The first variety store was started by Frank W. Woolworth in 1879. His idea came from an experience he had while working as a clerk in a dry-goods store in Watertown, New York. Setting up a counter of small items, he placed a sign over it reading "Anything on this table, 5¢." When the counter was almost sold out on the first day, Mr. Woolworth decided to start a store that sold 5-cent items only. In 1879 he opened for business in Lancaster, Pennsylvania, selling merchandise he had obtained with his own savings and with borrowed funds. The store was so successful that he opened other branches. In 1970 there were more than 2,000 Woolworth stores in the United States, Canada, and Mexico. The Woolworth idea has been copied widely, resulting in other variety stores, including McCrory's, S. H. Kress, S. S. Kresge, W. T. Grant, and H. L. Green.

The range of merchandise in the variety store has been greatly extended since Mr. Woolworth opened that first store, but the merchandising policy is still to sell goods that lend themselves to a quick transaction, with little consultation between customer and salesperson. This means that the merchandise must be relatively minor items in the customer's budget, nothing that would require him to shop around. Within these limits, the variety store sells many types of goods, including an economical assortment of cosmetics, toys, and school supplies. Many variety stores are now in the discount field; for example, Woolworth's operates Woolco and Kresge operates the K-Mart.

General Stores

The general store still survives in some rural communities. In earlier times it was a gathering place as well as a store, famous for its potbellied stove, cracker barrel, and bulk assortments of sugar, rolled oats, and flour. Today, it still carries groceries, housewares, and other necessities and convenience merchandise packaged in modern wrappings. However, because of its small size, the general store cannot offer a large selection in any of its lines.

A. Devaney, Inc., N.Y.

The traditional general store also served as a meeting place for residents of rural communities. Have you ever visited such a store?

LIMITED-LINE STORES

A retail establishment that sells only one kind of merchandise or several closely related lines of merchandise—such as greeting cards, gift wrappings, and writing paper—is called a *limited-line store.* Limited-line stores offer the consumer a wide selection within their own specialty. And, their selection is greater than that offered by any of the general-merchandise stores except the largest.

Limited-line stores include apparel and accessory stores, home-furnishings stores, automotive dealers, food stores, service stations, and hardware and building-material dealers.

Apparel and Accessory Stores

A retail establishment that sells dresses, suits, children's wear, shoes, millinery, lingerie, handbags, neckties, and other items of clothing is called an apparel and accessory store. An apparel and accessory store that sells only women's wear is called a *specialty shop.*

There are more than 110,000 apparel and accessory stores in the United States. The typical apparel and accessory store is fairly small, employing fewer than 20 people. The store owner must be especially aware of fashion changes. If he stocks up on a fashion that does not sell, he will lose his investment. On the other hand, if he does not have the latest fashions, his customers may desert him for the department stores, many of which are particularly strong in the field of fashion apparel.

Twigs

A limited-line store that is owned by a department store is called a *twig*. A department store may decide to build a twig in a location where there are not enough customers to support a general-merchandise branch store. The twig specializes in limited lines of merchandise—perhaps clothing, shoes, appliances, or low-priced bargain-basement goods.

The type of merchandise carried by a twig depends on the area in which it is located. A twig in a university town might specialize in sportswear, while a twig in a growing suburb might stock infants' and children's wear.

Home-Furnishings Stores

A retail establishment that sells furniture and other items for the home—such as radios, television sets, and major appliances—is called a home-furnishings store. There are about 99,000 home-furnishings stores in the United States.

Radios, television sets, and major appliances are largely presold by national advertising. Thus, competition is largely in terms of price. For this reason, chain stores have an advantage over the small independent store in selling this type of merchandise, because the chains can buy from wholesalers in quantity and at a discount. The small independent store can compete, however, by offering its customers such custom services as built-in television sets, specially designed complete kitchens, and better customer services in general.

Another disadvantage to the small independent store in the home-furnishings field is that it must make a large initial investment of capital in expensive items such as furniture and rugs. Also, allowing customers to buy on credit means that it takes the small independent store much longer to recover its initial investment. The small independent store relies more on this capital to make its future investments than does a large store, which can get more trade credit.

In general, the small independent store in the home-furnishings field stands a better chance by dealing in smaller merchandise such as china and glassware, gifts, drapery, or antiques. It might also do well by restricting its line to custom-designed furniture, which is manufactured to special order.

Automotive Dealers

A retail establishment that sells motor vehicles or the accessories that go with them is called an automotive dealer. There are about 105,000 automotive dealers in the United States.

Motor vehicle dealers are fortunate in that they have their field to themselves. So far, the trend toward selling unrelated items has not affected them, and department stores and chain stores are not their competitors. This is not true, however, of the auto accessory dealers; they are confronted with the fact that many chain stores, discount stores, and department stores are now selling accessories for cars.

Food Stores

There are about 295,000 food stores in the United States. They range from the traditional corner grocery to the supermarket. Butcher shops, candy stores, and bakeries are included in the food-store classification.

A large, departmentized self-service food store is called a *supermarket*. Many supermarkets now offer so much in the way of housewares, books, toiletries, and even apparel that they are almost combinations of food and variety stores. Each department within a supermarket may be owned by the store itself or may be leased by private owners.

Supermarkets date back to 1916, when the first Piggly-Wiggly store opened in Memphis, Tennessee. Although these early stores were not as large as the present supermarkets, they did use the idea of self-service. Supermarketing on a giant scale began in 1930 when Michael Cullen opened his King Kullen market in Jamaica, New York. Two years later the Big Bear supermarket was opened in Elizabeth, New Jersey, in an abandoned factory. King Kullen and Big Bear signaled the debut of the supermarket as a major marketing institution. From that point on, supermarkets began to appear all over the country; today there may be four or five supermarkets in a small town.

Price appeal is the strong point of the supermarket. The store depends on a large volume of sales to get a satisfactory profit. The convenience of well-organized self-service and one-stop marketing are other features that make the supermarket attractive to the customer.

To stress the advantages they have over supermarkets, some smaller grocery stores are now calling themselves convenience stores. One advantage the smaller grocery stores have is that they are often located in small shopping centers. Thus, if the shopper needs only one or two items, he does not have to cope with parking in a large shopping center or waiting in a long check-out line in a supermarket. In addition, convenience stores are often open every day of the week, usually from 7 a.m. to 11 p.m. Some are open 24 hours a day.

This factor is becoming less of an advantage, however, because many supermarkets are meeting the challenge by opening on Sundays or by remaining open for longer hours—even 24 hours a day.

The stock of the convenience stores is more limited than that carried by supermarkets. They do, however, carry all staple grocery items, some meats and delicatessen products, and convenience goods.

Hardware and Building-Material Stores

The smaller hardware and building-material stores traditionally carry such items as tools, garden hoses, and locks. Larger stores of this type include products such as wallpaper, paneling, lumber, housewares, and a host of do-it-yourself home-improvement items. During recent years, hardware and building-material stores have met much competition, particularly from discount department stores. They have tried to meet this challenge by increasing the selection of items they offer to the consumer.

NONSTORE RETAILING

When we say retailing, we usually think of stores. But there are ways of selling products and services to the consumer other than through the typical retail store. The selling of products and services direct to the consumer without the use of stores is called nonstore retailing. In nonstore retailing, products can be sold direct to the consumer through catalog retailing, telephone-order retailing, direct-to-the-consumer retailing, and automatic vending.

Catalog Retailing

Some merchants sell by means of a catalog. At one time, catalog retailing was done entirely by mail. Now a customer has the added choices of ordering by telephone or in person.

There are advantages and disadvantages in selling by catalog. On the positive side, merchandise can be kept in an inexpensive warehouse rather than in an expensive store. No salespeople are required, and delivery costs are usually paid by the customer. On the negative side, designing and printing of the catalog can be expensive. Also, clerical tasks are increased, such as computing shipping costs and completing more detailed order forms. Furthermore, there are more returns of merchandise in catalog retailing, because the customer cannot examine the merchandise until it has been delivered.

Two types of establishments deal in catalog retailing: mail-order houses and department stores.

Courtesy J. C. Penney
Seasonal catalogs are helpful marketing tools for mail-order houses.

Mail-Order Houses. General mail-order houses handle a complete assortment of goods similar to those found in a well-stocked department store. Specialty mail-order houses are comparable to limited-line stores in that they specialize in one type of merchandise. The two best-known general mail-order houses are Montgomery Ward and Sears, Roebuck and Company. These houses issue two major catalogs each year and several special catalogs. The customer can order merchandise from these catalogs at his home or at a company sales office.

Aaron Montgomery Ward established the first American mail-order house in 1872 in Chicago. His first catalog, a one-page handbill listing various items of goods and prices, was a far cry from the company's present catalog of more than 1,200 pages. Sears, Roebuck and Company had its beginning in 1886 as a mail-order watch and jewelry concern in Minneapolis. Both Montgomery Ward and Sears eventually opened retail stores, but their catalog business has continued to prosper.

Department Stores. Several department stores issue catalogs geared to a seasonal buying period. They also invite mail orders through newspaper advertisements and through miniature catalogs, or mailers, distributed to their charge customers. Department stores handle mail orders as part of their regular operations; usually they do not maintain a separate warehouse for mail orders but fill them from the current stock. Also, they do not issue catalogs offering merchandise available over a six-month period, as do mail-order houses. Rather, their promotional brochures are intended to cover a shorter period of time, such as a month, during which the promoted merchandise will be available.

Telephone-Order Retailing

Mail-order houses and most large department stores cultivate telephone business. Some department stores offer telephone-order service and free toll calls; in effect, this is a form of catalog retailing, for it uses newspaper advertisements to display goods from which the customer can make a selection. Formerly limited to Sunday newspaper ads, telephone-order service is now being offered all week, often 24 hours a day.

Ordering by telephone is a convenience for the customer, particularly the customer who is kept at home by bad weather, illness, or the lack of a babysitter. By offering telephone service, the department store puts itself within easy reach of the shopper.

Of course, the small independent store can also offer telephone-order service, but it may lack the facilities to deliver beyond a short distance. Also, it may not have the funds to advertise extensively in a newspaper. Without the help of a newspaper display, the customer would have to shop in person to make a selection. However, a small independent store that deals in staple goods, such as groceries, can serve its customers effectively by telephone.

Some businesses use the telephone as a primary means of contacting prospective customers. Magazine salesmen are particularly fond of this method of promoting sales.

Direct-to-the-Consumer Retailing

Direct-to-the-consumer retailing involves marketing to the consumer in his home. In the United States this type of selling dates back to the 1700s, when many young men began to peddle locally the merchandise they or their families had produced: leather, cloth, stockings, cheeses, butter, and rabbit skins. In 1741 two young Irish immigrants, William and Edward Pattison, set up shop in their home and proceeded to pound out plates, pans, and teapots from sheet tin. They packed sacks full of their tinware and set out on foot to nearby settlements to sell it door to door. Eventually other merchants started their own shops, loaded their tinware, brooms, and washboards into large horse-drawn carts, and set out to peddle their wares. These merchants came to be known as the Yankee tin peddlers, and they were a colorful addition to the life of early America.

In many cities street vendors sell refreshments from pushcarts.

Courtesy N.Y. Convention & Visitors Bureau

Although Yankee tin peddlers no longer roam the streets selling their wares from carts, the days of selling to consumers in their homes are far from over. In some areas, dairy products, baked goods, and farm products are still marketed and delivered direct to the consumer. Both the Fuller Brush Company and Avon are manufacturers who do their own retailing in that way. Consumers receive brochures describing the products of the Fuller Brush Company. The brochures are followed a few days later by the Fuller Brush salesman himself. "Avon calling" is the password of the Avon representative, who sells Avon cosmetics door to door.

Direct-to-the-consumer retailing falls into three categories: on-the-street selling, door-to-door selling, and party-plan selling.

On-the-Street Selling. The direct descendants of the Yankee peddler are those salesmen who travel residential streets in the sleek panel trucks from which they sell their wares. Among the most familiar street salesmen, or vendors, are those driving the Good Humor trucks.

Some street salesmen do not use trucks but set up stands to display their merchandise on the sidewalk. Their goods usually consist of toys, belts, or costume jewelry. In many cities the street salesmen are required to have a permit in order to set up such stands.

Door-to-Door Selling. In door-to-door selling the salesman attempts to sell his product in the customer's home. The simplest method of door-to-door selling is cold canvassing, in which the salesman literally goes from door to door in a particular neighborhood, without having had any previous contact with the customer. The cold-canvass method is used extensively in selling Avon products and the household wares of the Fuller Brush Company. This method is also used in selling vacuum cleaners, books, and magazine subscriptions.

A more sophisticated form of door-to-door selling is the appointment method. Companies that use this method provide their salesmen with "leads" —customers who may be expected to buy. The salesman telephones the lead and makes an appointment to demonstrate his merchandise. The prospect (lead) is usually more receptive to the salesman and more likely to be interested in the salesman's product than if he were approached by the cold-canvass method. Insurance companies and encyclopedia publishers use the appointment method.

Some companies use the route-selling method, in which they sell and deliver their products on a regular basis to customers who have ordered this service. Many dairies, bakeries, and beverage retailers still distribute their products in this way. The milk or bakery trucks cover regular delivery routes, servicing each customer several times a week.

Party-Plan Selling. In the party-plan selling method a company's representative persuades a customer to gather a number of friends in her home, where the representative will demonstrate the company's products. The representative takes orders at the party and seeks to have one of the guests agree to have a similar party in her home with her own group of friends. For her cooperation the hostess receives a substantial gift; she receives additional awards if the sales made in her home reach a certain figure. Tupperware, makers of plastic kitchenware, and Stanley Products, makers of housewares, often hold parties of this type.

Automatic Vending

The marketing of goods through the use of a machine operated by the customer is known as *automatic vending*. Goods are being marketed increasingly through vending machines. Many factories, schools, and offices have installed plant cafeterias that make food and drinks available to employees through vending machines. Soft-drink vending machines are everywhere—in retail stores, in train stations, in bus terminals, in motels, even in apartment buildings. By depositing a coin in the appropriate machine, a customer can buy his lunch, a handkerchief, a candy bar, or a cup of hot coffee (with or without cream or sugar).

The housewares party is a time for buying as well as socializing.

The first automatic vending machine was used in Egypt in 200 B.C.; a person could obtain holy water from the machine by depositing a 5-drachma coin. In the United States, automatic vending goes back to 1888, when Thomas Adams designed vending machines to sell his Tutti-Frutti gum on rapid-transit platforms. In 1902, Horn & Hardart created a sensation with their first automat, a cafeteria that sold entire meals on the vending-machine principle.

Today vending machines are able to sell hot food, refrigerated items, and frozen foods. Supermarkets have installed vending machines in front of their stores to serve the customer with basic food items during nonstore hours. Schools have installed vending machines that provide snacks and soft drinks, and railroad trains have installed vending machines that serve buffet dinners.

Automatic vending offers three advantages to the marketer. First, because the salesperson is eliminated, automatic vending makes it possible to sell many low-priced convenience goods more profitably. Second, even in stores that do employ salespeople to sell the same goods contained in the machine, automatic vending can provide assistance during busy periods and so prevent lost sales. Finally, automatic vending encourages impulse buying, as a customer is likely to buy from a machine what he might not buy if he had to wait for a salesperson to serve him.

◆ YOUR MARKETING VOCABULARY

On a separate sheet of paper define each of the following marketing terms; then use each term in a sentence.

Automatic vending
Department store
Discount store
General-merchandise store
Limited-line store
Specialty shop
Supermarket
Twig

◆ FOR REVIEW AND DISCUSSION

1. How are department stores organized?
2. What are some of the features of a department store?
3. What purpose does a discount department store serve?
4. Explain how variety stores originated.
5. Where are the general stores of today found, and what kinds of goods do they sell?
6. Through what means other than retail stores are goods and services marketed?
7. What three methods might a marketer use to sell goods direct to the consumer?
8. Name and describe two types of establishments dealing in catalog retailing.
9. List two advantages and two disadvantages of the catalog method of retailing.
10. Compare cold canvassing with the appointment method of door-to-door selling.
11. Describe the party-plan method of selling.
12. What kinds of goods can be bought in vending machines? In what three ways are vending machines advantageous to the marketer?

◆ ANALYZING MARKETING CONCEPTS

1. Prepare a form like the one below and list the following types of retail stores in the left-hand column: (a) general store, (b) variety store, (c) department store, (d) limited-line store, (e) specialty store, (f) supermarket, (g) discount store, (h) convenience store. In the right-hand column write one characteristic of each type of store listed.

Store	Characteristic
Example: Twig	Specializes in limited lines of merchandise—perhaps clothing, shoes, or appliances.

2. Prepare a form like the one below and list the following products and services in the left-hand column: (a) candy, (b) insurance, (c) loan, (d) car lubrication, (e) Fuller brushes, (f) electrical wiring, (g) groceries, (h) vacuum cleaners. Place a check mark in the appropriate center column to indicate whether the product or service listed would be sold by a retail store, a nonstore method, or both. In the right-hand column give the reason for your choice.

Product or Service	Store Retailing	Nonstore Retailing	Reason for Choice
Example: Landscaping		✔	Done by a service specialist on customer's property.

◆ MARKETING PROJECT 16
Comparing Types of Retail Stores

Project Goal: Given the types of retail stores, compare the characteristics of two competitive types.

Action: Select two competitive types of retail stores in your community, such as a department store and a discount store, or a supermarket and a small convenience food store. Visit one store of each type that you are comparing. During your visit, observe the characteristics of each type of store and make notes on your findings.

Prepare a form like the one below. In the left-hand column, list the following characteristics of a retail store: (a) merchandise, (b) selling prices, (c) layout and appearance. In the center column, list what you observed about each of those characteristics in one store. In the right-hand column, do the same for the other store. Your completed form will therefore compare the similarities and differences between the two types of stores.

Characteristics of Store	Store A	Store B
Example: Customer services	Department store has many services and customer conveniences, such as credit, delivery, several salespeople, play area for children, restaurants, lounges.	Discount store is generally self-service and has limited customer services. Few people, no delivery, one snack bar and lounge area.

part 17

Problems and Opportunities for the Retailer

YOUR GOAL

Given a retail business, identify the problems and opportunities facing the retailer because of changes in his market, competition, and technology.

Since the end of World War II, retailing has been undergoing a revolution. Many of the traditional methods of retailing have been discarded, and new methods have been developed. No longer is shopping confined to small stores on narrow streets or department stores in a teeming city. No longer are there such clear-cut distinctions between the products carried by different stores. No longer are shopping areas quiet every evening except Thursday.

The reasons for the changes in retailing have been given in previous parts. For example, the consumer market continues to grow in size and change in composition. People in general have more money to spend than ever before, and the average customer is much more knowledgeable today about what he wants to buy and what is available. There is more competition for every customer's business. Although the number of retail outlets in the country has not increased, stores today tend to be bigger and carry a larger variety of merchandise. Because of advances in technology, machines can perform a greater number of tasks more quickly and more accurately.

Although these changes have produced problems for the retailer, he has also been able to benefit from the many new opportunities which have been brought about by the changes.

PROBLEMS FOR THE RETAILER

Among the important problems facing retailers are a serious cost-profit squeeze, an alarming increase in losses due to shoplifting, and the changing character of many inner cities. These problems and some of the ways in which retailers are trying to solve them are discussed in this part.

Cost-Profit Squeeze

Retailers are doing more business than ever before. According to statistics both the dollar sales volume and the amount that the average person spends increases each year. However, costs are going up even more rapidly than sales, resulting in less and less profit for the average retailer each year. A condition in which costs rise more rapidly than sales and thereby decrease profits is called a *cost-profit squeeze*.

Marketers often face a cost-profit squeeze.

Most goods for resale now cost the retailer more. This is because the goods cost the supplier more to produce, and he passes along that added cost, if possible, to the retailer. Moreover, rent, building maintenance, transportation, utilities, labor, and all the other operating expenses also keep going up.

Ideally, the retailer should be able to keep setting his prices higher, but this is not always possible. One reason is that today's marketplace is highly competitive, and the consumer is very economy-minded. Thus a retailer could price himself right out of business. A second reason is that there is strong pressure, particularly from the federal government, to keep costs and profits from rising. Rapidly rising costs and profits could result in serious inflation, which is very bad for the economy.

What all this means to the retailer is that more of every dollar he earns must be earmarked for day-to-day expenses. It also means that he ends the year with less profit available for future investment in his business. And because much of the economy is in the same situation—facing a cost-profit squeeze—it is not easy for him to get investment money from other sources.

The solutions being tried are aimed at cutting costs—doing the same job for less money—and increasing operating efficiency—doing a better job for the same money.

Shoplifting

The theft of merchandise from a store is called *shoplifting*. Retailers used to consider shoplifting a minor problem. But as the loss figure has crept higher and higher, many retailers have come to consider it a major threat to their business. One large New York department store estimated its losses in one year in the early 1970s to be 4 percent of sales.

Two factors are probably responsible for the increase in shoplifting. The first, and more important, is the increased use of self-service selling in stores. The second is the life-styles or philosophies adopted by some groups.

To cut costs and speed up the selling process, many stores have brought their stock out into the open and put it on self-service racks, fixtures, and displays. This in turn has decreased the number of salespeople on a selling floor. Thus the opportunities to steal are greater than ever before. Customers or just browsers wander about, picking up goods and carrying them from one counter to the other. They are expected to pay for what they decide to take, dealing with either a salesperson or a cashier—but not all do.

Who steals? Some stealing is done by disturbed people who have a mental illness that compels them to steal. A larger amount of stealing is done by people who steal "just for the fun of it." A third group is made up of professional shoplifters, people who are habitual criminals. Professional shoplifters probably account for the largest losses of all.

In recent years a new group has been added to the list. This group consists of people who have adopted a philosophy which holds that all property is communal; that is, they believe that everything belongs to everyone. As long as they practice their philosophy within their own group, there is no problem. However, when they take something from a store without paying, they are guilty of theft.

Whatever the motivation for shoplifting may be, the act hurts the retailer and probably the customer, who may be forced to pay higher prices to cover the store's losses.

Retailers have not yet found an ideal solution to the shoplifting problem. Store security has been tightened in an attempt to protect the store against shoplifting. Marketers are enlisting psychologists to explore the reasons for nonprofessional shoplifting to determine what can be done to prevent the growth of this practice.

Crisis of the Inner City

Cities have always had their problems, but today's problems are growing in seriousness. Many of the problems involve the central, or inner, city. This is the area of a city in which many middle-income people once lived and which once supported major department stores and a variety of shops. However, the middle-income groups have gradually moved to the suburbs, leaving the inner city to the lower-income groups. The lower-income groups do not have the money to support the stores that once thrived in their areas. Moreover, with the increase of convenient shopping facilities in the suburbs, people from suburban areas have little or no reason to make shopping trips to the city.

The retailers who are caught in such areas sometimes try to sell a lower-priced line of merchandise in an attempt to find a level at which they can serve their new customers, but many cannot do enough business to survive. Some do not wish to change their store image and would prefer to move out of the area but find it difficult because of lack of funds.

Occasionally the frustrations of people who live in these areas erupt into violence. The 1960s and early 1970s saw riots in several major cities. During these riots, people often vented their anger on the stores and shops in their area. Some merchants had windows broken and merchandise stolen because the rioters felt they had been cheated by them. Other merchants, honest and fair retailers, suffered the same losses simply because they were located in the area of the riot.

Urban renewal projects are providing partial solutions in some cities. Perhaps even more important is the effort to make sure that people really do have equal opportunities for education, jobs, and housing. Many social scientists believe that a man with a chance to achieve his goals does not riot. This is one more reason why retailers are becoming active in civil rights efforts and the cause for equality.

OPPORTUNITIES FOR THE RETAILER

Retailers are trying in various ways to overcome their problems. They are increasingly taking their stores to the customer and keeping them open longer hours. They are using more self-service selling and are reverting to a policy called "scrambled merchandising." They are increasing their rental of goods and their sales of services. They are using automation. Finally, they are expanding their operations both vertically and horizontally. In so doing, they have been able to broaden their assortment of merchandise.

Suburban Shopping

To serve the rapidly growing number of customers in the suburbs, retailers developed the shopping center. The shopping center is and will continue to be a good retailing opportunity, because each time a new residential development goes up, a shopping center usually goes up nearby.

As the number of consumer products and services on the market continues to grow, so do the number of retailers competing to sell them. This means that stores must cater to the customer to get his business. One convenience that the customer has shown an appreciation for is a change in the traditional shopping hours, and retailers are responding by making their shopping hours more liberal.

Shopping Centers. The modern shopping center, almost a city in itself, usually contains at least one large department store, a supermarket, and numerous specialty shops. After parking their cars in the space surrounding the center, shoppers stroll along weather-protected malls or walkways. There they can leisurely window-shop through the rows of fine stores or go directly to the stores carrying the products they seek.

Today, shopping centers are becoming more than just buying-and-selling centers; increasingly, cultural and recreational activities are being offered. People can relax in public gardens, look at art exhibits, attend the theater, and eat in restaurants. Auditoriums are in constant use by social and civic organizations. Other meeting rooms are busy with cultural activities. There are dancing schools, music schools, amusement centers for children, and sometimes ice-skating rinks. The shopping center not only provides a place to buy the material needs of living but also makes a social contribution that enriches many lives.

Reprinted with permission of Architectural Record
This attractive, enclosed mall is typical of the modern shopping center.

Shopping Hours. The first stores to liberalize their shopping hours were the discount stores. They began to stay open evenings, and some opened on Sundays.

Gradually other types of stores decided that some kinds of Sunday shopping were convenient. Today many discount houses, garden shops, supermarkets, and drugstores are open on Sundays. In addition, many stores have increased their evening hours so that now, some stores are open four or five nights a week.

Evening and Sunday shopping has resulted in more convenience for consumers, particularly those who work; more jobs for retail salespeople, particularly those who want to work on a part-time basis; and more sales volume for the stores.

Some communities still have laws restricting shopping hours, especially Sunday shopping, but efforts are being made for more liberal laws.

Self-Service Merchandising

Before the 1950s, discount stores were warehouse outlets that sold mainly major appliances. Then discount stores began selling all kinds of goods, and they challenged traditional stores by selling those goods at lower prices. They accomplished this by cutting out some of the expenses of traditional stores. The discount-store interior was usually plain—"pipe-rack merchandising," it was sometimes called—and little sales assistance was given customers. To help customers make their choices, the stores featured self-service fixtures.

Traditional stores watched this development and decided to turn it into an opportunity. They adapted some self-service fixtures and turned their selling effort into what could be called a semi-self-service arrangement. Many goods were placed on self-service racks, where they could be examined by customers without the help of a salesperson. Some goods, such as jewelry and better dresses, were still kept in display areas where they could be examined only with the help of a salesperson.

It is interesting to note how similar the two types of stores are today. Discount stores are offering more expensive merchandise, various customer services, and some sales assistance. Traditional stores have installed self-service fixtures and thus have reduced the number of salespeople.

Self-service, then, not only makes shopping more convenient for the customer but also helps a retailer keep his labor costs down. For these reasons, self-service will continue to be an important marketing principle for the retailer.

Self-service merchandising permits shoppers to browse and make decisions to buy at their convenience.

Courtesy Two Guys Department Store, a subsidiary of Vornado, Inc.

Scrambled Merchandising

It is becoming increasingly difficult to identify stores just by the kinds of merchandise they sell. Department stores have added garden shops and auto service centers. Gas stations may sell garden equipment and supplies. Drugstores may sell stockings, books, small gifts, and greeting cards. The stocking and selling of untraditional lines of goods by a store is called *scrambled merchandising*.

Scrambled merchandising is one of the oldest forms of retailing. The old general store that served as the main retail outlet for an entire community used scrambled merchandising. The store always started with a basic stock of food, fabrics, and tools. Then, as people showed needs or wants for other goods, the store would bring in a new line. It did not matter whether the shopkeeper had ever sold such a line before; if he thought people would buy it, he would stock it.

The supermarket is the best modern example of the use of scrambled merchandising as a profit builder. For food retailers the cost-profit squeeze has been particularly severe. To raise their profit margins, many supermarkets have expanded into nonfoods—mostly convenience items that a customer will buy anywhere. They include notions, cosmetics, various nonfood kitchen supplies, some kinds of hardware, inexpensive toys, pet supplies, magazines and paperbacks, and even some clothing items.

The customer finds scrambled merchandising very convenient. He no longer has to go to the hardware store for cup hooks because he can toss them into his cart while doing the weekly food shopping. The supermarkets find scrambled merchandising very profitable. They average an approximate 3 percent net profit on food and a 20 percent net profit on nonfoods. Moreover, nonfoods usually do not cause the supermarkets any stocking or housekeeping problems because supplier representatives take care of the racks. The representatives supply the racks, stock them, check and restock them at regular intervals, and remove old stock.

Rentals and Service Sales

For a long time, almost the only items that a consumer could rent were a home and evening clothes. Today, consumer goods ranging from camping equipment to musical instruments can be rented. This merchandise is being offered for rent by rental companies as well as large retailers. The Hecht Company in Silver Spring, Maryland, offers do-it-yourself tools, hospital equipment, and party, guest, and baby needs. Montgomery Ward rents tuxedos. Alexander's offers car rental service. Some department stores even rent apartments.

Retailers view the sale of services in various ways. Some see services primarily as a customer convenience and a means to win new customers. These stores are interested only in breaking even on the cost of the services. Other retailers see services as profit makers and are interested only in the amount of profit the services produce. Most retailers, however, see the importance of services halfway between these two extremes: they offer some services to win and keep customer loyalty but also expect profits on overall sales.

Technology

The age of the computer has come to retail stores by way of electronic data processing. *Electronic data processing* (EDP) is the handling of information by electronic machines. In the case of stores, EDP handles sales and inventory information. Through EDP the retailer is able to relieve his store personnel of tedious clerical work and to obtain more timely and accurate data than possible through manual operations. Computers and other EDP equipment keep a check on which goods are being sold, the quantity of goods being sold, and the stock on hand. In some cases the computer can be programmed to tell when it is time to reorder an item.

At Woodward & Lothrop, a large department store in Washington, D.C., computers do a large part of the recordkeeping. The first step in the procedure is taken when a salesperson makes a sale and records it on an electronic cash register. The cash register prints on a machine-readable tape the department number, type of item, amount of sale, and the number of the salesperson. Every night these tapes are fed into computers that summarize the day's sales and prepare a report of sales by departments. In addition, this system maintains an automatic inventory control. Every week the computer prepares an inventory analysis report showing sales and remaining stock.

EDP is also being used with increasing frequency by smaller stores. These stores can buy professional help in setting up a system and then rent time on machines at a computer center.

The use of EDP means much more efficient operation for stores of all sizes, and every improvement in technology is a very important opportunity for retailers. In fact, sometimes retailers initiate the improvements. They tell the technology experts what they need, and the experts develop the equipment and systems to do the job. Electronic data processing is discussed further in Part 43.

Expansion

Many large retailers are meeting the challenges of growing competition and the growing consumer market in one of two ways: they are expanding vertically, or they are expanding horizontally.

The electronic cash register is an important technological development in retailing.

Courtesy The Singer Co.

The process by which a retailer branches out into other kinds of businesses, such as wholesaling or manufacturing, is called *vertical expansion* (sometimes vertical integration). Genesco, Incorporated, is a good example of vertical expansion. Genesco is a manufacturer, wholesaler, and retailer of footwear, underwear, and outerwear. Its operations handle a product from the time it is planned until the time it is sold to the ultimate consumer.

The process by which a retailer increases the number of his retail units is called *horizontal expansion.* For example, horizontal expansion occurs when a retailer opens a branch store near a new housing development.

The larger department and specialty stores have added branches to increase the number of their retail units, but their expansion is modest compared to the expansion of supermarket, drugstore, and variety store chains.

Expansion of retail establishments has not been easy in recent years because of the cost-profit squeeze. But as long as there is a consumer market, there will be retailers ready to serve that market. And the most successful of those retailers will be the ones who make the best use of the opportunities that present themselves.

YOUR MARKETING VOCABULARY

On a separate sheet of paper define each of the following marketing terms; then use each term in a sentence.

Cost-profit squeeze
Electronic data processing
Horizontal expansion
Scrambled merchandising
Shoplifting
Vertical expansion

FOR REVIEW AND DISCUSSION

1. Explain what is meant by the statement, "Retailing has been undergoing a revolution."
2. What three important problems face retailers today?
3. List two factors probably responsible for the increase in shoplifting.
4. What is meant by the statement, "Some people consider all property to be communal"?
5. Why will the shopping center continue to be a good retailing opportunity?
6. How is a shopping center more than a place to shop?
7. Name six consumer goods that you can rent today.
8. How do retailers sometimes initiate improvements through technology?
9. Give an example of vertical expansion in retailing.
10. Give an example of horizontal expansion in retailing.

ANALYZING MARKETING CONCEPTS

1. Assume that you are a member of a committee which must plan a shopping center in your area. You must suggest the types of stores to be included in the shopping center and the number of each type. You must also recommend special features that the center as a whole will need. Prepare a form like the one below and write your suggestions in the appropriate columns.

Number of Stores	Type of Store	Special Features of Shopping Center
Example: One	Supermarket	Have parking facilities and police patrol.

2. Scrambled merchandising is used in many types of stores that sell the same kinds of merchandise. Prepare a form like the following. Using your shopping-center plan in Problem 1 as a guide, list in the left-hand column an item that would be sold in at least four of the stores in your shopping center. In the right-hand column, list the four or more stores.

Repeat this procedure, item by item, for five more items of merchandise. (Of course, the four or more stores will not necessarily be the same for each item.)

Item of Merchandise	Stores in Which Item Is Sold
Example: Cosmetics	Drugstore, supermarket, department store, variety store.

◘ MARKETING PROJECT 17
Identifying Retailing Problems and Opportunities

Project Goal: Given a retail business, identify the problems and opportunities facing the retailer because of changes in his market, competition, and technology.

Action: Select a retail businessman in your community and ask the businessman for permission to interview him. With your teacher's guidance, plan your interview with other members of your class so that each of you visits a different business.

Prepare a form like the one below. In the left-hand column, list the following topics to be discussed with the businessman: (a) cost-profit squeeze, (b) shoplifting, (c) store location, (d) shopping hours, (e) self-service, (f) scrambled merchandising, (g) customer services, (h) electronic data processing. In the center column, write a question to ask the businessman about each topic.

When you interview the businessman, ask each question. Write a summary of his answers, comments, and key points in the right-hand column.

Prepare a 10-minute oral report to present in class on the overall reaction of the businessman to the problems and opportunities facing him. Be sure to give the name and address of the business and the name of the businessman at the beginning of your report.

Topic	Question	Businessman's Response
Example: Shoplifting	What techniques do you use to prevent shoplifting?	We have an antishoplifting training program for all personnel; also, detectives disguised as customers, and publicity on prosecution of shoplifters caught.

part 18
The Wholesaling Business

YOUR GOALS

1. Given a wholesale business of your choice, explain the kinds of work that business performs for retailers.
2. Given a wholesale business of your choice, identify the customer services that business performs.
3. Given the types of wholesalers, locate and classify three types found in your business community or in a nearby city.

Most consumers buy many of the goods and services they need through retail stores and institutions. But where do retailers buy the goods they have for sale? In some cases, buyers for retail stores buy direct from the manufacturer, but more often they deal with wholesalers. A *wholesaler* is a person or firm that buys merchandise from the manufacturer and sells it either to retailers for subsequent resale to the consumer or to business firms for industrial or business use.

Because wholesalers do not actually sell direct to the consumer, many consumers may not be aware of their importance. Manufacturing and retail businesses would have a difficult time marketing their goods without the contributions made by wholesalers.

WHOLESALER FUNCTIONS

Wholesalers perform several major functions that aid in the flow of goods from the producer to the consumer. These functions include buying, selling, warehousing, bulk breaking, and transporting, and offering credit, promotional assistance, and market information.

Buying

A wholesaler often makes purchases for retailers. To have on hand the merchandise that retailers will want to sell, the wholesaler of consumer goods studies fashion trends, consumer demand, and retail prices so that he can make the best possible purchases. The wholesaler keeps in constant touch with many manufacturers, looking at their new lines, noting prices, and checking the time it will take to obtain delivery. From the lines he has studied, he chooses the products that the retailers are most likely to buy.

The small retailer would find it impossible to contact all the manufacturers whose products are sold in his store and to make all the decisions necessary in selecting the products that will sell. For these reasons, he relies on the wholesaler to have close contact with sources of supply and to exercise judgment in the choice of the most appropriate merchandise.

Selling

Wholesalers buy goods for the purpose of resale to other business firms, and most wholesalers maintain a trained sales force to do the selling. A wholesaler's salesmen make regular visits to retail-store buyers, to industrial firms, and to institutions such as schools and hospitals. The salesmen carry samples, catalogs, and displays showing the wholesaler's complete line of products. The salesmen hope to persuade buyers to become regular customers of the wholesaler.

Wholesale salesmen perform a variety of services in connection with their selling activities. They sometimes check the stock remaining in the store and actually prepare order forms for items that need to be restocked. They often advise retailers on advertising new products. They may suggest retail prices, and offer ideas and materials for displays. Some wholesale salesmen of technical equipment give advice on proper installation and maintenance.

Wholesalers often take over the complete selling functions of manufacturers. This is particularly so in the case of manufacturers who do not wish to be involved in selling activities or who are too small to afford hiring and training a sales force. They depend on the wholesalers to find customers for their products.

The warehousing of goods is an important function of wholesalers.

Photograph by Guy Gillette

Warehousing

Many wholesalers bring the various products they handle together in one place. The process of handling and storing goods in one place is called *warehousing*. Warehousing by the wholesaler provides several advantages for the retailer. First, because the warehouse is generally nearer the retailer, he can expect much quicker delivery than he could get from a manufacturer whose plant may be hundreds of miles away. Second, the retailer need not use his own limited space for the storage of large quantities of goods.

Warehousing offers the retailer still another advantage. Because the warehouse keeps wanted merchandise on hand, the retailer need not buy a large amount of goods. He can simply reorder when his stocks are almost exhausted.

Bulk Breaking

The wholesaler buys his goods in truckloads or in railroad carloads. At his warehouse he divides these large quantities into smaller ones. The process of dividing large quantities into smaller quantities for the purpose of selling in small units is called *bulk breaking*.

Bulk breaking provides a service both to manufacturers and to retailers. Many manufacturers will not ship their goods in quantities smaller than truckloads or railroad carloads, and it would be impossible for the majority of retailers to buy and store such huge quantities. Bulk breaking, therefore, helps manufacturers to dispose of their goods and helps retailers by allowing them to buy goods in small quantities for resale.

Transporting

Because manufacturers deliver goods in railroad carloads to wholesalers, the cost of transportation is not so great as it would be if they shipped in small quantities direct to many retailers. Retailers who buy from wholesalers benefit indirectly from this saving because it reduces the total cost they have to pay.

Many wholesalers operate their own fleets of trucks. Therefore, they are able to maintain tight control over their delivery schedules. The retailer knows he can depend on these schedules. If, however, the retailer were ordering direct from the manufacturer, the exact arrival date of the shipment would be far less predictable.

Credit

Many wholesalers extend financial assistance to their customers through the practice of delayed billing. For example, wholesalers of lawn and garden supplies may deliver seed to retailers in February but not require payment until May or June. They may send toys and Christmas decorations to retailers in the fall but not expect payment until January. This form of credit allows retailers to pay wholesalers out of their income from the sale of the goods.

Promotional Assistance

Some wholesalers provide merchandise display aids to retailers for certain products. In some instances they help retailers in setting up effective window and counter displays. They also offer retailers help in designing store layout and in doing a better job of selling and advertising. Often they enter into a joint advertising effort with retailers in a particular area. Also, some wholesalers have cooperative advertising policies, in which they share the cost of a retailer's advertising program.

Market Information

The wholesaler is in a good position to know exactly what is happening in the market, and he benefits both his customers and himself by keeping his customers informed. By telling them what new products have been introduced, and what products seem to be gaining or losing popularity, he can help them increase their business and thus improve his own sales. Some of his information may come from his own market research. Other information and ideas may come through his contacts with numerous retailers. By distributing such information and ideas, the wholesaler often is able to assist customers in improving their operating methods and in making marketing decisions.

TYPES OF WHOLESALERS

Wholesalers are classified into two main groups according to whether they take title to the goods they handle. These two groups are merchant wholesalers, who do assume ownership of goods, and agent wholesalers, who do not assume ownership but assist manufacturers and retailers in buying and selling activities. The merchant wholesaler is a merchant middleman and the agent wholesaler is an agent middleman (both types of middlemen are discussed in Part 14).

Because the merchant middleman becomes the owner of the goods he handles, he assumes the responsibility of selling them and of accepting a loss if he cannot sell them. The agent wholesaler, however, does not have this responsibility because he does not assume ownership of goods.

Merchant Wholesaler

The merchant wholesaler may perform all wholesaling functions, or he may offer a limited number of functions. The merchant wholesaler who performs all wholesaling functions for his customers is called a *service wholesaler* or regular wholesaler. The wholesaler who offers partial service is called a limited-function wholesaler. A merchant wholesaler usually deals in large quantities and buys goods for resale to retailers and business firms.

Service Wholesaler. A service wholesaler gives complete wholesaling service. He carries full lines of merchandise, extends credit, buys in large quantities, and resells in smaller ones. He provides transportation services, accepts risks, and assembles and stores goods.

A service wholesaler may carry merchandise in a wide variety of lines, or he may deal in a specialty. The service wholesaler of a specialty line carries only one or two types of products within a certain field. For example, instead of handling footwear in general, he may handle only boots. Because he specializes in one area, the specialty wholesaler may be regarded as an expert who can provide dependable market information to his customers.

If a service wholesaler serves the industrial market, he is usually called an industrial distributor. An *industrial distributor* is a wholesaler who sells

This line of rug-cleaning and floor-polishing equipment is typical of the kind of merchandise displayed in stores by rack jobbers.

Courtesy Glamorene Products Corp.

equipment, accessories, standard parts, and supplies to industrial and business firms. He performs much the same services for his customers as do wholesalers in the consumer market.

Another type of service wholesaler is the *rack jobber,* who sells specialized lines of merchandise to certain types of retail stores. The rack jobber is most common in the food industry. He supplies supermarkets and other food stores with nonfood items such as health and beauty aids, housewares, and certain wearing apparel. Recently, rack jobbers have begun to display specialized lines of merchandise in drug, hardware, and variety stores.

Although he is a wholesaler, the rack jobber performs many of the functions of the retailer as well. The retailer usually takes ownership of the goods, but the rack jobber has complete responsibility for selecting the merchandise to be displayed, setting up the display facilities, removing old merchandise, substituting fresh items, and marking prices.

Limited-Function Wholesaler. In contrast with the service wholesaler, the limited-function wholesaler performs only certain services. The three main types of limited-function wholesalers are the drop shipper, the cash-and-carry wholesaler, and the truck jobber.

A *drop shipper* is a wholesaler who takes orders from retailers and arranges for delivery of goods directly from the producer. Often the drop shipper operates with little more than an office, a note pad, and a telephone. Because he does not maintain a warehouse, break bulk, or offer a delivery service, he sells at lower prices than service wholesalers. The drop shipper assumes ownership of the goods before reselling them, but he does not handle the goods physically.

The advantage of a drop shipper to retailers is that he reduces freight costs to a minimum. He arranges for shipments to be sent direct from the producer to the customer. A drop shipper deals almost exclusively with bulky items, such as coal, coke, lumber, and building materials. These are products which do not require bulk breaking and which customers are willing to accept in railroad carloads or truckloads.

A cash-and-carry wholesaler is one who maintains a warehouse at which customers pick up their merchandise in their own trucks. He provides no transportation service to his customers. He also provides no credit, requiring immediate cash payment. Because of the lack of such services, the cash-and-carry wholesaler offers goods at lower prices than the service wholesaler.

A truck jobber is a wholesaler who combines storage, selling, delivery, and collection into one operation by using his truck for storage and transportation. Because he carries his stock in his truck, he is able to sell and deliver merchandise during his calls on retail stores. His advantage to retailers is immediate delivery of small quantities of merchandise.

The truck jobber sells for cash and limits his stock to nationally advertised specialties and fast-moving items of a perishable or semiperishable nature. Most truck jobbers are concentrated in the food field where they carry only a few specialties, such as mayonnaise, cheese, potato chips, and candy.

One disadvantage of the truck jobber is that his costs are high because of the relatively small orders he receives from each customer. Consequently, he must charge a higher price for his goods.

Agent Wholesaler

The agent wholesaler does not take title to goods. His main function is to assist manufacturers and retailers in buying and selling. Three important agent wholesalers are brokers, selling agents, and manufacturer's agents.

Broker. An agent wholesaler who represents either buyers or sellers in arranging purchases by business firms or sales by producers is called a *broker*. A broker does not physically handle the goods or take ownership of them. His main function is to bring the buyer and seller together for the purpose of working out a sales transaction. If a sale results, the broker is paid a commission, which is a percent of the total amount of the sale.

The broker often arranges a meeting between the buyer and the seller.

A broker usually deals in one type of product. He may deal in food, stock, real estate, iron and iron products, wood, or dry goods. Because he deals in only one product, he is regarded as a specialist who can offer his principals (the firms or individuals he represents) important information about the conditions of the market. Such information includes the current prices being asked, the available supply of the product, the current demand for the product, and the best method of distribution. A broker has no continuing relationship with his principals. Instead, each transaction that he handles for a firm or individual is complete in itself.

A wholesale broker is important in the food industry, where he handles products such as sugar, grain, and fruits and vegetables (fresh, canned, or frozen). He is of particular service to producers of seasonal goods, such as tomatoes. The canning season for tomatoes is short, and small canneries open up for a short period to conduct the canning operation. These canneries do not maintain a sales force because they have only a seasonal operation. As a result, they rely on the experienced food broker to sell the entire output of the cannery. When the entire stock has been sold, the relationship between the broker and the cannery is temporarily discontinued. Their relationship may, of course, be resumed in the following season.

Selling Agent. An independent specialist who sells the entire output of a line of goods for one or more manufacturers is known as a *selling agent.* The selling agent usually has full authority with regard to setting prices, terms, and other conditions of sale. He has his own trained sales force, and he maintains showrooms in which he displays the goods that are for sale. He does not have a warehouse and prefers to have the goods shipped directly from the manufacturer's plant.

The selling agent usually operates under a long-term contract with his principal and is considered almost part of the manufacturer's organization. Since the manufacturer depends entirely upon the selling agent for the job of selling his goods, it is understandable why such a close association develops between them.

Manufacturer's Agent. An independent salesman who handles part of the output of one or more manufacturers within a particular territory is known as a *manufacturer's agent.* The manufacturer's agent is much more limited in scope than the selling agent. He does not have wide freedom in adjusting prices or making promises on behalf of the manufacturer. He can make sales only in accordance with the terms set by the manufacturer.

Sometimes a manufacturer will have a number of manufacturer's agents, each with a definite territory. In some cases the agents will conduct all the manufacturer's selling activities; in other cases a manufacturer will use the agents along with his own sales force.

The relationship of the manufacturer's agent to his principal is not usually as continuous as that of the selling agent. On the average, a selling agent works for the same manufacturer for a period of 1 to 5 years, although many have done so for as long as 20 years. In general, a manufacturer uses a manufacturer's agent when he is introducing a new product, when his own sales force is not fully developed, when the reputation of the agent is better known than his own reputation, or when the agent deals with customers that the manufacturer could not otherwise reach. When a manufacturer is ready to take over his own selling activities, he may end his relationship with the manufacturer's agent.

◘ YOUR MARKETING VOCABULARY

On a separate sheet of paper define each of the following marketing terms; then use each term in a sentence.

Broker
Bulk breaking
Drop shipper
Industrial distributor
Manufacturer's agent

Rack jobber
Selling agent
Service wholesaler
Warehousing
Wholesaler

FOR REVIEW AND DISCUSSION

1. What major functions do wholesalers perform?
2. How do wholesalers assist retailers in buying goods?
3. How do wholesalers assist manufacturers in selling goods?
4. What service does bulk breaking provide to manufacturers? to retailers?
5. Explain the benefits which wholesalers' warehousing and transportation services provide to retailers.
6. Explain the credit, promotional, and informational services that the wholesaler may offer his customers.
7. Name the two main groups into which wholesalers are classified, and explain why they are so classified.
8. List several functions of the service wholesaler.
9. Name three types of limited-function wholesalers and list one advantage that each type offers to retailers.
10. Identify three types of agent wholesalers and describe their functions.

ANALYZING MARKETING CONCEPTS

1. Wholesalers may be broadly classified into two groups: merchant wholesalers and agent wholesalers. Prepare a form like the one below. List the following types of wholesalers in the left-hand column: (a) rack jobber, (b) broker, (c) industrial distributor, (d) truck jobber, (e) manufacturer's agent, (f) service wholesaler, (g) drop shipper, (h) selling agent, (i) limited-function wholesaler, (j) cash-and-carry wholesaler.

    For each type listed, place a check mark in the appropriate center column to indicate whether that wholesaler is a merchant wholesaler or an agent wholesaler. In the right-hand column give an important characteristic of each.

Type of Wholesaler	Group — Merchant	Group — Agent	Characteristic of This Type
Example: Regular wholesaler	✔		Carries full lines of merchandise and extends credit.

2. Prepare a form like the one below. In the left-hand column, list the following types of agent wholesale middlemen: (a) broker, (b) selling agent, (c) manufacturer's agent. In the other columns, compare the services performed by each in handling consumer and industrial goods.

Agent Wholesale Middleman	Services Performed for Consumer Goods	Services Performed for Industrial Goods

MARKETING PROJECT 18
Identifying Types of Wholesalers

Project Goal: Given the types of wholesalers, locate and classify three types found in your business community or in a nearby city.

Action: Use the Yellow Pages of your telephone directory to locate the names of three types of wholesale businesses. Look for the names of wholesalers under headings such as these: brokers, grocers, florists, industrial equipment, office supplies, warehouses, hardware. With your teacher's approval, arrange to talk with each type of wholesaler to find out the kind of products he sells, the businesses he serves, and the services he performs.

Prepare a form like the one below and record your answers in the appropriate columns.

Name of Wholesaler	Type of Wholesaler; Products He Sells	Customers and Services of Wholesaler
Example: Industrial Supply Company	Merchant-service wholesaler and industrial distributor. Sells machines, tools, and supplies.	Sells to small factories, repair companies, construction firms, and mechanics. Offers credit, delivery, large inventory, and professional advice.

part 19

Selecting Channels of Distribution

YOUR GOALS

1. Given several consumer and industrial goods, determine a suitable channel of distribution for each.
2. Given four distribution policies, determine how each of them is being used in your community.

When a product comes off the production line, the manufacturer must select the distribution channel that he thinks will be the best means of getting his product to the consumer or industrial user. Much of the success of a product depends on the methods used to get it from the factory to the final user. No matter how good a product is, it can be a total sales failure if it arrives in the marketplace too late, if distribution costs are too high, or if it is not distributed as widely as a competing product. In distributing his product, a manufacturer may decide to sell direct to the consumer or industrial user, or he may choose appropriate middlemen. In either case, he must know the available distribution channels and must consider the advantages and disadvantages of each channel. Armed with that knowledge and careful consideration, the manufacturer can choose the channel which will result in the most efficient marketing of his product.

TYPES OF DISTRIBUTION CHANNELS

A middleman usually specializes in handling either consumer or industrial goods. Thus a manufacturer of consumer goods usually deals with middlemen who distribute only consumer products, and a manufacturer of industrial goods deals with middlemen who handle only industrial products. In other words, the channels of distribution for consumer products are separate from those for industrial products.

Channels for Consumer Goods

The illustration below shows the channels used for consumer products. Notice that the manufacturer of consumer goods has five channels to choose from in marketing his goods. The channels range from the most complex, which uses three middlemen between the manufacturer and the consumer, to the simplest, which uses no middlemen.

Manufacturer to Agent to Wholesaler to Retailer to Consumer. A manufacturer uses all three types of middlemen when he wishes to avoid all the activities necessary to get his product to market. The job of the agent is to

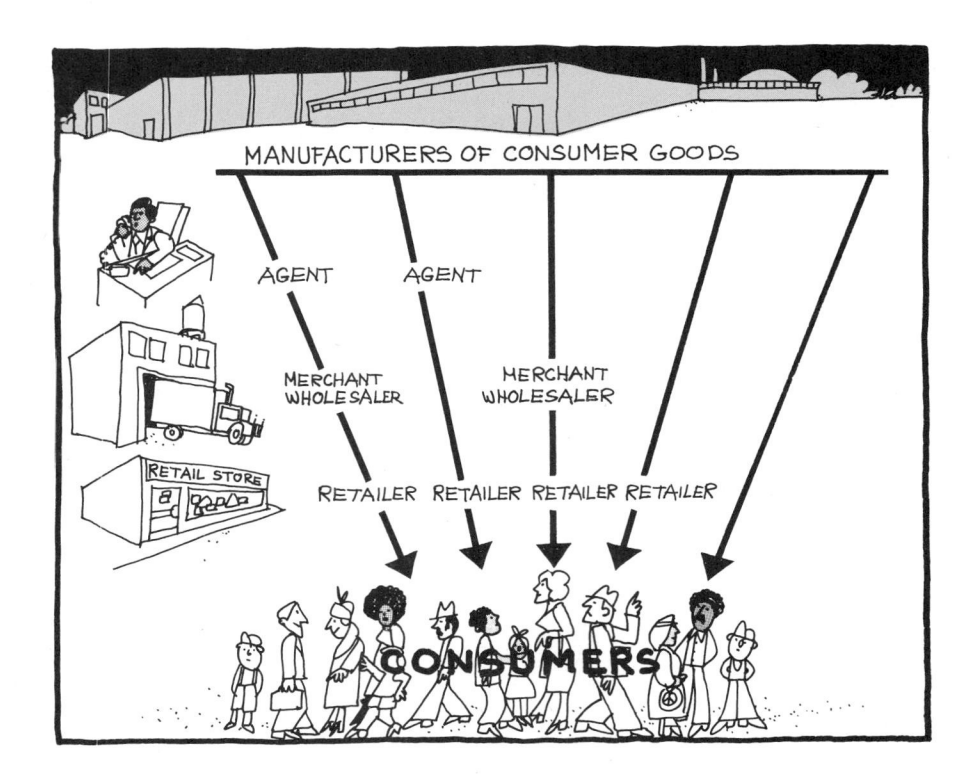

218 / Unit 5 / Marketing Channels

persuade the wholesaler to carry and distribute the manufacturer's product. The wholesaler performs the activities of bulk breaking, storing, selling to retailers, and transporting the goods.

Manufacturer to Agent to Retailer to Consumer. If a manufacturer is prepared to handle his own storage and transportation but does not want to hire and train his own sales force, he may use an agent to handle the selling activities. After the sale is made, the manufacturer takes over the rest of the wholesaling functions himself. The agent does not take possession or ownership of the goods at all; he merely brings the buyer and seller together.

Manufacturer to Wholesaler to Retailer to Consumer. The most frequently used channel of distribution is that of manufacturer to wholesaler to retailer to consumer. Most retailers are too small to buy goods in large quantities from manufacturers. In turn, many manufacturers do not have the facilities or personnel to handle many small shipments to retailers scattered across the country. They therefore prefer to ship their goods to wholesalers in various geographical areas and let the wholesalers handle sales and shipment to retailers in their particular regions.

Manufacturer to Retailer to Consumer. Some manufacturers feel that they do not need the services of agents or wholesalers in marketing their goods to retailers. Such manufacturers perform their own wholesaling functions; they do their own selling, warehousing, bulk breaking, delivering, and financing. This is the channel of distribution used when manufacturers are dealing with very large retail stores that can afford to buy and accept delivery in large quantities.

Manufacturer to Consumer. In the manufacturer-to-consumer channel, the manufacturer sells direct to the consumer, and no middlemen are involved. It is thus the simplest channel of distribution for consumer products. This channel is used when a manufacturer sells from his factory, when a farmer sells from a roadside stand, when a manufacturer sells through the mail, and when a manufacturer's salesman sells products door to door.

Channels for Industrial Goods

Channels for the distribution of industrial goods are separate from those for consumer goods; however, they are similar in nature to the consumer channels. Agents are used to assist in selling activities, and industrial distributors, who are merchant wholesalers, perform much the same activities as do wholesalers of consumer goods. See the illustration on the next page.

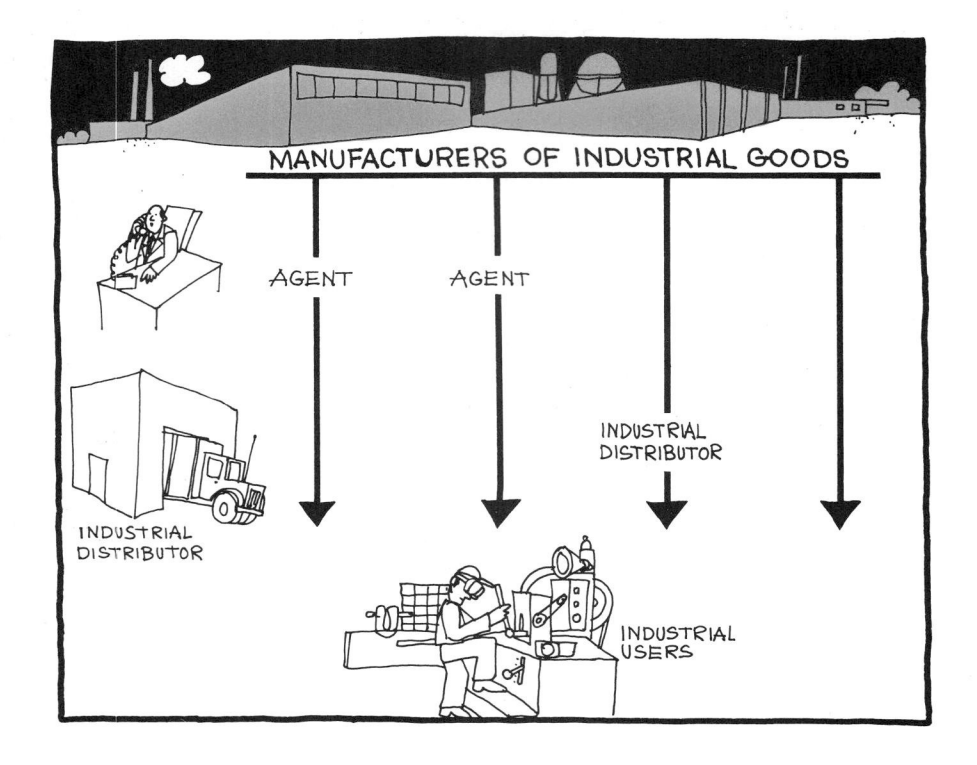

Manufacturer to Agent to Industrial Distributor to Industrial User. Small manufacturers of industrial goods often feel that it is better for their business if they concentrate on production and leave the distribution completely to middlemen. Thus a manufacturer will have an agent take over the activities involved in selling his product to an industrial distributor. After the sale is completed, the industrial distributor takes over the functions of storage, reselling, and shipping.

Manufacturer to Agent to Industrial User. When a manufacturer does not want to hire and train his own sales force to sell his industrial goods but is prepared to perform all other distribution activities, he will often use the selling services of an agent. The agent does not take ownership of the goods but is responsible for arranging details of the sale. Shipment is made direct from the manufacturer to the industrial user.

Manufacturer to Industrial Distributor to Industrial User. The industrial distributor deals chiefly in small standardized parts and in operating supplies needed on a continuous basis by the industrial user. Unlike an agent, the industrial distributor actually takes ownership of the goods he handles and keeps the products in stock in his supply house. The manufacturer uses industrial distributors to be sure that his products are readily available to users. Since an industrial distributor is usually located close to his customers, he generally can do a more effective job than the manufacturer in reaching users within a geographic area. Furthermore, an industrial distributor is often so well respected by his customers that they depend on him to fill their orders. In that case, a manufacturer can sell his products only through the industrial distributor.

Manufacturer to Industrial User. The direct channel of distribution for industrial goods is from the manufacturer to the industrial user. It is the channel usually used by producers of installations and accessory equipment. For example, a machine shop buying a South Bend lathe would order it direct from the South Bend Corporation in Indiana. The lathe would then be shipped direct from the factory to the machine shop.

SELECTING A DISTRIBUTION CHANNEL

In selecting the method of distribution for his product, the manufacturer considers both the length and the width of the channels available. The length of a channel refers to the number of middlemen through whom the product will pass on its way to the consumer or industrial user. The width of the distribution channel refers to the number of channels through which a product will be distributed. For example, a manufacturer may decide to use the retailer as a middleman in marketing his product to the consumer. After deciding to market his product through retail stores, the manufacturer next decides how widely he wants his product distributed; that is, he determines the number of retail stores that he wants to carry his product. The length and width of such a manufacturer-to-retailer-to-consumer channel is shown in the illustration on the following page.

In determining his distribution policy, then, the manufacturer must decide first on the length and then on the width of the distribution channel. In doing so, he must consider a number of factors.

LENGTH OF THE DISTRIBUTION CHANNEL

Three major considerations in selecting the length of a channel of distribution are the nature of the product, the nature of the market, and the characteristics of the middleman chosen to handle the product.

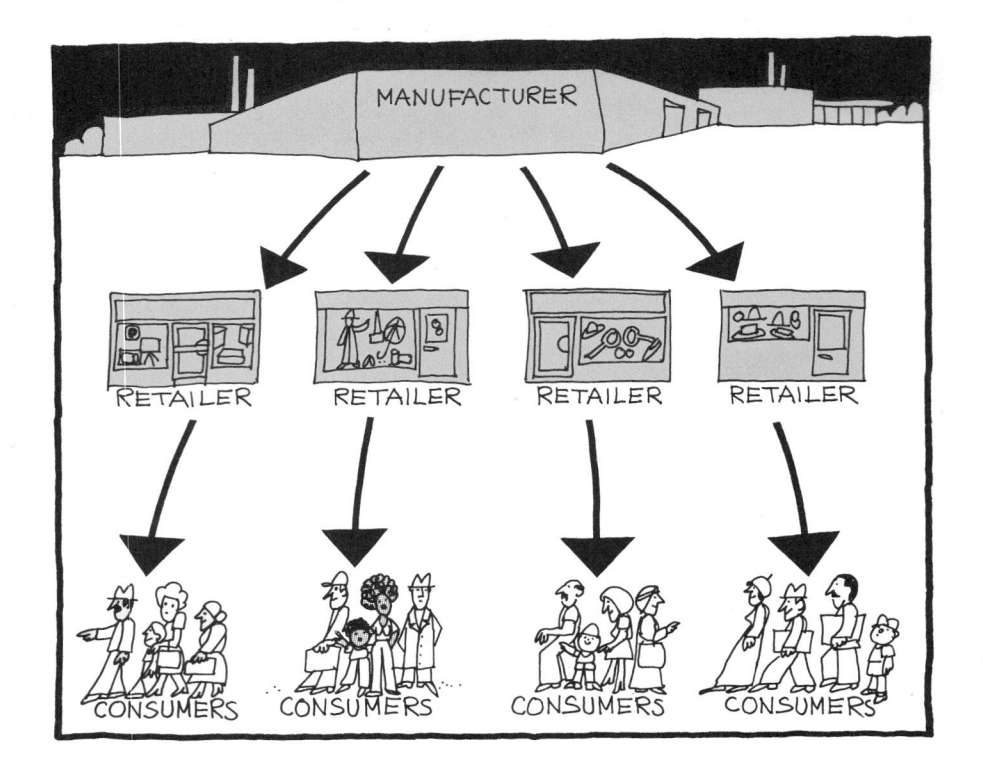

Nature of the Product

The product itself influences the manufacturer's choice of a distribution channel. If he produces a consumer product, the last stop in the channel is the consumer. Any middlemen that the manufacturer chooses will be among those who specialize in consumer goods. If the manufacturer produces an industrial product, the last stop in the channel is the industrial user. That manufacturer will choose among middlemen specializing in industrial goods. However, in deciding which specific industrial or consumer middlemen will guide his product to its final destination, a manufacturer must consider several factors. They are the product's perishability, value, size and weight, and the service required to maintain the product after purchase.

Perishability. If a food product will spoil rapidly or if a fashion product is subject to rapid style changes, the manufacturer must choose a distribution channel that will get the product to the consumer quickly. Usually, a manufacturer of fashion products sells to large retailers, who will make his goods available to consumers while they are still in style. A producer of perishable foods will choose a distribution channel that will get them to the consumer or industrial user as quickly as possible and will protect them from spoilage during transit. For example, to carry his lettuce to the supermarket, the producer would use a middleman who could transport the lettuce rapidly in refrigerated carriers.

Value. If a manufacturer of industrial goods markets his product direct to the industrial user, the product must have a high unit value[1] to cover the costs of marketing. On items of low unit value, the marketer of industrial goods could not possibly absorb the cost of selling, packing, shipping, and billing to many purchasers over a wide geographic area. He therefore finds it necessary to use an industrial distributor whose shipping and delivery charges are lower because he operates in a smaller geographic area. In addition, because the industrial distributor handles the products of many manufacturers, his total sales volume is much greater than that of the individual manufacturer. The increased sales volume makes it possible for him to absorb the marketing costs involved.

Size and Weight. If a product is very large, heavy, or bulky, moving it from warehouse to warehouse becomes difficult and expensive. To reduce the physical handling of this type of product, the manufacturer prefers to deal with an agent who can help him find a buyer, but who does not need to take possession of the heavy equipment. The equipment can stay in the manufacturer's warehouse until the agent has found a buyer and completed all other details connected with the sale. Then the equipment is shipped by the manufacturer direct to the buyer. Drop shippers are a good example of agents dealing in bulky goods. They do not physically handle the product; they simply make arrangements for the direct shipment of the goods from the manufacturer to the purchaser.

Service Required. Manufacturers of highly technical equipment prefer to sell direct to industrial users, so that they can back up their products with service and periodic maintenance checks. Often the manufacturer does not want to risk using an industrial distributor for fear that the equipment will be poorly serviced, causing the manufacturer to lose future sales. As for consumer goods sold through retailers, the manufacturer usually relies on franchised dealers or exclusive dealers to provide any servicing that his product may require.

---

[1] Unit value is the value of one unit of a product. For example, the book you are reading is one of thousands of copies produced. It is a unit and its price is its unit value. A diamond ring has a high unit value; a candy bar has a low unit value.

Nature of the Market

The market is determined by the product itself. A consumer good is, of course, destined for the consumer, and an industrial good is destined for the industrial user. But beyond that, factors such as competition, location of buyers, and total volume of sales determine the channels through which the product is distributed to the consumer or industrial user.

Competition. Every successful manufacturer must consider how the goods of his competitors are marketed, for even a superior product will lose to its competitors if it is not distributed efficiently. Sometimes a manufacturer, by studying the distribution techniques of a competitor, will be able to devise an even more successful method of distribution. Knowing what his competition is doing will help the manufacturer distribute his products effectively.

Location of Buyers. If the customers for a product are located within a small geographic area, direct marketing is a suitable method of distribution. The manufacturer can easily train a sales force and keep in touch with all his customers. However, if the customers are scattered over a large area, it is then more practical for the manufacturer to employ wholesalers and retailers as middlemen.

Volume of Sales. If the demand for his product is great, a manufacturer may perform large-scale wholesaling functions himself. Some large manufacturers of special products even sell direct to the consumer. Unless his total sales volume is very substantial, however, a manufacturer must employ the services of middlemen.

Characteristics of the Middleman

An important question that every manufacturer must ask himself in selecting the length of his distribution channel is "Which middleman is best suited to handle my product?" Manufacturers must analyze carefully the characteristics of each middleman—the services he can provide, his reputation, his selling ability, and the cost involved in using his services.

Services. A manufacturer expects a middleman to perform those services which he himself is not equipped to perform. The less a manufacturer wants to be involved with selling and distributing his product, the more he will depend on agents and merchant wholesalers to perform those functions for him. If he desires more control over the distribution of his product but does not want to be involved in selling to the consumer, he will market his product through retailers. Should he want complete control over selling and distributing, he will market direct to the consumer. The first factor, then, in choosing a middleman is to determine which services the manufacturer needs.

Reputation. Manufacturers may want to use a middleman who has a good reputation in a geographic area. Often a middleman is so firmly established in a local area that the manufacturer would find it almost impossible to sell through any other middleman. If, however, such a middleman is already carrying a line of a competitor's products and cannot take on a new line, the manufacturer must find another means of reaching the market. For example, he might choose to open his own sales branch in the area and adopt aggressive selling methods to compete with the established middleman.

Selling Ability. A very important factor which any manufacturer must consider when choosing a middleman is the middleman's ability to sell the product. Undoubtedly, the more successful a middleman is in achieving a high volume of sales, the more attractive he will be to the manufacturer as a channel of distribution.

Cost. A channel that offers excellent sales possibilities may also be a channel with high costs. These high costs must be studied carefully, however, in relation to the amount of service offered in return. A manufacturer might assume that selling the product direct to the consumer would be less expensive because it would eliminate the costs of the middleman. However, this manufacturer must consider the costs of direct selling, such as hiring and training a sales force, providing storage facilities, risk bearing, and financing. Often an established middleman can provide these services at a lower cost than a manufacturer can. Cost is always a vital consideration in selecting a middleman because the costs of marketing are reflected in the final selling price of the product; and this selling price is an important factor in the consumer's acceptance of the product.

WIDTH OF THE DISTRIBUTION CHANNEL

In choosing a distribution channel, the manufacturer must answer not only the question "Which channel of distribution shall I use?" but also "How widely shall I distribute my product?" His decision on the width of the distribution channel will depend chiefly on the nature of his product and the degree of aggressive selling required to market it. For a convenience item such as aspirin, a manufacturer will want to have it distributed to all possible outlets to compete with rival brands. But if his product is unique, the manufacturer can choose fewer selling outlets because the customer will seek out the brand rather than choose a substitute.

At first thought, it would seem that every manufacturer would want to distribute his product as widely as possible and that the only reason preventing him from doing this would be the marketing costs involved. But there are other reasons why a manufacturer might limit the distribution of his product or why he would refuse to allow it to be handled by every middleman willing to do so. How a manufacturer determines the width of product distribution can best be understood by studying the various distribution policies from which he can choose: intensive distribution, exclusive distribution, selective distribution, and integrated distribution.

Intensive Distribution

The form of distribution in which a manufacturer distributes his product to any middleman who agrees to stock and sell it is called *intensive distribution.* Intensive distribution is used for products that face much competition. Manu-

Courtesy Modern Packaging Magazine

Which distribution policy would be used to market these canned goods? Why?

facturers of convenience goods, such as toothpaste, shampoo, and shaving cream, know that these products must be readily available so that the customer will not buy a substitute. Most food-product manufacturers strive for intensive distribution in supermarkets and smaller food stores, because a customer will usually accept a substitute if a particular brand is not available. For the same reason, marketers of industrial operating supplies such as lubricating oil, nails, floor wax, and nuts and bolts try to distribute their goods to all possible outlets.

Exclusive Distribution

The form of distribution in which a manufacturer selects only one middleman within a geographic area to handle his product is called *exclusive distribution*. The manufacturer guarantees the middleman a protected territory; that is, no other middleman within the territory will be able to handle and distribute the same product.

In some cases of exclusive distribution, the middleman is allowed to handle certain competitors' products. For example, many car dealers handle a foreign car as well as an American car.

Sometimes a manufacturer will grant a franchise to a middleman handling his product. As discussed in Part 15, a franchise is an agreement by which a manufacturer gives a distributor the exclusive right to sell and distribute the manufacturer's product within a certain territory. Most soda-bottling companies operate under franchise. Each of these franchised distributors agrees to buy all its syrup, bottles, and other manufacturing materials from the parent company. In return, each of these franchised distributors is guaranteed a certain area as its exclusive territory in which to promote and sell the product.

Exclusive distribution has several advantages for the manufacturer. The cost of marketing is often reduced, since the manufacturer does not have to deal with a large number of middlemen. Exclusive distributors often do a large amount of sales promotion in their selling areas; they know that this will mean increased sales since the product cannot be bought elsewhere. Their participation thus relieves the manufacturer of the responsibility for promoting his product.

Since high quality is usually associated with a product available only through selected dealers, exclusive distribution brings prestige to a product. Exclusive distribution gives a manufacturer greater control over prices because he can threaten to withdraw an exclusive distributorship if the middleman tries to cut prices below the established level. The right of a manufacturer to maintain prices is often set down in the original contract between the manufacturer and the exclusive distributor.

Courtesy Sears, Roebuck and Co.
In what kind of store would you be likely to see a display like this one? Why?

Selective Distribution

The form of distribution in which a manufacturer carefully chooses a number of middlemen to market his product within a geographic area is known as *selective distribution*. Manufacturers using selective distribution choose those middlemen who are best equipped to maintain the image of the product and to attract suitable customers. A manufacturer of fine china would therefore select only fine department and jewelry stores as distributors of his product. The manufacturer would not be likely to deal with variety stores or discount houses for two reasons: First, sales of his product from these stores would probably not be very large. Also, the china might lose its reputation as a high-quality product.

Integrated Distribution

The form of distribution in which a manufacturer handles the functions of a retailer or a wholesaler in addition to his manufacturing functions is called *integrated distribution*. Fanny Farmer candy stores provide an example of integrated distribution. The Fanny Farmer Company makes its own candy and sells it in its own stores. In this way, Fanny Farmer is assured of always having an outlet for its products. Also, the company can maintain control over the display and storage of its products in the retail stores, as well as the selling techniques used by its retail salespeople.

While integrated distribution may seem to be an ideal means of controlling the production and distribution of products, it does have limitations. Retail stores controlled by manufacturers usually sell at prices set at the factory. Consequently, they cannot quickly adjust their prices to meet local competition, and the result is often lost sales. Also, the product selection is limited to one brand, and many customers prefer a store where they can select from several brands.

YOUR MARKETING VOCABULARY

On a separate sheet of paper define each of the following marketing terms; then use each term in a sentence.

Exclusive distribution   *Intensive distribution*
Integrated distribution   *Selective distribution*

FOR REVIEW AND DISCUSSION

1. Describe five channels of distribution available to manufacturers of consumer products.
2. Which channel of distribution do manufacturers of consumer goods use most frequently? Why?
3. What are the channels of distribution that are used by manufacturers of industrial goods?
4. Explain the difference in function between an agent and an industrial distributor.
5. Explain what is meant by the length of a channel of distribution. Explain, also, what is meant by its width.
6. What three major considerations must a manufacturer keep in mind in selecting the length of a channel of distribution?
7. How do such factors as a product's perishability, value, size and weight, and servicing requirements affect the manufacturer's selection of a channel of distribution?
8. In selecting a channel of distribution, what factors must the manufacturer consider about the nature of the market?
9. What characteristics of middlemen does a manufacturer seek in selecting a channel of distribution?

10. For what kinds of products is intensive distribution used? Why is it used for these products?
11. What advantages does the exclusive form of distribution provide the manufacturer?
12. What are some of the advantages of integrated distribution? What are its limitations?

◻ ANALYZING MARKETING CONCEPTS

1. The product itself influences the manufacturer's choice of a distribution channel. Prepare a form like the one below. In the left-hand column, list the following products: (a) coal, (b) diamond ring, (c) automatic washer, (d) television set, (e) piano, (f) lathe, (g) lubricating oil, (h) typewriter, (i) cola syrup, (j) carpeting for a store, (k) butter for a bakery, (l) computer (for electronic data processing).

    For each product listed, place a check mark in the appropriate column or columns to indicate those aspects of its nature to be considered in selecting a channel of distribution.

Product	Nature of the Product			
	Perishability	Value	Size and Weight	Service Required
Example: Cabbage	✓			

2. The selection of a channel of distribution for a product is affected by the nature of the market and the characteristics of middlemen. Prepare a form like the one below and list the following products in the left-hand column: (a) coal, (b) diamond ring, (c) automatic washer, (d) television set, (e) piano, (f) lathe, (g) lubricating oil, (h) typewriter, (i) cola syrup, (j) carpeting for a department store, (k) butter for a bakery, (l) computer (for electronic data processing).

    For each product listed, place a check mark in the appropriate column or columns to indicate the characteristics of middlemen to be considered in selecting its channel of distribution.

Product	Characteristics of Middlemen			
	Services	Reputation	Selling Ability	Cost
Example: Cabbage	✓		✓	

MARKETING PROJECT 19
Investigating Distribution Policies

Project Goal: Given the four distribution policies discussed in this part, determine how each of them is being used in your community.

Action: Visit a shopping area near you that has at least ten stores, and make a list of the products sold in these stores. From your list, select one or more products that are marketed by each of the distribution policies discussed in this part.

Prepare a form like the one below. In the left-hand column, list the distribution policies: intensive, exclusive, selective, and integrated. In the "Product" column, list the products that are marketed by each policy. For intensive distribution, list a convenience product. For exclusive distribution, find one well-known product that is available in only one store in your community. For selective distribution, list one high-quality product (other than that used in the example below). For integrated distribution, list two or three products.

In the "Stores" column, list the stores in which each of the products is sold. In the right-hand column, give a reason why the manufacturer of each product might have selected the distribution policy.

Distribution Policy	Product	Stores	Reason Policy Was Selected
Example: Selective	Luggage	Plaza Department Store; Julie's Luggage Shop	Stores will maintain image of product.

CASE STUDY
Selecting a Channel of Distribution for a New Product

Spring Foods Company was determined to make its entry into the pet food market a success (see pages 96-97). It had developed a formula for quality dog food that had passed all testing very successfully. It had designed unique packaging: a squat, sealed foil box which, when cut open, could serve as the dog's dish. The package was to be stocked in a special display unit that the company also had designed.

"We've got the right product," marketing director Pete Marconi said to his boss, Leon Hamil. "Now we've got to make the final decision about how to handle this line. It certainly would be easy if we could handle it exactly as we handle our other products, but I'm not sure whether that's the best way."

Spring Foods was very satisfied with the distribution arrangements it had made with the three supermarket chains that handled the products on a shared exclusive arrangement. The chains took ownership and responsibility for shipments right at Spring Foods' factory door. They then moved the shipments to their warehouses and from their warehouses to the store units—all of which were located within a hundred-mile radius. For this service, Spring Foods figured it was able to set prices about 6 cents lower on every dollar's worth of goods than it could have if it handled its own distribution. Last year, Spring Foods sold approximately one-half million dollars' worth of products on this basis.

"I'm not sure either," said Leon. "Look at this report I just got in." The report showed that every store manager surveyed by the chain organizations had commented favorably on the potential of the new dog food, but that there was some hesitation. According to the report, this was how one store manager phrased it: "The product has real quality, and that's what my customers want. But the display rack bothers me. Sure, we have lots of racks in our store, but the rack jobbers take care of most of them. My clerks don't really have the time."

"I've just been checking over the names of the rack jobbers who operate in our area," Leon continued. "Alonzo's is the only outfit that services all three of the chains we deal with. They've never handled a food product, but they probably would be willing to try it. Their rate for handling a single line would probably cost us about 2 cents more on the dollar than having the chains pick it up."

"Would our exclusive arrangements allow us to use a jobber?" Pete asked.

"Yes," Leon replied. "Our arrangements cover only our present lines for the coming year. They don't cover any new lines we add. The chains are willing, by the way, in spite of the worry about the display rack."

"I don't want to give up those racks," Pete said. "I think they're important to our sales. But using a rack jobber—that would sure add to our bookkeeping complications. And Alonzo's, if I remember correctly, likes to advertise that it can offer stores a large variety of any product it handles. If Alonzo's takes on our pet food, they might well solicit a couple of other pet food accounts, too."

"Of course, we could start thinking again about our own distribution system," Leon said. "We've been talking about that ever since the company got started. We're going to need it some day if we continue to expand. What were those figures you worked out last year?"

"Let me see," Pete said. "It seems to me we figured that after the basic investment in a warehouse and equipment, handling distribution to our present customers would begin at about $35,000 a year—everything included. That's figured on the basis of distribution to our present customers. Adding the pet food shipments, as long as they're going to the same customers, would add very little to those operating costs. When we start taking on new customers in new locations, however, operating costs are going to increase."

"All right, then," Leon said. "We seem to have three alternatives. Let's get all the facts together and put them before the management committee."

Questions

State the advantages and disadvantages, both financially and in terms of the future of the company, of each of the alternatives that Spring Foods may choose from. The three alternatives are as follows:

1. To leave the distribution of all its products, including the new pet food line, to the chains.
2. To sell the pet food through a rack jobber.
3. To set up its own distribution system.

Marketing Research

UNIT 6

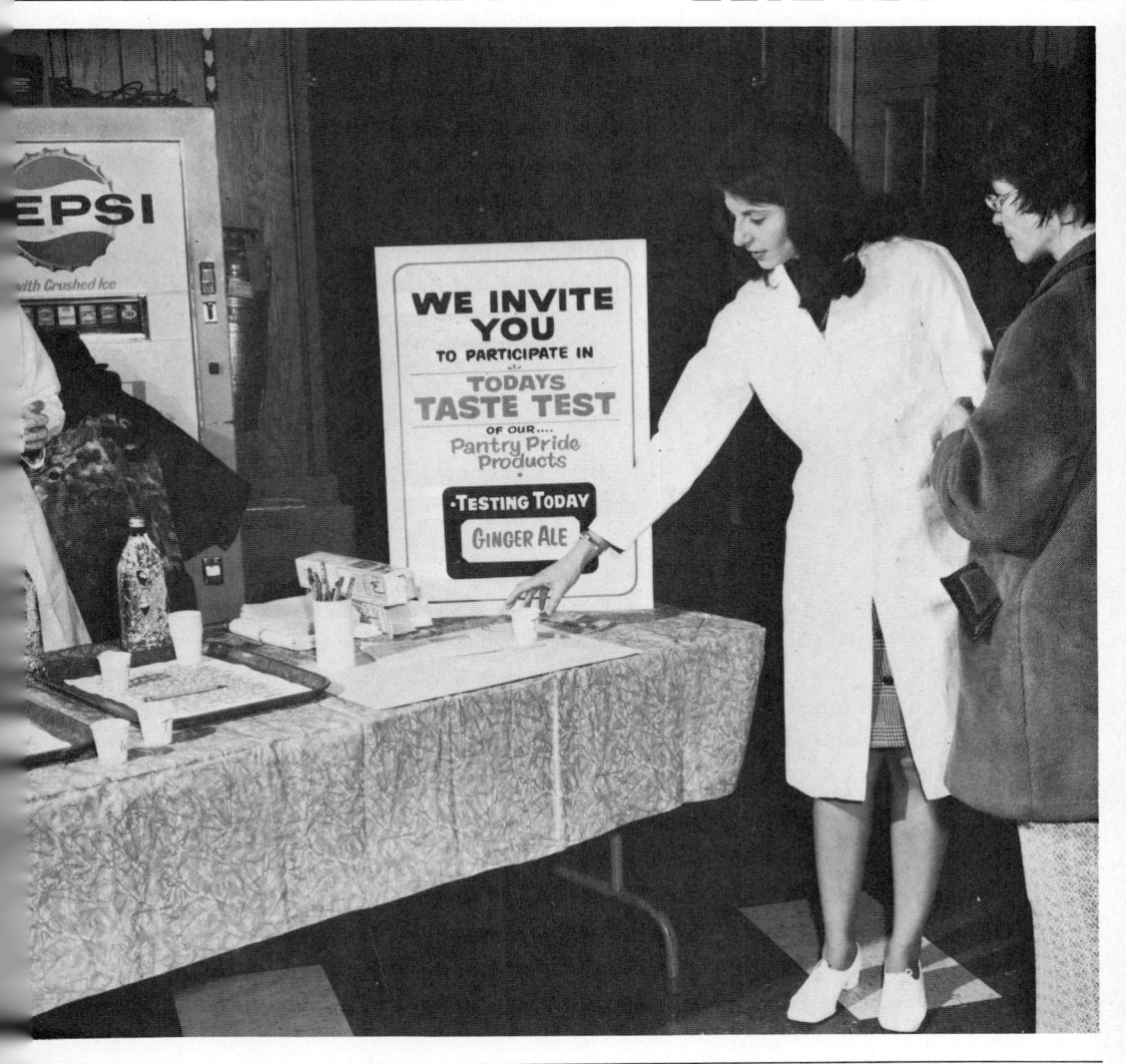

part 20

The Importance of Marketing Research

YOUR GOAL

Given a marketing problem involving one or more local retailers, determine how marketing research could aid in solving the problem.

In a bright, cheerful, windowless conference room deep inside a large office building, a group of people were gathered around a table. The walls of the room were covered with displays of wool sportswear, samples of the company's products. On the table were a half-dozen sport shirts. Examining the shirts were the company's marketing director, the sales manager, the advertising manager, and the marketing research manager.

"We want these to become big business for us," the marketing director said as he examined a shirt. "They're the first product we've ever offered that isn't made of wool. That means they're our way into what is a new market for us. Research shows that the market for sportswear made of man-made fibers isn't just a temporary thing—it's here to stay, it's big, and it's growing. Our woolens will continue to be important to us, but it's time we got a share of the market for man-made fabrics, too."

"They have a quality look, all right," the sales manager said. "Should fit in neatly with our other products, even though they aren't wool. According to the research reports, though, we're going to have to push hard to get a piece of that market. There's plenty of competition in that market, and we're known only for woolens."

"We can handle it," the advertising manager said. "Those reports showed that the best way to sell the shirts is by stressing both quality and ease of care. You know, 'Looks like wool, feels like wool, but washes like a handkerchief'—that kind of thing. I've got a folder of promotion ideas here."

"All right," the marketing director said, "let's get down to work and see if we can map out a plan to show to the board of directors this Friday."

The discussion of those executives illustrates an important point: In today's increasingly competitive marketing world, more decisions are being made on the basis of marketing research results. "Research" is the careful study of a subject; thus "marketing research" is the careful study of a marketing subject. According to a more detailed definition given by the American Marketing Association, *marketing research* is "the gathering, recording, and analyzing of all facts about problems relating to the transfer and sale of goods and services from the producer to the consumer."

Every business does some marketing research, although the research is often informal. The manager of a small diner studies customer demand to decide whether he should add barbecued beef to his menu or stick to hot dogs, hamburgers, and pizza. The service station owner keeps a record of the requests for car-washing service to help him decide whether to add this service. A shoe-store manager thinks it would be good for business to give toys to toddlers, and he watches to see if this practice pays off in more sales and happier customers. These are forms of marketing research.

The larger the business, the more detailed and elaborate its marketing research activities. Firms such as General Motors, Du Pont, and Procter & Gamble spend millions of dollars on marketing research each year. They not only have their own large marketing research staffs, but they also hire the services of independent marketing research organizations.

However, any marketing research, whether done informally by a small organization or formally by a large organization, takes time and costs money. It is worth the cost only when the results of the research are used in practical ways to help improve a business.

KINDS OF MARKETING RESEARCH

Marketing research activities can provide vital information about the potential market for a product and about customer likes and dislikes, sales trends, and the effectiveness of advertising. To obtain this information, businesses often use various kinds of marketing research. Four of these kinds are market research, sales research, product research, and advertising research.

Marketing research consists of four types of research activities, each appropriate to a different kind of marketing problem.

Market Research

The study of the nature and characteristics of a market is called *market research*. (Note that market research is one kind of marketing research.) Through market research the marketer can determine whether his products are likely to sell successfully in a particular area.

For example, a marketer of outboard motors who is considering selling his product in southern California would want to know certain facts about the area. He would want to know whether the climate is mild the year round, whether the area has many lakes, and whether boating is a popular sport in the area.

Similarly, a marketer who is considering selling his line of snowmobiles in the East would want to know the frequency of snowfalls in this region, the average number of inches of each snowfall, and the months during which the heaviest snowfalls usually occur.

By using market research to obtain such information, the marketer can accomplish a more effective job of planning his advertising program and his sales efforts.

Sales Research

A question often asked by the marketer is "How does my product sell in comparison to my competitor's?" Automobile manufacturers, insurance companies, cosmetics distributors, retail stores, and food processors all keep careful track of their competitive position through sales research. *Sales research* is the study of sales data.

For example, each Fanny Farmer candy store learns through sales research how many people in its area buy chocolate candy regularly, what percent of those customers buy their candy from Fanny Farmer, and what percent prefer the candy made by competitors. With such information the Fanny Farmer managers can take the necessary action if they are not getting their expected share of business. Such action might involve the arrangement of a more effective window display, a new and more colorful package design, or possibly a new type of chocolate.

Sales research also involves a careful study of a company's own sales figures. Are sales up? Is it a real increase, or have expenses increased even more rapidly? Are sales in line with the sales estimates? If not, why not? If a product showed one rate of sales last year and another rate of sales this year, how should future sales be forecast? The answer to each one of these questions can help a marketer improve his operations.

Product Research

New products are designed and old products are modified every year in the laboratories of American businesses. Before these new or changed products are manufactured in large quantities, however, product research is done to see how consumers are likely to accept them. *Product research* is the study of consumer reactions to a product.

Sometimes the reactions of consumers toward a product are totally negative, in which case the product is changed drastically or abandoned entirely. For example, at one time a salt company decided to produce a salt-based toothpaste because salt has cleansing properties. Preliminary research by the manufacturer showed that those people tested were enthusiastic about the sample toothpaste. This research, however, had been conducted among the employees of the salt company! When an independent organization tested nonemployees, the results showed overwhelmingly that people disliked the taste of the new toothpaste, and plans for marketing it were abandoned.

In another case, a well-known wax company planned to market a new and more durable floor polish. Research showed that the new polish tended to yellow light-colored linoleum and vinyl floors and that consumers would object to this feature. By eliminating the product's yellowing qualities, the company made it suitable for the market.

These panelists are tasting different brands of instant coffee and indicating their preferences without knowing which brands are being tested.

Courtesy Consumer Reports

Advertising Research

A study conducted to determine the effectiveness of a company's advertising is called *advertising research.* The following example illustrates how valuable this form of research can be in providing information about a company's advertising efforts.

At one time the Greyhound Corporation stressed only low fares in its advertising. When the company surveyed its riders to determine the effectiveness of its advertising in attracting new customers, it learned that its riders traveled by Greyhound not only because of the low fares but also because of Greyhound's use of the new express highways and its frequent departure times. Furthermore, Greyhound riders stressed the convenience of taking the bus instead of driving their own cars. Once Greyhound knew the real reasons that people had for riding its buses—low fares, fast service, frequent departures, freedom from the strain of driving—the company undertook a completely new advertising program. The program centered on the slogan "Go Greyhound and leave the driving to us."

Most retailers keep scrapbooks of their advertising efforts. They paste their ads in the scrapbooks and note next to each ad such information as when it appeared, how much it cost, and the sales just before and immediately after the ad appeared. The scrapbooks not only serve as treasure houses of ideas for the marketer, but they also tell the marketers which types of ads have proved the most successful.

THE PROBLEM-SOLVING PROCESS

When a company decides to undertake marketing research, it usually does so because it faces a problem. The problem may be a decline in sales or the need to develop new products to meet competition. The company uses marketing research to help it solve the problem. There is a definite procedure that is followed in marketing research to solve problems. It involves these five steps:

1. Identify the problem and establish the goal of the research.
2. Develop a research plan for achieving the goal.
3. Collect information about the problem.
4. Analyze the information.
5. Apply the results of the research to the problem.

The first two steps—identifying the problem, establishing the goal, and developing the research plan—are called preliminary research. *Preliminary research,* then, is the process of identifying a problem and devising a plan for solving the problem. These two steps are discussed in this part.

The next two steps—collecting information about the problem and analyzing that information—are called formal research. *Formal research* is the process of collecting and analyzing information about a problem. These two steps are discussed in Part 21.

The final step involves implementing the results of the research. This step is discussed in Part 22.

Identifying the Problem and Setting the Goal

The goal of a company's marketing research is always to increase profits or avoid losses. But the goal of a particular marketing research project—that is, one part of a total marketing research program—is to solve a certain marketing problem. For example, the purpose of one marketing research project might be to determine how consumers like a new type of shoe that keeps a shine without polishing. Another project might try to find out how customers like a disposable window-washing cloth that contains its own glass cleaner. Although the specific goal of each project would be to determine consumer acceptance of a particular product, both projects would be undertaken with the ultimate goal of making more sales, and thus increasing profits, for the company.

Sometimes a company knows only that its sales are falling off and wants to find out why this is happening. No research activity, however, could be set up around the goal of finding out why sales are declining; the objective has to be more specific.

When a businessman is faced with declining sales, marketing research might be useful in helping him find a solution to the problem.

Courtesy National Petroleum News

Consider Mr. Owens, owner and operator of a drive-in hamburger stand, who sells hamburgers, french fries, coffee, and soft drinks. He is faced with one big problem: Not enough people are stopping at his drive-in, so that his sales are declining.

Mr. Owens could look at his empty parking lot all day and wonder why his sales are falling off without getting any closer to a solution. But once he has asked himself, "Is my hamburger as good as the one served at Chili Joe's?" he has set a specific goal for a marketing research activity—to find out whether Chili Joe's serves a better hamburger. Or he could ask himself, "Do people think my stand is unattractive or unclean?" Again, he has set a specific goal— to gather opinions about the appearance of his stand.

To establish a specific goal for a marketing problem, then, a marketer must focus his attention on a specific marketing problem. And, once he decides how to solve that problem, he helps to answer the important question "How can I increase profits or avoid losses?"

Developing the Research Plan

When a marketer has decided on a specific goal, he must choose the methods that will bring him the information he needs. If he runs a small business, he will likely do his own research. If Mr. Owens's goal was to compare Chili Joe's hamburger with his own, he could simply drive over to Chili Joe's, have a hamburger, and compare the difference in appearance and taste.

Research planning for a larger project, however, is not that simple. A *research plan* is a step-by-step outline of everything that is to be done during a research project. It lists the kinds of formal research that are to be done, when they are to be done, and in what order. It specifies the kind of personnel needed to do the work. It specifies the amount of money to be budgeted for the project and details how it is to be spent.

A research plan, then, usually consists of a set of lists, specifications, and schedules. The marketer or the person in charge of the research project has a master outline of the entire plan. Each person involved is given the individual lists, specifications, or schedules that concern him.

Just as all good plans do, a good research plan serves both as a guide and as a control. The plan shows each person what is to be done and indicates that each phase is kept within the limits of the budget.

When the marketer has identified the problem and set up the research plan, his preliminary work is done. He is then ready to do the formal research.

◘ YOUR MARKETING VOCABULARY

On a separate sheet of paper define each of the following marketing terms; then use each term in a sentence.

Advertising research
Formal research
Market research
Marketing research
Preliminary research
Product research
Research plan
Sales research

◘ FOR REVIEW AND DISCUSSION

1. In today's increasingly competitive marketing world, what is the role of marketing research?
2. What does the term "research" mean?
3. Does every business do some kind of marketing research? If so, what kind of marketing research might a manager of a small diner do?
4. How does marketing research justify its cost?
5. What vital information can marketing research activities provide?
6. How can a large chain of candy stores such as Fanny Farmer use marketing research to determine its competitive position?
7. Give an example of how marketing research might lead a company to decide not to market a new product.
8. List the steps that a marketer must follow in solving a marketing research problem.
9. What is the goal of a company's marketing research?
10. How does the research plan serve both as a guide and a control?

◻ **ANALYZING MARKETING CONCEPTS**

1. Many sources of information are available for marketing research. Prepare a form like the one below and list the following types of businesses in the left-hand column: (a) shoe store, (b) television dealer, (c) service station, (d) life insurance agency, (e) motel, (f) wholesale automotive equipment dealer, (g) furniture wholesaler, (h) ice cream manufacturer, (i) car manufacturer. In the middle column, write a research question that might concern the business listed in the left-hand column. In the right-hand column, describe a research activity that might be used to answer the research question.

Business	Research Question	Research Activity
Example: Small diner	Should we add barbecued beef to the menu?	Our waitresses will tally the number of customer requests for barbecued beef.

2. Certain products and services can be marketed more successfully in one area than in another. Prepare a form like the one below. Then list ten products or services that you feel could not be marketed successfully in your area because of the area's climate, geography, or customs or because of lack of customer interest. In the right-hand column give the reason why the product would be unsuccessful.

Product or Service	Reason for Poor Market Potential
Example: Water skis	No lakes and only a shallow river within 35 miles.

◻ **MARKETING PROJECT 20**
Initiating Marketing Research

Project Goal: Given a marketing problem involving one or more local retailers, determine how marketing research could aid in solving the problem.

Action: With the guidance of your teacher, interview a local retailer. Ask him to discuss a marketing problem either within his business or within the local business community. Ask him to suggest alternative ways of reaching solutions to the problem and to indicate how marketing research could aid in achieving each solution. Write a preliminary plan for conducting this marketing research.

part 21

Collecting and Analyzing Data

YOUR GOAL

Given a problem requiring marketing research, identify four marketing research activities to be used in collecting data about the problem.

In operating a business, many important marketing decisions must be made. These decisions are more likely to be right when a businessman has accurate information about his product and his market. Gathering this information is the job of marketing research people who study markets, consumers' reactions to new products, and selling and advertising methods. Marketing research data—when carefully collected, summarized, and interpreted—help the businessman determine business trends, product acceptance, potential markets, and the effectiveness of selling and advertising efforts.

COLLECTING THE DATA

The word "data" means facts or information. In research work, data can be classified as primary or secondary. Data that are gathered by the researcher himself for current use are called *primary data*. Data that have already been collected by someone else for another purpose but which may be of use for the task at hand are called *secondary data*. The words "primary" and "secondary" in no way refer to the value or usefulness of the data. They simply identify the source of the data.

Primary and secondary data can be further classified as either internal or external. Data collected from sources within the company itself are called *internal data*. Data collected from sources outside the company are called *external data*.

Most marketing research involves collecting both primary and secondary data. The nature of the research project determines how much and what kinds of each are collected. Each type of data has its own characteristics as well as its own advantages and disadvantages.

Primary Data

Randolph Brown, the manager of the Lucky 7 Supermarket, is faced with a problem. Two new supermarkets have recently been built in his area, and Mr. Brown is concerned that the increased competition will hurt his business. Since Mr. Brown lacks the money to expand his business, he feels that offering special services to his customers may be his best means of meeting that competition. His first idea is to offer a home-delivery service, allowing customers to telephone their orders and have them delivered to their homes for a small service charge. Mr. Brown, however, operates on a tight budget. Therefore, before renting a delivery truck and hiring a driver, he wants to be reasonably sure that the service will pay for itself. He also wants to know whether this is the kind of service that will keep his present customers and perhaps attract new ones. Thus, Monday morning, Mr. Brown is stationed at the check-out counter, notebook in hand, asking his customers questions such as these:

- Would you be interested in a home-delivery service?
- Would you like to telephone your order, have it delivered, and not come to the store at all?
- Would you prefer to do your own shopping in the store and then have your purchases delivered?
- If you prefer a telephone-order service, would you want to have a price list mailed to you every week to help you with your ordering?
- How often would you use such a service?
- Would you be willing to pay a service charge of $1.50 on all telephone orders under $20, and $1 on all orders over $20?
- If you prefer to come into the store, shop for your order, and then have it delivered, does a delivery charge of 50 cents on all orders seem fair?
- All orders placed before noon will be delivered by 4 p.m. the same day. Would this be satisfactory?

From the information he will gather, Mr. Brown will be able to estimate the desirability of instituting a home-delivery and telephone-order service. If the customers' reactions indicate that such a service would not be popular, Mr. Brown will have to find another way to keep his present customers and attract new ones.

In the example above, Mr. Brown served as the researcher in his own marketing research project. He gathered his primary data through one of the commonly used methods of collecting primary data: the survey. The other methods are the panel, experimentation, and observation.

The Survey. One of the most widely used ways of obtaining primary data is the survey. The *survey* is a method of collecting opinions by questioning a limited number of people chosen from a larger group. The people to be surveyed are chosen as representative of the larger group and are called a sample. The use of a sample in conducting a survey is necessary because it is usually too costly to contact every person who could give information on a research subject. The people included in a survey may be chosen at random, or according to specific characteristics, such as age, sex, education, or income.

The personal interview is very useful in gathering primary data.

Part 21 / Collecting and Analyzing Data / **247**

For example, suppose the executive of an automobile-insurance company wants to know how his firm is regarded by its 500,000 customers in such matters as cost, service, and dependability. He cannot possibly question every customer. Instead, he selects a random sample of about 500 on the assumption that the answers of this group will be a fairly accurate indication of the opinions of the rest of his customers.

There are several types of marketing research surveys. Three common types are the personal interview, the telephone interview, and the mail questionnaire.

Probably the most effective type of survey is the personal interview, in which the researcher questions a person face to face. Although the personal interview is the most expensive type of survey, it often yields the most information. Besides obtaining answers to his questions, the interviewer can gather additional information from watching the expressions and reactions of the person being interviewed.

The telephone interview can be conducted more rapidly and less expensively than the personal interview, but often it does not yield as much information. This is because many people are reluctant to give information freely to someone they do not know and cannot see.

The mail questionnaire is a list of questions that is mailed to the people to be surveyed. The recipients are asked to answer the questions and mail the questionnaire back to the researcher. When a group to be surveyed is widely scattered geographically or when the marketing researcher wants a cross section of opinion from the entire country, a mail survey may be cheaper and more convenient to conduct than either a personal or telephone survey would be.

Mail surveys, however, require simple and clearly worded questions. Often people are slow in returning them to survey headquarters, and many people do not return them at all. Thus, the response rate to the mail questionnaire is typically low.

The Panel. When it is necessary to study the buying habits of people over a period of time, researchers use a panel. A *panel* is a selected group of people who serve as subjects of a continuing survey. At one time the Chicago *Tribune* made effective use of a panel in its consumer research. The panel consisted of 576 families that kept a diary of all grocery and pharmaceutical purchases. They recorded the brand name, size, price, and place of purchase of these items. The diaries were collected every week and summaries of their contents were sent to companies advertising in the *Tribune.* The advertisers receiving this information were thus able to judge the appeal of their products, the effectiveness of their advertising, and the strength of the competition.

Because a consumer panel records buying patterns over a long period of time, it can provide valuable information about sales trends and customer loyalty to certain brands and stores. In radio and television, many programming decisions are made on the basis of the research of radio and television rating organizations, which sometimes use panels to determine the listening and viewing habits of selected audiences.

Experimentation. A form of research involving a scale model or representation of a real marketing situation is called *experimentation*. All elements of the real marketing situation are present, but each one is scaled down in size. Experimentation thus enables the researcher to judge the effectiveness of his marketing efforts on a small scale before attempting a full-scale operation.

For example, a retailer may want to find out whether an advertisement is more effective in color than in black and white. He prepares two circulars — one in black and white and the other in color. The color circular is sent to one group of customers, and the black-and-white circular is sent to a similar group of customers.

An order reply form, coded to identify the circular that the customer received, is included in both mailings. If the response to the color circular is much greater than that to the black-and-white circular, the retailer can justify the added expense of using color in his mail promotions.

Experimentation is carried on constantly in business. Probably the most important use of experimentation is in test marketing. *Test marketing* is the marketing of goods to consumers in several carefully selected areas before the goods are released on a wide scale. Through test marketing a marketer may determine the appeal of a proposed package design or consumers' acceptance of an entirely new product.

Observation. The process of collecting information about customers, product acceptance, and sales effectiveness by watching the actions of people without actually interviewing them is called *observation*.

Customers may be observed while shopping for products. An investigator could note whether they compare prices before selecting a brand, read the labels, or hesitate before making selections. In much the same way, a retail store that wants to know how well its sales staff is performing may hire a marketing research firm to find out. The representatives of the firm would go into the store posing as customers. In this way they would be able to observe the selling effectiveness of the salespeople, their knowledge of the merchandise, and the brands they seem to favor in their selling efforts.

Customers may also be observed by mechanical or electronic means. For example, in a retail store a hidden camera may be used to record how carefully customers read brand labels, or how many customers stop to look, handle, or buy a product. In a home a mechanical device (called an audimeter) may be attached to a family's TV sets to record how often the sets are used and to what stations they are tuned. In short, mechanical or electronic devices may be used to gather data about customers and consumers that would otherwise have to be collected by less convenient or more expensive methods.

Secondary Data

When a marketing researcher makes use of information that has been collected by someone else for another purpose, he is using secondary data. For example, suppose the Super Cola Company wants to set up four distributorships in Wisconsin, each to have a territory that represents a fair division of the state in terms of population and average income. The company's marketing manager uses secondary data to decide how to divide the state. He consults the U.S. Census population reports for the state of Wisconsin. He also consults reports for each county within the state, and those for the large cities. He determines that the population is denser in the southeastern end of the state and along the shores of Lake Michigan. Because the marketing manager knows that family income is an important factor in sales, he next consults state publications that list average family income for each county. He also studies sales reports of the soft-drink industry to determine the probable size

Courtesy Today's Secretary
The researcher may obtain valuable secondary data from company records.

250 / Unit 6 / Marketing Research

of the Wisconsin soft-drink market. Secondary data have given him all the details he needs to do the job.

Using secondary data offers several advantages. Usually the information is considerably less expensive to collect, and it can be collected easily. In some cases, information that cannot be collected in primary form is available in secondary form. For example, no individual marketer could collect age and income statistics about every single individual in the country; yet this information is collected by and available from the federal government.

On the other hand, there are certain disadvantages in using secondary data. Because the data have been collected for another purpose, any particular group of facts may contain some information that the researcher does not need, and may not contain some information that he does need. Furthermore, because secondary data have been collected by someone else, the researcher cannot be sure how carefully the collection was made and thus how accurate the data are.

Important sources of secondary data include company records, libraries, outside organizations, and the government. To use any of these sources effectively, however, the researcher must have identified his problem, established his goals, and developed a plan for achieving his goals.

Company Records. Usually the first source that a researcher checks for data is the company itself. Company records include salesmen's reports, customers' invoices, and complaints and suggestions received from customers. These sources provide information about past sales records, the size of the market, and customers' reactions to the company's products or services.

Company information should be easy to find. However, this is not always true. Even though everyone in a company is ideally working for the same goal—the success of the company—sometimes one department may not be cooperative and let another department examine the information in its files. At other times, people may simply lose track of information they already have. Because of these possibilities, more and more marketers are placing all useful information where it is readily available to everyone in the company.

Libraries. Many marketing research problems can be solved by using material in a library, whether it be a library maintained by a school, a university, a city, or a company. The modern, well-equipped library carries a wide assortment of magazines, periodicals, and up-to-date reports that are of value to those doing marketing research.

Outside Organizations. Advertising agencies, the media they serve, and marketing research firms are among the outside organizations that are good sources of secondary data.

Both advertising agencies and advertising media are likely to have their own research departments. These departments concentrate their research on the customers reached by advertising. The research reports they prepare are usually available to any interested person.

Marketing research firms are of two types: the syndicated data firms and the consulting firms. The syndicated data firms specialize in collecting certain types of information and then selling that information on a regular basis. They generally collect information about brand recognition, public opinion, and fashion trends. The consulting firms undertake specific jobs for clients. They are not direct sources of secondary data but can be hired to collect them.

The Government. The largest single source of secondary data is the federal government. Surveys by the Bureau of the Census provide the foundation of marketing knowledge in this country. These surveys are supplemented by research done by other bureaus and agencies of the federal government,

The Statistical Abstract *is widely used in business research.*

such as the Bureau of Labor Statistics and the Federal Power Commission.

The information collected by the federal government is available at a very low cost to anyone who wants it. Perhaps the greatest bargain in the secondary data field is the *Statistical Abstract*. This annual publication of the U.S. Department of Commerce consists of approximately 1,000 pages of summarized statistics about the country.

PREPARING THE DATA

Earlier in this part we discussed Mr. Brown, who collected the data he needed by standing at the check-out counter and asking his customers questions. When Mr. Brown had filled his notebook with the customers' answers, he still was not ready to make his decision, because the information in his notebook was raw data—a jumble of facts, opinions, and figures. The data still had to be checked and classified before they could be analyzed.

Checking for Accuracy

After the raw data have been collected, they can be checked for accuracy by a two-step procedure. First, a spot check is made to see whether the data were collected properly. Second, several facts or figures are checked to verify that they were recorded correctly.

If the data were collected in the way specified, and if the facts and figures chosen for verification prove to be accurately recorded, then it is assumed that the data are accurate enough to be useful.

Classifying

The next job is to organize the data into meaningful categories. These categories are usually decided upon at the time the research plan is made, although some changes may be made after examination of the data begins.

For example, suppose a researcher is to classify the data obtained from women who were questioned about their purchases of hair-care products. He might first classify the answers according to the age and hair color of the customers, as had been decided when the survey was arranged. However, after looking at some of the answers, the researcher might decide to add one more classification: women who use tint or dye on their hair.

The grouping of those customers is an example of "qualitative classification," which is a classification made according to differences in kind. The other common type of grouping is called "quantitative classification," which is a classification made according to differences in amount. In using quantitative classification, the researcher would group the women who were asked about their purchases of hair-care products according to the amount of money spent by each customer. One group would contain the answers of those who spent less than $2; another, the answers of those who spent between $2 and $5; and so forth.

Once the data have been checked for accuracy and classified, they are no longer considered raw data. They are now ready to be analyzed.

ANALYZING THE DATA

To "analyze" means to study the various parts of something in order to understand the whole. Marketing research began with a problem to be solved. That problem was divided into parts, and data were collected on each part. Now the data about each part of the problem must be examined and interpreted by the researcher. His job is to determine from the data a possible solution or several possible solutions to the problem.

Suppose a fashion magazine wants to know whether to aim its editorial content at women between 18 and 35 or women between 35 and 55. The magazine does a survey among a representative group of women of both age groups. The survey shows that women between 18 and 35 spend an average of 12 percent more on apparel and 46 percent more on cosmetics than do women between 35 and 55. This is true even though the family incomes of the women aged 35 and over tend to be higher than those of the younger women. Based on this information, the magazine decides to aim most of its editorial content at the younger women.

While collecting and analyzing data, the researcher must take steps to eliminate all forms of bias. In marketing research, "bias" is a prejudice for or against an idea or object. In spite of a researcher's determination to be fair, bias can creep in through a number of ways. For example, a person who is being interviewed about a product may prefer a particular brand because she has used it for a long time and has never tried the competing brands. To minimize bias when interviewing, the researcher may try to conceal the identity of the product.

Sometimes the problem of eliminating bias is made more difficult when the researcher himself has certain preferences related to the product or idea being researched. He may deliberately influence answers for or against a product or idea or misrecord them. Therefore, a researcher should always be on guard against his own personal bias.

The job of collecting and analyzing data is not a simple task, nor is it necessarily inexpensive. If the marketing researcher gathers and studies biased or unnecessary data, he has wasted both time and money. For this reason, the researcher must be competent and objective and able to determine what data are appropriate to solve the problem.

◆ YOUR MARKETING VOCABULARY

On a separate sheet of paper define each of the following marketing terms; then use each term in a sentence.

Experimentation *Primary data*
External data *Secondary data*
Internal data *Survey*
Observation *Test marketing*
Panel

◆ FOR REVIEW AND DISCUSSION

1. How can reliable research data help the marketer?
2. Of the three types of surveys, which type can yield the most information? Why? Which type is the most expensive?
3. What are the advantages of telephone surveys? What are their disadvantages?
4. When are mail questionnaires likely to be used?
5. Explain the use of a consumer panel.
6. What is probably the most important use of experimentation?
7. Must observation always be conducted in person by the researcher? Explain your answer.
8. List four important sources of secondary data.
9. What steps are involved in preparing data?
10. What does the term "bias" mean in marketing research? How can bias be controlled?

◆ ANALYZING MARKETING CONCEPTS

1. Assume that you manage a record shop. One of your major problems is deciding which records to buy and how many of each to stock. Prepare a form like the one below, and list primary and secondary sources of information that will aid you in making these marketing decisions.

Primary Source	Secondary Source
Example: Your own sales records.	A published list of the nation's best-selling records.

2. You want to be sure that your goods and services are satisfying the customers of your record shop. Therefore, you decide to conduct an informal survey of their likes and dislikes about your business. Develop a list of ten survey questions to ask your customers when they make a purchase.

MARKETING PROJECT 21
Collecting Research Data

Project Goal: Given a problem requiring marketing research, identify four marketing research activities to be used in collecting data about the problem.

Action: Identify four marketing research activities that can be used to collect data concerning the research problem you dealt with in Project 20. Determine whether each activity involves primary data or secondary data. For primary data, identify the methods to be used in collecting the data. For secondary data, list the sources from which the data can be obtained.

Prepare a form like the one below, and write your answers in the appropriate columns. Use a check mark to indicate whether the research activity involves the collection of primary or secondary data. Be sure to state your research problem at the beginning of the form.

Marketing Research Activity	Kind of Data		Collection Method Used (for Primary Data)	Source of Secondary Data
	Primary	Secondary		

part 22

Preparing the Research Report

YOUR GOALS

1. Given the collected data for a marketing research project, write a formal research report.
2. Given a research report, organize an oral presentation and illustrate it with tables, charts, graphs, or other relevant materials.

After the data have been collected, prepared, and analyzed, they still must be assembled into a final, usable form—a research report. A *research report* is a document that contains the results of research and is the basis for action. Only after the research report has been prepared can the research project be considered complete.

If a research project is of substantial size, then a formal report is usually prepared in written form. In addition, the marketing executives concerned may want to hear an oral presentation of the report as well.

THE WRITTEN REPORT

One of the most important skills that a researcher can develop is that of writing a clear, concise, well-organized research report. To do this, he must know the elements that make up a research report and the way in which these elements should be organized. The following are the elements of the research report in the order in which they should appear:

- Title page
- Table of contents
- Introduction (purpose, scope, and goals of the project)
- Organization of the project
- Methods
- Results
- Conclusions
- Recommendations
- Appendix (including any tables, charts, graphs, and pictures)
- Bibliography (a list of the secondary sources of information)

The body of the report can be divided into two parts. The first part (introduction, organization, and methods) tells what was done and why. It explains the background of the project and the activities that took place. To someone unfamiliar with research work, it may seem unnecessary for a research report to go into such detail about the purpose, scope, goals, and organization of the project, as well as the methods used in research. But that information is always valuable to anyone who reads the report.

The second part of the report (results, conclusions, and recommendations) gives details about what was learned and may include the conclusions and recommendations of the researchers. (To speed up the decision-making process, sometimes the recommendations are placed after the statement of the problem in the introduction.)

The results of research are frequently called *research findings*. In the research report these results, or findings, are given as clearly and precisely as possible. Often findings are presented in tables, charts, or graphs that dramatize the major points of the study.

The conclusions in the research report are summaries and interpretations based on the findings. The researcher who has a knowledge of marketing as well as research techniques will usually include his recommendations.

Supporting material is included at the end of the report. The kind of supporting material included depends upon the project. In one project the supporting material might consist of maps of certain areas; in another project, it might consist of a detailed description of the procedures for tabulating data.

Near the end of the report is the appendix. The appendix may include a sample of the questionnaires used, a sample of the instructions given to interviewers, and a sample of every letter or other piece of written material distributed during the course of the project. Finally, there is the bibliography, which lists all the secondary sources of information.

The oral report should be both informative and interesting.

THE ORAL PRESENTATION

While most formal research projects are reported in written form, sometimes researchers are asked to give the results of the project orally before a group. Marketing people are busy, and decisions need to be made quickly. Often these decisions must be made by groups or committees. By making an oral presentation of the findings to the group, the researchers can help speed up the decision-making process.

An oral presentation of the research report provides those present with detailed information about the project and its results. In addition, the chief researchers are usually on hand to answer any questions the decision makers may have.

In an oral presentation the findings, conclusions, and recommendations are usually given the most emphasis, and only a brief outline of the background and activities of the project is included. Frequently, charts, slides, or films are used to illustrate the findings. This gives the group the information it wants quickly and enables it to move right on to decision making. In case any person wants more background information or more details about the results, the researcher usually provides everyone at the presentation with a copy of the written report for reference.

When preparing the written research report or presenting it orally, the researcher must be aware of bias just as he is when collecting and analyzing the data. He may, for instance, be prejudiced in favor of a particular solution to a problem. Thus, he may emphasize in the report those data that favor that solution and give considerably less attention to those data that favor other possible solutions. Because of this, it is important that marketing managers be aware of the possibility of bias when they evaluate the research studies presented to them.

ACTING ON THE PRESENTATION

Marketing research costs money, and the marketer considers it worth the cost only when the results of the project can be used to help the company. Thus the conclusions of the project must be acted upon.

Here is how the Shop-Rite supermarket organization set up a research project and then implemented the results of that research. The project involved the establishment of a supermarket in a small town. The town was typical of communities that were settled long before city planning boards helped plan and organize the growth of cities. The town had the usual narrow main street, with a small "downtown" shopping area that consisted of a men's clothing store, a variety store, a butcher shop, a drugstore, a shoe store, several small grocery stores, and a stationery store. When supermarkets came along, they were built on the edges of the town because there was no room for them in the downtown shopping area. Although customers were delighted with the new supermarkets, they wished they could combine their downtown shopping chores with their supermarket shopping.

Then the Shop-Rite food chain came to look over the town for a possible location for a supermarket. The management of Shop-Rite felt that if it could provide a supermarket near the town's main shopping center, the store would attract as customers the many people who prefer to combine their food shopping with other kinds of shopping. But there was no available land. Part of the area surrounding the downtown shopping center was residential, and some of it was industrial. All the land was in use.

Shop-Rite's research staff went to work, and their research uncovered a good possibility: Just behind the downtown shopping area was a large lumberyard. Its only building was a decrepit wooden shed; the rest of the property was used for open storage. With very little work, this property could be cleared for a building site.

Then came the action: Shop-Rite executives approached the owner of the lumberyard, offering to buy his land and pay the costs of transferring his business to another part of town. When the owner agreed, Shop-Rite began construction of the supermarket.

Today the area is a huge shopping plaza, with the new supermarket and generous parking space. As expected, customers are attracted to Shop-Rite because of its central location, where they can combine their supermarket shopping with their downtown shopping. Only through careful research of many factors—location of competing businesses, convenience to shoppers, availability of parking space, availability of land for purchase—was Shop-Rite able to make a decision that led to outstanding success for the new store.

STUDENT RESEARCH

Marketing research can be an exciting adventure not only for professionals but also for students. Students have shown that they can conduct worthwhile marketing research, and some of their projects have influenced marketing practices in their communities.

In one chapter of the Distributive Education Clubs of America (an organization of vocational marketing students, often referred to as DECA), the members were concerned about declining sales in their town's shops. Their town was located near a state line, and the neighboring state, unlike their own state, did not have a sales tax. The students' first guess was that shoppers went to the neighboring state to shop in order to avoid the sales tax. They set out to do some research on ways and means of bringing shoppers back to their community despite the sales tax.

However, the students learned by surveying local residents that avoidance of a sales tax was not the only reason shoppers left their own community.

These DECA members are compiling the results of their research.

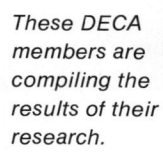

Courtesy DECA-Distributive Education Clubs of America

The out-of-state stores, they discovered, were open late four nights a week, compared with two nights for the local stores. The out-of-state stores carried a wider variety of brands and offered more liberal credit terms. They also provided larger parking areas. The DECA group compiled the results of their survey, tabulated the information, and gave a clear summary of their findings to the local chamber of commerce.

It was not long before the local merchants instituted some of the changes proposed in the DECA market survey—longer shopping hours, a new credit plan, and a wider selection of merchandise.

Another student project aided an entire industry. A DECA chapter in Iowa conducted research on consumers' opinions about certain foods, especially dairy products. When the survey was completed and the results tabulated and summarized, these DECA members sent a copy to the state's dairy council, which found the results valuable in increasing sales of dairy products. The DECA chapter received not only state but national recognition for its marketing research project.

DECA sponsors three types of research activities for high school students. They consist of two types of Creative Marketing Projects and one activity called Studies in Marketing.

Creative Marketing Projects

Activities conducted by a local group or chapter of DECA members in cooperation with Sales and Marketing Executives International (SMEI) are called *Creative Marketing Projects*. SMEI is a professional organization of sales executives.

The first type of Creative Marketing Project is the activity project. Although not a formal research project, it sometimes involves research. Its goal is to bring about a measurable improvement in the local economy through increasing sales, improving services, providing more employment, increasing income, or improving shopping facilities. The activity project must be completed within the school year. Here are some of the results of successful DECA activity projects:

- Improved customer gift-wrapping service offered by a store.
- Increased availability of sales personnel in a community during peak sales periods.
- Improved public parking facilities in a business district.
- Greater student patronage of local businesses because of more effective advertising in a school newspaper.

The second type of Creative Marketing Project involves a research report. The project is a marketing study that is planned, conducted, and reported by

This member of DECA has been recognized for outstanding marketing research.

Courtesy DECA-Distributive Education Clubs of America

an entire DECA chapter. Its goal is to improve the economy of a community by finding new markets for local products, promoting the community's resources, or otherwise increasing trade. The students use the formal research techniques of collecting and analyzing data and carry the work through the preparation of the formal research report.

Listed below are some examples of research projects completed by distributive education students throughout the country. These research projects will give you some idea of the size and scope of student research studies in various communities and of the usefulness of such studies to local marketers. The project reports were displayed at DECA national leadership conferences as examples of what students can do in research.

- A study to investigate how to expand tourism.
- A survey to determine the purchasing patterns of high school students.
- A survey of the effectiveness of newspaper advertising in drawing shoppers to the central business district.
- A survey to identify the manpower resources of the community in order to attract new businesses.
- A study of the flow of traffic in a retail store.
- A survey of customer taste preferences in canned pineapple.
- A study of the safety programs of selected marketing businesses.

Studies in Marketing

Individual research activities for DECA members are called *Studies in Marketing*. These individual studies cover marketing fields such as the automotive and petroleum industries, department store merchandising, the home furnishings industry, the food industry, service enterprises, and specialty store and variety store merchandising. Students who want to explore a future career field can undertake one of these studies in the area of their interest. Listed below are some of the topics for Studies in Marketing.

- Determine the traffic patterns of customers of a given industry during selected shopping periods.
- Determine employee reactions to management practices in a given industry in a selected marketing area.
- Determine the customer services offered by a given industry in a selected marketing area.
- Determine reasons for continued customer patronage of a given industry in a selected marketing area.
- Evaluate sales techniques in a given industry in a selected marketing area.
- Determine training needs of new employees in a given industry in a selected marketing area.

DECA publishes an official handbook as well as special bulletins listing areas needing more research.

Perhaps you will have the opportunity to take part in a student marketing research project or even conduct individual research in a marketing area of your choice. You will find either activity an exciting experience.

◻ YOUR MARKETING VOCABULARY

On a separate sheet of paper define each of the following marketing terms; then use each in a sentence.

Creative Marketing Projects   *Research report*
Research findings   *Studies in Marketing*

◻ FOR REVIEW AND DISCUSSION

1. Describe the elements contained in the two parts of the body of a research report.
2. List the kind of supporting material that might be included in a research report.
3. What kind of material is included in the appendix of the research report?
4. What information is usually emphasized most in an oral presentation?

5. Why are research reports often presented orally to the decision makers?
6. Why is everyone at the oral presentation usually supplied with a copy of the written report?
7. Explain why action should always be considered a part of marketing research.
8. List and explain the three types of research activities that DECA sponsors for its members.
9. Give one example of a successful marketing research project conducted by DECA members.
10. List one topic which you feel would be a worthwhile activity for Studies in Marketing.

ANALYZING MARKETING CONCEPTS

1. If the results of marketing research are to be usable in a business, the research project must be based on specific questions. Assume that you manage a department store. Prepare a form like the one below. Then list the following areas of business research in the left-hand column: (a) merchandise, (b) salespeople, (c) merchandise displays, (d) customer services, (e) credit sales, (f) prices, (g) advertisements, (h) store location, (i) competitive stores. In the right-hand column, write a specific research question for each item listed in the left-hand column.

Area of Business Research	Research Question
Example: Customers	Where do most of our customers live?

2. Assume that you have conducted research based on the research questions you developed for Problem 1. Prepare a form like the one below. In the left-hand column, list the same research areas as in Problem 1: (a) merchandise, (b) salespeople, (c) merchandise displays, (d) customer services, (e) credit sales, (f) prices, (g) advertisements, (h) store location, (i) competitive stores. In the right-hand column, describe a marketing action that might result from your research findings.

Area of Business Research	Marketing Action Resulting From Research
Example: Customers	Might increase amount of advertising in specific newspapers in surrounding communities.

SAMPLE QUESTIONNAIRE

Characteristics of customers shopping in ____*Belk's*____ store.

Directions: For each item, place a check mark in the appropriate blank.

1. Sex:

    __✓__ a. Female   _____ b. Male

2. Age:

    _____ a. 12 to 16   __✓__ d. 30 to 49

    _____ b. 17 to 22   _____ e. 50 to 69

    _____ c. 23 to 29   _____ f. 70 or older

3. What method of transportation do you use to reach the store?

    __✓__ a. Car   _____ c. Taxi

    _____ b. Public transportation   _____ d. Other_____
                                                  (Specify)

4. How far do you travel to reach the store?

    _____ a. 1 mile or less   _____ d. 11 to 15 miles

    _____ b. 2 to 5 miles   _____ e. 16 to 25 miles

    __✓__ c. 6 to 10 miles   _____ f. 26 miles or more

5. How often do you shop at the store?

    _____ a. Four times a week   _____ d. Once a week

    _____ b. Three times a week   __✓__ e. Once every two weeks

    _____ c. Twice a week   _____ f. Once a month or less

6. What is your main reason for coming to this shopping center?

    _____ a. Availability of parking   __✓__ d. Variety of merchandise

    _____ b. Prices of merchandise   _____ e. Quality of merchandise

    _____ c. Attitude of salespeople   _____ f. Other_____
                                                  (Specify)

7. What is your favorite day of the week for shopping?

    _____ a. Monday   _____ d. Thursday

    _____ b. Tuesday   __✓__ e. Friday

    _____ c. Wednesday   _____ f. Saturday

MARKETING PROJECT 22
Preparing the Research Report

Project Goal: Given the collected data for a marketing research project, write a formal research report.

Action: If you have worked on Projects 20 and 21 and have gathered primary or secondary data on a topic, use those data to complete this project. If you have not worked on Projects 20 and 21, choose a topic with your teacher's help and proceed to collect data. If you or your teacher decide not to select an original topic, complete the following one.

Take a random sampling of about 25 customers entering a particular business in a shopping center near you. Prepare a questionnaire like the one on the opposite page. Have the questionnaire approved by your teacher.

Explain the purpose of your project to the store manager and ask for his permission to interview a number of his customers as they enter the store. Show him your questionnaire; he may have suggestions for questions to be included.

Prepare a written report summarizing your findings. Follow the outline on page 258 in writing your report.

The Product

UNIT 7

part 23

Product Planning

YOUR GOALS

1. Given a new product, describe the marketing techniques used to introduce and promote the product, and analyze its position in the market.
2. Given the four stages of the product life cycle, identify one characteristic of each stage.

The direction and control of all stages in the life of a product—from the time of its creation to the time of its removal from the company's line of products—are called *product planning.*

A decision involving the planning of a product may be the most important one the marketer makes, because his decision commits the company's money, or capital. In addition, a great deal of time and effort are needed to plan new products or to change established ones. The marketing research involved and the designing of a test product may be very expensive; manufacturing and equipment costs may be high; and inventory development, handling, and storage may become major expenses. It is easy to see why a mistake in product planning can cost millions of dollars.

The importance of product planning is closely related to the growth of technology. Manufacturers can produce more products in less time today than ever before. More new products have been introduced in the past 30 years than in all previous history. Within each product class, customers are being offered a much larger selection. This means that to remain competitive, marketers must develop new and better products.

Product planning is also important because markets are always changing. A product profitable today may not be profitable tomorrow. Because of this, marketers believe in the motto "Innovate or perish."

PRODUCT TERMS DEFINED

To discuss product planning in detail, it is necessary to define four important terms: product, product item, product line, and product mix.

A *product* is all the physical features and psychological satisfactions received by the customer. In the broadest sense, then, a product may be a service that provides satisfactions for the customer, as well as a tangible object to be sold at a profit.

A *product item* is a specific, unique product. For example, a pocket-sized AM-FM transistor radio with unique styling and design would be a product item. A product item often carries a specific name or number designation, such as the Minolta SRT-101 camera.

A *product line* is a group of similar types of product items that are closely related because they satisfy a class of customer needs, are used together, or are sold to the same customer groups. One marketer might say that he has a product line of sporting goods. His line might include golf clubs, baseball equipment, tennis rackets, and other sporting-goods items. Another marketer might consider tennis rackets alone as a product line; he would carry numerous brands, models, and sizes of tennis rackets, with prices that varied according to the quality of the product.

A *product mix* is the total of all product items and product lines offered for sale by a company. Some large manufacturing firms have hundreds or thousands of products in their product mix. Most large companies develop a broad product mix for growth and diversification, and so that profits in one product line might offset losses in another.

PRODUCT PLANNING OBJECTIVES

Product planning involves finding answers to such questions as the following: What products do our customers need and want? When should we introduce a new product? How broad a product mix should we offer? Should we expand or modify any product line? What product or products should we drop? When should the product be changed? How can we develop new uses and a new

Choosing the proper time to introduce a new product is an important factor in the successful marketing of that product.

image for our product? How should the product be styled and designed? How should the product be packaged and branded?

The answers to these questions will be guided by the product objectives of the company. Product objectives vary widely from company to company. It would be impossible to list all the product objectives of all companies. However, here is a list of typical product objectives.

- Growth in sales volume by the introduction of new products.
- Steady sales growth through the improvement of existing products.
- Increasing sales volume by creating new uses for established products.
- Developing a complete line of products. (An example of this objective would be making or selling every type of appliance that might be used in a kitchen.)
- Maintaining or improving market share.

There will always be limitations in the ways of achieving product objectives. How these objectives are achieved is influenced by changes in the consumer market, competition, and the company's production capabilities.

Changes in the Consumer Market

The demands of a constantly changing consumer market are a powerful influence on product planning. A company may add a new line of sporting goods because of the growth of the leisure-time market. Increased purchasing power and higher average incomes may influence a company's decision to manufacture higher-priced and better-quality products. The increased demand by consumers for more built-in conveniences will persuade a company to enter a new market with, for example, a line of battery-powered, portable electric appliances. Changes in life-style, such as increased participation in active sports, may cause a marketer to create a new line of outdoor and indoor games involving physical exercise.

Competition

One of the strongest influences on products is competition. Some marketers constantly seek to make their products different from the products of their competitors. If two competing products are very similar, one marketer may try to make his a better-quality product, or he may offer better service with his product. Another marketer may attempt to avoid competition by planning products that offer unique advantages. Other marketers may compete by developing products that copy the features of a successful product. For example, General Electric reports that within two years after it introduced its automatic electric toothbrush, there were more than 52 competing brands on the market.

Production Capabilities

Although a marketer may feel that a product needs to be changed, production limitations may prevent this change. For example, the machines used to produce a given product may not be adaptable for adding a new feature. The cost of changing existing machines from production of a metal body for an appliance to production of a more colorful plastic body may be too great. In many cases, however, the marketer has been able to successfully adapt existing methods of production or to discover new and better ones. With such changes the marketer can modify a product so that it is significantly better than a competing brand.

DEVELOPING A PRODUCT

New products do not just appear. Once a consumer need is established and product planning objectives are known, the company is ready to begin the actual development of the product.

The product development process can be divided into six steps: (1) collecting ideas, (2) screening ideas, (3) evaluating ideas, (4) preparing a prototype of the product, (5) testing the product, and (6) introducing the product into the marketplace.

Collecting Ideas

Ideas for new products can come from customers, from a company's employees, and from various organizations that know the market well. Sometimes an idea can even be born from a mistake.

Marketers collect new product ideas from customers in a number of ways. They conduct customer surveys, they invite product suggestions, and they study what customers prefer to buy. Customers are perhaps the most important source of new product ideas because their reactions to a new product will determine whether that product is going to be a success.

Research organizations and trade associations also are sources of new product ideas, because of their general knowledge both of a particular industry and the market it serves. Such organizations suggest new product ideas, and often they screen and evaluate them.

Even a mistake may result in a new product idea.

How can a product idea come from a mistake? In 1878 a Procter & Gamble workman went to lunch without remembering to turn off his blending machine. As a result, tiny air bubbles were beaten into a batch of soap, making it buoyant. Procter & Gamble has been selling floating Ivory soap ever since.

Screening Ideas

Usually a company interested in developing a new product starts out with a large number of ideas. They then screen, or quickly review, the ideas, saving those that have special merit and eliminating those that seem unsuitable. One or more persons within the company who know product development problems and possibilities usually screen the ideas.

Screening saves time and money. On the other hand, it may discard some good ideas whose value was not recognized. However, the company knows that those ideas which do pass the screening test deserve serious attention. Of course, a marketer could choose to examine every single idea very carefully and thoroughly, but such a practice might alone use up the entire development budget.

Evaluating Ideas

The ideas that pass the preliminary screening stage are given very careful study and evaluation. These are some of the questions asked about them:

- Will the product meet a definite customer need?
- Will the product be a logical addition to the company's product mix?
- Can the product be developed and produced with a reasonable expenditure of the company's resources?
- Will the product produce a profit for the company?

That last question is very important. A marketer is in business to make a profit. Only when a product idea shows strong evidence of being profitable is it considered seriously by a company.

This careful evaluation usually eliminates a few more ideas. When the evaluation is completed, the company will have reduced the original large collection of ideas to one, two, or three ideas that offer enough promise to make further investment in their development reasonable.

Preparing a Prototype

After a new product idea has been screened and evaluated, work on the product itself begins. The product is designed, the kind and quality of materials to be used in manufacturing the product are selected, and the method of manufacture is determined.

When all the specifications for the product have been planned, the company usually makes a prototype. A *prototype* is a model of the new product; it is the first form of the product that the company makes.

Because of the unexpected problems that may arise and the time needed to solve them, a prototype is usually made by hand rather than on the production line. The handwork involved makes the prototype very expensive to produce. However, making a prototype is a necessary step in the development of a product. The prototype is needed because it enables the company to see how the specifications for the proposed new product work and how the finished product will look.

Testing the Product

After the prototype of a product has been made, it is tested. It may be tested in a laboratory, by a special group of customers, or under actual market conditions. Often a newly developed product is tested under all three of these conditions.

For example, a new line of sew-them-yourself dolls' clothes might be put through several tests. First, the fabrics in the kit are laboratory-tested to make sure that they are fire-resistant. They are also tested to make sure they are colorfast and will not shrink, since the instructions in the kit claim that the clothes can be washed and ironed.

Next, a group of parents are asked to test the product. The parents are given samples of the kit for their children. Later, they are questioned about the children's interest in the kits and about whether the handwork required was done by their children.

Finally, a market test is arranged. Test marketing is the introduction of a product in a small marketing area to check customers' reactions. The test-marketing area is chosen as representative of the total market. Thus the kits are distributed to dealers in a single city, and the sales results and customers' reactions are carefully studied by the company.

Introducing the Product

When a new product passes all the tests, it is ready for full-scale introduction. Production, distribution, promotion, and selling efforts are all aimed at making the product a success in the market.

Introducing a new product to the market is expensive. Seldom do sales repay that expense immediately. However, if a company has done its product development work carefully—and if the market accepts the new product—then sales will gradually pay off the development costs and begin to yield a profit for the company.

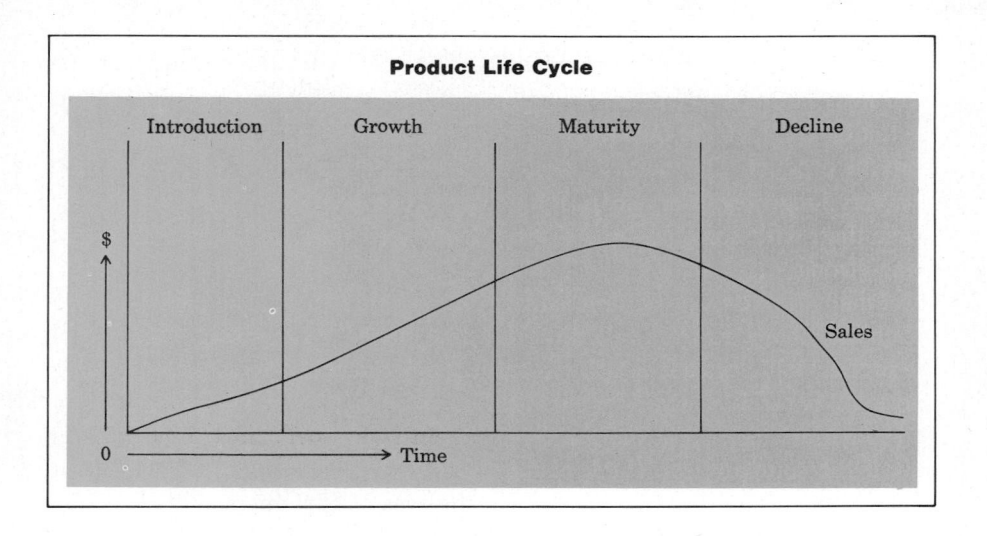

Product Life Cycle

| Introduction | Growth | Maturity | Decline |

Sales

$ / Time

PRODUCT LIFE CYCLE

A product has a definite life cycle. A *product life cycle* is the period from the introduction of a product to the market until it is withdrawn. The product life cycle can be divided into four stages: introduction, growth, maturity, and decline. Each of these stages can be affected by fashion, which is one of the strongest influences on the length of a product life cycle, but one of the hardest influences to predict.

Stages of the Cycle

The "introduction stage" of a product life cycle is the first appearance of the product on the market, accompanied by full-scale production and strong marketing effort. This is the same as the full-scale introduction stage in the product development process. The company puts all its effort into making the product a marketing success.

Immediately after the introduction stage comes the product's "growth stage," the period when sales are rising. How long the growth stage lasts depends upon the product and the marketing techniques used. One product may catch the market's interest, and sales may grow very rapidly. Another product may have a long growth stage during which sales rise steadily but very slowly. In any case, if a product is to experience growth, it is important that sales increase at this time. If sales do not increase, the marketing strategy must be changed.

The next stage occurs when sales begin to level off. This period, in which sales remain at a fairly even level, is called the "maturity stage." The leveling off of sales can occur for several reasons. The market for the product may be saturated, perhaps because competing products have been introduced and are taking much of the business. The market's interest may be shifting away from the product. The maturity stage for a product can last a very short time or a very long time. Ivory soap, for example, can be said to have a maturity phase that, with some ups and downs, has lasted many decades and is still going strong.

Finally, there comes a time when sales begin to drop. The period during which sales slow down is called the "decline stage." At this stage, the end of the product's life cycle is usually in sight. Sometimes an increased marketing effort will boost sales again for a while, but the sales gain is usually temporary and sometimes not worth the cost. The end of the product's life can be delayed only if the company can think of interesting new uses for the product that would make it almost a new product in the eyes of customers.

At the end of the decline stage producers take the product off their production schedules, and retailers remove it from their inventories. The product life cycle is completed.

Fashion Influence

The style preferred by the majority at any given time is called *fashion*. Fashion affects many products. Clothes and cars, for example, are greatly influenced by fashion. However, the length of time that different products remain fashionable varies greatly. In women's clothing, so-called "high-fashion" usually lasts for one season. On the other hand, fashion in architecture may not change for a number of years.

To a large degree, fashions change because people are interested in the new and the different. Because people tire of wearing the same styles, they can often be persuaded to wear different styles. And because people are attracted by innovations, they can often be persuaded to trade in their old cars for new ones, even if the old cars still work.

For some products, such as food and clothing, the companies that make the products sometimes try to create the desire for change. Yet the manufacturers can never be sure that their new products will catch on and spark sales. In any fashion market the manufacturer lives from one season to the next, wondering what trend is going to be popular and trying to keep up with consumers' preferences.

If a new product becomes an "in" fashion, its growth stage will be strong, and the sales during its maturity stage will be high. However, when the consumers decide that the product is no longer fashionable, a marketer can do very little to keep that product from going into its decline stage.

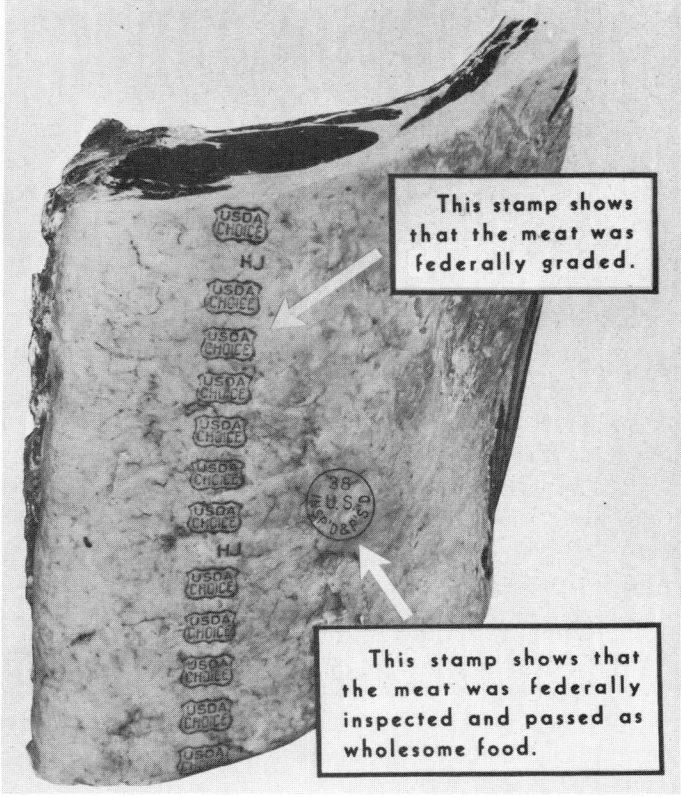

Meat is graded and stamped accordingly by the federal government.

This stamp shows that the meat was federally graded.

This stamp shows that the meat was federally inspected and passed as wholesome food.

USDA Photo

STANDARDS AND GRADES

To satisfy a customer, the products he buys must have the quality he is seeking. Sometimes he may want only minimum quality at a low price. At other times he may want the finest quality, even though the price is high. Marketers, too, have a choice of quality when they purchase raw materials; and their selection will depend on the level of quality most in demand by customers. Standards and grades help marketers identify levels of quality in the materials they buy and thus help them maintain the quality of the finished products they sell.

Standards are measurements of the quality of both manufactured goods and natural and agricultural products. Standards can be set by private industry for its own products, by consumer groups, or by the government. *Grades* are the letters, numbers, or descriptive words used to indicate that a product has met certain standards. Canned fruit, for example, has three grades: grade A, or fancy; grade B, or choice; grade C, or standard. The fruit is graded on the basis of size, color, and ripeness. Only the most perfect fruit would meet the standards of grade A, but even grade C fruit would have to be edible to meet the established standards for that grade. Standards and grades are important because they regulate marketing practices and assure customers of getting a certain level of quality each time they buy a product.

Some standards are developed by producers and retailers, others are set by consumer groups, and still others are established by the government.

Standards Set by Producers and Retailers

Every producer wants his products to have a good reputation. Most producers are proud of their products and believe that they are equal to or better than competing products. This is why many manufacturers maintain their own testing laboratories, which test the company's products long before they ever reach the market.

To protect their industry's reputation, producers often form trade associations to establish standards for their industry's products. Some trade associations establish standards for more than one industry. One organization, the American National Standards Institute, is supported by business firms for the purpose of working out standards used as guidelines by all industries.

Some retailers, in order to guarantee the quality of the products they sell, test those products before selling them. Large retail chains, such as Sears and J. C. Penney, have elaborate merchandise testing laboratories. These laboratories have established standards that products must meet before the chains will carry them.

Standards Set by Consumer Groups

Independent testing organizations, such as Consumers' Research and Consumers Union, test products already on the market. Their ratings of various products are published in their monthly magazines. The recommendations made in these magazines carry great weight with readers and influence their purchases.

Some general-interest magazines, such as *Good Housekeeping* and *Parents' Magazine,* have their own testing laboratories. Products that meet the standards set forth by these magazines have a right to use the magazines' "seal of approval."

Standards Set by Government

The government is one of the most powerful forces in the standards and grades field. Local governments usually have laws concerning measuring devices, such as scales, pumps, and meters, and employ inspectors to check

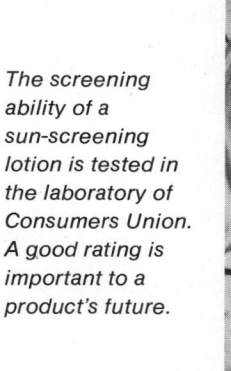

The screening ability of a sun-screening lotion is tested in the laboratory of Consumers Union. A good rating is important to a product's future.

Courtesy Consumers Union

these devices within the area of local authority. State governments are particularly concerned about agricultural and food products, and many require grading of those products according to specified standards.

The federal government is especially interested in standards and grades. The Department of Agriculture develops standards for agricultural products, and the Food and Drug Administration enforces laws and regulations controlling the marketing of foods, drugs, and cosmetics. Nearly every other kind of product comes under the jurisdiction of the Federal Trade Commission, which prepares "industry guides" suggesting basic standards for products. Some of the government's work is of an advisory nature, but much of it has the actual or implied force of law.

◘ YOUR MARKETING VOCABULARY

On a separate sheet of paper define each of the following marketing terms; then use each term in a sentence.

Fashion
Grades
Product
Product item
Product life cycle
Product line
Product mix
Product planning
Prototype
Standards

FOR REVIEW AND DISCUSSION

1. What are some of the questions that marketers must answer in doing product planning?
2. What are some typical product objectives for a marketing firm?
3. Name and explain three important influences on product planning.
4. List the six steps in product development.
5. What methods may be used to test a new product?
6. Explain why the sales of a product may level off.
7. Describe the decline stage of a product.
8. Why is fashion a strong influence in marketing?
9. Name three groups that set standards for products.
10. Why are standards and grades important?

ANALYZING MARKETING CONCEPTS

1. A company may decide that it needs to expand its product mix. Prepare a form like the one below and list the following types of businesses in the left-hand column: (a) ice cream company, (b) retail shoe store, (c) self-service laundry, (d) office-furniture manufacturer, (e) dry-cleaning business, (f) grocery wholesaler. For each business, suggest a new product that it might add to its product mix. Write your suggestion in the center column. In the right-hand column, state why each product might be added.

Type of Business	Suggested New Product	Reason for Adding Product
Example: Cash register manufacturer	Small electronic calculating machine	Machine is needed by same businesses that buy cash registers.

2. The more uses a product has, the greater will be its sales potential. Prepare a form like the one below. In the left-hand column, write the following products: (a) small plastic cabinet, (b) dish detergent, (c) cellophane tape, (d) scouring pad, (e) paper towels, (f) plastic sandwich bags. In the center column, write the primary use of each product. In the right-hand column, describe two other uses for each product.

Product	Primary Use	Other Uses
Example: Baby shampoo	For babies' hair.	For adults who shampoo their hair often; for small pets.

MARKETING PROJECT 23
Analyzing a New Product

Project Goal: Given a new product, describe the marketing techniques used to introduce and promote the product, and analyze its position in the market.

Action: Select a new product that has been introduced on the market recently. Obtain information about the product from sources such as advertising, businessmen, salespeople, customers using the product, the manufacturer's written material, and your own observation of the product. Collect advertisements, booklets, tags, labels, and other materials about the product. Based on the information you gather, answer the following questions:

1. At what market is this product aimed?
2. How was the product introduced and promoted?
3. What is the product's relationship to competition?
4. Why, in your opinion, will this product be successful or unsuccessful?

Using your answers to the above questions and your collected product materials, give an oral report in class on the marketing of this new product.

part 24

Brand Names and Trademarks

YOUR GOALS
1. Given the brand names for actual products, evaluate the characteristics and marketing effectiveness of each brand name.
2. Given specific types of products and their target markets, create new brand names with desirable characteristics to serve the target markets.

Imagine the problems a customer would have if products in the marketplace were not identified by brand names. Shopping would be chaotic. The customer would have to spend hours in a retail store comparing products to make sure that he was getting the particular product he wanted. Brand names help the customer avoid such problems by enabling him to quickly and easily identify products.

The manufacturer uses brand names for several purposes. He wants to give his product a personality of its own, to say to the customer that his product has a certain quality that makes it superior to other products. He wants to build a reputation for a quality product so that consumers will try it, grow to like it, and buy it regularly. In short, he uses brand names to set his product apart from other products, to build a reputation for quality, and to encourage repeat sales.

TYPES OF BRANDS

Business firms use several marketing strategies to make their products more appealing than those of their competitors. One of their most effective techniques is to identify their products by giving them a brand. A *brand* is a name, symbol, design, or any combination of these that identifies the goods or services of a seller and sets them apart from those of his competitors.

A *brand name* is that part of a brand that can be spoken. It may be a word, a group of words, a letter, a number, or any combination of these. Almost all the products in the marketplace carry brand names. The American consumer is familiar with such brand names as Kellogg's, Kleenex, Betty Crocker, and 7-Up.

The distinctive symbol that is used along with a brand name on a product is called a *brand mark.* Some familiar brand marks are the shell sign of the Shell Oil Company, the lightning symbol of Zenith, and the Colonel of Kentucky Fried Chicken.

A *trademark* is that part of a brand that has been legally registered with the U.S. Patent Office. A trademark cannot be used by anyone else without the permission of the person or company that owns it. Trademarks are usually identified in printed matter by a small encircled R (registered) placed immediately after the trademark. Sometimes the abbreviation "T.M." (trademark) or the abbreviation "Reg. U.S. Pat. Off." (Registered in the United States Patent

Courtesy Procter & Gamble

Do the brand names on these products identify them effectively?

Office) is used. The registration and protection of trademarks are discussed later in this part.

Manufacturers and middlemen brand their goods and services. Because much of their business depends upon how well their brands are respected and remembered by consumers, they try very hard to make their brand names well known and recognized as symbols of reliability.

Manufacturer's Brand

The branded product of a manufacturer is called a *national brand*. National brands are also referred to as name brands, brand-name products, producers' brands, and manufacturers' brands. The term "national brand" does not refer only to products that are distributed on a national scale. In fact, several national brands are distributed only on a regional or statewide scale. The term merely indicates that such products carry the labels of their manufacturers. Examples of national brands are Coca-Cola, Eastman Kodak, Pillsbury, and NEHI.

Middleman's Brand

A product that carries the label of the middleman (wholesaler or retailer) who sells it is called a *private brand*. Private brands are also referred to as middlemen's brands, retailers' brands, distributors' brands, and private-label brands. Examples of private brands include the Kenmore brand of Sears, Roebuck and Company, the Finast brand of the First National Food Stores, and the Signature brand of Montgomery Ward. Although a private brand may be sold on a national scale, it remains a private brand because it carries the label of the middleman rather than the manufacturer.

Most private-label goods sold through retail stores are made by manufacturers of nationally known brands. For example, Whirlpool manufactures the Coldspot refrigerator sold by Sears, and Hotpoint makes the Penncrest washers sold by J. C. Penney. Because he usually does not know the name of the manufacturer, the customer who buys a private brand puts his trust in the reputation of the retailer selling it. He depends on the retailer rather than the manufacturer to stand behind his merchandise. And the retailer generally does stand behind his product. He reasons that if he can build customer loyalty for his private brands, then he is assured of repeat sales, because his store is the only place where these brands can be obtained. Sometimes a middleman's brands are different from any other products on the market, because the middleman has had the manufacturer make certain changes in their design.

Private-label merchandise is often in direct competition with national-brand merchandise. Middlemen may push the sale of their private brands by vigorous selling programs, by displaying private-brand goods more prominently than national brands, and by special advertising campaigns.

Sometimes in building the reputation of his own brand, a middleman may lean on the national brand names of the materials used in his product. Sears, Roebuck, for example, advertises that its Premiere brand of men's shirts are made of SuPima broadcloth; Montgomery Ward notes that its own Style House brand of carpeting is made with Acrilan; and Allied Stores point out that their Millay brand of women's stockings use Du Pont nylon. A customer unfamiliar with the retailer's brand is often reassured by the fact that the materials that make up the product are those of a familiar, nationally known manufacturer.

Sometimes a private-label brand becomes so well established in its own right that customers respect it as much as a national brand, or even prefer it. Many professional carpenters and amateur do-it-yourselfers purchase Craftsman tools by Sears and Powr-Kraft tools by Montgomery Ward because these brands have come to stand for excellent quality and dependability.

WHY BRAND?

Every manufacturer takes pride in his product. Marking his product with a brand name is one way in which he shows this pride. However, he has three other important reasons for using a brand name: to create a favorable impression of his product, to build a reputation for a quality product, and to encourage repeat sales.

To Create a Favorable Impression

A brand name plays a large role in the impression a product makes on a prospective customer. If he is favorably impressed by the brand name of a product, he is likely to buy the product. Customers may buy certain brands of cosmetics because they convey the image of love, strength, or increased charm. House hunters may be attracted to model homes whose names create the impression of luxury and elegance, such as the "Aristocrat" or the "Excelsior."

In recent years several large companies have changed the brand names of their products to create a more favorable impression. Cities Service Oil Company, for example, changed the name of its gasoline to CITGO to create an active, modern image. The name was selected from more than 80,000 possible choices. The first syllable of the new brand name—CIT—came from the company name Cities Service. The second syllable—GO—was selected to suggest power, energy, and progress—qualities that symbolized the new image the company wanted to convey.

This ad emphasizes the quality of the product.

Courtesy Schwinn Bicycle

To Build a Reputation for Quality

Customers learn to depend on and trust a quality brand-name product. A company working to build and maintain its reputation must provide the customer with brand-name products of consistently high quality regardless of where he buys the products.

A customer, for example, expects a Schwinn bicycle to have the same qualities whether he purchases it from a dealer in Miami, Indianapolis, or Seattle. Schwinn advertises its bicycle as "America's Favorite Bicycle," a product that is built to last longer.

A company with a reputation for a quality product usually invests much time and effort in improving its product. Such improvement is essential in order for the product to stay ahead of competition. The aim is always to offer a product that maintains a reputation for quality and that continues to satisfy the customers' needs and wants.

To Encourage Repeat Sales

If customers receive satisfaction from a particular brand, they tend to buy the same brand again. Branding, then, encourages repeat sales by making it easy for the customer to find the product that gave him satisfaction in the past. Moreover, once the customer has found the brand he likes, shopping for the particular product becomes easier; he no longer has to bother making a decision about which product to buy each time he shops. He has already used the product, and he knows that it fits his needs; hence he has little reason to take a chance on another brand.

In retail stores the products of various manufacturers are often stocked together on the shelves. A customer without a strong brand preference is likely to buy any brand. To prevent this, a manufacturer must build strong customer preference for his brand. Only then will his product be able to withstand the intense competition in the marketplace.

BRAND-NAME STRATEGIES

A business organization usually follows a certain strategy in choosing a brand name. This strategy has a strong influence on the marketing methods used to promote and sell a product. An organization may decide to use one brand name for all products, one brand name for each product line, one brand name for each product, or one brand name for each grade or price line.

One Brand Name for All Products

A brand name that is used for all the products of a company is called a *family brand*. Examples of well-known family brands are Campbell's, Heinz, Sunbeam, Gerber, and Kodak. A major advantage of using a family brand is that any new products introduced by the company will benefit from the established reputation of the existing products. Each marketing effort for any given product in the "family" tends to promote all the products sold under the family brand.

A family brand is best suited to products that are in the same category. The inclusion of a product outside the category could lower the image of the other products. Consider what customer response would be if a manufacturer of baby foods were to extend his line to include floor wax. Quite possibly, the dissimilar product could lessen the customers' faith in the line of baby foods. The word "family" suggests that all the products in a line have a similar quality, use, or other characteristic. Thus the name "Kodak" on a package immediately tells a customer that he has a product related to photography, "General Electric" signifies an electrically operated appliance, and "Kellogg's" means breakfast foods. To maintain consumer acceptance of the brand name, all products in the family should be of a similar type and should meet similar standards of quality.

One Brand Name for Each Product Line

Most distributors have their own private lines of products. They may give each line a brand name. The trend today is to use fewer single-product brand names and to promote the image and reputation of product-line brand names. This strategy has the same major advantage as the family brand name: Any new products introduced into the line will benefit from the established reputation of the existing products.

Some large retailers use separate brand names for their various private lines of sporting goods, appliances, clothing, and automobile accessories. For example, Montgomery Ward has established brand names for a number of its product lines. Some of them are Powr-Kraft for tools, Signature for appliances, and Western Field for outdoor sporting goods.

One Brand Name for Each Product

Many manufacturers develop separate names for each of their products, especially when the products face stiff competition. Individual branding allows the product to be advertised more intensively than if a family brand were used. For example, Procter & Gamble makes the soaps Safeguard and Ivory. Rather than use a common name for both products (such as Procter & Gamble's soaps), the manufacturer assigned each a brand name. In this way, the products can be more heavily promoted individually than if a single name were used for both.

Sometimes a company wants to enjoy the advantages of both a family name and a product name. Post's Grape Nuts is a typical example. The Post family name helps the product to gain consumer respect, and the brand name "Grape Nuts" helps to individualize the product and publicize it in advertising and sales promotion. The paper products of the Scott Paper Company—Scott towels, Scotties, and Scotkins—are other examples of products that benefit from using the company name.

One Brand Name for Each Grade or Price Line

Sometimes, within the same line of products, a company will offer different grades of the product. Because each grade represents a different price line, the company assigns a different brand name to each grade. WEO A&P Food Stores use this strategy. They carry three different grades, or price lines, of private-label canned fruit and vegetables. Ann Page is the most expensive brand, Sultana is next, and Iona is the least expensive brand.

A fighting brand must take on the competition.

Automobile manufacturers also brand according to price lines. General Motors, for example, uses a series of brand names to identify its lines of automobiles: Chevrolet, Pontiac, Oldsmobile, Buick, and Cadillac. Each line represents a specific quality and price range that appeals to the needs and incomes of different consumers. The different automobiles within each line also represent differences in quality and price. Nevertheless, the customer would expect the least expensive brand of Cadillac to cost more than the most expensive brand of Chevrolet.

Sometimes car dealers and other manufacturers use the least expensive brand as a fighting brand. A *fighting brand* is a low-priced brand used to compete aggressively with other companies that use low-price strategies. The prestige of the higher-priced brand name is protected by using only the fighting brand for such competition.

CHARACTERISTICS OF BRAND NAMES

When a manufacturer or distributor selects a brand name for his product or service, he wants a name that will help him to make as many sales as possible. The accumulated experience of a large number of business organizations has shown that many successful brand names have certain characteristics. Such brand names are brief, they are distinctive, and they suggest ideas that appeal to the customer.

Brevity

When choosing a brand name for its products, a company wants a name that will be easily remembered and recognized by the customer. For this reason, brief brand names are popular. In any supermarket the shelves are filled with an array of products with short brand names, such as Crest, Bold, Swan, Tab, Jif, and Kool-Aid. Short brand names have been found to have greater impact on customers than long ones. In fact, the average customer insists on short brand names and will often shorten long names for convenience. For example, he may shorten "Pepsi-Cola" to "Pepsi" and "Coca-Cola" to "Coke."

Distinctiveness

Since the purpose of brand names is to distinguish the goods of any marketer from those of his competitors, it is important that the brand name be different from any other. A distinctive brand name positively identifies a marketer's product and prevents confusion with similar products of other marketers.

Some brand names have lost their distinctiveness through overuse. The names American, Imperial, and Supreme, for example, have been used so often by manufacturers, retailers, and service businesses that they are no longer unique.

On the other hand, some brand names are so distinctive that they instantly bring to mind the product or line of products that they identify. For instance, Mr. Clean is immediately recognized as the name of a household cleaning liquid, Timex is readily associated with a brand of watch, and Gerber is instantly identified with baby foods.

Suggestion of Appealing Ideas

Most customers need to have a favorable impression of a product before they will buy it. A customer is not likely to buy a detergent called Gloom nor a car named Turtle. A shopper looks for cleaning products that suggest optimism or satisfaction, such as Joy, Dash, Bravo, or Cheer. Car manufacturers try to convey vitality and sleekness through the choice of names such as Thunderbird and Wildcat, or strength and power through such names as Charger and Mustang. Because the image conveyed by the brand name greatly affects a customer's product choice, it is important that the name be one that will appeal to the customer and encourage him to buy the product.

REGISTRATION OF TRADEMARKS

The registration of a trademark, that part of a brand which is given legal protection, is really a matter for a company's legal department. But it is important for the marketer to know what is involved in securing legal protection for his own brand.

In the United States, trademarks are registered with the U.S. Patent Office. Such registration establishes ownership of a trademark and guarantees exclusive right to its use.

Four kinds of trademarks may be registered with the U.S. Patent Office: trademarks used to identify goods and distinguish them from goods manufactured or sold by someone else; service marks used to distinguish the services of one company from those of another (such as the trademark "Martinizing," which describes a dry-cleaning process); collective marks used by associations of marketing companies (such as the "Grown in Idaho" trademark used by the Idaho Potato and Onion Commission, an association of Idaho farmers); and certification marks, which indicate that goods or services meet certain standards (such as the seal of approval used by *Good Housekeeping* magazine for products that have met the standards of its testing laboratories).

Legal protection of trademarks dates back to 1870, when the first Federal Trademark Act was passed. The Lanham Trademark Act of 1946 gave additional protection to owners of trademarks. These federal laws and some state laws prohibit the use of a company's trademark by another company or an individual.

The laws, however, do not protect trademark owners from another danger: the possibility that the trademark will become a generic term through repeated use. A "generic" term refers to all products of a certain kind, rather than to a branded product made by one specific manufacturer. The word "typewriter" is a generic term, but Royal is a trademark for a specific manufacturer's typewriters.

The marketing problem is that a brand may become so popular that it becomes legally generic. Aspirin, for example, was once Bayer's trademark for acetylsalicylic acid. But as this pain reliever became more popular, Bayer lost its exclusive right to use the term. Thus now the products of any manufacturer may be called aspirin.

Marketers today take definite action to prevent their trademarks from becoming generic terms and therefore available for use by any manufacturer making a similar product. In their advertising campaigns, they emphasize that the product's brand name is registered by including the encircled R after every use of the brand name. The firm often uses the generic name of the

The symbol ® to the right of each of these trademarks indicates that the trademark has been registered with the U.S. Patent Office.

product in connection with the trademark to keep the trademark from being applied to any other company's version of that product. Examples are Kleenex tissues, not Kleenex; Kodacolor film, not Kodacolor; and Dacron polyester fiber, not simply Dacron. In addition, many marketers adopt distinctive ways of writing their names. They may write in an unusual script or in a special style that customers can recognize and remember.

◆ YOUR MARKETING VOCABULARY

On a separate sheet of paper define each of the following marketing terms; then use each term in a sentence.

Brand	Fighting brand
Brand mark	National brand
Brand name	Private brand
Family brand	Trademark

FOR REVIEW AND DISCUSSION

1. Explain why brand names are important to both the consumer and the marketer.
2. When the term "national brand" is applied to a product, does it mean that the product is sold only on a national scale? Explain.
3. How does branding help establish the reputation of a quality product?
4. Explain how branding encourages repeat sales of a product.
5. List some advantages of using a family brand name.
6. What are some of the advantages of branding by product line?
7. What are some of the advantages of using both a family brand name and a product name? Give one example of a product branded in this way.
8. List the advantages of branding by price line.
9. Give the characteristics of a successful brand name. Tell why each characteristic is important.
10. What are the three principal ways of protecting a brand?

ANALYZING MARKETING CONCEPTS

1. An effective brand name is a valuable part of a product. Prepare a form like the one below. In the left-hand column, list the following brand names: (a) Cheer, (b) Holsum, (c) Turf-Builder, (d) Friskies, (e) Tang, (f) Baggies, (g) Bugles, (h) Silk'n Satin.

    In the next column, list the following products: (a) detergent, (b) bread, (c) lawn fertilizer, (d) dog food, (e) orange drink, (f) plastic bags, (g) snack treat, (h) hand lotion. Note that each of these products corresponds to the brand name with the same letter, which you listed in the left-hand column.

    Place a check mark in one or more of the appropriate columns at the right to indicate the desirable characteristics of each brand name.

Brand Name	Product	Brevity	Distinctiveness	Appealing Ideas
Example: Timex	Watch	✔	✔	

2. Creating a brand name is an important task. Prepare a form like the one at the top of the next page. List these products in the left-hand column: (a) detergent, (b) soft drink, (c) automobile, (d) ball-point pen. In the next two columns, briefly describe the product and write the brand name you invent for it. In the right-hand column, explain your reason for choosing the brand name.

Type of Product	Description of Product	Brand Name Chosen	Reason for Choice
Example: Breakfast food	Pieces of cereal shaped like popular cars.	Car Snaps	Name has only two syllables; relates to the shape of the cereal; has crisp, lively sound.

MARKETING PROJECT 24
Evaluating Brand Names

Project Goal: Given the brand names for actual products, evaluate the characteristics and marketing effectiveness of each brand name.

Action: Select five brand names of actual products. Then collect examples of the use of each brand name in magazine and newspaper advertisements. Prepare a form like the one below, and list each brand name and the manufacturer's name in the left-hand column. In the center column, briefly describe the product that the brand name represents. In the right-hand column, evaluate the marketing effectiveness of each brand name. You may want to refer to the characteristics of a good brand name discussed in this part. Support your evaluation by asking others how they react to each brand name.

Attach the brand-name ads you collected to your completed form.

Brand Name	Description of Product	Evaluation of Brand Name
Example: Pinto by Ford Motor Company	Small economy car	Creates the impression of a colorful, spirited pony. Ties in effectively with Ford's family of horse names: Mustang, Maverick. Name is short and easy to say and remember. Seems to associate well with economy, durability, freedom, and fun.

part 25

Packaging and Labeling

YOUR GOALS

1. Given a product package, evaluate the materials used in the package, the form of the package, and the functions of the package.
2. Given actual labels on several kinds of products, list the desirable characteristics of the most informative labels.

In the days of the country store almost everything was sold in bulk. Milk was ladled from a large milk can into the containers that customers brought from home. Huge barrels held crackers, dried fruit, sugar, and flour. As customers ordered these foods, the storekeeper picked them by hand or with a scoop and wrapped them in paper. Cheese of all types lay on the counter in huge slabs, and slices were cut and wrapped to the customer's order.

Today many products are sold in packages that have been specially designed for them. In supermarkets and many warehouses, few actual products can be seen; instead there are packages in hundreds of different sizes, shapes, colors, and types. Almost all manufactured or processed products are packaged today.

Packaging is the use of containers and wrapping materials to protect, contain, identify, promote, and facilitate the use of the product. Some of those

Courtesy Modern Packaging Magazine

The trend in food packaging is to include nutritional information on the label. Can you think of some reasons for this trend?

functions are performed in part by the package's label. A *label* is an informative tag, wrapper, or seal attached to the product or the product's package.

Labels may be classified as brand, grade, or descriptive. A brand label simply gives the brand name of the product. The name may be that of the manufacturer, such as Heinz ketchup, or it may be a name chosen by the manufacturer, such as Bold detergent, produced by Procter & Gamble. A grade label identifies by letter, number, or word the exact quality or grade of a product, such as "prime" beef or "fancy" canned peaches. A descriptive label gives information on the use, care, performance, construction, ingredients, or other characteristics of the product.

Packaging and labeling are important for nearly all consumer products and for a large number of industrial products. They add to the value, the usefulness, and the appeal of the product.

FUNCTIONS OF PACKAGING

Packaging protects a product, contains it, identifies it, promotes it, and makes it easy to use. The jobs of protecting and containing are closely linked. So are the jobs of identifying and promoting.

Consider salt, for example. After salt has been processed, it is packaged in a container and ready for sale to the consumer. The container does not change the flavor of the salt in any way; yet customers prefer to buy packaged salt rather than loose salt. What then does packaging do for the salt? The tough moisture-resistant cardboard of the carton keeps the salt dry and clean, and safe from insects, dirt, and foreign matter. The art and printing on the carton attract the customer and describe the product. The convenient flip-

298 / Unit 7 / The Product

open spout makes measuring and pouring easy. In addition, packaging makes shopping easier and faster; the customer can choose the product he wants without having to wait while a salesperson weighs the desired quantity and wraps it.

Contains the Product

In this country, almost no one takes along a container or wrapping material when he goes shopping. A person may take along his own shopping cart, but that is usually the only exception. A person shopping in a supermarket expects many of the products he buys to be in containers: boxes, cans, jars, and plastic bags. And if he buys any product that is not in a container, he expects it to be wrapped. When he has finished making his selections, he expects the checker to place his purchases in large carrying bags.

The function of packaging as a container is widely evident in all types of food stores. Even when foods are displayed unpackaged—as is often true with fruits and vegetables—they are placed in bags for the customer's convenience when he buys them. Of course, supermarkets now prepackage many fruits and vegetables in amounts considered convenient to shoppers. But even these prepackaged foods are put into large bags at the check-out counter.

Identifies the Product

A package would be useless if it did not identify its contents. Usually, the contents are identified by the label on the package. However, using a special design or color on the package also helps customers identify the contents.

This identification is very important to a marketer in distinguishing his products from those of his competitors. Often competing products look very much alike, even in their packaging. When one company first introduced canned soup that was not concentrated, it placed the soup in a can that was somewhat larger than the standard-size soup can. In this way, the size of the can as well as the label helped identify the product. Then other companies introduced similar unconcentrated soups and put them in larger-than-standard cans. Because all the larger cans now contain ready-to-heat-and-eat soup, a customer must read the label to find out which manufacturer's soup he is buying.

Promotes the Product

The package is the natural place for promotion. It is the part of the product most visible to the customer. Sometimes it is the only part visible. Often a product that is plain or unexciting in itself can be livened up with the use of cheerful packaging.

An attractive shape and a bright, effective design are necessary to help draw customers to the product, because often the product is competing with many similar ones. Bold design and a "catchy" promotional slogan or message on the package help to make sales. Information on the uses of the product as well as the offer of a premium or refund can also encourage sales.

Makes the Product Easy to Use

Cartons with spouts for easy pouring, boxes with zip-strip openings, butter wrappers with measurements marked on them—all are examples of the conveniences offered by packaging. In each of these examples the package is designed with the user's needs in mind.

The idea of adding convenience to packages has extended into the industrial area. Products for food markets, for example, often come in shipping cartons that open into attractive displays of the products. All the retailer needs to do is slit open the top or pull a zip strip and he has a self-standing product display that can immediately be placed in an aisle or on a counter.

WHO DOES THE PACKAGING?

Manufacturers take packaging seriously because studies indicate that the company that takes the time to design and produce suitable packaging sells more products. One study, for example, showed that companies that did packaging research had a sales volume 50 percent higher than those selling similar products without doing packaging research. Since attractive packaging leads to more sales, some manufacturers give nearly as much thought to the packaging as they do to the product.

Package design may be handled by the packaging department within the company that manufactures the product. In other cases an advertising agency or an independent packaging company may design the package for the manufacturer. In addition, suppliers of packaging often develop new ways of packaging products. One such supplier is the American Can Company, which has been responsible for many new developments in metal cans, such as the pull tab that allows the consumer to easily remove the entire top of a can without using a can opener.

Whether a manufacturer chooses to meet his package-design needs through his own packaging department, an advertising agency, an independent packaging company, or his packaging supplier, the actual work of package development involves the study and the availability of materials. After suitable designs have been developed and materials chosen, samples of the package are produced and then tested in laboratories and in actual markets before they are adopted for use in the mass distribution of a product.

Some retailers, such as food marketers, do their own packaging. Food marketers receive their fresh meat, vegetables, and fruits in bulk lots. Then either at the warehouse or the store, they divide the lots according to cut, weight, or a convenient number of units and package the food in plastic bags or plastic or cardboard trays covered with plastic wrap. Finally, they add a tag to each of the packages. This tag identifies the item inside the package. In addition, the tag states the weight of the item, as well as its price per pound and its total price.

PACKAGING MATERIALS AND FORMS

The basic materials of packaging are paper, cardboard, metal, glass, wood, and a wide assortment of plastics. All kinds of foods are sold in metal cans and glass jars. Nuts are sold in small cellophane envelopes or in cans; potatoes, in bags made of heavy plastic or paper; and crackers, in cardboard boxes or paper bags. Dried codfish is often packed in small wooden boxes, and ammonia is sold in glass or plastic bottles.

In addition, each of the basic packaging materials can be seen in a variety of forms in the supermarket. The new forms of packaging include aerosol cans, blister packages, and flip-top cans.

Packaging Materials

Paper and cardboard are among the most widely used packaging materials. Paper is inexpensive, lightweight, fairly strong, and easy to print on. Cardboard has all the advantages of paper and is heavier and stronger. Both paper and cardboard can be corrugated for additional toughness, or they can be soaked in wax for added protection against moisture. Cellophane (transparent paper) is used for see-through packaging. Cellophane is particularly useful when the sight of a product is apt to encourage sales, as is true of meat, for example.

Wood and glass are traditional materials for the sturdier or more specialized forms of packaging. Wood makes sturdy shipping crates, which are often reused many times. Glass is used mainly to hold liquids or products containing liquids. It is completely seepage-proof and has no taste or smell to permeate the liquid.

Plastic is used in many forms for packaging. It is shaped into jars and bottles; it is molded into boxes, baskets, and trays; it is processed into sheets for packaging toys, bed linens, small articles of clothing, and a wide variety of food products; and it is expanded into plastic foam for use in packaging fragile items, such as Christmas-tree decorations, glassware and china, and delicate instruments.

Courtesy Modern Packaging Magazine
Cellophane is a popular packaging material for some snack foods.

Metal is a material that has long been used to package liquids and food products. The most commonly used metal container is the can. At one time, all cans were made of steel with a tin plating. Today, aluminum cans are popular, particularly as containers for soft drinks. Self-opening metal cans have been a great help in the automatic vending of soft drinks because they are unbreakable and disposable.

Metallic foil, extremely thin sheet metal, is widely used in commercial packaging. It can be folded and wrapped almost like paper and yet has the strength and moisture resistance of metal. Heavyweight metallic foil is sometimes molded into semirigid shapes and used for holding bakery products.

Packaging Forms

Some of the most familiar forms of packaging are boxes and crates, bottles and jars, and bags and wrappers. One of the newer forms of packaging is called *skin packaging,* in which plastic film is molded tightly over a product mounted on a card. The film keeps the product clean and protected, yet leaves it visible to the customer. The card gives rigidity to the package and provides a surface for printed information.

Very similar to skin packaging is *blister packaging,* in which a plastic bubble is preformed in a plastic sheet. The product is placed on a card, and the bubble is placed over it. The plastic sheet is then sealed to the card.

Another form of packaging is the *aerosol dispenser,* which is a can that releases its contents in spray or foam when a valve is pressed. Aerosol dispensers are popular for such products as hair sprays, shaving creams, perfumes, starches, waxes, paints, room deodorants, and insecticides.

Other interesting developments in forms of packaging include the flexible pouch, the shrink pack, the multipack, and the package with a dispensing closure.

The *flexible pouch* is a package formed from plastic film or paper that is filled with the product and sealed by a heat process. The flexible pouch is used to package an almost limitless variety of products, including candy bars, corn chips, liquids, cake mixes, and hardware items.

The *shrink pack* is a package made by placing clear film around the product itself. The shrink film fits the contour of the product, which may be a book, a record, a small electrical appliance, or even a very large product.

The *multipack* is a special package design that groups two or more packaged products into a unit for easier display, carry-home utility, or user convenience. Many examples of multipack can be found in food stores, drugstores, and hardware stores.

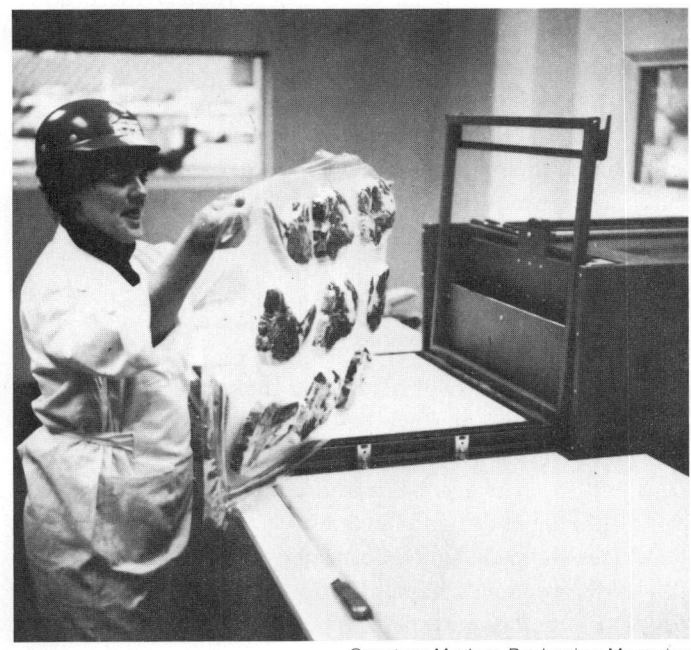

Meats packaged in clear plastic film are well protected and visible to the customer.

Courtesy Modern Packaging Magazine

Part 25 / Packaging and Labeling / 303

A *dispensing closure* is a cap, lid, or seal through which the contents of the container can be dispensed in a controlled manner. Hand lotions, deodorants, liquid soaps, medicines, and household cleansers often come in this type of package. The dispensing closure eliminates spillage. Because of this, consumers usually select a product with this feature rather than a similar product without it.

DESIGNING THE PACKAGE

A package must be designed from the standpoint of how well it does each of the jobs expected of it. A well-designed package can do the following:

- Promote market acceptance.
- Reduce costs.
- Preserve the product for a long time.
- Increase sales and profit.
- Help customers make better use of the product.
- Introduce new products and new uses for existing products.
- Promote a company, its products, and its image.
- Give an established product a modern image.

The planning stage of package design is very important. Several questions must be answered: Must the package protect the product against moisture, leakage, and temperature changes? Must the package be resealed or closed after it has been opened? Will the product be processed in the package?

After such questions have been answered, the next step is to study the market for the product. The producer wants to know the ages of the potential customers, their income group, their geographical location, and their buying habits. The producer also wants to know the sizes and shapes that the retailer can handle most conveniently and the type of store in which the product will be sold.

Next, the actual work of designing the package begins. Here, too, several questions must be answered:

- What material will be used to make the package?
- How will the package be opened?
- How will it be sealed?
- Will the package withstand handling?
- Is the label design effective?
- Does the package conform to government regulations?
- Is the product's name clearly visible?
- Does the design reflect the quality of the product?
- Will the package make a good impression on the customer?

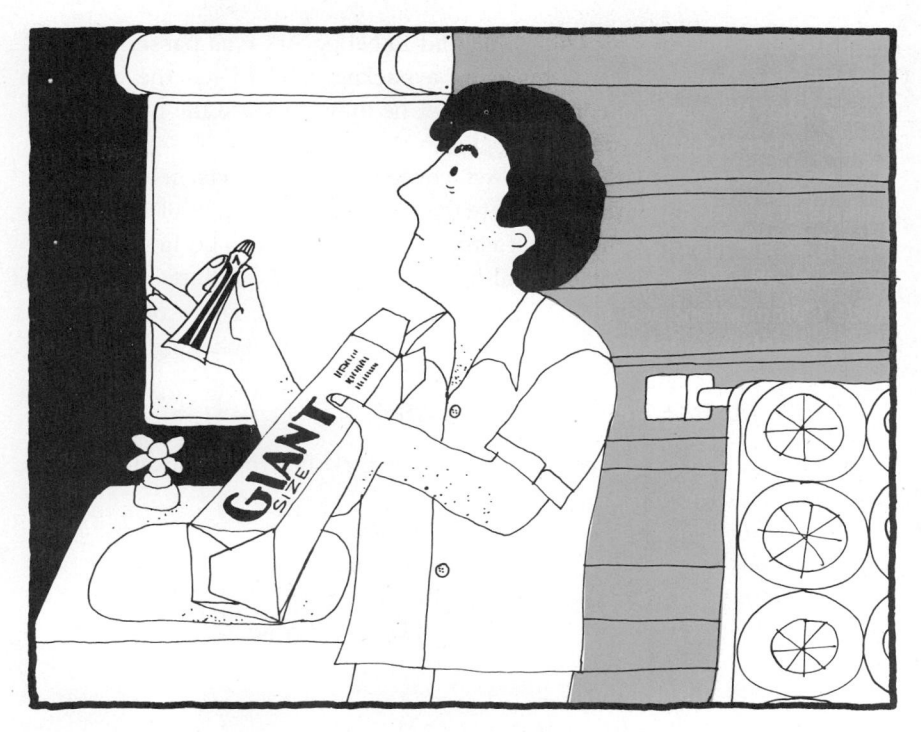

Labels should not be misleading.

Once the package design has been decided, the manufacturing process can begin. Many details must be worked out. For example, a production schedule must be established. A decision must be made whether to install new equipment to make the package or to use an outside firm to manufacture the package.

It is easy to see that developing a package design is almost as complicated as developing the product itself. But to those who recognize the impact of packaging, the work is well worth the effort and the cost.

PACKAGING AND LABELING LAWS

Many packages and their labels must conform to standards established by local and state governments and the federal government. These standards, for the most part, have been established in an attempt to prevent sellers from using misleading labels and packaging.

Sometimes the labels on packages can be misleading. Terms such as "giant economy size" or "super half-quart" used to describe quantity have been found to be confusing to consumers. To protect consumers against deceptive labeling, the Fair Packaging and Labeling Act was passed in 1967. It states that the information given on a package should tell the consumer exactly what the package contains, so that he may compare the product with those of other manufacturers.

The Packaging and Labeling Act covers most products sold in supermarkets. It requires that the label state the contents and weight of the package as well as the name of the manufacturer or distributor. The law is administered by the Department of Health, Education, and Welfare; the Federal Trade Commission; and the Department of Commerce. These organizations review complaints about unfair or deceptive methods of packaging or labeling.

◻ YOUR MARKETING VOCABULARY

On a separate sheet of paper define each of the following marketing terms; then use each term in a sentence.

Aerosol dispenser
Blister packaging
Dispensing closure
Flexible pouch
Label
Multipack
Packaging
Shrink pack
Skin packaging

◻ FOR REVIEW AND DISCUSSION

1. What are the five functions of packaging?
2. Give two examples of packages that offer convenience.
3. Explain the importance of packaging in promoting sales.
4. How is a product usually identified? Why is identification important?
5. What kind of information is given on a brand label? a grade label? a descriptive label?
6. Why is packaging sometimes called a company's "second product"?
7. Who designs the package for a manufacturer's product?
8. Name three packaging materials, giving characteristics and uses of each.
9. What factors must a package designer consider?
10. Why do we have the Fair Packaging and Labeling Act of 1967?

◻ ANALYZING MARKETING CONCEPTS

1. Packaging increases the value, usefulness, and appeal of a product. Prepare a form like the following. In the left-hand column, list these products: (a) popcorn, (b) potato chips, (c) window cleaner, (d) detergent, (e) milk, (f) paper cups, (g) cheese, (h) dry soup mix. For each product, study the materials used to make the package as well as the form of the package. Record your information in the appropriate columns.

Product	Materials Used in Package	Form of Package
Example: Ice cream	Cardboard	Box-shaped

2. The convenience offered by good package design provides an opportunity for an interesting marketing study. Prepare a form like the one below. In the left-hand column, list five products with convenient package designs. In the right-hand column, describe the convenience that each package design offers.

Product	Convenience Offered by Package Design
Example: Bread	Wire fastener reseals air-tight plastic bag.

◊ MARKETING PROJECT 25
Studying a Product Package

Project Goal: Given a product package, evaluate the materials used in the package, the form of the package, and the functions of the package.

Action: Select an actual product package that you believe meets the purposes of packaging as discussed in this part. Study your product package carefully and then answer the following questions:

1. What materials are used in the package?
2. What is the form of the package?
3. How does the package protect the product?
4. How does the package identify the product?
5. How does the package promote the product?
6. What are the special convenience features of the package?

Using your answers to those questions and your actual product package, present an oral report to your class evaluating the marketing effectiveness of the package.

part 26

Pricing the Product

YOUR GOALS

1. Given an increase or decrease in the price of a product, identify the marketing factors causing the change in price.
2. Given a list of consumer products, identify those that are competitive either because they are similar or because they are good substitutes.

Prices are so much a part of our lives that the question "What is price?" seems almost too simple to deserve discussion. Simply stated, price is what a customer pays for something. In a more specific sense, *price* is the amount of money a customer must have at a particular time in order to acquire a particular product or service that he needs or wants.

To command a price, goods and services must have utility—that is, they must be able to satisfy a human need or want—and they must require human effort to make them available to the consumer. For example, cotton cloth helps to satisfy the human need for clothing; therefore it has utility. To make cotton cloth available to the consumer, human effort is required in planting and harvesting the cotton, spinning it into thread, and weaving it into cloth. Cotton cloth and other goods that have utility and require human effort to bring them to market are called *economic goods* and are said to have economic value. The price of such economic goods is in part a reflection of their economic value.

FACTORS AFFECTING PRICING

Deciding on the price at which to sell a product or service is not just a matter of tallying production costs, adding the expenses of operating the business, and providing for a reasonable profit. If that were true, pricing could be done easily by anyone good with figures. But much more than mathematical skill is required in making pricing decisions. Skillful pricing requires judgment. The responsibility for setting the prices of a firm's products, therefore, is usually assigned to key executives in the organization. Such executives are chosen because they have a thorough knowledge of the product, the market, and many other factors that affect price.

Among the important factors considered when setting a price are the costs and business expenses involved in the manufacture or distribution of the product, the fashion and seasonal appeal of the product, the competition, and government price regulations.

Costs and Expenses

Many costs and expenses are involved in the manufacture and distribution of a product. These costs and expenses include expenditures for materials used in making the product, employees' wages, shipping charges, advertising and selling costs, business taxes, costs of major accessory equipment and operating supplies, and costs connected with the research and development of new products. Manufacturers often use these costs in calculating the break-even point for a new product. The *break-even point* is the point at which the money from the sales of a product equals the total costs involved to produce and market the product. After the break-even point has been reached, the company may begin to make a profit on each item sold.

For example, suppose a record manufacturer is planning to produce 5,000 copies of a new record that will sell for $4 each. His cost to produce and market each record is $3, or $15,000 for 5,000 copies. The question now is, "How many records must he sell at $4 each to get back his original cost?" Dividing $15,000 by the selling price of $4 gives him an answer of 3,750 records. The sale of 3,750 records would mark his break-even point. Only after this point has been reached will the sale of the records begin to yield a profit. Manufacturers find the use of break-even analysis very helpful in determining what price to set for achieving their profit goals.

The price of this coat would probably be affected by seasonal changes.

Courtesy J. C. Penney

Fashion and Seasonal Appeal of the Product

The marketer of fashion merchandise knows that its value to the customer is highest at the beginning of the fashion cycle. Thus the price for fashion goods is likely to be high when a style is just appearing. The price drops when the style is well established and drops further when it becomes outdated.

In seasonal merchandise, too, prices are likely to be higher at the beginning of the season than at the end. Ice skates are usually reduced in price in February; women's white shoes generally cost less in late July than in May; and children's school clothes usually go on sale in April.

Competition

When a manufacturer is setting prices, he must always keep in mind competition from three sources: similar products (Pepsi-Cola watches the prices of Coca-Cola, for example), substitute products (manufacturers of leather wallets watch the prices charged for plastic wallets), and dissimilar products or services that could be chosen in preference to his own products or services (a bowling alley's business could be affected by a skating rink built in the same town).

The retailer's competition comes from similar stores or from discount stores seeking to sell similar items at lower prices. If a retailer expects to get a high price for an item that is being sold for less at a discount store, he must be prepared to offer customer services usually not offered by a discount store, such as credit, gift wrapping, and extra sales help.

Government Price Regulations

Many federal and state laws control what businesses may and may not do in setting prices. Some of these laws are very complex, and considerable study is required to understand them fully.

In general, the federal laws are directed toward the prevention of unfair competition and monopoly. *Monopoly* is the control by one company of the supply of one kind of economic goods. The Sherman Antitrust Act of 1890 outlawed monopolies as a form of unfair economic competition. The Clayton Act of 1914 defined price discrimination as unlawful when it creates unfair competition. The Robinson-Patman Act of 1936 strengthened the provisions of the Clayton Act. Briefly, the Clayton and Robinson-Patman laws state that a seller cannot offer one customer one price and another customer a different price if both customers are buying the same product.

Most state laws concern resale price maintenance, and they are called fair-trade laws. These laws allow a manufacturer to set a price at which his products must be sold at retail, or to set a price below which his products may not be sold at retail. For a time, almost all states had fair-trade laws. In the past few years, however, many states have revoked them, usually on the ground that they tend to eliminate price competition at the retail level. Discount stores are a major force in the battle against fair-trade laws.

CAUSES OF PRICE CHANGES

Regardless of the amount of care taken in setting a price for a product when it first appears on the market, the prices of many goods change frequently. The prices of certain foods soar one season and go down the next, fashion merchandise is "marked down for clearance" when new styles appear, and bathing suits are less expensive at the end of the summer than in June. Yet a $19.95 swimsuit bought for $9.98 at the end of the summer is the same bathing suit that was available at the beginning of the season. Its appearance has not changed—it is still in good condition, still in style, still useful to the consumer. Tomatoes might cost 59 cents a pound in June; by August, they are likely to be 39 cents a pound. Yet the tomatoes available in August are bigger, riper, and more flavorful than those sold in June. Why, then, did prices drop in August?

The economic value of the bathing suit has been affected by a decrease in demand, because there are fewer customers for swimsuits in late summer. When demand for a product decreases, prices tend to drop. Tomato prices fall when there is an increased supply of tomatoes, which is likely in late summer. When supply of a product increases, prices usually fall. These two factors—the supply of a product and the customer demand for it—are basic considerations in pricing.

Nature of Supply and Demand

The amount of a product that a supplier decides to sell at a specified price is called *supply*. A supplier may decide to hold back some of his goods if he expects prices to rise; the goods that he withholds would not be considered part of supply until they are offered for sale at a specified price.

The amount of a product that consumers are willing to purchase at different prices is called *demand*.

Effect of Supply and Demand

Although other factors also affect pricing, supply and demand are the basic considerations in determining the market value of goods. It is important to understand the relationship between price, supply, and demand. The following rules and examples help to clarify this relationship.

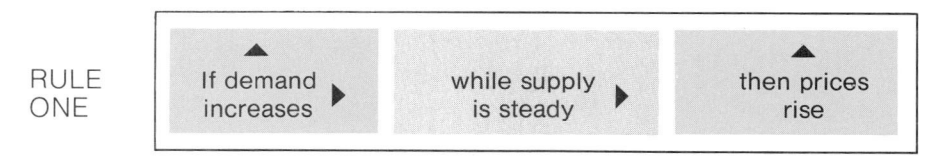

RULE ONE | If demand increases ▶ while supply is steady ▶ then prices rise

EXAMPLE 1. Florida is a popular spot for tourists. The most desirable months to go there are February, March, and April. Florida attracts more tourists during those months than at any other time of year (increase in demand). The number of hotel and motel rooms in Florida is about the same throughout the year (supply is steady). As a result, the rate for room rentals increases during February, March, and April (prices rise). For example, a one-room efficiency apartment that costs approximately $150 a week during the month of August might cost about $200 a week in the prime months of February, March, and April.

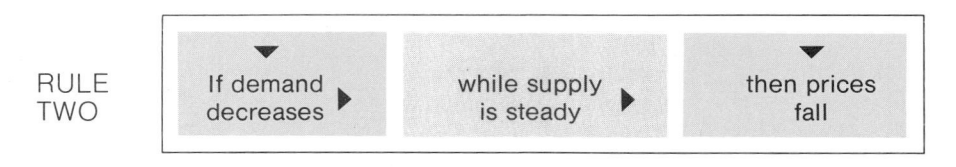

RULE TWO | If demand decreases ▶ while supply is steady ▶ then prices fall

EXAMPLE 2. Cranberries are very popular at Thanksgiving; they are part of the traditional holiday feast. Some years ago, just before Thanksgiving, consumers were warned to beware of that season's cranberry crop. Health authorities reported that the cranberries had been sprayed with an insecticide just before harvesting, and this insecticide might possibly make the cranberries unfit to eat. Despite all efforts of the cranberry growers to reassure the public that there was no danger in eating the cranberries, many consumers were afraid to buy fresh cranberries or canned cranberry sauce (demand decreased). The cranberries were already being harvested in large quantities, and nothing could be done to reduce the supply (supply was steady). Cranberries came to market, but at greatly reduced prices (prices fell).

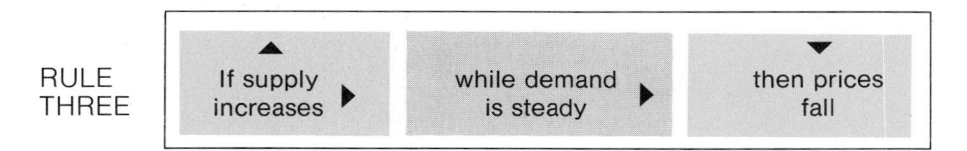

RULE THREE | If supply increases ▲ | while demand is steady | then prices fall ▼

EXAMPLE 3. During World War II almost all available nylon was used in the war effort, and very little of it was used to make women's stockings. The few pairs of nylon stockings available were very expensive, even higher in price than they had been before the war. After the war, nylon was again available to the consumer market and nylon stockings began to be manufactured in large quantities (supply increased). After an initial rush of buying, the demand for nylon stockings became fairly consistent (demand was steady). Therefore, as the supply increased, prices fell drastically.

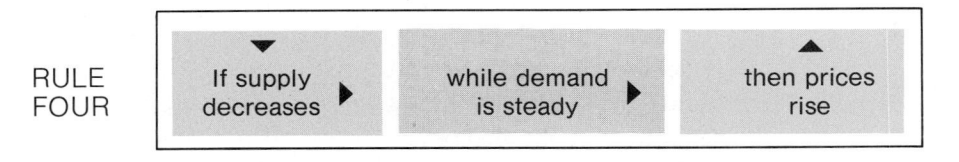

RULE FOUR | If supply decreases ▼ | while demand is steady | then prices rise ▲

EXAMPLE 4. Many people like hamburgers, and the demand for ground beef, which is used to make them, is fairly constant all year (demand is steady). But if a widespread epidemic of hoof-and-mouth disease were to kill many steers and make others unfit to eat (supply decreases), beef prices would rise sharply and hamburgers would cost more.

GOALS OF PRICING

Every marketer is in business to make a profit, and prices are usually set with this profit motive clearly in mind. However, building a successful business involves more than earning a certain profit each year. Often a company will adopt a pricing policy that seems to sacrifice some of the profit that it could earn. In such a case, the company feels that this policy will help achieve a specific marketing goal that could make the company even more successful and profitable in the long run.

Companies, then, have certain goals that they hope to achieve through careful pricing. Three of these goals are the following: to obtain a specific share of the market, to achieve a specific return from sales, and to match the competition.

Obtaining a Specific Share of the Market

Rather than be guided by the profit motive, many companies strive to obtain a specific percentage of customers. If, for example, there were ten record companies in the United States, it might seem fair to expect the market share for each one to be 10 percent of all money spent on records. But a record company that produced more than 10 percent of the records and had a larger-than-average sales staff would expect a higher market share, perhaps 15 percent.

To achieve a higher market share, that record company might cut its prices. Although cutting prices would give the company a lower profit on each sale, it could also increase total sales. If this pricing policy succeeded, the increase in total sales would more than make up for the lower profit on each record.

By setting a specific share of the market as its marketing goal, a company is more likely to maintain its market position than if its goal is profit alone. *Market position* is a company's competitive standing based on its sales volume compared with that of the other companies in the same industry. To maintain its market position, a company must continually note any changes in the size of the market and keep track of the growth of competing companies. A company directed toward profit alone might be satisfied if it were able to maintain an annual profit of $100,000 for five succeeding years. Yet its market position might be steadily declining because of competing companies increasing their advertising programs and enjoying more sales from an expanding market.

Achieving a Specific Return From Sales

Many companies set their own guidelines for pricing, particularly those that are industry leaders or are in industries with little or no competition. Of course, they want to earn as high a profit as possible, but they also want to avoid being accused of unfair trade practices. To justify the profit they earn, these companies often set a target return on sales. *Target return* is a method of pricing that involves setting price levels according to the rate of profit that

A marketer may cut his prices in order to increase sales.

a company wants to earn from its sales. In this approach, the rate of desired profit return on sales is decided first; then prices are set to bring about this rate of return. Such a practice protects a business organization from the accusation that it has made unreasonable profits, since its records will show that it has earned profits at a just and reasonable rate.

Utility and telephone companies usually determine their prices according to target return. These companies operate largely as monopolies and are therefore subject to close government control. They need to earn a reasonable profit to pay dividends to their stockholders and to have money to invest in their businesses, but it is to the benefit of the public that this profit be limited. Pricing according to a target return that is acceptable to the government allows the companies to meet their own needs and yet serve the public as economically as possible.

Matching the Competition

Sometimes a company lets its competitors set the price and then follows with a matching price. This strategy is useful if the market has become very competitive or if a company is trying to win a share of a new market.

For example, a furniture manufacturer may want to go into the unfinished-furniture business. However, until he gets a foothold in that market, the amount he sells will be relatively small. He must therefore manufacture items in small volume, and the cost of each item will be relatively high. Rather than set his prices high enough to cover those costs, he may choose to charge the average prices of his competitors. By matching the prices of his competitors, he should be able to win customers; and once his sales volume increases, his cost for each unit will drop and his prices will begin to bring a profit.

YOUR MARKETING VOCABULARY

On a separate sheet of paper define each of the following marketing terms; then use each term in a sentence.

Break-even point   *Monopoly*
Demand   *Price*
Economic goods   *Supply*
Market position   *Target return*

FOR REVIEW AND DISCUSSION

1. What characteristics must goods and services have in order to command a price?
2. Who usually has the responsibility for pricing products and services in a business organization? Why?
3. Name four important factors that a company must consider in setting the price of a product.
4. When is the value of fashion merchandise highest to the customer? What causes price changes in fashion goods?
5. What three sources of competition must the manufacturer always keep in mind when he is setting prices?
6. List the four rules that explain the effect of supply and demand on prices.
7. What is the main purpose of federal price-regulation laws?
8. What is the chief concern of pricing laws enacted by the various states?
9. List three goals that a company may hope to achieve through careful pricing.
10. Why is it to a company's advantage to seek a specific share of the market rather than a specific profit?

ANALYZING MARKETING CONCEPTS

1. When pricing a product, a marketer must consider his competition. Prepare a form like the following one. In the left-hand column, list these products: (a) TV set, (b) toothpaste, (c) business magazine, (d) economy

car, (e) luggage, (f) typewriter. In the right-hand column, write the brand names of five competing products for each product listed in the left-hand column.

Product	Competing Products

2. Supply and demand are important considerations in setting the prices of goods. Prepare a form like the one below and write the following situations in the left-hand column: (a) A department store reduces the price of its Christmas cards by 50 percent two days before Christmas. (b) A concession stand sells 10-cent candy bars for 20 cents at a ball game. (c) An appliance dealer encourages customers to buy an air conditioner before a certain date and receive a camera free.

In the right-hand column, explain how supply and demand influence the pricing of the product in each situation.

Situation	Influence of Supply and Demand on Price
Example: A department store reduces the price of its winter coats by 30 percent in the spring.	Spring weather reduced the demand for winter coats; store wants to sell its winter stock to make room for spring clothing.

◊ MARKETING PROJECT 26
Studying Price Changes

Project Goal: Given an increase or decrease in the price of a product, identify the marketing factors causing the change in price.

Action: With your teacher's permission, visit a business of your choice and ask the manager to identify a specific product that has increased or decreased in price in the past six months. Discuss with him the marketing factors that could have caused the change in price.

Make a written report of your findings, and be prepared to give an oral report to your class.

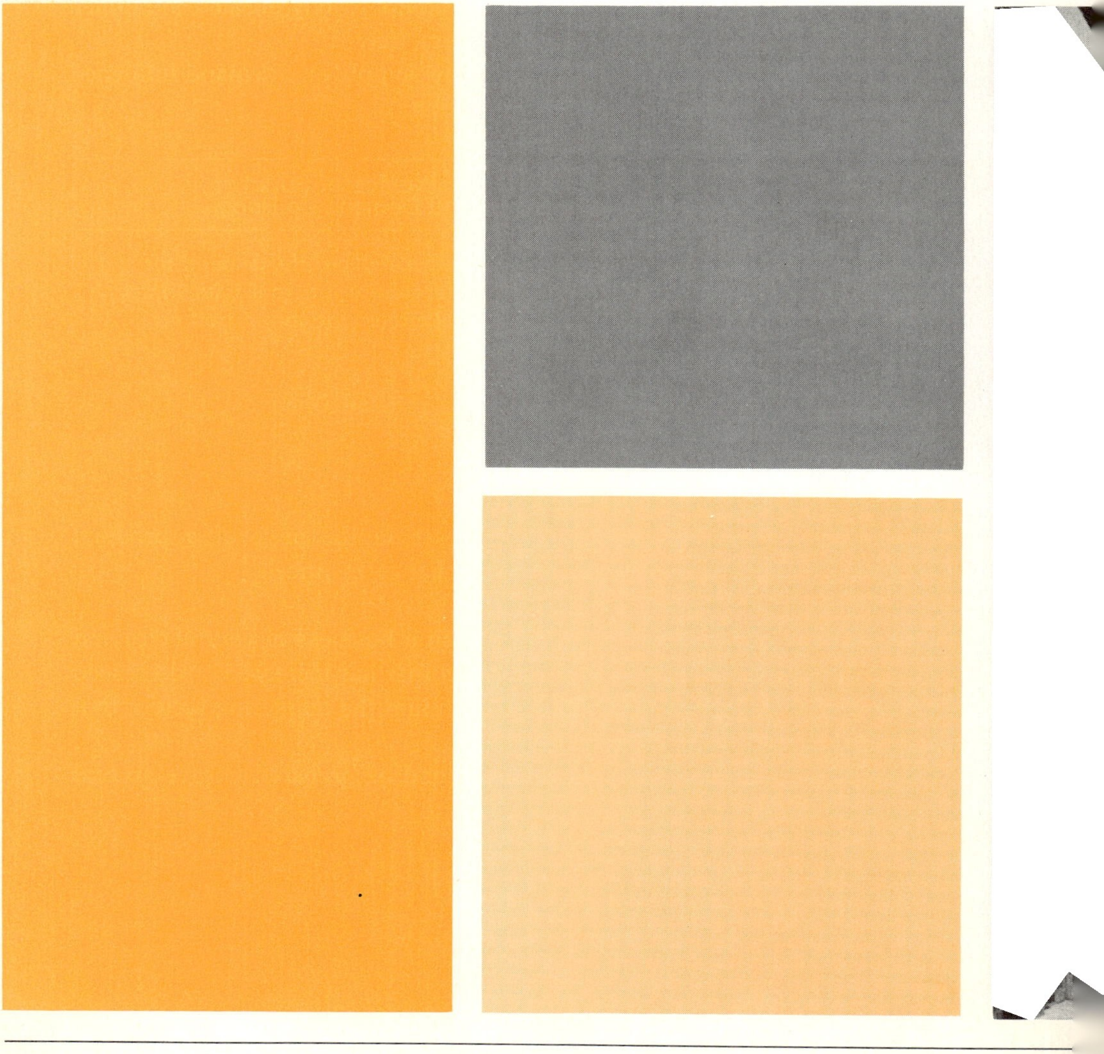

Physical Distribution

UNIT 8

part 27
Transporting the Goods

YOUR GOALS

1. Given a number of products to be shipped to your community, determine the best means of transporting those products.
2. Given a list of transportation services, determine which services are available in your business community and who uses them.

Throughout the United States, trucks, planes, trains, and machinery are constantly involved in moving goods to various destinations. A trailer truck carries a cargo of fresh asparagus to the wholesale vegetable market. A jet cargo plane flies a load of high-fashion suits to an airport for movement to a department store. A freight train delivers a shipment of new automobiles to a siding where they are removed for delivery by truck to an authorized dealer. A forklift truck in a giant warehouse lifts a load of books off the loading platform, moves it to the proper area, and unloads it into a storage space.

Each of these activities is concerned with *physical distribution,* the total process of moving, handling, and storing goods on the way from the producer to the final user. Physical distribution, then, includes both transportation and warehousing of products. Transportation is discussed in this part, and warehousing is discussed in Part 28.

CARRIERS AND THEIR OWNERS

A company that transports goods between the producer and the consumer or industrial user is called a *carrier*. Carriers can be classified into three types: common, contract, and private.

A *common carrier* is a transportation company that provides equipment and services to any shipper for a fee and takes full responsibility for the safe arrival of the goods. Some common carriers haul all kinds of goods. Other common carriers specialize in a single kind of good or a related group of goods, such as fresh vegetables, grain, or liquid petroleum products.

A *contract carrier* is a transportation company that owns transportation equipment and rents it to other companies for specified lengths of time. A contract carrier is often responsible for servicing and maintaining its rented transportation equipment. However, the company that rents the equipment is responsible for the goods being transported. Some contract carriers rent on a short-term, one-time basis. Others work so closely and for so long with a company renting their equipment that they almost become part of that company.

A *private carrier* is a transportation facility owned and used by a firm to transport its products. A baking company that delivers bread in its own company trucks is using a private carrier. A mining company that ships ore in its own barges is using a private carrier.

Each type of carrier has certain advantages and disadvantages for the marketer. A large company involved in considerable and continuous transportation of freight may prefer to buy and operate its own transportation equipment. A smaller company with a special kind of product to ship may rent specialized transportation equipment from a contract carrier on a regular basis. Still another company may find it most economical to ship its goods via a common carrier.

Many marketers use a combination of transportation methods. They may own and use a small fleet of trucks for local shipments and rent trailer trucks from contract carriers for long hauls. They may also send some shipments by rail transportation and some by air or water transportation.

RAILROAD TRANSPORTATION

The most important kind of freight transportation in the United States is the railroad. Before the spread of highways and the growth of airports throughout this country, the railroads carried more freight than all other forms of transportation combined. Although that overall percentage has dropped, the railroads still carry more freight than any other single form of transportation.

Railroad Equipment and Services

One reason for the wide use of railroads is that they will carry almost any kind of good, in almost any amount, size, and weight. Most types of freight are carried in boxcars, but the railroads are buying an increasing number of specialized cars adapted to the needs of certain shippers (the companies that are sending out goods). Gondolas and hoppers carry gravel, coal, and other kinds of loose material. Covered hopper cars carry grain and malt. Multilevel auto racks carry new automobiles. Tank cars haul liquids. Refrigerator cars carry perishable foods. Flatcars transport bulk goods that cannot be hurt by bad weather.

Piggyback and Fishyback. Piggyback, or TOFC (trailer on flatcar), service has been developed to give freight cars more uses and to meet the growing competition from trucks. In this system, loaded trailer trucks are driven or swung right onto railroad flatcars and are carried to freight terminals by rail. This gives a shipper the advantages of both rail and truck travel, without the need to unload and reload for each form of transportation.

A citrus grower in Florida might use TOFC (pronounced: tof-see). When his fruit is ready, he wants to ship it north quickly and safely and at a cost low enough to make a reasonable profit. He crates his fruit and loads it carefully onto a trailer truck. The truck is driven to the nearest railroad terminal and loaded onto a flatcar. A freight train speeds the flatcar to a northern railroad terminal. There the trailer truck is taken off the flatcar and driven the

Courtesy National Petroleum News

In piggyback freight service, loaded trailers are driven on and off railroad flatcars. Piggyback service combines the convenience of truck transportation with the economy of long-distance rail transportation.

final few miles to its destination. Because of TOFC, the shipper receives both the door-to-door advantage of truck transportation and the lower-cost rates of long-distance rail transportation. Moreover, he avoids possible damage to his shipment by not having to unload and reload the fruit.

Fishyback is a further development in freight service. It adds water transportation to the piggyback pattern. Trailer trucks are carried piggyback to the port, and then loaded onto ships or barges.

Less-Than-Carload. The two basic classifications in rail freight service are carload lots (CL) and less-than-carload lots (LCL). A *carload lot* is a shipment that completely fills a freight car. A *less-than-carload lot* is a shipment that does not fill a freight car. A CL shipment is carried at a somewhat lower rate for its weight and size than an LCL shipment, because a shipment that fills a car is easier to transport than one that does not.

Many railroads offer special LCL services. In most of these plans, shipments from different senders that are destined for the same general area are combined at a shipping point. They travel as a single carload shipment and get the benefit of the lower carload rate. They are divided into individual shipments again when they reach their rail destination.

Pros and Cons of Railroad Shipping

Railroads are particularly useful for hauling large quantities of goods long distances. Their long-distance rates are generally lower than those of other forms of transportation, except for some forms of water transportation. Thus shipping by railroad is often the most economical way to transport coal, ore, logs, grain, and other bulky low-value products.

The services offered by railroads are increasing. Freight cars today are larger, and they offer shippers such improvements as wider loading doors and better springs to reduce damage in transit. Shippers now have a much wider selection of types of cars to haul their freight. To speed service, railroads have automated switching, the transferring of trains from track to track. In addition, computers give the shipper instant and constant information on the progress of the freight car carrying his goods.

One of the main disadvantages of rail shipping is that door-to-door service is not part of regular service and costs extra.

MOTOR TRANSPORTATION

The railroad's biggest transportation competitor is the truck. The use of trucks has increased rapidly in recent years, particularly for long-distance freight shipments. As the number of roads and highways in the United States increases, truck transportation is likely to experience continued growth. One can hardly take a walk or even look out a window without seeing a local delivery truck. It may, for example, be delivering bread, soft drinks, gasoline, fuel oil, or mail. The procedure for delivering each of these goods is similar in many respects. Workers load the trucks at a plant or outlying station, and during the day a routeman or driver makes stops according to a prearranged schedule.

Long-distance delivery, on the other hand, takes trucks from one city to another, frequently from coast to coast. The trucks used for long-distance delivery are usually trailer trucks. Trailer trucks are a familiar sight on highways. They consist of a cab, in which the driver sits, and a trailer, in which the goods are carried. Trailer trucks are larger than those used for local deliveries. Superhighways enable these trucks to move rapidly.

Trucking Equipment and Services

To handle the variety of products to be delivered, motor transportation companies have developed specialized types of equipment. Van trucks carry household furniture, machinery parts, and dry goods. Refrigerator trucks carry perishables, such as lettuce, ice cream, and meat. Platform trucks haul bars of steel and bales of cotton. Tank trucks carry fluids, such as oil, milk, molasses, and gasoline. Dump trucks transport gravel, sand, crushed rock, and chemicals. Pole trucks carry logs, large pipes, and telephone poles. Armored cars, garbage trucks, and cement trucks are other examples of specialized equipment.

Although many shipments fill a truck completely, less-than-truckload (LTL) shipments are the backbone of the trucking business. Trucking companies offer a variety of special route services to meet the needs of LTL shippers and they give these shippers special rates.

Pros and Cons of Trucking

Although shipping by truck usually costs more than shipping by rail, the total transportation cost can be lower. Truck shipping is a door-to-door service, and there is no need to pay extra for pickup and delivery. The flexibility of truck routes is also an important advantage. Trucks are often the preferred form of transportation for shipments that are more compact and of higher value than those sent by rail, and for shipments where door-to-door handling is important.

The main disadvantage of trucking is the fact that a truck is vulnerable in the same way that the family car is vulnerable. Traffic tie-ups, road accidents, bad weather, and equipment breakdowns—any one of these can slow down or halt service.

Courtesy Fruehauf Div., Fruehauf Corp.
This stainless-steel trailer can carry up to 7,000 gallons of chemicals.

WATER TRANSPORTATION

Ships and barges are among the oldest forms of transportation. They were in use on waterways long before railroads and trucks were even dreamed of. Of course, the ships and barges of today bear little resemblance to their crude ancestors. Modern vessels have been developed to haul railroad cars and truck trailers. Others have been designed specially for dry cargo, such as grain, sugar, and coal. Double-hulled tankers carry liquids. Insulated barges haul goods requiring a constant temperature. The size of some of these ships, particularly those engaged in foreign trade, is startling. Some oil tankers, for example, are among the largest ships afloat.

In this country, a considerable amount of freight is carried from one place to another on intracoastal and internal waterways. Intracoastal shipping is from one port to another along the coasts or from ports of one coast to ports of another coast (the route from the Atlantic coast to the Pacific coast takes ships through the Panama Canal). Internal shipping is from one port to the other on waterways such as the Mississippi River and Great Lakes.

Intracoastal and internal water transportation are most likely to be used by shippers who have extra-large quantities of a low-value product to move. Although such transportation is slow and its routes are limited, it does offer the capacity for carrying very large loads at very low rates.

With the growth of international trade, overseas water transportation is increasing. This shipping is mainly of two types: liner service and tramp service. Liner service provides freight transportation on regular routes on a scheduled basis. Tramp service is mostly contract business; the ship route is determined by the type of goods being shipped. Almost all overseas freight is transported by ship and barge; only comparatively small amounts are carried by airplanes.

These workmen are laying a gas pipeline. Pipelines are a usually unseen but very important form of transportation.

Courtesy Columbia Gas of Ohio

PIPELINE TRANSPORTATION

Few people think of pipelines as a major form of transportation equipment, yet pipelines rank third in volume among freight carriers. While oil and gas are the principal products transported by pipelines, other products include wood pulp and finely ground ores. These solids are transported by mixing them with liquid and flushing them along the pipeline.

Most pipelines are owned by the companies using them and are therefore really private carriers. The federal government has ruled, however, that because pipelines cross state borders, they must technically be considered common carriers and must abide by the rules and regulations governing common carriers.

AIR TRANSPORTATION

Airlines are the newest form of freight carrier and the smallest in terms of volume of freight carried, but their share of the transportation business is growing rapidly. Air shipment is usually the costliest form of transportation, but it offers a speed unmatched by other forms. Shipments sent by air, therefore, are usually light in weight, small in size, high in value, and often perishable.

The advantages of air transportation are the speed and frequency of flights and the accessibility to overseas areas not reached by trains or trucks. The disadvantages include the greater expense and the danger of delay because of weather conditions.

Airlines are increasing their appeal to shippers by developing larger equipment, thus enabling a single aircraft to carry more freight. They are also offering reductions in price for air freight shipped at certain times or on certain scheduled flights.

SPECIAL SERVICES

A number of special services are available to shippers. These services are offered by the Railway Express Agency, the federal postal service, and freight forwarding companies. The services of these organizations are particularly useful to companies that want to transport smaller shipments and packages. A shipper can get the help of transportation specialists, a combination of several types of transportation, and door-to-door service.

Railway Express Agency

The Railway Express Agency, or REA as it is now known, began more than a hundred years ago as a small package service offered by one railroad. Today it is a large company that handles shipments on railroads, trucks, ships, and planes, and is owned jointly by all railroads.

REA Express specializes in small-package and less-than-carload shipments. It handles almost any kind of freight, including perishables and animals. It moves shipments on special express trains that travel faster than normal freight trains. REA Express no longer relies exclusively on rail transportation. It may use truck, air, and ship transportation for all or part of the freight journey.

Parcel Post

Sometimes the simplest way to ship a small package is through the postal service. Parcel post is the fourth class of mail accepted by the postal service. Rigid regulations control the type and size of package, its contents, and how it should be wrapped, tied, and identified. If a package meets these requirements, it can be shipped at a very low cost by parcel post.

Although parcel post is noted for its low cost, it may be slow because of its low priority on the postal service's transportation facilities. For shippers who want quicker service, postal service does offer air parcel post and special delivery service at a higher cost.

Freight Forwarders

Some shippers simplify the transportation of their products by using freight forwarders. *Freight forwarders* are independent companies that collect the small shipments of various businesses, combine them into truckload or carload lots, and ship them by truck or rail. Although they work mainly with railroads and trucking companies, freight forwarders also work with some air and water transportation companies.

The freight forwarder's job is to arrange and watch over shipments. He collects small- or odd-sized shipments from various shippers in an area and charges each shipper less-than-carload (LCL) rates. He then puts these shipments together in carload or truckload lots and arranges for their transportation. He also takes care of distributing the shipments at their destination.

Because his shipments are in carload or truckload lots, the freight forwarder pays carload or truckload rates to the common carriers; these rates are lower than the LCL rates which he charges the shippers. The difference in these rates provides for his operating expense and a reasonable profit.

Perhaps you are wondering why a shipper would use a freight forwarder instead of a common carrier when both charge the same LCL rates. The answer is that the shipper gets four advantages from using a freight forwarder: speed, and minimum handling in shipping, the freight forwarder's services as a transportation manager, and pickup and delivery of his goods to and from the common carrier.

◻ YOUR MARKETING VOCABULARY

On a separate sheet of paper define each of the following marketing terms; then use each term in a sentence.

Carload lot
Carrier
Common carrier
Contract carrier

Freight forwarders
Less-than-carload lot
Physical distribution
Private carrier

◻ FOR REVIEW AND DISCUSSION

1. What factors does the marketer consider in selecting a carrier?
2. Why are railroads popular as a method of transportation? Name and describe two shipping services offered by railroads.

3. For what reasons is shipping by truck often selected over shipping by rail?
4. Describe some of the specialized equipment that trucking companies have developed for shipping different types of products.
5. Name and describe the two main forms of water transportation to foreign ports.
6. Why are most of the privately owned pipelines technically considered common carriers?
7. What are the advantages of air transportation?
8. What service does the Railway Express Agency offer?
9. Why is parcel post one of the slowest methods of transportation?
10. Describe the responsibilities of freight forwarders.

◆ ANALYZING MARKETING CONCEPTS

1. On a form like the one below, write the following descriptions of carriers in the left-hand column: (a) Union Transport owns its trucks and hauls gasoline for other companies. (b) Ace Baking Company delivers its goods in its own trucks. (c) Jackson Hauling Company rents trucks to other firms. (d) Harris Trucking Company owns its trucks and hauls coal from local mines. (e) Murphy Mining Company ships ore in its barges.

   Based on this information, classify each carrier as common, contract, or private by placing a check mark in the appropriate column of your form.

Description of Carrier	Type of Carrier		
	Common	Contract	Private
Example: Hayes Freight Lines owns its trucks.			✓

2. On a form like the one below, list the following methods of transportation in the left-hand column: (a) truck, (b) ship, (c) pipeline, (d) air carrier. For each method of transportation, think of a type of company that might use it, and record your answer in the center column. In the right-hand column, describe the purpose for which the company would use the method of transportation.

Method of Transportation	Type of Company	Transportation Purpose
Example: Freight train	Automobile manufacturer	To ship new automobiles to distributors.

MARKETING PROJECT 27
Selecting Methods of Transportation

Your Goal: Given a number of products to be shipped to your community, determine the best means of transporting those products.

Action: Assume that you own a combination discount house-supermarket in your community. You have ordered several shipments of merchandise from various parts of the country and must arrange for the most suitable methods of shipment. You will pay all shipping charges. Assume that water transportation is the cheapest but slowest method, that air freight is the fastest but most expensive method, and that truck and rail transportation offer moderate speed at costs between those of air freight and water transportation.

Using a map of the United States, determine the best means of transporting the following products to your community:

1. From Oregon: 100 spruce trees, 3 feet tall, planted in bushel baskets.
2. From California: 275 bathing suits.
3. From Maine: 200 live lobsters.
4. From Florida: 400 crates of oranges.
5. From Georgia: a carload shipment of canned peaches.

Prepare a form like the one below in which to record your answers.

Product	Approximate Shipping Distance	Suggested Transportation Method	Reason for Choice

part 28

Warehousing the Goods

YOUR GOALS

1. Given a list of goods, indicate how a warehouse can add value by storing and handling those goods.
2. Given a list of warehouses in your community, select one and determine the services it offers and the types of products it handles.

A *warehouse* is a storage and handling facility. It is the heart of the physical distribution system. Nearly every shipment of cargo is either coming from or going to a warehouse. Nearly every product marketed has traveled through or been stored in at least one and often several warehouses.

Storage is the biggest job of warehousing, but handling and processing jobs such as dividing and assembling shipments, packaging certain products, and controlling inventory are also important.

WHY WAREHOUSES ARE NEEDED

Warehousing serves many purposes. It protects goods, increases their value, helps stabilize prices, and eases financial burdens. The warehouse keeps products in good condition. It protects them against theft, fire, flood, heat

This meat is being graded during its stay in a refrigerated warehouse.

and cold, and insects and animals. The warehouse building itself—sturdy, weathertight, and fireproof—is enough protection for many products, but others need special care. For example, meat and vegetables need a warehouse with refrigeration facilities to keep from spoiling; and grain must be protected from excess heat or dampness by means of special temperature and humidity controls.

Of prime importance to the marketer is the fact that warehouses add time utility to the value of goods. The production of goods and the demand for them are rarely identical. When the rate of production is higher than the rate of demand—that is, when there are more goods available than there are buyers—the excess goods are stored in warehouses until there is a demand for them. At that time the goods are released from the warehouses to the market. Storage has given those goods time utility.

The condition of some products is improved during their stay in the warehouse. This adds to the value of the products. For example, lumber is seasoned in the warehouse, certain meats and cheeses are aged, and hides are cured. These products need time to reach the peak of condition, and their stay in the warehouse gives them that time.

Warehouse storage helps to avoid sharp changes in the selling price of many products by keeping excess supply off the market until it is needed. Without storage the price of potatoes, for example, would be very low during the harvest season, when they are plentiful, and very high the rest of the year. During the harvest season, the low prices would hurt the potato growers, who have put considerable time and money into their crops. During the rest of the year, prices could be so high that many families could not afford to buy potatoes. Because potatoes are stored while they are plentiful and are therefore available throughout the year such extreme price variations are avoided.

Products that are sitting idle in a warehouse represent frozen capital. Not until these products are sold can the marketer turn his frozen assets into cash. There are times, however, when the marketer may need to borrow money to cover business expenses until the goods are sold. This he can do by obtaining a warehouse receipt. A *warehouse receipt* is a statement given by the warehouse management indicating the value of the goods placed in the warehouse for storage. The marketer can use these warehouse receipts as security to borrow the money needed to meet business expenses.

TYPES OF WAREHOUSES

Warehouses are usually found near transportation facilities in manufacturing and marketing centers. There are two basic types of warehouses: public and private. Both public and private warehouses may also be bonded. These terms are defined and discussed in the following paragraphs.

Public Warehouses

An independent business that provides the service of storing and handling goods for other businesses is called a *public warehouse.* The public warehouse owns its building and equipment but does not own the goods it handles. It is, however, responsible for providing reasonable protection for the goods.

Fees charged by the public warehouse are based on the amount of space the customer uses, the length of time the goods are stored, and the kind of handling or processing requested.

The most common type of public warehouse is the *general-merchandise warehouse,* which stores any kind of product that needs only protection from the weather.

A public warehouse used for agricultural products that need special care, such as grain and cotton, is called a special-commodity warehouse.

Perishables, such as peaches and melons, need a constant cold temperature to avoid quick deterioration. Some other foods, such as apples and potatoes, can be stored at room temperature but will last a good deal longer if placed in cold storage. To preserve these foods for the longest possible time both types are stored in a cold-storage warehouse.

Private Warehouses

Most warehouses are privately owned by manufacturers, wholesalers, or retailers. A *private warehouse* is a storage and handling facility owned by the company that uses it. Private warehouses are of many types. Each company designs its warehouses to suit its own products.

Companies that own their own warehouses try to locate them close to where the goods will be needed. As goods come off the production line at the factory, for example, they are shipped by carload or truckload to regional warehouses owned by the company. When orders for those goods are received, the factory notifies the regional warehouse in the appropriate area to ship the product to the customer. In this way, goods do not accumulate at the factory. Once the goods are manufactured, they are transported as inexpensively as possible and stored in a location from which orders can be filled quickly.

Wholesalers and retailers locate their warehouses close to where the goods will be needed for the same reasons. In the food industry, for example, a wholesaler may locate his private warehouse within a short trucking distance of the supermarkets he serves. Likewise, a retailer of television sets and radios may locate his warehouse in an area near most of his customers.

Bonded Warehouses

A particular type of warehouse used to store products requiring a federal tax is called a *bonded warehouse.* Sometimes the federal tax agents place their own seal on the warehouse or sections of the warehouse containing bonded products. A "bonded product" is any domestic or imported product that cannot be removed from a warehouse and sold until taxes are paid. Bonded warehouses are either public or private.

To the marketer the advantage of using a bonded warehouse is that he does not pay the required federal tax until he removes his goods from storage. Thus he does not tie up that money in stored inventory.

INSIDE THE WAREHOUSE

How efficiently the warehouse does its job helps to determine the cost of distributing a product. A good warehouse system can mean lower costs and more efficient service to customers. On the other hand, a poor warehouse system can hurt the sales of even a good product.

Mechanization in materials handling has increased warehousing efficiency.

Courtesy National Petroleum News

Warehouse efficiency has been greatly improved by new materials-handling methods. *Materials handling* is the process of assembling, packing, weighing, and moving products from a producer to a warehouse, from a warehouse to a carrier, or from one carrier to another.

At one time, warehouses were primarily storage centers. Today they still store goods but usually for as short a time as possible. The modern concept of warehousing puts emphasis on order fulfillment. Storage means inventory dollars sitting idle. Order fulfillment means inventory dollars making money. The warehouse now is thought of by some companies as a distribution center. A *distribution center* is the link between the supplier and the customer; it is the place where products are received, stored, and processed, and the place from which products are shipped.

Receiving

The first job at the warehouse is to see that shipments are received safely and intact. This means safe unloading and careful inspection of each shipment to assure that it is in the condition claimed by the shipper. Any discrepancies or damages discovered at the warehouse are noted and reported to the shipper.

Unloading in a modern warehouse may involve automatic conveyor belts or carts that travel to preset destinations. Or it may involve pallets that travel along the floor in the way that a hydrofoil boat travels on water, keeping a friction-free cushion of air between the pallets and the floor. These systems and other tools operated by the unloaders and the movers, such as the driverless forklift truck and the driverless tractor, are all designed to make the unloading job more efficient.

The shipment received by the warehouse may be containerized. *Containerization* is the transportation of goods in specially built shipping containers. The containers are loaded by the shipper at his warehouse and their contents are not unloaded until the containers reach their destination. The containers used are large and can hold much more than a normal shipping crate. They protect the shipment and enable it to be moved easily from one type of carrier to another. Containerization reduces transportation time and expense as well as damage and theft by eliminating the separate loading and unloading of numerous shipping crates each time the shipment is transferred to a new carrier. Only the single container needs to be loaded and unloaded.

Storing

Once goods are accepted by the warehouse, they are placed in a storage location. This location is selected to protect the particular type of shipment. The location must also be accessible for inspection.

One of the more advanced types of storage equipment for small items is a bank of shelves that swing like pages in a book, thus taking up less space than ordinary shelving while remaining accessible. Warehouse storage equipment also includes bins used for small items, island stacks used for larger products, and overhead racks used for hanging products in spaces that would otherwise be unusable.

Processing

The amount of processing a shipment receives in a warehouse depends on the number of services available and on the wishes of the owner of the goods. Many marketers find the warehouse a convenient and inexpensive place for some processing. Shipments may be split up and stored by units. Units may be price-marked and repackaged. Various products may be put together for an outgoing shipment. Transportation may be arranged and paperwork handled.

Warehouses near garment manufacturing centers, for example, bring in shipments from various manufacturers in the area and sort those shipments

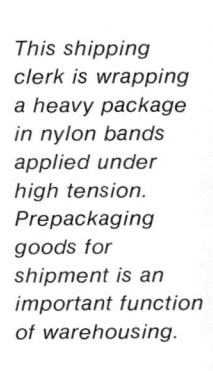

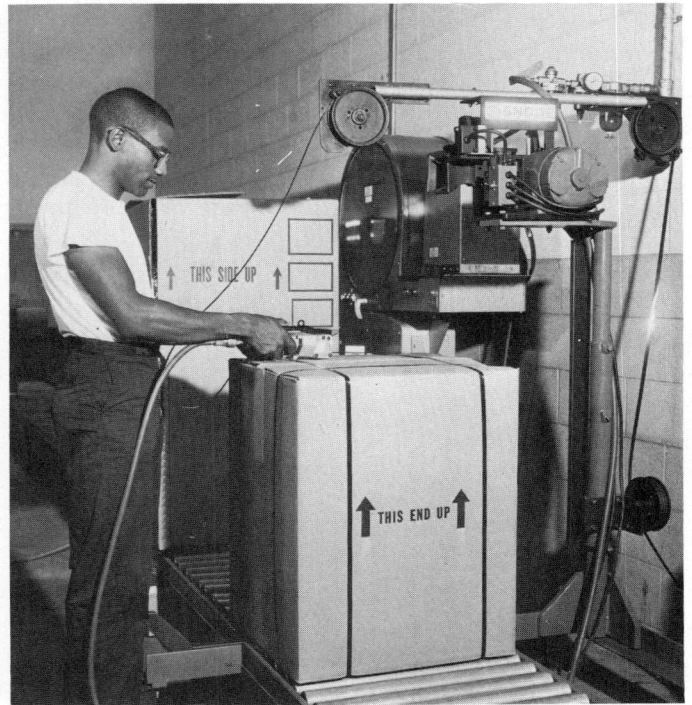

This shipping clerk is wrapping a heavy package in nylon bands applied under high tension. Prepackaging goods for shipment is an important function of warehousing.

Courtesy Signode Corp.

according to the orders placed by stores. The garments are then put on hangers, and fabric and price tags are attached. Each store's shipment, still on hangers, is loaded onto a truck for express delivery.

Shipping

The final job of the warehouse is to see that a shipment is moved out of storage safely and started on the way to its next destination. The orders to ship goods may come from the owner of the shipment, or sometimes they may be part of a routine order-fulfillment service provided by the warehouse. Public warehouses usually ship in response to the direct orders of the owners of the merchandise. Private warehouses sometimes function as distribution centers.

In the distribution-center-type warehouse, customer orders are transmitted to the warehouse. There the order-filling department checks the orders for accuracy and makes sure the inventory is in the warehouse. The department then prepares the invoice, requests that the specified items be withdrawn from storage, and makes arrangements to transport the items to the customer. The customer receives his bill from the distribution center and responds by sending his payment to the center.

The way a distribution center operates shows how warehousing can greatly increase the efficiency of physical distribution systems and thereby benefit both the marketer and his customer.

◆ YOUR MARKETING VOCABULARY

On a separate sheet of paper define each of the following marketing terms; then use each term in a sentence.

Bonded warehouse
Containerization
Distribution center
General-merchandise warehouse
Materials handling
Private warehouse
Public warehouse
Warehouse
Warehouse receipt

◆ FOR REVIEW AND DISCUSSION

1. While storage is still the biggest warehousing job, what other warehousing jobs have become important?
2. What purposes do warehouses serve for the marketer and the manufacturer?
3. How does the warehouse add time utility to the value of goods?
4. In what ways does warehouse storage avoid sharp changes in the selling price of a product?
5. Where are warehouses usually located?
6. What is the most common type of public warehouse? What kinds of products are stored in special-commodity warehouses? in cold-storage warehouses?
7. Who owns most warehouses?
8. What is a bonded product?
9. Does the warehouse have any effect on the cost of distributing a product? Explain.
10. Name and describe four functions of a warehouse.

◆ ANALYZING MARKETING CONCEPTS

1. Warehousing serves many purposes. Prepare a form like the one below. In the left-hand column, list the following services that a warehouse can provide: (a) protection of goods, (b) increasing the value of goods, (c) helping to stabilize prices, (d) easing financial burdens. In the right-hand column, explain how a warehouse can provide each of these services.

Services of Warehouse	How Warehouse Provides Services

2. While storage is the biggest job of warehousing, handling and processing goods are also important. Prepare a form like the one below and list the following products in the left-hand column: (a) furniture, (b) soft drinks, (c) potato chips, (d) lumber, (e) clothing, (f) appliances, (g) vegetables. For each product, indicate in the right-hand column several services that a warehouse might perform in handling and processing the product.

Product	Services of Warehouse

◆ MARKETING PROJECT 28
Studying Warehousing Services

Project Goal: Given a list of warehouses in your community, select one and determine the services it offers and the types of products it handles.

Action: With your teacher's guidance, arrange to interview the manager of a warehouse in your community. The Yellow Pages of your telephone directory will help you find the name of a local warehouse. During the interview, determine and write down the services the warehouse offers and the kinds of goods it handles.

Prepare a form like the one below. Write the name of the person you interviewed at the top of the form. In the left-hand and center columns, list the name of the warehouse and the services it offers. In the right-hand column, list the types of products that the warehouse handles.

Name of Warehouse	Services Offered	Types of Products Handled

Promotion and Selling

UNIT 9

part 29

The Elements of Promotion

YOUR GOALS

1. Given a new product, identify the techniques that a manufacturer uses to promote it.
2. Given a new product and a budget, develop a promotion program for the product. Be prepared to discuss the promotional mix that you choose.

In our highly competitive business economy, every organization must keep prospective customers continually aware of its products or services through promotion. *Promotion* consists of those means or activities that are designed to bring a company's goods or services to the favorable attention of potential customers.

Promotion takes many forms. A person may be encouraged to try a new product because he has seen it advertised in a newspaper or on TV. Or he may have been given a free sample. He might have been attracted by a colorful travel exhibit in a hotel, by a demonstration in a variety store, by an advertisement on a bus or train, or by a radio commercial delivered by a well-known personality. The following are some other examples of promotional activities:

■ A record company arranges for a group of singers to appear on a disk-jockey program to discuss their latest recording.

- A camera company plans an advertising campaign to announce its new color film. The campaign includes sponsorship of a national television show, spot commercials on 300 radio stations, full-page ads in 1,500 newspapers, and advertising messages on billboards throughout the country.
- At a large banquet attended by businessmen, a local insurance agent places at each table ball-point pens on which an advertising message is printed; a florist furnishes free flowers in exchange for a credit line on the printed program; and an employment agency gives each person a memo pad imprinted with its name and telephone number.
- A farm-implement dealer sets up an exhibit at the state fair and hires a country-music group to draw farmers to his exhibit.
- A dealer of a particular make of automobile writes a letter to people who have bought cars from him during the past three years, inviting them to a "sneak preview" of new models.
- A service station sponsors a local softball team and provides them with uniforms on which the name of the business appears.
- A local soft-drink distributor supplies his product free to student delegates attending a career development conference.
- An automobile manufacturer publishes a monthly magazine for owners of his brand. The name of the local dealer appears on the back cover.

Marketers are always developing new promotional activities to bring their products or services to the attention of the public. The alert marketer knows how to make the elements of promotion work for him.

PROMOTIONAL ELEMENTS DEFINED

The elements of promotion are advertising, advertising media, sales promotion, visual merchandising, publicity, public relations, and personal selling. Each of these activities plays an important role in marketing.

Advertising is a nonpersonal sales message which is paid for by an identified company. It promotes the company's products, services, or image and is directed toward a mass audience. The company that pays for the advertising is called the *sponsor*. The fact that advertising is paid for distinguishes it from free publicity. The nonpersonal approach of advertising distinguishes it from personal selling.

Advertising media are the channels of communication used by advertisers to send their messages to potential customers. Advertising media include radio, television, newspapers, magazines, direct mail, and billboards.

Sales promotion is any sales activity that supplements or coordinates advertising and personal selling. Sales promotion includes free samples, coupons, contests, and other special incentives intended to stimulate sales.

Which elements of promotion do you see here?

Visual merchandising is the display of a product at or near the point of purchase. Visual merchandising includes attractive window and interior displays and eye-catching exterior signs.

Publicity is free advertising for a company or its products. Public relations is the total process of building goodwill toward a business organization. Personal selling is the direct effort made by a salesperson to convince a customer to make a purchase.

THE PROMOTIONAL MIX

To achieve desired sales results, marketers must consider all forms of promotion and decide which ones should be used and in what proportion. Naturally, the aim of every marketer is to get the most from every dollar he spends for promotion. If he has $50,000 to spend on promoting an existing product or on launching a new product, he must budget every cent as intelligently as possible. Should he spend it all on advertising or should he spend most of it for salesmen? How much should he invest in contests, giveaways, exhibits, and premiums?

An efficient marketer studies the problem carefully and mixes the various forms of promotion in the right proportion for his product. This combination of different forms of promotion is called the *promotional mix*. The marketer may decide to spend $20,000 on advertising, $11,000 on sales promotion, and $19,000 for new salesmen. The makeup of the promotional mix varies with the product being promoted, the nature of the potential customers, the general market conditions, and the funds available.

A CASE HISTORY

To develop a better understanding of the elements that may go into a promotional mix, let us follow a product—the Ford "Maverick"—from the time of the car's development through its successful promotional campaign to the time when it was first introduced to the public.

Background

The Maverick, introduced in 1969, received one of the most thorough promotional campaigns in marketing history. Behind it all was a highly intensive marketing research program. Through this research program, the Ford Motor Company learned some very significant facts about car buyers. Research showed that there are two groups of potential customers for smaller cars: the compact-car buyers, who are older, generally college-educated people with modest incomes; and the imported-car buyers, who are younger, fairly well-educated people with average or higher-than-average incomes. Only a few people in the older group own more than one car, while a great number of the younger group have more than one car per family.

Marketing research showed that although the two groups of buyers are dissimilar, their buying motives are alike. Both groups buy small cars mainly for economy of operation and for low purchase price. Durability is another reason for their choosing small cars. The small-car market, then, is an economy market. However, the desire for economy is sometimes mixed with the desire for the glamor of an imported item.

Armed with these data, the company began to visualize the kind of car that would best suit this market. After a great deal of research and planning, designers and engineers produced the car. They thought of it as a different combination of automotive qualities, a blending of foreign-car lower cost and economy of maintenance with American roominess, quietness, and road performance.

Because of this unusual combination of qualities, Ford settled on the car name "Maverick"—which means "something different." As if to prove its point, the company even decided on "maverick" paints, using colors such as

The Maverick was designed to combine the advantages of small foreign cars with the desirable qualities of American cars.

"Thanks Vermillion," "Hulla Blue," and "Anti-Establish Mint." Promotion personnel determined to launch the Maverick with the greatest possible impact on the market. The promotional mix decided upon can be divided broadly into two main categories: national advertising and sales promotion.

National Advertising

Ford's advertising goal was to give the Maverick more impact on potential consumer consciousness than any other competitive car. To accomplish this goal, Ford decided to use these major media for its national advertising: radio and television, newspapers, magazines, and displays.

Radio and Television. As marketing research had shown, Ford could have dwelt on the car's economy of operation or used a Western theme for advertising ("maverick" is a Western term commonly applied to unbranded calves or colts). Instead, the company decided upon what it called an "offbeat" advertising approach. For example, television commercials featured opera singers vocalizing their disbelief in the car's price and performance.

The night before the Maverick was introduced to the public, Ford sponsored commercials for the new car on every prime-time television network show except one. In radio, Ford purchased time on news and sports shows on 500 stations that weekend. Also, 100 commercial minutes on one station featured recorded interviews with personalities such as the comedian Jonathan Winters.

Newspapers. Long before the Maverick was introduced, Ford designed newspaper ads to lure potential buyers away from other cars. These ads announced the Maverick's arrival and gave every important technical detail about the car. Buried in the middle of the ad was the sentence, "You don't have to read it all, but isn't it nice to know it's all there?" Five months later, when the competing Chevrolet model appeared, Ford ran a newspaper ad featuring Maverick's price: "still $1,995."

Magazines. Ford made extensive use of advertising in nationally circulated magazines. Three-page gatefolds made the point that Maverick was the first 1970 car at a price below $2,000. Follow-up ads were also used.

Simultaneous cover stories (not ads) on the Maverick appeared in automobile magazines such as *Motor Trend, Car and Driver,* and *Car Life.* Editors of automobile magazines had been briefed at press conferences months before, and all publications in the automotive field carried articles and pictures during the week of Maverick's debut.

Displays. The Maverick was put on display in selected busy areas and in major hotels and motels across the country. It was displayed at some 80 airport terminals in major cities. At the same time, large outdoor billboard posters — 22,775 in all — appeared along American highways. These posters gave the car a particularly important exposure, because dealers initially had only limited quantities of the product.

Sales Promotion

Maverick's sales promotion consisted of direct company promotion and promotional tie-ins. Five direct promotional efforts by Ford are worthy of mention because they were extremely successful.

- Copies of a carefully prepared talk on the Maverick's qualities were distributed to Ford executives. They delivered the talk to selected groups of community leaders in all sections of the country.
- For the car's introduction to the press, automotive writers from all over the country were brought to the Arizona desert for a news conference. The last leg of their journey was in buckboards and carriages, which carried them to Mavericktown, a desert movie set that had been built especially for the car's debut. There the writers were presented with Western entertainment and a Western steak cookout. A covered wagon rumbled into town escorted by a group of horsemen. Suddenly bandits staged a gunfight, whereupon the sides of the covered wagon fell away, revealing the first Maverick the writers had ever seen — in "Thanks Vermillion" (a bright red).

Advertising photos emphasized that Maverick's trunk space was much greater than that of the leading competitive foreign automobiles.

■ The company was interested in reaching young people. Because the car was introduced around spring vacation time, Ford placed Mavericks at several resort towns in Florida, Texas, and California, where young people from all over the country gather. Along with the car, Ford gave away hats, towels, and sweat shirts. Ford also staged contests to select a Miss Maverick or to stuff a Maverick, for example. Students returned to school wearing their Maverick hats and talking about the new car they had seen, before it was actually put on general public display. Soon a half-million Maverick posters were placed on 300 college campuses.

■ The formal debut of the Maverick was held at the New York Auto Show. Here, the car generated a great amount of buyer activity and interest.

■ Maverick was also the center of attention at another, more unusual, place for a car—the United States Senate. Shortly after Maverick's introduction, a Senate subcommittee investigating the automotive repair business examined the car to see what Ford had done to give it ease of maintenance and servicing. In a demonstration the Maverick was partially dismantled on the Capitol lawn and reassembled by experienced mechanics. This activity became news, and radio and television crews filmed and recorded the event, which later was broadcast throughout the country. The story also appeared in newspapers.

Ford also used promotional tie-ins, which are cooperative promotional efforts involving the manufacturer, other advertisers, and the media. For example, Mavericks were given as prizes on some TV programs. This, of course, put the car's name before millions of people. In addition, Ford dealers throughout the country conducted "Win-a-Maverick" contests. Also, about a thousand prizes, including some new Mavericks, were offered to people visiting Ford showrooms.

Local Follow-Ups

Ford worked closely with its dealers throughout the country in staging the promotional and advertising activities just described. Suggestions were sent out to dealers, and dealers were encouraged to develop their own ideas to capitalize on exposure gained by the national campaign.

In addition, events of a purely local nature were encouraged, such as using Mavericks in parades, sporting events, and other community activities; in tie-ins with local merchants' promotions; and in sneak previews for service-station and garage operators.

Various promotional materials were sent to local dealers. These included picture postcards to announce the car in as wide a local mailing as possible, special trims for showrooms, framed photographs of the Mavericks, and other attention-getting devices.

Information for Dealers and Salesmen

Not to be overlooked were the special business and educational meetings held between Ford's top management and the dealers who would introduce the new car. Here product comparison films were studied and new marketing procedures were introduced. The dealers had the opportunity to learn about the new car firsthand from the men who made the production and marketing decisions.

Ford made sure that all dealers and their salesmen were themselves sold on the Maverick. They were thoroughly familiarized with its features, so that they could answer any questions put to them about the car. Special sales manuals were prepared, and sales training sessions were held, in which motion pictures and other aids were used extensively.

Did the company reach its advertising goals? Did its efforts pay off? Ford's marketing research showed that within four weeks of the Maverick's introduction, 85 percent of the nation's car owners knew about it and 75 percent remembered the advertising related to it. In addition, Maverick's sales during the early months of its existence proved to be in line with its manufacturer's expectations.

PROMOTION—A BROAD FIELD

The story of the Maverick has been greatly condensed and simplified; a complete account of this multi-million-dollar effort would require hundreds of pages. However, even this brief account illustrates how broad the term "promotion" is and how the elements of promotion may be mixed. Exciting stories could also be told about the launching of other products—from breakfast cereals to motion pictures.

It should be understood, however, that the promotional mix always varies with the product and the market. The owner of a roadside fruit stand has his own promotional mix—modest though it may be—which is just as individual as the promotional mix of a large national airline. The mix is rarely the same for any two businesses or for different time periods in the same business. The promotional mix is of vital importance not only to the successful launching of a new product but also to the maintaining of the life of already established products.

◻ YOUR MARKETING VOCABULARY

On a separate sheet of paper define each of the following marketing terms; then use each term in a sentence.

Advertising
Advertising media
Promotion
Promotional mix
Sales promotion
Sponsor
Visual merchandising

◻ FOR REVIEW AND DISCUSSION

1. Give three examples of promotional activities.
2. What are four types of advertising media?
3. Give one example of the use of sales promotion.
4. In order to achieve the sales results he is aiming for, what must a marketer consider?
5. What qualities were included in the design of the Maverick? Why were they included?
6. What does the term "maverick" mean?
7. Discuss Ford's national advertising of the Maverick on radio and television.
8. How was the press utilized to introduce the Maverick?
9. What are promotional tie-ins? Give two examples.
10. How did the Ford management prepare its dealers and their salesmen to introduce the Maverick?

ANALYZING MARKETING CONCEPTS

1. Promotion consists of those activities which are designed to bring products to the attention of the consumer. Think of promotional activities for five different products that you have observed recently. On a form like the one below, list each product and describe the activity used to promote it.

Product	Promotional Activity
Example: Reader's Digest	Materials received in the mail to promote condensed books through a lucky-number sweepstakes.

2. Assume that you own a record shop. Your business is highly competitive, and therefore your promotional mix must be effective. Prepare a form like the one below. Then list and describe each activity that you would include in your promotional mix.

Promotional Activity	Description of Activity
Example: Placing of weekly newspaper ad.	Small but consistent ads featuring current hit songs and special prices on traffic-building items.

MARKETING PROJECT 29
Identifying Promotional Techniques

Project Goal: Given a new product, identify the techniques that a manufacturer uses to promote it.

Action: Choose a new product sold in your community. Visit a particular business that sells this product and note the advertising and display materials used to promote it. Also, read newspapers and billboards, watch TV, and listen to the radio to determine the promotional techniques used by the manufacturer.

On a form like the one below, list the name of the product you have chosen and the techniques used to promote it.

Product	Promotional Techniques

part 30

The World of Advertising

YOUR GOAL

Given several advertisements in various media, describe each advertisement and identify the advertiser, determine the main message of the advertisement, and explain why the advertising medium was chosen.

The typical consumer encounters advertising throughout the day. Her first encounter comes when the clock radio wakes her in the morning with music and news and weather reports. From time to time the program is interrupted by commercials that tell her of the virtues of Minute Maid orange juice or *The Wall Street Journal.*

While eating breakfast she glances at a magazine in which many colorful advertisements suggest that she "Fly to Hawaii" or "Try Chef Boy-ar-dee Spaghetti."

As she travels to work by bus, advertising pursues her. Inside the bus, car cards attract her attention, urging her to buy Lay's potato chips, see a movie, or contribute to the Heart Fund.

Our typical consumer opens her morning newspaper, glances at the day's headlines, and then turns to the fashion pages. Mingled with the fashion news are ads of various sizes, promoting ladies' coats, shoes, and dresses. She makes a mental note to stop at Rich's Department Store later in the week to see the Italian knit dresses being featured.

On her way to lunch she notices a large ad painted on the side of a building. Once in the restaurant, she studies a menu that has several ads tucked in the corners. All around her are display signs, one of which encourages her to "Try a hamburger with a Coke."

Arriving home in the evening, she finds in her mailbox shopping coupons, a neighborhood shopper's guide, and an invitation from a magazine publisher to take advantage of a special subscription rate.

As she sits down later to enjoy her favorite television program, she sees and hears advertising messages which tell her that a certain toothpaste will make her teeth whiter and prevent tooth decay and that a certain soap will make her skin softer.

Like this consumer, all American consumers are surrounded by advertising. This part discusses the basic types of advertising and how they help marketers promote their products.

TYPES OF ADVERTISING

Advertising is important to all types of companies. Through advertising, business organizations keep consumers aware of specific products and services that are available. This type of advertising, which stresses products or services, is called *product advertising*. Advertising may also publicize a firm's name and build a reputation for it. This type of advertising, which builds an image for a business organization without mentioning a specific product, is called *institutional advertising*.

Product Advertising

The primary aim of product advertising is to make consumers buy a specific product or use a specific service. But product advertising can be adapted to fit many types of promotional activities. For example, product advertising can perform the following functions:

- Support personal selling.
- Create consumer interest in a company's products or services.
- Keep the consumer aware of the products and services of an established company.
- Introduce a product to a new market or age group.
- Introduce a new business to a community.
- Encourage stores to carry a product by creating consumer demand for it.

Institutional Advertising

Institutional advertising is geared toward establishing and maintaining a company's image and prestige. Usually, little or no mention is made of a company's product in this form of advertising. At times, the only reference made to the company sponsoring the message is the company name at the end of the advertisement. Institutional advertising is often concerned with these objectives:

- Demonstrating the organization's role in community affairs.
- Presenting information and viewpoints on public questions.
- Presenting general or health information of interest to the consumer.
- Keeping the company's name before the public.

TYPES OF ADVERTISERS

Business organizations can be divided into three advertising groups: national, retail, and industrial. National and retail advertisers promote consumer products, whereas industrial advertisers promote industrial goods.

National Advertisers

A manufacturer of consumer goods who advertises his product by its brand name is called a *national advertiser*. The advertising itself need not be directed at the entire country to be classified as national. Some brand-name products, for example, are sold only in certain sections of the country, and advertising for these products is placed only in the media reaching people in those areas. Such advertising, however, is still referred to as national advertising. National advertising differs from retail advertising in that the emphasis is on the brand name of a product rather than on the place of purchase.

Retail Advertisers

A store or service organization whose advertising message encourages consumers to shop at its place of business is called a *retail advertiser*. A retail advertiser may advertise a huge assortment of products, or he may feature only one product. But the emphasis in the ad is on the place of purchase. The retail advertiser's goal is to persuade consumers to come to his store to shop. Retail advertising is also called "local advertising," since ads are limited primarily to newspapers and radio and television stations that reach a consumer market located within shopping distance of the advertising store.

   Manufacturers of brand-name products frequently join with retailers

If we do say so ourselves—Montgomery Ward and Container Corporation get around pretty well for companies whose collective age is 145.

How do we stay fit? It's simple, really. By hiring the youngest, brightest executive talent we can find.

Expanding opportunities in packaging and retailing, a working environment based on performance and self-fulfillment, and corporate commitment to our social responsibilities create exciting challenges for our young management.

A typical Montgomery Ward and Container manager is from 30 to 40 years old, and he functions in a highly charged organization offering almost unlimited potential.

For, what Wards and Container have both found is this: when you let young managers grow up in an environment of maximum responsibility, they invariably grow into a very young-thinking senior management team.

Youth is a precious commodity and Marcor's philosophies recognize it as such.

MARCOR
Montgomery Ward   Container Corporation of America

We're very young for our age.

Courtesy Montgomery Ward

The main purpose of this institutional advertisement is to maintain a youthful as well as efficient image for the company.

Part 30 / The World of Advertising / 355

in cooperative advertising programs. The brand-name product is featured in such a cooperative ad, and the name of the retailer selling the product appears in a prominent spot. Manufacturers often provide retailers with complete advertising material for cooperative advertising. The retailer merely adds the name and address of his establishment and buys space for the ad in a local newspaper.

Industrial Advertisers

Industrial advertisers promote goods to the industrial market. Four basic types of industrial advertising are trade, business-directed, professional, and farm advertising.

Trade Advertising. To encourage retailers to carry their products, manufacturers place ads in magazines that circulate among retailers. Wholesalers and distributors also advertise in trade magazines to stimulate sales to retailers. For example, *Musical Merchandise Review* is intended for owners and managers of stores that stock and sell musical instruments. Manufacturers and wholesalers of such instruments place full-page ads in this magazine to tell retailers why they should stock their brands. Almost every industry has a trade publication through which manufacturers can reach retailers and try to get the retailers to stock their products.

Business-Directed Advertising. Business-directed advertising appears in publications meant for manufacturers of consumer or industrial goods. Industrial advertising promotes products used by industries in the manufacture of goods or in the operation of their businesses. For example, ads in *American Machinist* explain how the use of certain machines will reduce production costs in machine shops. Ads in *Textile World* describe the merits of various yarns, fabric dyes, and cones for holding thread on cloth-weaving machines. Ads in *House & Home* urge home-building contractors to use certain building materials, kitchen equipment, or flooring material in the houses they construct.

Professional Advertising. Professional advertising is addressed to professional people such as doctors, dentists, and hospital and school administrators who are in a position to recommend a product to others or to buy a product for use by others.

To inform professionals of the merits of their products, manufacturers advertise in professional journals, such as *The Nation's Schools* and *Modern Hospital.* In addition, they may send out samples of their products or letters telling how the associates or clients of these professionals can benefit from the use of the product.

Nonwoven fabrics start here

—with FMC rayon fiber. Most nonwoven fabrics are made from rayon fiber, and we make more rayon fiber than anybody else.

Whatever the nonwoven fabric you make or are planning to make—whether wet or dry process—we can help you make it better. Ask us to prove it. Call FMC Fibers, New York, N.Y. 10036.

FMC Fibers

Courtesy FMC Corp., Fibers Div.

This industrial ad is directed toward fabric manufacturers. Which of the four basic types of industrial advertising does it represent?

Part 30 / The World of Advertising / 357

Farm Advertising. Several magazines, such as *The Progressive Farmer, Farm Journal,* and *Prairie Farmer,* are directed toward families living on farms. The ads for consumer products in these magazines are basically the same as those that appear in general consumer magazines. The difference is that farm magazines also carry ads for products appealing mainly to farmers, such as tractors and other vehicles, milking and other farm equipment, animal feed, and fertilizer.

THE ADVERTISING BUSINESS

The typical large business organization manages its advertising through the resources of various groups, two of which are the company's own advertising department and advertising agencies.

The Advertising Department

Many medium-size and most large companies maintain their own advertising department, usually directed by an advertising manager. Companies which sell a variety of products may appoint an advertising manager for each product line. For example, the Scott Paper Company, which manufactures paper products for both industrial and consumer use, has a manager in charge of advertising its industrial products and another manager in charge of advertising its consumer products.

The advertising manager and his department work closely with the marketing director, the promotion manager, and others who have the responsibility for promoting and selling the product. Together they determine policy and prepare advertising budgets. If the company also uses an advertising agency, the advertising manager works with the agency in preparing ads and selecting media in which to place the advertising. The advertising manager is assisted by several people.

Copywriter. The copywriter writes the message that is to appear in the ad. This message is known as the *copy.* A good copywriter must be a master of expression and have an unusually good understanding of psychology. He must be able to write advertising copy that will create the desired impression of the product in the consumer's mind. To do so, he must have a thorough knowledge of the product and of the market for the product. Preparing good copy is an art that requires both talent and training.

Art Director. The art director designs the ads and supervises the artists who prepare the cartoons, drawings, and other illustrations. He also directs the layout specialists, who arrange the ads on the page, combining the work of the artists and the copywriter. The job of the layout specialist requires a knowledge of balance, design, and psychology.

Other Advertising Personnel. The advertising department may also include photographers, editors, writers, and various office personnel. In very large advertising departments, there may also be a media director and a research director. The media director studies the effectiveness of each type of media, and the size and kind of audience represented by each type. The research director specializes in testing the appeal of the ads (often before they are used) and measures their effectiveness. He sometimes makes surveys of consumer preferences, buying motives, and shopping habits.

Advertising Agencies

Most companies that use a wide variety of advertising media seek the help of advertising agencies. An *advertising agency* is a business that specializes in creating, planning, and placing ads for other businesses and organizations. The companies that use these advertising agencies are referred to as *clients*.

Growth of Advertising Agencies. Advertising agencies started more than 100 years ago, when a group of men bought "white space" in newspapers and then sold this space to various advertisers. In return for getting this business, the newspaper paid a commission to the group.

In time these groups, or agencies, realized that they had something to offer the advertiser besides white space. They could offer him copywriting, artwork, layouts, and assistance in selecting media. The agency became a specialist, working with the advertiser not only in advertising but also in other promotional activities.

A good description of the work of the modern advertising agency was given in a talk by William J. Colihan, past executive vice president of Young and Rubicam, one of the country's largest advertising agencies.

> The agency helps the manufacturer find out what wants people have that he can fill. It helps him develop and style his product, package it, set a budget for advertising, and pick the media in which to advertise. Then it decides what the advertising should say or show; thinks up, writes, and designs the ads and commercials; buys the art and type; helps produce the radio or TV commercials; orders the space and time; sends out the advertising and checks to make sure it ran, checks the bills, pays the bills, and tries to find out how the ads worked.

Today there are thousands of advertising agencies in the country. The large agencies employ artists, designers, copywriters, layout artists, and TV scriptwriters. They also employ account executives, who are responsible for managing the advertising activities of clients.

Method of Paying Agencies. Most of the income of advertising agencies comes from the commissions they receive for placing clients' advertising. A commission is a percentage of sales received. The typical commission that an agency receives is 15 percent of the price charged by the media for space or time.

To illustrate the commission system used for paying agencies, let us assume that an advertising agency has placed a full-page ad in a magazine for one of its clients. The normal cost of the magazine space is $10,000, but the magazine bills the agency for only $8,500 ($10,000 less 15 percent). (Had the client himself placed the ad, the magazine would have billed him for the full $10,000.) Although the agency must pay only $8,500, it bills its client for $10,000. The difference of $1,500 ($10,000 less $8,500) is the agency's commission. From the commission the advertising agency must pay its costs for creating and placing the ad and make a reasonable profit.

In recent years, more than 90 percent of all advertising has been placed with the media by commercial advertising agencies. The remaining 10 percent is placed by large companies that maintain their own advertising agencies, known as "house agencies." The media usually grant the house agencies the same 15 percent discount given independent advertising agencies.

SELECTING ADVERTISING MEDIA

The chief advertising media are newspapers, magazines, radio, and television. Advertisers try to find the best media in which to promote their products. They read reports published by the media, study government documents, and keep up to date with advertising trends by subscribing to trade magazines. They also conduct their own research. Basically, they select advertising media by asking themselves, "How can I reach the largest number of customers for my product with the amount of money I have available?"

Reaching the Customer

The audience that an advertiser hopes to reach usually determines the media that he selects and the kind of advertisement he prepares. If he wants to promote a hair shampoo for women, he may advertise in magazines such as *Ebony* or *Mademoiselle.* Often an advertiser finds that he can reach a specific audience best through television. If he wants to promote a cereal that will likely appeal to children, he may choose to advertise on TV programs for children. In promoting its cameras and film, Kodak sponsors family-type shows, because it knows that cameras are bought by almost everyone. Delco, a manufacturer of batteries, sponsors shows such as professional football games, which are likely to be watched by men.

Every marketer must decide how he can best advertise his product with the amount of money he has on hand for advertising.

Sometimes the audience that the advertiser wants to reach is located in a specific geographic area. In this case, he will choose media that will reach that area most effectively. A local or regional retailer, for example, does not advertise on network TV or in national magazines, since a great portion of the audience is not within shopping distance of his stores. Instead, he uses local newspapers and local radio stations to advertise his goods.

Considering Cost in Choosing Media

The cost of advertising is based largely on the type of media used, the number of people reached, and the amount of space or time purchased. For example, the cost of advertising on a national television network is more than the cost of advertising on a local station. Also, the cost of television advertising is affected by the hour of the day the advertising is scheduled, because this has a bearing on the size of the audience. For example, advertising for a program scheduled for eight in the evening costs more than comparable advertising scheduled for an afternoon program, because the evening program is likely to attract a large audience.

Similarly, a full-page ad in a Sunday newspaper costs more than an identical one in a weekday newspaper, because the Sunday newspaper has more readers. A billboard placed in the middle of a large city is more expensive than one placed in the country, because more people are bound to see a billboard in the city.

While the cost of advertising is very important in choosing media, cost is relative; that is, money for advertising should be spent on the media that will reach the largest number of possible customers at the lowest cost per person. A national advertiser of a brand-name orange juice may spend $50,000 for a full-color ad in *Reader's Digest* and figure that the cost is low in view of the millions of people who will see the ad and be encouraged to buy the product. On the other hand, if a TV manufacturer were to spend $100 for space in the classified advertisement section of a local newspaper, he may regard the cost as expensive in terms of the number of potential buyers who would read the ad. Thus, advertisers must always determine whether the amount of coverage offered by a particular type of advertising media is worth the cost.

◆ YOUR MARKETING VOCABULARY

On a separate sheet of paper define each of the following marketing terms; then use each term in a sentence.

Advertising agency
Clients
Copy
Institutional advertising

National advertiser
Product advertising
Retail advertiser

◆ FOR REVIEW AND DISCUSSION

1. List five examples of advertising that the typical consumer is exposed to throughout the day.
2. List four services that product advertising can provide.
3. List four objectives of institutional advertising.
4. Explain the difference between national advertising and retail advertising.
5. At what audience is trade advertising aimed? And professional advertising?
6. What resources do large businesses have available to them for managing their advertising?
7. Explain how a company's own advertising department may work, and discuss the staff it may have.
8. Discuss the staff that an advertising agency may have. From what source does the agency receive most of its income?

9. How do advertisers seek to find the best media in which to advertise their products?
10. How does cost affect the selection of advertising media?

ANALYZING MARKETING CONCEPTS

1. Advertisers try to find the best medium in which to promote their products. Prepare a form like the one below and list the following marketers in the left-hand column: (a) a retail store with a new line of clothing, (b) a manufacturer of medicines, (c) a manufacturer of electronic office machines, (d) soil-fertilizer producer. In the center column, list the advertising medium you would suggest for each marketer. In the right-hand column, explain the type of advertising that each marketer should place in the medium.

Marketer	Medium	Type of Advertising
Example: A local grocery store	Local newspaper	Full-page ads once a week to reach local market.

2. An important factor in selecting media is the audience that the advertiser wants to reach. Prepare a form like the one below. In the left-hand column, list the following five products: (a) sports cars, (b) cosmetics, (c) gas and oil, (d) food items, (e) phonograph records. In the center column, write the name of a specific magazine, newspaper, radio program, or TV show that would be a suitable medium for advertising each product. In the right-hand column, write the reason for your selections based on the audience reached through each medium.

Product	Specific Medium	Reason for Choice
Example: Sporting goods	*Sports Illustrated*	Magazine is read widely by sports fans.

MARKETING PROJECT 30
Studying Media Selection

Project Goal: Given several advertisements in various media, describe each advertisement and identify the advertiser, determine the main message of the advertisement, and explain why the advertising medium was chosen.

Action: Select an advertisement from each of the following media: (a) a current issue of a magazine or newspaper, (b) a radio program, and (c) a television program.

Prepare a form like the one below. In the left-hand column of your form, write a description of each advertisement and identify the advertiser. (Attach the magazine or newspaper ad to your form.) In the center column, indicate the main message of each advertisement. In the right-hand column, explain for each advertisement why you think the advertiser chose the particular medium.

Advertisement and Advertiser	Message of Advertisement	Reason for Choice of Medium

part 31

Advertising Media

YOUR GOALS

1. Given a product, list the advantages and disadvantages of advertising that product in each of seven types of media.
2. Given a number of ads in your local newspaper, justify the placement and pattern of the ads during a one-week period.

As described in Part 29, advertising media are the channels used by advertisers to inform customers about products and encourage potential customers to buy them. This part discusses the following ten types of advertising media: newspapers, magazines, radio, television, direct mail advertising, outdoor advertising, transportation advertising, specialty advertising, directories, and program advertising.

NEWSPAPER ADVERTISING

People depend on newspapers for detailed coverage of national, international, and local happenings. While radio and television present the news more frequently, the reporting is brief and often lacking the depth. Newspapers not only give depth in news coverage but also offer something for everyone—world news, editorials, society news, sports news, fashion trends, and comics. Of course, tucked into these same pages are numerous ads. Many people are just as interested in the ads as they are in the news. They study the ads to learn what is new in fashions, home furnishings, and cars, and to compare prices on foods and other necessities. The Wednesday and Thursday supermarket ads and Friday weekend bargains offered by discount houses, department stores, appliance stores, and other retailers are of special interest to many readers.

Newspapers offer a number of benefits to the advertiser:

- Newspapers can give readers market information about local merchants, their products, and prices. Only radio offers this advantage at a comparable cost.
- Newspapers combine copy with illustrations, and the ads can be removed and used as shopping guides.
- Newspaper ads can include shopping coupons, which the shopper can use toward the purchase of a product.
- Newspapers are timely and flexible. Ads can be prepared and inserted just a few hours in advance of publication. For example, when a heavy snow falls, newspaper ads can be changed quickly to feature sleds, snow tires, skis, and cold-weather clothing. Magazines do not have this flexibility.
- Newspapers saturate the local market. Because of the wide variety of coverage, the newspaper is read by the whole family. In the United States it has been found that at least 88 percent of all families read one or more daily newspapers.
- Newspapers are read consistently. There is no significant seasonal fall-off as there regularly is, for example, in television viewing during the summer months.

Two types of newspaper advertisements are display and classified. *Display advertisements* appear throughout a newspaper and use pictures, art, or different styles of type, or print, to attract attention. Display ads are used primarily by business firms.

Unlike display ads, *classified advertisements* are grouped in special pages of newspapers or magazines by the product or service advertised and generally contain only copy. The type style and format of most classified ads follow the pattern set by the newspaper. Classified ads are used to sell household furnishings, pets, and other belongings and to advertise personal services, such as yard work, house painting, and floor repair. They are also used by real estate agencies, employment agencies, and automobile dealers to advertise their goods or services.

Magazine advertising is often directed to a specific audience. At what group is this ad aimed?

You've got a lot to live
Pepsi's got a lot to give

Things are getting better. People are learning to live every day to the fullest. Pepsi-Cola belongs in this kind of world. Enjoy it. You've got a lot to live.

Courtesy PepsiCo, Inc.

MAGAZINE ADVERTISING

Magazines are a favorite medium of the national advertiser. It is estimated that almost 80 percent of all national advertisers each spend at least $25,000 a year on magazine advertising.

Magazines offer a number of benefits to the advertiser:

■ Magazines permit the advertiser to be selective about his audience. Some magazines appeal primarily to homemakers, such as *Ladies' Home Journal,* or to teen-age girls, such as *Seventeen.* Car "buffs," sportsmen, and businessmen are attracted to magazines such as *Hot Rod Magazine, Sports Illustrated,* and *Business Week.* Other magazines concentrate on an area of the country, such as *Sunset* (for readers in the West).

Part 31 / Advertising Media / **367**

- Magazines can present superior color reproductions, whereas newspapers generally cannot. Thus magazine ads generally can stimulate the desire for foods better than newspaper ads; magazine ads can also show greater product detail and better illustrate the textures of fabrics.
- While newspapers are usually thrown away soon after they are read, magazines are likely to be saved for future reference. This gives the advertiser more exposure. Studies have shown that each issue of some magazines is passed along to as many as eight or nine readers.

RADIO ADVERTISING

In the years before television, radio was the prime form of entertainment, and national advertisers spent huge sums of money on national network programs. When television became popular in the 1950s, national advertisers quickly turned their attention to this new medium and radio network programs declined sharply. While television became a source of home entertainment especially in the evening hours, the radio became a source of entertainment for listeners wherever they happened to be. The development of the transistor has made the radio an even more popular entertainment medium. Transistor radios can be found in the home, workshop, automobile, boat, and at the beach. During the summer months more people are reached by radio than by television.

Radio provides advertisers with more outlets than any other major medium. There are 1,749 daily newspapers in the United States, but there are about 4,330 commercial AM radio stations and more than 2,000 FM stations. The national advertiser can select those areas that he considers prime markets for his product or service and advertise on stations serving those areas. Of course, the local businessman confines his advertising to those stations within his trading area.

Today most radio advertising consists of spot announcements ranging from ten seconds to one minute in length. However, some programs are sponsored, which means that a company pays for an entire 15-minute or half-hour program and has exclusive advertising rights. For example, an oil company may sponsor the six o'clock news every Sunday evening on a local radio station.

TELEVISION ADVERTISING

From very modest beginnings in 1948, television has grown to be a powerful advertising medium. It has done so by taking business from other media, especially radio and newspapers. Television is now the prime family entertainment medium; more than 90 percent of all homes in the United States contain at least one set, and the average set is on for five hours a day.

Television offers certain advantages to advertisers. It brings the advertiser's message to the viewer with the dramatic impact of sight, sound, motion, and in many cases, color. It commands fairly close attention of the person watching it. Finally, all members of the family are likely to watch TV. This makes it a powerful advertising medium for a great number of products. In addition, family members often watch TV together and may make comments and suggestions to each other regarding certain products.

Programming

Television is primarily a national medium of advertising. It is dominated by the three major networks—American Broadcasting Company (ABC), Columbia Broadcasting System (CBS), and National Broadcasting Company (NBC). Many television stations are owned by one of these three major networks. Others are locally owned but affiliated with a network, in which case they devote most of their time to hookups with national networks for certain programs. In return, the local stations receive about 30 percent of the time charges paid by the advertisers for national network time.

Types of Television Advertising

The two basic types of television advertising are network and local. Network advertising is carried across the country by the local stations owned by or affiliated with one of the major networks. Network advertising is very expensive. To sponsor a program broadcast during prime-time hours on a major network and place three one-minute commercials within it costs more than $5 million for a one-year period. Network rates vary with the appeal of the particular program and the time of day. Prime time, the evening hours when television audiences are largest, is also the time when network advertising is most expensive. Prime time generally is from about 7 to 10:30 p.m.

Because only a limited number of companies can afford advertising on such a grand scale, many television stations offer two variations of network advertising, which reduce the cost to a national advertiser. One variation permits two advertisers to alternate the weeks in which they sponsor a program. Another allows two or more advertisers to sponsor a show, dividing the advertising time and costs among them. The trend is toward more sharing of programs among advertisers.

Local advertising may be placed on local or network programs. Local stations affiliated with a network depend on the network for national shows. However, they produce a number of their own programs which are chiefly news, sports, movies, local current events, and musical and variety shows.

Courtesy Montgomery Ward

Direct mail pieces such as those shown here can be very effective in promoting and selling various kinds of merchandise.

DIRECT MAIL ADVERTISING

A form of advertising that is sent to prospective buyers by mail is called *direct mail advertising.* Direct mail advertising is popular among both large and small businesses because of its personal effect. For small businesses it is also an economical way to deliver an advertising message direct to potential customers. Types of direct mail include letters, postcards, circulars, folders, price lists, broadsides (large folders), brochures, catalogs, and house organs (newspapers or magazines prepared by the advertiser). The type of mailer an advertiser selects depends on the kind of impact he wants to make on his market and on the size of his promotional budget. Most direct mail advertising is sent third class, which costs less than first-class mail.

The primary advantage of direct mail is that the advertiser can select his customers and aim his message at them exclusively. For example, a local dress shop that is planning an advance showing of new fashions can send special invitations to its important customers. A sporting-goods store can send a circular to members of a local country club, advertising a special sale on golf clubs. A manufacturer of hospital supplies can send literature to doctors and hospitals throughout the country.

Direct mail offers the advertiser several other advantages. The direct mail advertiser does not compete with other advertisers; he has the reader all to himself. Direct mail can be highly creative; it is not limited to any size, color, or shape beyond observing certain postal regulations. Moreover, direct mail can make the sale, because readers of direct mail advertising are often asked to place their orders on an enclosed order form or coupon. Finally, the results of direct mail advertising are easier to measure than those of other advertising media.

Most small businesses use direct mail extensively. The medium is also used by national firms that include magazine and book publishers, record clubs, book clubs, mail-order firms, and insurance companies.

Using Direct Mail

In small businesses, direct mail is often handled by the owner or manager himself with the assistance of a clerk-typist. Large businesses that use direct mail have staffs of experts, including copywriters, artists, and layout specialists. Some large businesses hire organizations that specialize in direct mail to conduct their campaigns. Two leading organizations of this type are the Reuben H. Donnelley Corporation and R. L. Polk and Company.

Using Mailing Lists

The key to any successful direct mail campaign is a good mailing list. A *mailing list* is a list of the names and addresses of potential buyers for the goods or services of a firm. One excellent mailing list is the names of the firm's present customers. Some businesses use this list exclusively. Mailing lists may be compiled from telephone directories, newspapers, and business and professional directories. They may also be purchased or rented from businesses specializing in developing lists. In some cases, businesses often exchange mailing lists.

Mailing lists require constant examination and revision to remain current. Some people may have moved, some may have died, and others may have changed their names. A company's advertising dollars are wasted on mailing lists that are out of date.

OUTDOOR ADVERTISING

Outdoor advertising started in the days when radio and television did not exist and traveling circuses and vaudeville acts were popular forms of entertainment. Several days before one of these troupes was to appear in a community, an "advance" man came and plastered huge, gaudy signs on fences,

Political candidates often use outdoor advertising to reach voters.

trees, posts, barns, and buildings to announce the big event. Often he hired a local bill poster. Today *outdoor advertising* is a form of modern traffic media that includes signs and posters displayed on billboards, building walls, and other rented outdoor spaces.

Outdoor advertising offers three primary advantages to the advertiser. First, it can be highly localized. For example, in a Spanish-speaking neighborhood, the advertiser can feature his copy in Spanish. A political candidate can restrict his "showing" to the districts in which his voters reside. Second, the message remains in the same position for a long period of time, and passersby can see it again and again. Finally, the message can be made very large, employing dramatic use of color, art, and even movement.

Outdoor advertising is used by both national and local advertisers. National advertisers who make extensive use of billboards usually have their messages printed on posters and pasted to the structures. Local advertisers usually have their signs painted. The cost of billboards and signs depends on the size of the sign, the location in which the sign will be posted, and the length of time the space will be used.

TRANSPORTATION ADVERTISING

Advertising that is used in buses, subways, and taxis, and in railroad, bus, and airline terminals is called *transportation advertising.* It is estimated that 10 billion passengers ride public vehicles each year, and transportation advertising is aimed at this group. Three basic types of transportation advertising are car cards, traveling displays, and station posters.

Car cards are advertising signs found in the interiors of buses, subways, commuter trains, and taxis. Most of them are 11 by 28 inches in size. They are used by banks, chewing-gum manufacturers (Wrigley is the largest user of car cards), private schools, and many other types of businesses, as well as by various nonprofit organizations.

Traveling displays are ads placed on the outside of moving vehicles, mostly buses. As the bus travels its route, the message is exposed to those waiting to ride the bus and to pedestrians and motorists as well.

Both car cards and traveling displays are purchased in what is called a "showing." A "full-run showing" is one card in or on every vehicle owned by the transportation company. A "half-run showing" is one card on every other vehicle. A "double-run showing" is two cards on every vehicle. Rates are by the month. A full-run showing in one large city subway system costs about $10,000 a month.

Station posters are ads located in subway and railroad stations and bus and airline terminals. Like traveling displays, station posters are purchased by showings, the cost depending on the number of displays used and the length of time they are shown.

Courtesy New York City Transit Authority

This traveling display can be seen by people wherever the bus travels.

Transportation advertising offers two primary appeals to advertisers. It reaches people who are likely to be in or near the business area, and it is economical, considering the number of people it reaches.

SPECIALTY ADVERTISING

Advertising that consists of providing a useful item to a potential customer and placing an advertising message on it is called *specialty advertising*. The list of specialty advertising products is limited only by the imagination of the advertiser. The following are examples:

Address books	Coasters	Money clips
Almanacs	Cookbooks	Note pads
Appointment books	Desk calendars	Paperweights
Auto-bumper signs	Diet guides	Pens and pencils
Auto-license frames	First-aid kits	Phone indexes
Badges and buttons	Key rings	Place mats
Balloons	Kitchen reminders	Record books
Blotters	Litter bags	Rulers
Book covers	Luggage tags	Shopping bags
Calendars	Maps	Travel guides

Specialties have certain characteristics that make them popular as an advertising medium. First, they are useful items. The recipient is actually receiving a gift for looking at the advertising message. Second, they provide repeat advertising. Every time a person picks up a pencil or a memo pad advertising a bank, for example, he sees the bank's advertising message. Third, specialties do not require high-priced advertising campaigns, and the cost per item is very low. Finally, specialties can be planned specifically for potential customers; for example, free sewing needles can be given to potential customers by a yard-goods store.

DIRECTORIES AND PROGRAM ADVERTISING

Many trade and business directories accept advertising. These include city, medical, educational, building, and professional directories.

The most important directory for advertisers is the classified section, or Yellow Pages, of the telephone directory. All businesses that have telephone numbers are automatically listed by classification in the Yellow Pages, which may be bound as a separate volume. While all businesses are automatically listed, the telephone company encourages them to buy large ads in addition to the listing. Families moving into a new neighborhood rely on the Yellow

Pages to locate and establish regular buying sources. Even established residents and business firms turn to the Yellow Pages when looking for distributors or suppliers of goods and services.

"Program advertising" refers to advertising that appears in church bulletins, school-play and athletic programs, and school yearbooks. Most businessmen look upon this type of advertising as a donation, since they expect to receive little benefit from it. For this reason, many do not try to sell their products in the ad but take advantage of the public relations value by including a statement such as "Compliments of XYZ Store."

YOUR MARKETING VOCABULARY

On a separate sheet of paper define each of the following marketing terms; then use each term in a sentence.

Classified advertisements
Direct mail advertising
Display advertisements
Mailing list
Outdoor advertising
Specialty advertising
Transportation advertising

FOR REVIEW AND DISCUSSION

1. Explain four benefits of newspaper advertising to the advertiser.
2. State three benefits which magazine ads offer the advertiser.
3. What advantage does radio have as an advertising medium?
4. What are three main advantages of TV as an advertising medium?
5. List three advantages of direct mail as an advertising medium.
6. List three primary advantages of outdoor advertising as a medium.
7. How is the cost of outdoor advertising determined?
8. Name three types of transportation advertising.
9. In traveling displays, what is meant by the terms "full-run showing," "half-run showing," and "double-run showing"?
10. Cite three characteristics of specialty advertising that make it popular as an advertising medium.
11. What is the most important directory in which advertisers may place their messages?
12. Explain program advertising.

ANALYZING MARKETING CONCEPTS

1. Prepare a form like the one near the top of the next page. List the following descriptions in the left-hand column: (a) primarily a national medium, (b) a family entertainment medium, (c) a personal entertainment medium, (d) saturates the local market, (e) permits audience selectivity,

(f) commands a person's entire attention, (g) can be saved and referred to again at the person's convenience.

Place a check mark in the appropriate column at the right to indicate the type of advertising medium described.

Description of Advertising Medium	News-paper	Maga-zine	Radio	Tele-vision
Example: Increased audience during summer months.			✔	

2. Prepare a form like the one below. List the following advertising media in the left-hand column: (a) newspaper, (b) magazine, (c) radio, (d) television, (e) direct mail, (f) outdoor advertising, (g) specialty advertising, (h) methods of transportation. In the other two columns, describe how a manufacturer and a large department store might use each medium listed. If you feel that one of the businesses would not use a specific medium, explain your reason.

Advertising Medium	Used by Manufacturer	Used by Department Store
Example: Telephone directory	Might buy a special ad in the Yellow Pages for each major city.	Might buy a large special ad in the Yellow Pages of the local telephone directory.

◻ MARKETING PROJECT 31
Studying Advertisements

Project Goal: Given a number of ads in your local newspaper, justify the placement and pattern of the ads during a one-week period.

Action: Study the display ads in the issues of a daily newspaper for one week to find answers to the following questions:

1. Which types of businesses run the largest ads most often?
2. What is the approximate ratio of local to national ads?
3. Which types of businesses usually seek the best placements?
4. Do some businesses use certain days of the week?
5. Is there a relationship between the location of articles and ads?

Write the results of your findings, and prepare to discuss them in class.

part 32

Sales Promotion and Visual Merchandising

YOUR GOALS

1. Given the various types of premiums used in promoting a product, collect an example of each type.
2. Given five point-of-purchase displays, determine the basic objective of each.

Sales promotion includes all activities in the promotion process except advertising, publicity, and personal selling. Among the most important forms of sales promotion are premiums, contests, product samples, container promotion, exhibits, price-oriented promotion, and visual merchandising. These elements are used to stimulate sales and increase dealer effectiveness.

PREMIUMS

Something given without charge with the purchase of a product is called a *premium.* The purpose of a premium is to attract customers who otherwise would not buy a product or would not buy it as often if the premium were not given. Premiums used as consumer-promotion devices come in many forms. Five of the most common are trading stamps, coupons, factory packs, direct-sales premiums, and sales-lead premiums.

Coupons serve as effective premiums. This one offers a 10-cent discount on a carton of a popular soft drink.

Trading Stamps

Trading stamps are offered by supermarkets as well as service stations, department stores, and car-rental agencies. The stamps are given to the buyer when he makes a purchase. When he has filled a certain number of stamp books, he can trade them in for merchandise at a redemption center.

The main purpose of trading stamps is to attract new customers and to build the loyalty of all customers so that they will come back to the retail establishment again and again.

In recent years, trading stamps have been under attack by various consumer groups that claim the shopper actually pays for the premiums he gets through higher prices charged by the retailer. Some retailers agree and have discontinued the use of stamps. Nevertheless, trading stamps are still popular as premiums.

Coupons

Many firms issue coupons that offer a discount on an article. Coupons encourage shoppers to try a new product or to continue buying an old one. A typical coupon might say, "Eight Cents Off On Liquid Vel!" or "Five Cents Off On Skippy Peanut Butter!" Manufacturers of soap and other household and personal grooming aids use this type of premium frequently. People may receive coupons by mail, by door-to-door delivery, or in newspaper or magazine ads. Sometimes the coupon comes with the product. Like trading stamps, some coupons that come with the product may be exchanged for valuable merchandise.

Factory Packs

Manufacturers of cereals that appeal to children often place in the package a free gift, such as a toy or comic book. Such a gift is called a "factory pack." Manufacturers of detergents use factory packs widely. They may include a piece of silverware or china inside the box of detergent to encourage the buyer to keep buying their product until she has a complete set.

Direct-Sales Premiums

Door-to-door salesmen often use premiums to build sales. Fuller Brush salesmen, for example, may give away a small brush or other article to each person they call on, whether or not a sale is made. Encyclopedia salesmen may offer a free bookcase with the purchase of a set of books. With higher-priced items, such as appliances and automobiles, a gift is sometimes offered to those who come to the store to watch a demonstration.

Sales-Lead Premiums

The sales-lead premium is a gift or a price discount that is offered to customers in return for the names of friends who may be induced to purchase the product. These premiums are used widely with higher-priced items that are sold door to door. Often, the salesman must pay for the premium out of his commission, and the person who furnishes the lead receives a gift or a price discount only if the referral results in a sale.

CONTESTS AND SWEEPSTAKES

Both contests and sweepstakes are very popular sales promotion devices. A contest requires some degree of skill on the part of the entrant. It may involve writing or completing a jingle or slogan, submitting a name, working a puzzle, and so forth. The entrant may be asked to provide a proof of purchase with each entry submitted.

Pillsbury sponsors what is one of the better-known contests, the Pillsbury Bake-Off Contest. In it people send in recipes, and from those submitted, 100 people are selected to bake their particular specialty in a "bake-off" contest. This contest has received nationwide publicity and has been a source of extremely effective promotion for the Pillsbury Company.

A sweepstakes, on the other hand, does not require skill on the part of the entrant. Sweepstakes winners may be selected at random from all entries, or they may hold winning numbers or matching portions of a trademark, symbol, or design.

PRODUCT SAMPLES AND CONTAINER PROMOTION

A small sample of an advertiser's product that is given away free is called a *product sample*. Examples are small tubes of toothpaste, small bottles of shampoo, and small cans of household cleanser. Manufacturers of pharmaceuticals use samples heavily in promoting their products to doctors. Advertisers send some product samples through the mail, deliver some door to door, and give away others at stores. Food manufacturers offer samples of their cheeses, meat spreads, candy, and crackers to shoppers in supermarkets. Food manufacturers also use "container promotion," in which a product is made more appealing to customers by packaging it in a reusable container. Examples of container promotion are coffee in glass percolators, jelly and cheese in useful tumblers, and candy in attractive vases.

EXHIBITS

The marketer has many opportunities to promote his product at exhibits and various shows. Some of the most popular events are county and state fairs, automobile and boat shows, and hobby and sports shows. One company, Hickory Farms, uses its company symbol, a red barn, as the setting for its exhibit booths at fairs and other places. At the booths, people can see, smell, and taste Hickory Farm crackers, cheeses, dips, mustards, meats, and candies. The appeal of good food and the "food-from-the-farm" theme lures customers to the exhibit and later to a similar red-barn display in food stores.

Generally, exhibits are used more often for industrial products than for consumer products. When held for industrial products, the exhibits are called trade shows. At these shows, manufacturers display the merchandise they will offer for sale during the coming season. Home-furnishings shows may occur semiannually, and other merchandise shows may take place annually. In many cities, manufacturers hold an annual business show at which they display their office supplies, machines, and equipment, and demonstrate their products to office executives and industrial buyers.

Although direct sales are made at exhibits, this is not necessarily the main purpose of exhibiting. Manufacturers hope to interest prospective buyers in placing their names on the company's mailing list so that they may be sent more information at a future time.

PRICE-ORIENTED PROMOTION

Promotion that offers a special price reduction to the buyer is known as *price-oriented promotion*. It is of two types: a combination offer and a special price reduction.

A "combination offer" gives the customer two products which, if purchased separately, would be more expensive. Toothpaste manufacturers sometimes include a toothbrush with their product, and charge only a slightly higher price for the combination than they do for the toothpaste alone. A typewriter dealer might offer a complete typewriting course with each typewriter purchased. A razor manufacturer might include a bottle of his new shaving lotion with the purchase of a razor.

Sometimes, to introduce customers to a new product or to keep them buying an old one, manufacturers offer a special price reduction for a limited time. One of the most successful price-reduction promotions is the Rexall Drug Company's famous one-cent sale. When a customer buys one article, he gets another just like it for an additional penny. These special promotions are held twice a year, in the spring and fall.

VISUAL MERCHANDISING

While advertising and various promotional techniques can create interest in a product or a company, the results come when the buyer approaches the store. What will his decision be? Marketers try to make the decision favorable by providing visual encouragement. They strive to make the interior and exterior of the store as attractive as possible. Inside the store they use point-of-purchase advertising to call the customer's attention to their products and to remind or encourage him to buy.

Exterior of the Store

If a prospective customer is attracted by the exterior of a store, he is more likely to want to shop there. One important factor is the sign identifying the store. A good sign provides clear identification and reflects the image the store is trying to create.

Gaudy store signs somehow scream "Bargains here!" while tasteful, sophisticated signs make the shopper feel that he is about to enter a first-class establishment. Compare, for example, the signs of used-car lots that light up the skyline, with those that identify stores specializing in exclusive fashions. Of course, loud signs are not always bad and quiet signs are not always good. In some cases a flashy, colorful sign is a must if the marketer is to get his share of business. Service stations, roadside eating places, movie theaters, and amusement parks depend on their signs to attract customers. On the other hand, because of its location, a downtown department store has less need for a sign to draw attention.

Of vital importance to the store image is the storefront. An effective storefront provides an attractive "picture frame" for the store. It harmonizes

The sign should suit the store.

with the image the store is trying to create and provides an inviting entrance, so that customers will want to stop and enter the store.

A trend in storefront design is the use of glass fronts which enable customers to see inside the store. In other words, marketers want to remove barriers that separate the outside and inside of the store. See-through glass fronts have become especially popular in banks, automobile showrooms, and appliance stores.

Another important part of the storefront is the window display. Some retailers give window displays credit for as much as one-third of their business. The best results are obtained on streets with heavy pedestrian traffic.

Creating an effective window display requires special skill, and most large retailers employ specialists to handle this job. Smaller businesses receive help with their displays from representatives of manufacturers and wholesalers. There are four basic rules concerning window displays:

1. They should maintain a clean, crisp appearance—they must never appear dusty, faded, or worn.

2. They should be related to the season or show some connection to current events.
3. They should reflect the personality of the store and the merchandise it carries.
4. They should be related to the store's advertising and promotion.

Interior of the Store

Because customers like to shop in attractive surroundings, retailers spare no expense in designing store interiors that are pleasing to the eye. Lighting, color schemes, floor coverings, and display equipment are given special attention.

One of the most important parts of the store's visual image is the display of merchandise. Merchandise is pleasing to the eye when it is grouped by type, displayed appealingly, and kept fresh, clean, and well stocked. Four basic types of retail merchandise displays are open displays, closed displays, model displays, and wall and ledge displays.

Open displays are those in which the merchandise shown is not enclosed in a display case. Everything is out in the open, so that customers can pick up articles and examine them. Open displays are used by all types of stores.

Closed displays are those in which merchandise is housed inside a display case. Closed displays are used mostly for expensive articles, such as diamonds and watches, to prevent theft, or for fragile items, such as glassware, to prevent breakage. In addition, closed displays are used when special lighting and display effects are desired. Closed displays that have dramatic lighting can often attract customers more effectively than open displays.

You have probably seen model kitchens, bedrooms, and recreation rooms in department and furniture stores. These are called model displays. *Model displays* are used to show merchandise as it would look in actual use with related items.

"Wall and ledge displays" occupy space that would otherwise be wasted in the store. Merchandise on these displays is usually not accessible to shoppers, but the displays are used to attract attention to identical goods that are being featured at nearby counters. Sometimes wall and ledge displays are used mainly to improve the appearance of the store or to set a particular mood. For example, a store may display baskets of artificial flowers to relate to the coming of spring.

For goods such as automobiles, boats, farm equipment, and office machines, the floor models serve as the displays. Stores featuring this type of merchandise find the see-through storefront an excellent inducement to the pedestrian to stop in and see a demonstration.

Closed displays are often used for small items of merchandise that might be susceptible to shoplifting.

Point-of-Purchase Advertising

The use of advertising or display material in and around a retail store is referred to as *point-of-purchase advertising*. The display material is usually supplied by the manufacturer for use in promoting his products where the goods are sold. Point-of-purchase (POP) advertising includes posters, counter cards, window display material, price cards, stands, racks, and barrels. POP advertising has several objectives. Among them are the following:

- To attract the shopper's attention
- To remind the customer to buy
- To introduce new products
- To get the customer to ask for more information about the product

To take advantage of the shopper's previous exposure to advertising, POP displays often feature the same illustrations and themes used in magazines and on television.

Retail food stores use POP displays to sell products such as canned goods, napkins and tissues, and cookies and cakes. Department and specialty stores use POP displays to sell cosmetics, hosiery, and other small items.

It is to the manufacturer's advantage if the dealer can place POP displays at strategic points in the store. Many companies spend a great deal of money developing POP devices and helping dealers make effective use of them. POP advertising is especially effective for impulse (unplanned) buying. Manufacturers, therefore, not only supply dealers with appropriate display material but also offer attractive display cases for the merchandise itself. The display case for Life Savers is a good example. Distributors of razor blades, magazines, candy, and other impulse goods also furnish special display racks and stands on which their products can be prominently shown.

POP advertising provides the dealer with excellent promotional assistance and, when used effectively, can greatly increase sales.

YOUR MARKETING VOCABULARY

On a separate sheet of paper define each of the following marketing terms; then use each term in a sentence.

Closed displays
Model displays
Open displays
Point-of-purchase advertising
Premium
Price-oriented promotion
Product sample

FOR REVIEW AND DISCUSSION

1. Explain what is included in sales promotion.
2. Name some of the most important forms of sales promotion.
3. What is the main purpose of trading stamps?
4. What is the difference between a direct-sales premium and a sales-lead premium?
5. Explain the difference between contests and sweepstakes.
6. What is the main purpose for manufacturers' exhibiting their products?
7. Describe container promotion.
8. Name and explain the two types of price-oriented promotion.
9. List two characteristics of a store sign.
10. What are three important qualities of an effective storefront?
11. Name four general rules concerning window displays.
12. List four objectives of point-of-purchase advertising.

ANALYZING MARKETING CONCEPTS

1. As a consumer, you are bombarded with sales promotion. You can learn a lot about marketing by analyzing sales promotion techniques. Prepare a form like the one near the top of the next page. List these techniques in the left-hand column: (a) trading stamps, (b) coupons, (c) factory

packs, (d) direct-sales premiums, (e) contests, (f) product samples. For each technique, list in the middle column a business you have observed using the technique. In the right-hand column, describe the marketing activity in which the business uses the technique.

Sales Promotion Technique	Business Using Technique	Marketing Activity
Example: Trading stamps	Food store	Stamps with every purchase; double-stamp day on Tuesday.

2. Point-of-purchase advertising is designed to get the customer's attention, to remind him to buy, and to introduce new products. Prepare a form like the one below and list the following products in the left-hand column: (a) bars of soap, (b) gum, (c) cans of soda, (d) magazines, (e) women's hosiery, (f) flashlight batteries, (g) greeting cards, (h) ball-point pens, (i) razor blades, (j) small hand tools. You have seen these products displayed regularly in drugstores, supermarkets, and variety stores. For each product, describe in the right-hand column one POP display you have seen for that product.

Product	Description of POP Display
Example: Candy	Plastic bags of candy in wire racks in middle of first aisle in a supermarket.

◻ MARKETING PROJECT 32
Determining the Objective of POP Displays

Project Goal: Given five point-of-purchase displays, determine the basic objective of each.

Action: Visit a local drugstore, supermarket, variety store, or department store and ask the manager for permission to record information on POP advertising. Walk through the store and select five products that have point-of-purchase displays.

Prepare a form like the following one; write the name of the store at the top of the form. In the left-hand column, list the five products you have selected. In the center column, describe the display for each product and indicate its location in the store.

Each numbered column at the right of your form represents a specific basic objective of POP displays, as follows:

Column 1: To attract shoppers' attention.
Column 2: To remind customers to buy.
Column 3: To introduce new products.
Column 4: To get a customer to ask for more information about a product.

Place a check mark in the appropriate column to indicate the basic objective of each POP display you have listed.

Product in POP Display	Description and Location of Display	Basic Objective			
		1	2	3	4
Example: Oyster crackers	Boxes of crackers in wire basket on floor beneath canned soups.		✓		

part 33

Publicity and Public Relations

YOUR GOALS

1. Given examples of publicity and public relations, determine their marketing value.
2. Given a type of marketing business, develop 12 ideas for special events, one for each month of the year.

Publicity and public relations both play important parts in a company's promotional efforts. The purpose of publicity is to gain free advertising for a firm by supplying the various media with news items about the company, its products, or its services. The purpose of public relations is to build goodwill toward the company. This may be done by presenting or sponsoring free shows, by offering free instruction in areas related to the company's products, or by participating in community activities.

PUBLICITY

Unpaid advertising for a company or its products is called *publicity*. Some companies have one department to handle publicity and another for public relations. Other companies combine the two into one department.

Publicity appears in print media such as newspapers and magazines, or in broadcast media such as television and radio. It is the job of the publicity department to get the company's name and products mentioned favorably wherever and whenever it can. The publicity director and his associates must know all the media and other channels of communication that might be interested in publicizing news about the company and its product. They must also know how to contact these various channels of communication. For one story, they may prepare press releases and send them to selected newspaper and magazine editors. For a second story, they may offer a magazine a full-length article with illustrations, on an exclusive basis. For a third story, they may contact the director of a local television station to see if live coverage can be arranged. A publicity department's success depends upon sending the right news to the right channel of communication at the right time.

Evaluation of News

A publicity department has to be careful in selecting what it chooses to publicize. This point is illustrated by the following example of a telephone conversation that might take place between the director of sales promotion (Keith) and the director of publicity (Susan) in a large department store.

KEITH: Good morning, Susan. Say, I think we've got something going in our outdoor advertising campaign that might be newsworthy. Interested?

SUSAN: Sure, Keith. What is it?

KEITH: You know, of course, that there's a good deal of public opposition to large billboards within the city limits these days.

SUSAN: I certainly do. I just read a statement by the Midvale Community Association in this morning's paper about it.

KEITH: Well, it's true that people are saying that some signs are eyesores. We're scheduled for 15 outdoor showings in and around Midvale to promote our new twig store in Greenfield County. They're going to be handsome billboards—colorful, three dimensional, and beautifully lighted.

SUSAN: That sounds pretty good, but what's new about that?

KEITH: Well, our idea is to completely landscape the area where the billboards are by planting grass, flowers, and shrubs—really beautifying the place. At the Bates Street intersection sign, we're even planning to build a fountain.

SUSAN: Sounds interesting enough to make a pretty good story.

KEITH: Do you think the papers might be interested in carrying it? How about Chet Farber's "TV News Roundup"?

SUSAN: I think they might be interested. Have you definitely decided to do this? Where does the project stand?

KEITH: We have the go-ahead; in fact, we're nearly ready with a couple of projects.

SUSAN: This sounds like something I can get newspaper and radio and maybe TV coverage on, Keith. We'll want some pictures, and . . .

Notice that Susan was cautious about promising Keith that his story would be used. The publicity director is always faced with the possibility

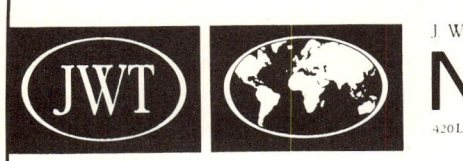

```
                J. WALTER THOMPSON COMPANY
  [JWT]  [globe]   NEWS
                420 Lexington Avenue · New York, N.Y. 10017
                        MUrray Hill 6-7000


from: _____ GENE SECUNDA _____


                        FOR IMMEDIATE RELEASE


        The First National Bank of Commerce in New Orleans has assigned
   its advertising to the J. Walter Thompson Company, it was announced
   today.
        JWT will service the bank, one of the largest in the South,
   from its southeast regional headquarters in Atlanta, and from its
   office in New Orleans.

        "We are delighted that our Atlanta Office has received this
   assignment," said Wyatte Hicks, Executive Vice President and Chair-
   man of JWT's North American Management Committee.  The First National
   Bank of Commerce is identified with progress and growth in the south-
   east.  Its contribution to the financial development of the Louisiana
   Superdome and its broad branch banking network, the largest in New
   Orleans Parish, are indicators of its burgeoning vitality."
                              ###
   6/28/73
```

Courtesy J. Walter Thompson Co.

A company's publicity department sends press releases such as this one to editors of selected magazines and newspapers. When an editor uses a release as the basis for a news story, the company receives publicity.

that the story he wants told will not find its way into the various media. All media are burdened with more news than they can handle, and they must make sure that whatever they accept is of genuine interest to the public. In preparing copy for the press and for the broadcast media, therefore, the publicity department must search for news that is unusual. The publicity director must also strive to keep the story free of blatant advertising and as brief as possible.

Samples of News Items

Nearly every organization uses publicity. Large and small business firms, colleges and universities, church groups, social clubs, fraternities, and civic groups—any or all of them may have a publicity director who strives to get the news of his organization's activities across to the public. Whether or not the news is publicized will depend on its uniqueness and its current interest to the public.

Here are some examples of good publicity ideas:

- The publicity director of a steamship line carrying vacationers to the Bahamas makes sure that pictures are taken of guests and sent to their hometown newspapers. The newspapers, knowing that local residents will be interested in reading about their fellow townsmen, will probably print the picture of the happy vacationers and mention the name of the steamship line.
- The publicity director of a private school asks all students for the names of their hometown newspapers. During the school year, any interesting event concerning any student—election to office, honors, a sports triumph, graduation, etc.—is written up as a news release and sent to his hometown newspaper. If the story is printed, the school is mentioned and thus gets free advertising.
- A glue manufacturer develops a glue powerful enough to hold two heavy blocks of wood together, even when the top block is lifted by a crane. The publicity director has pictures taken of the crane lifting the blocks, writes a story about it, and sends it to various media.
- The publicity director for a large savings and loan association writes a news release about the appointment of a new president and a new board chairman and sends it to various media.

PUBLIC RELATIONS

The total process of building goodwill toward a business organization is called *public relations*. The job of public relations is to create a favorable atmosphere for doing business. The public relations director and his associates strive to build within the public a friendly feeling for the company.

Public relations is involved with all aspects of a company. How a company's physical plant looks, what a company's policies are, how company representatives act and react all affect public relations. The "public" of public relations usually consists of four groups: customers, the community, stockholders, and employees. It is to a company's advantage to be on the best possible terms with these groups.

Customer Relations

Today many businesses think of their customers as guests and treat them as such. This not only means giving their usual courteous and friendly service but also means finding other ways to make shopping more pleasant and convenient. It is this attitude that has led some large stores to establish baby-sitting services and to provide piped-in music and comfortably furnished lounges. These services make customers feel more comfortable and relaxed in the store and thus encourage their patronage.

A few of the public relations efforts that a marketing firm may engage in include establishing a consumer advisory board, making consultants available to help customers with their shopping, and staging special events.

Consumer Advisory Boards. Many firms have established *consumer advisory boards,* which are panels of consumers who determine what customers want and do not want in the way of merchandise and services. A manufacturer of waxes may call on such a panel to test a new floor polish. Another manufacturer may call on the advisory board to determine what is desirable and undesirable about laundry bleaches. At one time an Eastern retail store appointed a panel of clubwomen representing 13 statewide organizations to study possible ways of improving store services. The panel surveyed some 5,000 women to learn their preferences regarding store hours, delivery services, and monthly billing procedures. Using the panel's findings, the store changed its policies greatly and was able to serve all its customers better.

High school, college, and career advisory boards are appointed by many stores. From these groups, marketers learn what young people prefer in fashions.

Perhaps the major value of consumer advisory boards is that they are excellent sources of marketing research information. The opinions expressed by customers help the store make its marketing policies. Consumer advisory boards also have an important public relations value. "We're really a part of that store," thinks the customer. "They want our advice and opinions, and we help them decide what to do."

Customer Consultants. Many large stores have various kinds of customer consultants who help make shopping easier for customers. The consultants are usually specially trained and are expected to put customer service ahead of sales. They may be fashion, bridal, or interior-decorating consultants.

Many large department stores keep a record of employees who speak foreign languages and assign these employees to help foreign customers. In one ad before Christmas, Macy's listed the languages in which it could serve customers. This was a very effective public relations effort that certainly aided sales promotion.

The interior-decorating consultant helps customers select home furnishings and accessories.

Special Events. Sometimes stores hold special events for their customers. They may sponsor fashion shows open only to charge-account customers and donate the proceeds to charity. Stores may have special sales and announce them to established customers before advertising the sales publicly. Sweepstakes drawings may be held exclusively for present customers, with the winner receiving a valuable prize. The object of all such special events is to make the customer realize that the store values his patronage.

Services to New Residents. Some stores mail gifts to new residents in the community and encourage them to open charge accounts. One of the largest gift programs of this kind is Welcome Wagon International, Inc., a private business which generally represents one store of each kind in a community. The hostesses of Welcome Wagon call on new residents. Each participating store pays a certain amount for each call and usually contributes one or more gifts. The newcomers receive gifts when the hostesses call and receive others when they visit the stores. In this way, new residents are welcomed to the community and, furthermore, are encouraged to become regular customers of the welcoming stores.

Courtesy Welcome Wagon International, Inc.
The Welcome Wagon hostess may be one of the earliest visitors to new residents of a community.

Community Relations

The activities a company engages in to acquire or maintain the respect of the community are referred to as *community relations.* One way that marketing businesses build good community relations is by sponsoring activities of public interest. Such activities, known as *special events,* can increase business and also contribute to the civic and cultural life of the community. Here are some examples of special events:

- A children's clothing store puts on a fashion show for a women's club. The club charges an admission, and the proceeds go to the local hospital.
- Several banks guarantee the costs of a special concert, enabling outstanding talent to appear in the community.
- A furniture store brings in a craftsman to demonstrate caning chairs, a weaver to show how fabrics are made on a loom, and a potter to demonstrate the use of the potter's wheel.
- A manufacturer of water skis speaks to sea scouts about water safety.

Just about everyone in a company has a role to play in public relations. Executives are encouraged to join local groups such as the Junior Chamber of Commerce (Jaycees), booster organizations such as Lions and Rotary, and city planning boards. Some companies give employees time off to work in community activities, such as United Fund campaigns and hospital drives.

Sometimes public relations activities are spontaneous. It may take an emergency to bring out the best public relations spirit in an organization. For example, a few years ago New York City was blacked out when electric power failed just as people were leaving their offices at the end of the day. Most New Yorkers use subways to get home, but without electric power the subway trains could not run. Thousands of people faced the prospect of spending a cold night in New York without food, light, or shelter. Macy's, a large department store located in the heart of the city, opened its doors to people stranded in that area, provided sleeping cots, set up a portable emergency lighting system, and served free coffee and sandwiches. While it is hard to measure the reactions of people, it is safe to say that most of those who found shelter at Macy's were left with a favorable impression of the store.

Stockholder Relations

A publicly owned company is responsible to its stockholders and must keep them informed of its financial operations. This information is usually given out through the public relations department. The department produces annual and quarterly financial reports and arranges and participates in periodic meetings with stockholders.

All communications with stockholders must be forthright and clear. A stockholder is likely to have confidence in a company that lets him know what it is doing with his money.

Employee Relations

To the customer, the employees he meets are the company. This does not mean only vice presidents and department managers. It also means salespeople, cashiers, deliverymen, repairmen, telephone operators, and credit personnel. The executives and managers who realize this fact know that happy, satisfied employees will present the company most favorably to the public, both inside and outside the store or office. They know that the thousands of dollars spent on advertising, promotion, and publicity mean very little if employees complain to outsiders or are rude to customers.

To build good employee relations, management continually studies ways of training, compensating, and promoting employees and providing good working conditions. Managers are also aware of the importance of employee benefits, such as insurance, hospitalization, vacations, and recreational activities. The extent of these benefits can greatly affect an employee's attitude toward his company.

PUBLICITY AND PUBLIC RELATIONS AT WORK

Let us look at an example of how publicity and public relations work together. Suppose that a nationwide retail chain store decides to open a branch store in a small city. How might management publicize the event and get support for the new outlet?

Long before the decision to establish a branch store is made, the company makes many surveys to determine the demand for the store in the community, traffic problems, probable location, and sources of labor. This involves research and discussions with leaders in local government, business, and the community. Once the decision to establish a store is made, the firm begins to plan its publicity and public relations campaign. One of the first things it does is to arrange for a company executive to speak at a chamber of commerce luncheon. This speech will announce the company's decision to enter the community and is likely to be reported in the local paper and on radio.

As soon as construction is ready to begin, a ground-breaking ceremony is held, with key executives, the mayor, and local civic leaders present. Photographs are taken, and the story appears on the front page of the local newspaper. It is also presented on radio and possibly on local television.

After the ground-breaking ceremony, a special luncheon is held for presidents of local banks, newspaper editors, television personnel, and various city government officials and civic leaders.

As construction progresses, the firm sends out a series of news stories. Some describe the company—its major executives, its national growth, and its merchandising policies. Other stories announce the appointment of local people to important jobs in the store, the opening of an employment office, and the training program planned for new employees. One point continually emphasized in the news releases is the importance of the new store to the growth and prosperity of the community. As the opening date approaches, the news releases become more frequent.

About a week before the opening, management holds a preview for the press. Newspaper, magazine, radio, and television reporters and cameramen are taken on a tour of the new store and given photographs and news releases. The day before the opening, another preview is held for the leading citizens. Executives greet guests and answer questions.

The *formal opening* is usually a brief but impressive public ceremony to open the business officially. The store manager and other key executives greet the people, and the mayor welcomes the store to the community. The ribbon-cutting ceremony is held, officially opening the store.

After many months of combining public relations and publicity to inform the public about the new store, business is finally begun, and the store is off to a good start. Now the job of keeping the goodwill of the community begins.

YOUR MARKETING VOCABULARY

On a separate sheet of paper define each of the following marketing terms; then use each term in a sentence.

Community relations
Consumer advisory board
Formal opening
Public relations
Publicity
Special events

FOR REVIEW AND DISCUSSION

1. What is the purpose of publicity? of public relations?
2. Explain the job of the publicity department.
3. What guides must the publicity department follow in preparing acceptable copy for news media?
4. What four groups make up the "public" of public relations?
5. In what ways might a company work toward establishing good public relations with its customers?
6. List three activities that a business could sponsor to build good community relations.
7. Explain the relationship that should exist between a company's public relations department and the stockholders.
8. Why must a company show concern for its employees? How does it show this concern?
9. What important people are likely to be present at a ground-breaking ceremony for a new retail store?
10. Describe the formal opening of a new business.

ANALYZING MARKETING CONCEPTS

1. Try to remember several publicity or public relations activities by businesses. Recall them from your experience, from newspaper stories, or from TV and radio news reports and interviews. Prepare a form like the one below and write the names of the businesses in the left-hand column. In the center column, describe the publicity or public relations activity sponsored by each business. In the right-hand column, tell why the activity was effective.

Type of Business	Activity	Why Activity Was Effective
Example: Sporting-goods store	Joe Namath at opening ceremony of new store.	Famous football star attracted large crowd.

2. Assume that you are about to open a record shop, and you want to prepare a publicity and public relations campaign for your opening. Prepare a form like the one below. In the left-hand column, list at least five activities that you would include in your campaign. In the right-hand column, describe each activity.

Campaign Activity	Description of Activity
Example: On the night before opening, sponsor a free dance.	Hold dance on the parking lot in front of the record shop. Provide free soft drinks. Have drawings for records.

◆ MARKETING PROJECT 33
Studying Publicity and Public Relations

Project Goal: Given examples of publicity and public relations, determine their marketing value.

Action: Look through local newspapers and magazines and tune in to radio and TV news broadcasts. Through these media locate five examples of publicity or public relations activities by different types of business firms, such as retail, service, and manufacturing.

Prepare a form like the one below. In the left-hand column, write the name of each business engaged in the activities you discovered. In the center column, describe the publicity or public relations activity, and estimate the value of this activity to the marketing firm. In the right-hand column, identify the source of your information.

Name of Business	Activity and Value	Source
Example: Lane Department Store	Sponsors an annual art contest for high school students in cooperation with schools. Awards many prizes. Displays the paintings in store for public viewing. Covered by local TV and newspapers. Creates goodwill and in-store traffic.	Local newspaper

part 34

The Importance of Personal Selling

YOUR GOALS

1. Identify the kinds of salesmen needed by several types of marketing businesses.
2. Identify the personal characteristics and abilities needed to become an effective salesman in a business of your choice.

Advertising, display, publicity, and sales promotion are important parts of the selling process. These activities are examples of nonpersonal selling, which is usually directed at large groups of people. Personal selling, however, is often needed to actually close the sale and put the product into the customer's hands. *Personal selling* is the direct effort made by a salesperson to convince a customer to make a purchase.

The commercial that interrupts your favorite television program with "a word from our sponsor, the National Tire Company," is an example of nonpersonal selling because it is aimed at a large audience. In that audience there are some who are interested in the sales message and some who are not. On the other hand, the salesman who tries to sell an insurance policy to a businessman is doing personal selling. This sales effort involves direct personal contact with the customer. As stated in an earlier part, the term "salesman" refers to both men and women.

THE IMPORTANCE OF SALESMEN

Salesmen are needed at all stages of the marketing process. When you pick up a carton of your favorite soft drink at the supermarket, you can be sure that many salesmen were involved in getting it to you. Sugar salesmen, flavoring salesmen, and coloring salesmen sold these ingredients to the manufacturer of the soft-drink syrup. Another salesman sold the manufacturer the machinery he uses to make the syrup.

Other salesmen called on the local bottler of the soft drink. They sold the bottler the carbonating ingredients, the bottles, the caps, and many other bottling supplies and equipment. Still another salesman sold him the carton.

The bottler employs drivers who are route salesmen. They sold the soft drink to stores and offices in the bottler's territory. Indeed, many salesmen participated in getting that soft drink to you.

Personal salesmen are needed to sell all types of products and services. Telephone companies employ salesmen to sell increased telephone usage by business firms and other organizations. Hotels employ salesmen to sell their meeting-room and banquet facilities to various groups and firms. Transportation companies hire salesmen to sell their charter services and other facilities to different organizations.

The modern professional salesman is one of the most valuable people in business. He does not exaggerate his product or pressure people into buying. He thinks of making a sale, but he also thinks of the needs of his customers. For this reason, people often rely on the professional salesman to show them how to get the most for their money; to give them information about new products; and to advise them on styles, colors, models, prices, and financing.

Personal selling is the most important and costly element of promotion. Some companies budget five times as much money for their salesmen's salaries and selling expenses as they do for all other advertising and promotional activities. Salesmen are usually expected to carry the major part of the selling effort in the following circumstances:

■ *When the customers for the product are limited in number.* For example, a manufacturer of printing presses has only a limited number of potential customers for his products, and he depends on his salesmen to seek out and sell to these customers. In fact, any salesman selling to the industrial market has far fewer people to contact than a salesman selling to the consumer market. If a company has a product which appeals primarily to the consumer, it will concentrate its personal selling efforts on the retailers who handle its product. A large bread company, for example, does not hire salesmen to call on consumers. (It can reach consumers

The modern professional salesman informs, advises, and sells.

far more effectively by spending a major portion of its promotion budget on consumer advertising.) Instead, the company's salesmen spend their time calling on the retailers who sell its bread.

■ *When the product or service requires a demonstration or explanation.* A company introducing a new electronic computer needs to explain how the use of this computer will help the potential customer to process more work in less time and with greater accuracy. A well-trained salesman is usually in a better position to demonstrate these advantages than is an advertisement, because the salesman can tailor his presentation to the particular needs of the potential customer and can answer questions.

■ *When the product or service is high-priced.* The customer in a variety store or a supermarket can be influenced to buy through an ad or an attractive POP display. The cost of items purchased in such a store is relatively low, and the customer is less likely to hesitate in buying an item once he is convinced he wants to own it. But that same customer will hesitate in buying a car, a major appliance, or a piece of furniture solely on the basis of an ad or a display. Here a salesman is needed to convince the customer to buy.

■ *When a trade-in is part of the sale.* Many industrial products and some consumer products may not be completely worn out at the time the customer is considering a new or an improved version of the same product. This creates a situation in which the salesman can offer a trade-in allowance to the customer. It takes a salesman to convince the customer that he is getting a good trade-in allowance. The closing of the sale often hinges on this very human element.

TYPES OF SELLING JOBS

Salesmen may work for manufacturers, wholesalers, or retailers. Their jobs for each of these marketers may vary tremendously. Even two salesmen working for the same type of wholesaler may have jobs that are quite different. However, there is one thing that all salesmen have in common: Each uses the techniques of personal selling.

Selling for Manufacturers

Manufacturers serve a wide variety of customers—other manufacturers, wholesalers, retailers, government agencies, hospitals, educational institutions, and individual consumers. The salesmen who represent the manufacturers in selling to these customers are called *manufacturers' salesmen.*

This manufacturer's salesman is pointing out the merits of a machine part to his customer, an industrial buyer.

Most manufacturers hire salesmen who are technically trained in, or willing to learn about, specialized fields. Salesmen trained in engineering or other skills may call on industrial buyers who buy goods to be processed or to serve the industrial user. Such goods may include metal parts for airplane manufacturers, plastics for radio and television sets, desks for schools, and tableware for restaurants. A manufacturer's salesman must know his customer's problems intimately and be trained to assist in solving them. The following story is an example of how a manufacturer's salesman can help a customer solve a problem.

Walt Larson is a manufacturer's salesman. He works for the Berwick Freight Car Company. Walt's job is to sell all types of freight cars to railroads. He calls on executives of railroads, listens to their needs, and tells them about the fine freight cars his company makes.

Several years ago, Walt hit a snag during a talk with Southern Railway executives. He found that the railroad did not need any new cars because it was losing business to truckers. Southern Railway had hauled large amounts of grain in standard hopper cars. Truckers, however, were now shipping the grain for less money than the railroad charged, and business was thus shifting from the railroad to the truck hauler. To make matters worse, Southern Railway could not afford to lower its price to a competitive level.

Walt Larson had uncovered a customer problem. He knew that Southern Railway could not buy new hopper cars until this problem was solved. Then Walt had an idea. What if his company were to build a hopper car at least twice as big as the standard model, so that it would cost far less per bushel to ship grain by railroad? The idea was tried, and it worked. The railroad was able to offer grain shippers a lower price using its new "Big John" hopper cars, and shippers began to switch their business back to the railroad. Now Southern Railway could place a substantial order for "Big John" hopper cars with the manufacturer's salesman Walt Larson.

Thus, by studying and finding a solution to his customer's problem, the manufacturer's salesman in the example above was able to help his customer (the railroad), his employer (the freight car manufacturer), and himself.

The typical manufacturer's salesman has an assigned territory and a list of customers on whom he calls regularly. Over a period of time he becomes almost a part of the organizations to which he sells. He learns his customers' special problems and needs and looks for ways of serving them better.

Selling for Wholesalers

Wholesalers employ salesmen to call on their customers, which include grocery stores, drugstores, hardware stores, service stations, hospitals, schools, lumber dealers, hotels, and business offices. A wholesale salesman often deals in hundreds, perhaps even thousands, of items. A salesman for a wholesale grocer may have as many as 3,000 items to sell. Some wholesale salesmen serve their customers so efficiently that they are trusted to decide what items the customers need and to order those items without consulting the customers. Often the wholesale salesman is required to be a specialist and consultant, capable of advising his customers on what to buy, how much to buy, and when to buy. The retailer welcomes the wholesale salesman, because the salesman keeps him up to date on the latest happenings in his field. The wholesale salesman also gives the retailer important information about which products are selling best and why.

Selling for Retailers

The most familiar form of personal selling is in retailing. The service-station attendant, the hardware-store clerk, the waitress, the clothing salesman, the dairy routeman, and the door-to-door household-products salesman are all retail salespeople. Retail salespeople are salespeople who sell direct to the consumer.

Often retail salespeople act as sales consultants to customers. For example, a busy person has little time to study new fashions in clothing. Therefore, when buying a new suit, he may consult with a salesperson for fashion and fabric information. The salesperson learns the tastes and needs of the customer and advises him on the most appropriate apparel. This type of selling helps to build higher earnings for the salesperson as well as to earn goodwill among customers for the store.

WHAT IT TAKES TO SELL

To sell effectively, a salesman must be enthusiastic about his job. Moreover, he must be able to get along well with people, have a thorough knowledge of his product, and be capable of managing his time wisely. A lack of any one of these qualities can seriously impair a salesman's performance.

Getting Along With People

A salesman must have a genuine liking for people. Successful salespeople enjoy being with others and learn not only to give a cheerful greeting but also to think in terms of the needs of other people. By thinking of others, salespeople learn to see the customer's point of view and can therefore find out his needs. They can then offer a solution to the customer's problem.

Many salespeople are outstanding because they have worked hard to develop a friendly and pleasing personality, so that customers will like them and will want to do business with them. They know that customers like to associate with and buy from salespeople who are pleasant, courteous, considerate, and willing to help.

Knowing the Product

The salesman who knows his product well and believes in its qualities has confidence in his ability to sell it. He need not bluff his way through a demonstration. Because he knows the product, he also knows how it can benefit the customer. The result is a magic ingredient called "selling enthusiasm." A salesman cannot "turn on" enthusiasm. He acquires it through experience and knowledge and confidence in his product or service.

A number of excellent sources of product knowledge are available to salesmen. Most companies provide brochures, descriptive booklets, merchandise manuals, and advertising pieces. They also hold sales conferences, which are in a sense schools where salesmen acquire product knowledge along with training in selling techniques. Manufacturers often attach to their products tags or labels that carry important information. Salesmen may also refer to a *merchandise manual,* which is a notebook of facts about a product. The manual is prepared by the manufacturer for his salesmen and customers.

This young saleswoman knows her product and explains it to her customer.

Managing Time and Territory

A salesman is a businessman. He must manage his time and his territory. Frequently, no one is around to remind him to get up and get going in the morning. He must be a self-starter. He must find the courage to make the tough calls along with the easier ones. He must resist the temptation to quit early, particularly after a disappointing day. He knows that those late-in-the-day calls can sometimes be the best ones. He must be willing to devote his evening to organizing his plans for the following day. He must telephone ahead for appointments and prepare his schedule to avoid unnecessary travel. He must see to it that he has the proper samples. At the end of each day he must prepare reports on his day's activities. In brief, the salesman must be able to operate effectively with a minimum of supervision. This takes the willingness and know-how to organize a work plan and the determination to stick to that plan.

Succeeding as a Retail Salesperson

A retail salesperson, whose "territory" is a counter or a department and who works regular hours, must have most of the qualities mentioned above if he is to be successful in his job. He is expected to be at his selling post on time, with his stock in order and his selling area ready for customers. He is expected to deal with difficult customers as patiently and carefully as he does with pleasant ones. He is expected to be as alert for the last customer of the day as he was for the first. He is expected to keep his records accurate and up to date.

Personal selling is a very important job in marketing, and the best salesmen are those who never stop training themselves to do the job better.

◻ YOUR MARKETING VOCABULARY

On a separate sheet of paper define each of the following marketing terms; then use each term in a sentence.

Manufacturers' salesmen   *Personal selling*
Merchandise manual

◻ FOR REVIEW AND DISCUSSION

1. Give one example of personal selling and one example of nonpersonal selling.
2. Describe the modern professional salesman.
3. Name four situations in which the salesman usually carries the major part of the selling effort.

4. Even though their jobs may vary, what do all salesmen have in common?
5. How might a creative retail salesperson help his customer?
6. Discuss the statement "A successful salesman thinks in terms of other people's needs."
7. To sell effectively, what abilities must a salesman have?
8. Of what use is product knowledge to a salesman?
9. What are some excellent sources of product knowledge for a salesman?
10. Describe the role that self-management plays in the life of a salesman.

ANALYZING MARKETING CONCEPTS

1. Some consumer problems require more emphasis on personal selling than do others. Prepare a form like the one below and write the following products in the left-hand column: (a) car, (b) gum, (c) necklace, (d) house, (e) aspirin, (f) TV set, (g) pocket radio, (h) bread, (i) shoes, (j) toothpaste, (k) lipstick, (l) dishwasher, (m) magazine, (n) notebook paper, (o) shirt. For each product ask yourself the following question: "In general, how often is personal selling needed for this product?" Answer the question by placing a check mark in the appropriate middle column. Write your reason for each answer in the right-hand column.

Product	\multicolumn{3}{c|}{How Often Personal Selling Is Needed}	Reason
	Always	Often	Seldom	
Example: Handkerchief			✔	Only special types for gift purposes need personal selling.

2. In a business organization dealing with the public, almost every employee at some time or in some way engages in sales work. Prepare a form like the one below and list the following types of employees in the left-hand column: (a) service-station attendant, (b) counterman, (c) photographer, (d) repairman, (e) delivery man, (f) gift-wrap specialist, (g) receptionist, (h) interior decorator. In the right-hand column, describe a job-related selling activity of each employee listed.

Employee	Job-Related Selling Activity
Example: Stock clerk	Helps shoppers to locate merchandise on shelves and may suggest different items.

MARKETING PROJECT 34
Studying Characteristics of Salesmen

Project Goal: Identify the personal characteristics and abilities needed to become an effective salesman in a business of your choice.

Action: Select a business that employs salesmen, and arrange an interview with its owner or manager. Ask the following questions during the interview:

1. What characteristics do you like in the salesmen who work for you?
2. What characteristics of salesmen do you dislike?
3. In what specific ways do your salesmen help their customers?
4. How important are these salesmen to you and your business?

Prepare a form like the one below. Write the name of the person you interviewed and the name of the business at the top of the form. Then write each of the questions above in the left-hand column. In the right-hand column, write the key points of the businessman's answers to each question.

Use this project as the basis for an oral presentation to your class.

Interview Question	Businessman's Answer
Example: What characteristics of salesmen do you dislike?	Dislikes salesmen who do not know the facts about their products, who waste time, who try to pressure customers into buying, who do not seem to care about the company and its business problems.

part 35

Principles of Effective Selling

YOUR GOALS

1. Given a product requiring personal selling, prepare a sales presentation for it and make the presentation before your class.
2. Given several salespeople in different selling situations, evaluate their use of specific selling techniques as effective or ineffective in satisfying sales prospects.

Many sales follow a definite sequence. Each step in the sequence presents its own challenges to the salesman and requires specific selling techniques. The salesman may accomplish the entire sequence in a matter of minutes, or it may take him weeks, months, or even years to complete all the steps of a sale.

The seven steps of a sale are (1) prospecting, (2) the preapproach, (3) the approach, (4) the sales presentation, (5) handling objections, (6) the close, and (7) the departure and the follow-up.

PROSPECTING

The word "prospecting" may bring to mind the California Gold Rush, when grizzled forty-niners searched for that yellow metal that would make them rich. These gold prospectors used different means of finding likely places in which to dig for gold. They listened to stories of other prospectors, they followed their own hunches, and they watched carefully to see where successful prospectors found their gold.

Sales prospecting is similar to gold prospecting, except that the salesman's "gold" is a sale. His efforts are concentrated on locating sales prospects. *Sales prospects* are potential customers who could benefit from and who are in a position to buy a product or service. Prospecting is the process of finding these potential customers.

Salesmen use several basic methods to find prospects. One is the "endless-chain method," in which the salesman secures names of prospects from customers who have already made purchases. Some salesmen use the "cold-canvass approach," in which they make as many calls as possible without any preliminary investigation. The salesman goes from door to door in a neighborhood, hoping to find a satisfactory number of good prospects for his product.

In addition to these methods, there are a great number of sources that a salesman can use in prospecting for customers: telephone directories, trade and professional directories, commercial lists, and local newspapers. The sources for prospecting are many, and they vary with the type of product being sold. The important point is that the salesman cannot afford to ignore a single source in locating prospects who are likely to buy his product.

THE PREAPPROACH

The part of the selling process that consists of gathering and analyzing information about the prospect and using it to construct the sales presentation is the *preapproach*. If the salesman is trying to sell a product for the prospect's own use, the salesman will want to gather certain information about the prospect: What are his hobbies and interests? What are some of his immediate problems? What are his previous buying habits? Does he like baseball or some other sport? Is he especially price-conscious? The average prospect likes a salesman who has taken the time to learn these facts. This tells the prospect, "Here's a man who cares."

If the salesman is trying to sell to an industrial buyer for a company, he will want to know certain facts about the prospect's company and about how the prospect operates: What does the company make or sell? Who buys its product? How well is its product accepted by the market? How could the product be improved? How would the purchase of the salesman's product benefit the company? Where has the company been buying products similar to those the salesman hopes to sell? How and when does the buyer for the company normally place his orders? Does he have many sources of supply?

Salesmen often use the endless-chain method to find prospects.

Why does he buy from another company? The salesman who obtains answers to these questions is well on the road to understanding the characteristics of this prospect.

In selling to a consumer or an industrial buyer, the salesman must determine the prospect's product need. Few people buy something just for the sake of buying. They buy because they are convinced they will benefit from their purchase. The experienced salesman knows his product so well that he can spot the various ways that it could fit a company's needs and produce real benefits. Consider the salesman who is planning to discuss the merits of his new electric typewriter with an office manager. He knows the office manager will be mildly interested in the durability of the typewriter, in the interchangeable typefaces, and in the one-year guarantee; but the manager's interest will really perk up when the salesman relates these product features to customer benefits. The new electric typewriter will make it easier to get and keep a competent secretary. The new typewriter will give the company's letters a nicer appearance and will create a more favorable impression. And, the one-year guarantee means that the office manager will not have to worry about expensive repairs.

After the salesman has collected all the necessary information about the prospect and analyzed it to determine the prospect's needs, he is ready to make the approach.

THE APPROACH

The process by which the salesman tries to gain the favorable attention of the prospect so that he will be willing to hear more about the salesman's product or service is called the *approach*. The approach, then, is made to gain an interview and make the sales presentation. Salesmen use a number of methods to gain interviews.

Timing is important in deciding when to approach the prospect. The salesman should ask himself: "Is the prospect prepared to buy at this time? Is there a best time of the day or month to make this call?" In general, the salesman should make an appointment with the prospect. This gives the prospect some time to think about his needs in terms of the salesman's product.

When approaching the prospect, most salesmen find it helpful to use a business card. This serves to identify the salesman and his company. No prospect is at ease if he does not know the salesman's name, or if he is in doubt about the name of the company and what it sells.

The first few sentences that a salesman says to the prospect are also considered part of the approach. They should be phrased to capture the prospect's interest and make him receptive to what the salesman is going to say afterward. Some salesmen begin the interview by encouraging the prospect to talk. In some cases, they begin with a general opening question such as "What is your biggest problem in the service-station business, Mr. Jones?" Other salesmen begin their interviews with several questions, or they simply talk about some recent happenings in the field, hoping to involve the prospect and to draw out his buying needs in the course of the conversation.

An approach is successful if it gains the interview and if it puts the prospect in a listening frame of mind. The success of an approach is often determined at the moment the salesman steps into the prospect's office. If the salesman is dressed nicely and greets the prospect with a smile and a firm handshake, the prospect is likely to regard him favorably. Moreover, if the salesman looks the prospect directly in the eye during the handshake and the interview and shows confidence in himself, his product, and his ability to sell, the prospect will be more likely to feel at ease with him and will be ready to listen.

THE SALES PRESENTATION

At the heart of the selling process is the *sales presentation,* in which the salesman demonstrates or explains his product and attempts to build a desire for ownership within the customer. This is the selling effort for which the salesman has planned so carefully in his preapproach.

An effective sales presentation often follows this pattern: the salesman organizes his story, involves the prospect's eyes and ears, brings the prospect into the act, and concludes the presentation with extras.

Organizing the Story

Every product or service has certain features that will benefit the prospect. These features may not be self-evident, in which case they must be explained by the salesman. For example, an industrial salesman trying to sell desks to a school may need to explain certain features about the desks. He may note the following characteristics:

1. There are no sharp edges on the desks.
2. The furniture is made of the best grade of Southern pine.
3. Desk tops have a vinyl coating to protect them against stains and scratches.
4. Each desk has an extra-roomy book-storage compartment so that the desk top need not be cluttered with books not in use.
5. The desks may be paired in several ways, depending on the space available.
6. The desks are adjusted to the size of the average student, with extra parts available for adapting them to bigger or smaller students.
7. Each desk can be securely fastened to the floor.
8. All desks can be washed with soap and water.

Each of these points can be fully developed as a part of the complete sales presentation. The organized sales presentation is in no way a "canned" sales talk. A canned sales talk is simply a recitation of product features without considering the feelings or attitude of the prospect. An impersonal recording might do the job just as well. An effective sales presentation, on the other hand, takes into account the fact that every prospect reacts differently, and it therefore depends on a salesman who can think and adjust his presentation to fit each situation.

The good salesman is ready to condense or omit parts of his talk. He stays in tune with the prospect's needs and presents his product in the way that best meets those needs. With one prospect he may give a simplified

This salesman's effective presentation may result in the customer's purchase of a large fleet of trucks.

three-minute talk, and with another he may present the entire story over a much longer period. A good sales presentation, then, is flexible. It can be expanded or shortened to suit the sales situation.

Appealing to Sight and Hearing

It is estimated that a person remembers 20 percent of what he hears, 40 percent of what he sees, and 80 percent of what he simultaneously sees and hears. Therefore, the effective salesman organizes his presentation so that the prospect sees and hears at the same time. He may do this by demonstrating his product. However, if the product is too large to demonstrate, he may use charts, filmstrips, posters, or models to help the prospect visualize it.

The use of visual aids gives the salesman an opportunity to dramatize his presentation. Most prospects react favorably to a presentation that is both factual and eye-catching.

Bringing the Prospect Into the Act

Every good sales presentation involves the prospect as much as possible. This gives the prospect a chance to sell the product to himself. After he has seen and heard the salesman's words, he has a natural urge to want to touch or handle the product. That is why so many automobile salesmen invite the prospect to take the keys and drive the car himself. The clothing salesman invites the prospect to feel the quality of the fabric and to try on the suit. Some salesmen place a product in the prospect's home for a free 30-day trial period to get him to experience the feel of ownership.

Concluding With Extras

Most salesmen like to conclude their presentation with some extras. These extras are no substitute for the body of the presentation, but they do dress it up and make it appealing. For example, to convince the prospect who is considering a product that is totally new to him, the salesman may introduce an extra by saying, "Best of all, Mr. Miller, these desks are guaranteed for one full year." If he wants to convince the prospect of the high quality of his product, he may say, "An independent testing laboratory has given these desks an exceptionally high rating." To reassure the prospect of the good reputation of the manufacturer, the salesman may point out, "The General Furniture Company will stand behind this product." Finally, the salesman may use a testimonial as an extra by saying, "Ten other school districts in the area are using this school furniture, and they all like it."

HANDLING OBJECTIONS

The experienced salesman is prepared for objections. They tell him that the prospect is listening and is interested in the product. The objections may be based on fear, uncertainty, or misunderstanding. In the case of fear or uncertainty, the salesman will attempt to remove all doubt that is causing the prospect to hesitate in making a buying decision. The prospect might say, "I like your product, but I don't think I can afford it now." The salesman could respond to such an objection by stressing the benefits of immediate ownership and by explaining to the prospect how he could purchase the product on the installment plan.

If the objection is based on a misunderstanding, the salesman listens to the prospect carefully and repeats the objection to show that he understands. He then proceeds to remove the misunderstanding. For example, the prospect might say, "I like your product, but your delivery service is too slow." The salesman could respond by mentioning the new warehouse that makes speedier delivery possible. He could even call his company from the prospect's office and find out how fast they can get the order to this prospect. This is a dramatic way to overcome the prospect's objection and close the sale at the same time.

Objections give the salesman a chance to take the pulse of the prospect and to judge how near the prospect is to the close.

THE CLOSE

The *close* is the completion of the sale. It is the main purpose of the selling process. With the close of a sale, the prospect becomes a customer because he has made a purchase. Much has been written about the right psychological moment to close a sale. The experienced salesman begins his close when he has thoroughly presented his product and overcome all objections. He very carefully watches the mood of the prospect to judge when it is the appropriate time to close the sale.

The salesman should avoid closing with a statement as blunt as "Do you want to buy?" This might make the prospect feel pressured. Instead, the salesman should say, "I know you need and want this truck now, Mr. Jones. I believe I can get you delivery next week if I can have your purchase order now." This approach assumes that the prospect wants to buy.

There are other types of closes that a salesman can use. One popular type revolves around the prospect's making a minor decision. Instead of asking the prospect whether he wants the color TV set, the salesman asks, "Would you like the cabinet in maple or mahogany?" Or, for some smaller item, "Would you like to take this with you or shall we deliver it?"

Another type of close is the price concession. The salesman agrees to give the buyer a discount or perhaps a generous trade-in allowance in return for the order. Still another type of close can be used if the product is in short supply. A mention of this fact by the salesman could influence the prospect to make a decision to buy.

The salesman who is making his first call on an important prospect does not necessarily expect to close the sale on that visit. His chief purpose is to learn more about the prospect and his needs. On the second and succeeding calls, he will be in a stronger position to present his product based on the real need of the prospect. A salesman who sells highly technical equipment, such as computers, may call on one company for several years before he is in a position to try for a close.

THE DEPARTURE AND FOLLOW-UP

When the sale is completed, the salesman should thank the customer and leave. The departure should be neither too abrupt nor too drawn out. Before leaving, the salesman should give the customer assurance of speedy delivery, dependable service, and whatever else was promised. Even when no sale has been made, the salesman should show appreciation for the time and attention that has been given to him. A good salesman is always interested in future business and sales. He wants the customer to be a permanent source of business and therefore seeks to keep the door open for future calls.

The test of good salesmanship comes when it is time for the salesman to live up to his promises. A good salesman does not promise the customer what he knows he cannot deliver. If he makes a sale, he takes the time and trouble to follow through on details in connection with a customer order or request.

The departure and follow-up are the end of the selling process. They are also the beginning of the next selling process, because a good salesman studies the reasons for his success or failure after each call. He wants to return to the customer for future sales or to be in a stronger position to make a sale for the first time. This leads him back to his preapproach "homework" and the start of another cycle of activity. With each of these cycles, he becomes a more accomplished salesman.

RETAIL SELLING

The steps in the selling process are used by all types of salespeople. However, whereas outside salesmen usually make their customer approach away from their office or store, most retail salesmen work in a store where their customers come to them. Therefore, the retail salesman must employ some special selling techniques. Unless the retail salesman is selling door to door, he has little opportunity to prospect for customers. He also has little chance to

The successful retail salesperson is friendly, sincere, and efficient.

Courtesy Montgomery Ward

Part 35 / Principles of Effective Selling / 417

prepare his preapproach. For him, the approach is the real beginning of the selling process. He must accomplish in the approach what outside salesmen accomplish through prospecting, the preapproach, and the approach.

The approach of the retail salesman should be prompt and friendly. A warm, pleasant smile from the salesman helps to put the customer at ease. The customer likes to feel welcome and important; therefore, he should not be ignored or kept waiting. The customer wants to have confidence in the salesman, and the well-groomed, polite, and friendly salesman will help develop this confidence. The words of greeting should vary and not develop into a dull stereotype such as "May I help you?" If the customer is inspecting particular merchandise, for example, the salesman could say, "We have several other ties in that same style" or "How are you, Mrs. Miller?" Customers can sense when a greeting has a ring of genuine enthusiasm and when it is offered in a routine or bored fashion. A customer feels especially good when the salesman greets him by name.

If the retail salesman is busy and cannot immediately get to a waiting customer, he recognizes the customer's presence with a nod or smile, or says simply, "I'll be with you in a minute."

Determining Customer Need

In determining customer need, the retail salesman must ask one important question: "For whom is this purchase intended?" Once the intended user of the purchase is established, the salesman can begin to show merchandise. The importance of first determining the intended user is illustrated by the following story.

A young man, neatly dressed in slacks and a sport coat, approached the store counter and told the salesman he wanted to buy a tie. Observing his youth and sporty clothing, the salesman showed him a series of brightly colored ties in reds, yellows, and blues. The young man did not like anything he saw and was about to leave the store when the manager arrived and asked, "Are you buying the tie for yourself?" "No, for my grandfather," the young man replied. Of course, the salesman then quickly brought out a conservative tie in dark blue, which the young man liked and purchased.

The salesman could have saved time had he first determined the customer's need instead of depending on an incorrect assumption.

Increasing the Sale

After the sale has been closed, the retail salesman should move into suggestion selling. *Suggestion selling* is the selling of related or additional items along with those items the customer has already purchased. Suggestion selling is a most effective way of increasing sales. It is not uncommon for more to be sold in suggestion selling than in the original sale, yet many salespeople overlook this important part of retail selling.

Consider the case of a company that made a wide variety of men's grooming aids, such as razors, razor blades, talcum powder, shaving cream, and after-shave lotions. Naturally, the company wanted salespeople to sell as many related items as possible. To determine how much suggestion selling was actually being done, the company sent one of its employees into a number of stores that carried its products. The employee, posing as a customer, was told to ask for a pack of the company's razor blades. In addition, he was authorized to buy up to $20 worth of any related items if a salesperson suggested them. In a few cases, a salesperson did suggest and sell both a razor and talcum powder, but in no case did any salesperson come close to exhausting the $20.

The salesperson who devotes time to suggestion selling increases the stores' profits, makes his job more interesting and rewarding, and enhances his value as an employee.

USE OF THE TELEPHONE IN SELLING

A great deal of selling is done by telephone. An industrial salesman is often in touch with his customers by telephone, informing them of new products, price changes, special discounts, and so on. The same is true of the wholesale salesman. He telephones retailers to tell them that a special purchase of merchandise is available or possibly to find out how a certain item is moving and whether it should be reordered. A manufacturer's representative may call customers to remind them of a successful product or to inform them of a new one.

Some stores encourage salespeople to keep card files of their customers and to call these customers when merchandise arrives that might be of interest to them. Other stores encourage customers to use the telephone-shopping service, in which trained switchboard operators accept orders from customers who make selections from ads or catalogs. Sometimes those switchboards are open 24 hours a day, seven days a week, for customer convenience.

Basically, the telephone is used in selling for the following purposes:

To build a strong prospect list
To make appointments
To service regular customers
To acknowledge orders
To close a sale

To revive old accounts
To notify customers of special events
To handle complaints
To take orders
To sell to new customers

Telephone shopping systems are widely used by department stores.

Courtesy American Telephone & Telegraph Co.

◊ YOUR MARKETING VOCABULARY

On a separate sheet of paper define each of the following marketing terms; then use each term in a sentence.

Approach
Close
Preapproach
Sales presentation
Sales prospects
Suggestion selling

◊ FOR REVIEW AND DISCUSSION

1. List the seven steps in making a sale.
2. In selling, what is meant by the term "prospecting"? Describe some methods of prospecting.
3. In the preapproach, salesmen try to find answers to certain questions about the prospect. List some of those questions.
4. What is the pattern of an effective sales presentation?
5. Explain the difference between a canned sales talk and an organized presentation.
6. How might the salesman make appeals to the customer through sight and sound?

7. How can the customer's objections to a product serve the salesman?
8. How can the departure and follow-up be the beginning of the next selling process?
9. Name two important factors in retail selling.
10. In what ways can telephone selling serve the industrial salesman? the wholesale salesman? the retail salesman?

◼ ANALYZING MARKETING CONCEPTS

1. Suggestion selling is an effective way of increasing sales, and it adds to customer satisfaction. It is therefore important for a salesperson to engage in suggestion selling whenever possible. Prepare a form like the one below. In the left-hand column, list the following items that a customer might purchase: (a) camera, (b) electric toothbrush, (c) record, (d) portable TV, (e) camping knife, (f) paint, (g) ice skates, (h) sweater, (i) bracelet, (j) shoes. For each listed item think of several related items that an alert salesperson might suggest following a customer's purchase of the listed item. List those related items in the right-hand column.

Item Purchased	Items for Suggestion Selling
Example: Camera	Flash bulbs, color film, photo album

2. The selling points of a product should be emphasized according to the needs of the particular customer. Prepare a form like the one below and list the following products in the left-hand column: (a) camera, (b) portable record player, (c) toy, (d) typewriter, (e) dishwasher, (f) model-car kit, (g) personalized stationery, (h) $3 ball-point pen, (i) electric can opener. For each product, select from the following customers the one who would be most likely to buy the product: (1) father, (2) mother, (3) high school student, (4) newlywed, (5) factory worker, (6) secretary. Write your customer selections in the middle column. In the right-hand column, describe a key selling point that might be appropriate in selling the item to the customer.

Product	Customer	Key Selling Point
Example: Tennis racket	Experienced player	Perfectly balanced for greater control and more power.

Part 35 / Principles of Effective Selling / 421

◇ MARKETING PROJECT 35
Making a Sales Presentation

Project Goal: Given a product requiring personal selling, prepare a sales presentation for it and make the presentation before your class.

Action: Select a product such as a camera, radio, recorder, or toy. Prepare a form like the one below and list the product in the left-hand column. In the center column, list the parts of the sales presentation: (a) organizing the story, (b) appealing to sight and hearing, (c) bringing the prospect into the act, and (d) concluding with extras. In the right-hand column, list the key selling points for each part of the presentation.

Use this material as the basis for delivering an oral sales presentation to your class.

Product	Parts of Presentation	Key Selling Points
Example: Camera	Organizing the story	Give product features, such as single-lens reflex; positive, fast shutter action; interchangeable lens; precise focus; fast, sharp viewfinder; through-the-lens electronic meter; built-in shutter-release timer; leather case.

part 36

Planning the Promotion Campaign

YOUR GOAL

Given a new or improved product or service, identify all the media in which it is being promoted, and estimate the role that research played in the promotion campaign.

A smart marketer looking at some healthy sales and profit figures does not think, "We're lucky." Instead, he thinks, "That worked out well. We did a good job of planning."

One of the major jobs in any marketing effort involves planning the promotion campaign. Promotion informs customers about the products and services that the marketer has for sale and encourages customers to buy these products and services. A promotion campaign helps determine just how healthy sales and profit figures will be.

Levi Strauss & Company knows this. Its story began in 1850, when Levi Strauss arrived in San Francisco with sail canvas that he hoped to sell to the gold miners for tent material. The miners, however, were more interested in sturdy pants than sturdy tents. Because Levi Strauss was versatile, he became a pants maker instead of a tentmaker. The miners were pleased. In fact, one was so delighted that he went around San Francisco boasting about his "pants of Levi's," a term that became the company's brand name.[1]

Today, Levi Strauss & Company is the country's largest manufacturer of branded pants for men and boys. The company's products are sold in 24,000 stores and in 30,000 departments.

Levi Strauss & Company uses promotion wisely to make its business grow. There may well be a Levi's ad in this month's issue of a magazine you read frequently. One of the commercials on your favorite radio program may he paid for by Levi's. This promotion campaign is one of the many competing for your dollar in the marketplace.

BEHIND THE PLANNING

For a century, Levi Strauss & Company specialized in making the rugged denim jeans and selling them to working men in the West. The company's customers were ranchers, cattlemen, and anyone else who wanted work pants with a Western look. Shortly after World War II, the company decided it was time to expand by widening its product mix and its marketing area. It decided to add new styles and new fabrics to its line. As a result, the company is becoming known today not only for its jeans but also for its complete sportswear line of casual pants for men, women, and teen-agers. It is also moving into the shirt, jacket, and belt market.

To expand its marketing area, which was primarily in the West, the company began to sell its products all over the country. Carefully planned promotion helped Levi Strauss & Company to get its expansion under way and is helping the company continue its expansion today. From an annual sales volume of $50 million in 1962, the company increased its sales almost tenfold to nearly $500 million in 1972.[2]

The Promotional Pattern

The following marketing goals describe the kind of expansion the company seeks for the 1970s.

- To continue sales growth, doubling sales every five years.
- To maintain leadership in the sale of jeans.
- To increase the company's share of the casual-pants market.
- To gain a foothold in several complementary markets, including the shirt, jacket, and belt markets.

[1] Milton Moskowitz, "The Levi Lifestyle," *The New York Times,* August 6, 1972, Sec. 3, p. 2, cols. 5-6.
[2] Ibid.

Gold miners of the 19th century were the first customers of Levi Strauss.

To achieve these goals, Levi Strauss & Company decided that its promotion should be divided into two programs. One was to be national in scope and fashion-variety–oriented in theme. The other was to be regional in scope and Western-image–oriented in theme.

In the national program the promotional efforts were to communicate a contemporary fashion message and to emphasize the variety of fashions that were now being sold under the Levi's brand. This program was designed to bring in new business. In the Western-image program the promotional effort was to help the company maintain its traditional strength in the Western market while expanding into the fashion sportswear fields.

This dual approach continues to be the pattern for the company's promotion campaigns. If you live in the East or South, you probably have seen some of the company's fashion-oriented promotion. If you live in the West, you probably have seen or heard much about the company's traditional jeans.

The Planning People

Several groups of people are involved in the promotional activities of Levi Strauss & Company. These groups include the company's public relations department, various advertising departments, the marketing department, and an outside advertising agency.

One current objective of Levi Strauss & Company is to improve its position in the casual-wear market.

Courtesy Levi Strauss & Co.

The public relations department handles both publicity and public relations for the entire company. Until recently, a central advertising department handled all the company's advertising work. Now the work is divided according to products. Jeans, sportswear, girlswear, and boyswear each has its own advertising manager with his own budget.

The marketing department gives advice and service to other departments and divisions within the company. It offers advertising, sales, and marketing services as follows:

- Advertising services include preparing display and cooperative advertising material and helping the company service its retail dealers. There is a cooperative advertising supervisor and an advertising services coordinator. They make sure that all the projects involving promotion fit into the general pattern set by the company.

- Sales services include collecting and supplying market statistics to both the sales force and retail dealers. This involves keeping track of all important developments in the merchandising field that might be useful to the company or to the retailers who handle the company's products.
- Marketing services include preparing sales estimates, analyzing sales results, and helping the various divisions prepare their marketing plans.

The company uses a great deal of outside help. Advertising managers hire free-lance artists and copywriters to develop much of their advertising material. They also employ an outside advertising agency to handle a large amount of the work. The tasks of the agency include preparing and placing network TV commercials, trade advertisements, and Western advertisements.

The Use of Research

There is always some guesswork in planning for the future. However, research helps a company make its guesswork as educated and logical as possible. At Levi Strauss & Company, the marketing department handles market research and media research. The market research is done to find out as much as possible about the company's target customers. The media research is done to find out which media offer the best means of reaching and influencing specific groups of customers.

Market Research. Some of the company's market research projects are continuing projects. For example, the company has a "consumer purchase panel." This is a group of families who record their apparel purchases each month and send the information to the company. The company uses this information to spot style and purchasing trends among its target groups of customers.

Other company market research efforts are one-time projects. For example, the company ran an important "consumer perception study" to learn more about why its customers buy and what they want. The project was handled in the following manner.

First, the marketing department worked with the appropriate divisional personnel in setting up the project. It decided what kind of information should be sought and what research techniques should be used to gather that information. Next, the department turned the actual field work over to an outside research organization. This organization set up interviews with various groups and individuals. It questioned individuals about their awareness of the various brands of pants, their shopping habits, their reasons for buying a particular type of pants, the kinds of words they used to describe the various types of pants, and the kinds of advertising that influenced the purchases that they made.

Then the research organization analyzed the data it had collected and submitted a detailed report, plus recommendations, to the company. The research organization reported that the ordinary customer does not make as much of a distinction between "slacks" and "jeans" as is made in the industry. It therefore recommended that the company take this into consideration when setting up product categories.

Finally, the company put what it had learned to work, primarily in its advertising approach and product labeling. Today, it no longer uses the term "young men's casuals" in its advertising, because research revealed that this term did not mean a specific product category to the average customer.

Media Research. In its media research the company has done both pretesting and posttesting. *Pretesting* is the process of measuring the probable effectiveness of advertising before it appears. *Posttesting* is the process of measuring the actual effectiveness of advertising after it has appeared.

An example of pretesting is the use of a panel of customers in testing advertising themes. The panel is shown a series of ad sketches, each similar in layout but different in theme. If the panel is representative of the target customers as a whole, then its reactions can help the company judge which theme will be most effective.

Posttesting is done to determine how many people noticed an ad, what reactions those people had, and whether the ad encouraged sales of the product advertised. If a particular ad, commercial, or other kind of promotion effort proves particularly successful, then the company will use it again.

THE NATIONAL PROGRAM

The promotion campaign that has helped the company expand both its product mix and its marketing area is the national program. This program is intended to build Levi's as a name that means smart styling—that is, contemporary colors, patterns, and fabrics—in casual pants and in slacks for all occasions. At the same time the program tries to convey the idea that the old reliability attached to the name "Levi's" applies to the new products as well.

In the early 1970s, Levi Strauss & Company used advertising, publicity and special promotions, and dealer aids as elements of the promotional mix in its national program.

Advertising

Levi Strauss & Company has put the major part of its advertising effort into network television commercials. It has done this because television reaches a broad audience. Moreover, television advertising has sight, sound, motion, and (for those with color TV sets) color, all of which combine to

This ad is a good example of the use of the marketing concept: Find out what customers want and then make it.

Courtesy Levi Strauss & Co.

be particularly effective in presenting a fashion and variety message. Generally, the company has run television commercials during the peak selling periods of spring, fall, and the Christmas season.

To reach teen-age audiences, the company has used radio advertising. Popular music stations in the major metropolitan areas have run commercials on a scheduled basis. One Levi Strauss commercial done by the Jefferson Airplane became a musical hit among teen-agers.

The company has also used magazine advertising to reach specific groups of customers. Ads designed for the adult male audience have appeared in such magazines as *Sports Illustrated.* Also, ads specially designed to appeal to black Americans and to military personnel have appeared in magazines widely read by those groups.

Levi Strauss & Company has also done some advertising in publications intended for retailers. As explained in Part 30, such advertising is referred to as "trade advertising." Most of the company's trade advertising has been of a special-impact type rather than a year-round type. For example, the company has used trade advertising when introducing a new product.

Publicity and Special Promotions

Levi Strauss & Company publicity has been aimed primarily at getting coverage in newspapers. Most of the effort has been made during the two peak selling periods—the back-to-school period and the spring-summer period. Fashion editors of major newspapers are sent stories and photographs of fashion-oriented products for use in either the women's section or the family section.

The company has also obtained considerable publicity through its tie-ins with various special events. For instance, it has provided pants for the Soap Box Derby contestants, for auto racing teams, and for the United States and Russian track-meet teams. The company has even set up its own special event, a ski rodeo program, which features competitive events in major ski resort areas.

Dealer Aids

Levi Strauss & Company has given its retail dealers both advertising and display assistance. This means that a coordinated promotion campaign can be carried through to the point of sale.

Dealers can participate in a cooperative advertising program. In such a program, 50 percent of the cost of advertising in local media is paid by Levi Strauss; television, radio, or newspaper copy, tapes, or films are supplied if requested.

Also, a wide selection of point-of-purchase display material is available to dealers. This material includes plaques, counter cards, posters, window displays, and special shopping bags.

THE WESTERN-IMAGE PROGRAM

Part of the Western-image program has consisted of year-round magazine advertising. The ads are in Western-type magazines, such as *Hoofs and Horns, Western Livestock Journal,* and *The Horseman.* A typical ad features boot jeans ". . . cut straight down from the knee. They fit over your boots—low and comfortable like."

Retailers in the West have received a special Western Wear catalog. They have also received point-of-purchase material designed specifically for the Western market.

An important part of the Western-image program has been the company's interest in rodeos. It has worked closely with the Rodeo Cowboys Association in promoting major rodeos. It has donated prizes in the form of Levi's jeans, championship belt buckles, and cash awards. It has sponsored films of the

The promotion of rodeos helps Levi Strauss maintain the Western image.

major rodeos and of the Miss Rodeo American Pageant. These films have been released nationwide for showing by local television stations. The company has even sponsored its own rodeo event, a revival of the old "Ride and Tie" contest, during which two riders alternately walk and ride one horse over rugged terrain.

RESULTS OF THE PROMOTION CAMPAIGN

Planning a promotion campaign the size of the one used for Levi Strauss & Company is not easy. It takes people, time, money, and talent. Levi Strauss & Company is just one of the many marketers who believe that effort put into promotion pays off. It believes this for three reasons: First, market research shows that the company's fashion-variety theme is beginning to click with customers. More and more people are thinking of Levi Strauss & Company as a fashion manufacturer as well as a work-clothes manufacturer. Second, sales increases have been consistent with corporate goals. Third, the company remains the country's number-one pants manufacturer and continues to open new accounts as well.

YOUR MARKETING VOCABULARY

On a separate sheet of paper define each of the following marketing terms; then use each term in a sentence.

Posttesting
Pretesting

FOR REVIEW AND DISCUSSION

1. What does one of the major jobs in any marketing effort involve?
2. For a century, what type of product did Levi Strauss & Company make? For whom did it make the product?
3. Explain how Levi Strauss & Company expanded its business after World War II.
4. To achieve its goals, into which two programs did Levi Strauss decide to divide its promotion? Explain the promotional efforts of each program.
5. Name four groups of people involved in promotion for Levi Strauss.
6. Identify and describe three services that the marketing department gives other departments and divisions within Levi Strauss.
7. Why does the Levi Strauss marketing department do market research and media research?
8. What is a "consumer purchase panel"?
9. Where has Levi Strauss put the major part of its advertising effort? What other means of advertising has it used?
10. When and to whom is Levi Strauss' newspaper publicity sent?

ANALYZING MARKETING CONCEPTS

1. Levi Strauss & Company uses advertising, publicity, and dealer aids for its promotional mix in its national program. Prepare a form like the one below and list the following promotional elements in the left-hand column: (a) advertising, (b) publicity, (c) dealer aids. In the right-hand column, describe two marketing actions taken by Levi Strauss to make each element of promotion effective.

Promotional Element	Marketing Actions
Example: Advertising	Used radio advertising to reach teen-age audiences.

2. Assume that you own and manage a clothing business that sells Levi's and appeals to a youth market. Assume also that you want to develop a

promotion campaign for your business. Prepare a form like the one below. In the left-hand column, list the following promotional elements: (a) advertising, (b) publicity, (c) dealer aids. In the right-hand column, describe at least two specific marketing actions you will take for each promotional element.

Promotional Element	Marketing Actions
Example: Publicity	Award a free pair of Levi's jeans to the top ten money collectors in a local charity drive conducted by high school students.

◘ MARKETING PROJECT 36
Studying a Promotion Campaign

Project Goal: Given a new or improved product or service, identify all the media in which it is being promoted, and estimate the role that research played in the promotion campaign.

Action: Select a new or improved product or service. Identify the different media in which this product or service is being promoted. You can do this by observing commercials on radio and TV, by reading ads in magazines and newspapers, and by watching for give-aways and other promotional devices.

Contact two or three people in the advertising business (an agency, a TV or radio station, or the advertising department of your local newspaper) and ask them how research was likely to have been used in this promotion campaign. Write a report of your findings.

◘ CASE STUDY
Planning a Promotion Campaign

"All right, John, you've got $10,000 to spend on Diamonds for the first six months. What are you going to do with it?"

Leon Hamil, executive vice president of the Spring Foods Company, was discussing the company's new pet-food line with Spring Foods' promotion director, John Ramanos (see pages 96–97 and 231–233). Spring Foods Company was a small but very successful food producer already selling several top-quality regular food lines through the outlets of three supermarket chains within a hundred-mile radius.

"That theme we've chosen, 'Your dog deserves Diamonds,' will fit just about any promotion," John said. "We could use television, radio, newspapers—and I'd like to get out a coupon campaign. Here are some of the possibilities."

John explained that the company could get prime television spots for about $500 each. These commercials would cover the company's marketing area and an additional area of about 200 miles. There were also spots available on local television shows that would reach about two-thirds of the audience in the marketing area and cost about $200 each. Regardless of which were used, John estimated that it would take a series of at least ten spots to make enough impact to justify the cost.

"Some of the biggest pet-food companies concentrate on television," he said. "For instance, Ralston Purina puts about 90 percent of its $30 million ad budget into television."

To get sufficient radio coverage, he continued, the company could use one station. This station covered about three-fourths of the marketing area. Spots were available for about $50 each, and it probably would take at least 20 of them—perhaps 30—to get the message across.

Good newspaper coverage would cost about $4,000, figuring two full pages at $800 each and 30 small ads at $80 each. Because the area is serviced by a newspaper chain that publishes a number of local editions, the company could pinpoint the exact coverage it wanted.

"And I think we might use a coupon campaign again," John added. "They've worked well for us. To date, we've been able to put on a good coupon deal for about $1,900, which includes $1,300 for the mailing and $600 for redemption payments, handling, and general expenses."

"What about publicity?" Leon asked. "Could we handle some of the coverage that way?"

"Carl Kline, our publicity expert, has a very good idea," John replied. "He says he can guarantee good newspaper coverage and very likely some television coverage for a total of about $800. He knows a dog-obedience trainer who puts on demonstrations and gives people advice on handling their dogs. He's been a hit wherever he's done his show. He'd do eight shows for us at $100 each, which should enable us to blanket the area nicely."

Leon liked the dog-trainer idea, but he had still one more question. "And now, what about dealers? We've got to spend some of that money on them."

"Signs and such, of course," John answered. "They'll cost us very little; say $50 a month. Since we're supplying a special display rack free, we don't need much more point-of-purchase material. But what about a special contest for dealers? We could offer cash prizes for the three stores that sell the largest volume of Diamonds in the first six months—no, make that cash prizes and a thoroughbred pup! Let me see . . . a rough guess is that we could do it for about $2,500."

"They're all good possibilities, John," Leon said, "but I just did some rough figuring, too. I figure that the ideas you've just listed would cost us over $15,000. We just haven't got that much to spend. Go over those ideas and prune them down. Fix me up a program that will sell Diamonds and not cost us more than $10,000 for the first six months. And make sure your calendar includes plenty of push at the beginning—we have some big competition in this field."

Questions

1. Without exceeding the $10,000 limit of spending for promotion, which activities would you choose for your promotion program?
2. Assuming that you are expected to spend one-third of your six-month budget during the first month that Diamonds is on the shelves, which promotional efforts would you schedule for that month?
3. How would you spend the remainder of your budget in the next five months?

Customer Services

UNIT 10

part 37

Credit as a Customer Service

YOUR GOAL

Given a store that offers credit as a customer service, analyze its credit system.

A marketer may use various methods to get ahead of his competition. He may reduce the prices of his products or offer products of higher quality. He may also offer a variety of customer services either free of charge or for a small fee. *Customer services* are extra aids, conveniences, or facilities offered to the customer to make him more willing to buy.

Manufacturers, wholesalers, and retailers offer customer services. These services are valuable to the customer because they reassure him that he is buying from a reliable marketer. They also make his shopping more pleasant and provide him with useful advice and assistance at little or no charge.

One of the most important and appealing customer services is credit. *Credit* is the power to obtain goods or services (or money) in exchange for a promise to pay later. The remainder of this part is devoted to a discussion of the various types of credit and their uses and applications. Other customer services are discussed in Part 38.

WHO USES CREDIT?

Credit touches almost everyone in our economy. Consumers use credit to buy goods and services ranging from clothes to airline tickets. There is very little that cannot be bought on credit. Businesses extend credit to other businesses. Both wholesalers and retailers use credit to obtain the goods and services they sell. Manufacturers use credit to buy raw materials and operating supplies. Towns, cities, counties, states, and the federal government all use credit. When the revenue a government collects is less than the amount of money it needs, the government borrows on credit to make up the difference. The principles of government credit are similar to those of other types of credit, with one important difference: Government has the power to tax as a means of raising funds to pay its debts.

Many economists believe that the high level of the American economy is due in part to the extensive use of credit. Without such emphasis on credit, they say, manufacturers would not have the money to design and produce the multitude of products that consumers enjoy. In addition, marketers would not have the money to develop extensive distribution networks for these products, and consumers would not have the money to buy them.

ADVANTAGES AND DISADVANTAGES OF CREDIT

One of the most important advantages of credit is that it makes business transactions easier. The charge plate and credit memo actually serve as mediums of exchange, in much the same way that paper and silver money are mediums of exchange. When consumers, businesses, or the government buy on credit, little or no money actually changes hands at the time of the transaction. This makes the buying and selling process quick and easy.

Because of credit, there are more automobiles in this country than in any other country in the world. Credit has made it possible for many Americans of average income to enjoy television sets, washing machines, and attractive furniture. Credit allows consumers to buy goods and services now and to pay for them later. Because it thus allows them to satisfy their needs and wants immediately, American consumers are buying more and more goods on credit.

Credit also has certain disadvantages. A credit system presents added complications and expense to a business. Applicants must be investigated, and information on them must be kept up to date. Bills must be sent out to customers periodically, and amounts owed must be collected.

While credit is convenient for the customer, it can also create problems for him. He must often pay interest on the items that he buys on credit.

Credit should be used wisely.

Moreover, he is more likely to buy items that he does not really need when he buys on credit. Some people use credit to buy things that they cannot afford and thus accumulate debts that they are unable to pay, or are able to pay only with great difficulty and hardship to themselves.

CONSUMER CREDIT

There are several forms of consumer credit. Department and specialty stores have offered credit for a long time, and an increasing number of hardware stores and drugstores are now offering it. Several companies are in the business of offering credit by means of credit cards, which they issue to their customers. A *credit card* is a card that entitles the holder to enjoy credit privileges with a variety of businesses throughout the country, sometimes throughout the world. This is possible through arrangements the credit-card companies have made with many stores and other business firms. In such arrangements, the stores and firms agree to give credit to holders of the company's credit card. The store or firm is usually charged a small percentage of the full purchase price by the credit-card company. Many banks now offer credit cards that enable the customer to make purchases in many states and be billed on one statement from the bank.

Sources of Information About Consumers

Some applicants seeking consumer credit simply walk into a business and ask for it. Others are informed about credit by salespeople. Still others are solicited by direct mail or newspaper promotion. Once the credit department of a company has the name of a person who wants credit, its first job is to determine whether the applicant is a good risk.

Information about the applicant may be obtained from a number of sources, one being the personal interview. In the personal interview, the credit department has a face-to-face talk with the applicant. At that time the applicant is usually asked to complete a credit application, on which he states his earnings and lists personal references. Employer and character references are also useful in helping a company determine whether a person is a good credit risk.

Another important source of credit information is the local credit bureau. A *credit bureau* is an organization that specializes in collecting and interpreting credit information. The information it collects about residents in its locality is available, for a fee, to any business that has a legitimate reason for wanting the information. Most towns and cities have credit bureaus.

Types of Accounts

When an applicant for credit has been accepted as a good risk, he may have a choice of several credit plans. Four credit plans that are commonly used today are the regular, or 30-day, account; the installment account; the revolving account; and the budget, or 90-day, account. Some companies offer all these plans; others offer only one or two types.

Regular, or 30-Day, Account. Those accounts that creditors allow to run for 30 days (in some cases, 60 days) are called "regular accounts." The customer is billed at the end of the 30-day period for any purchases he has made. Usually, there is no service charge if the customer pays within the given period.

At one time, regular charge-account customers received their bills in the first few days of each month. This meant an enormous work load for billing departments at the end of each month. Today large companies use *cycle billing*, a system which spreads the preparation of customers' bills throughout the month, so that the billing department always has an even

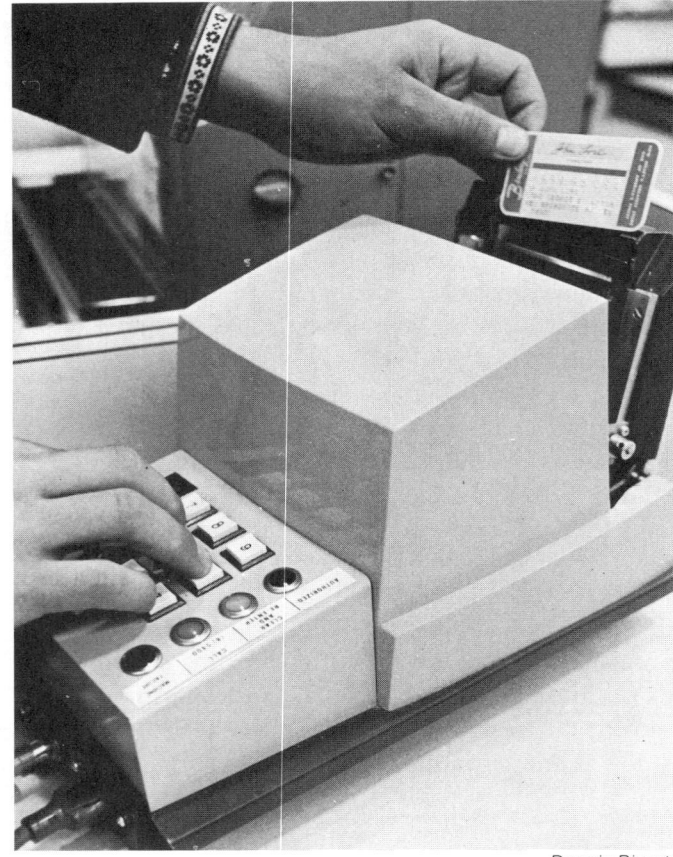

Credit cards are convenient for both the customer and the retailer. Here, a credit card is inserted into a special device that is linked to a computer. Within a short time, a light will flash on to indicate whether or not credit is authorized.

Dennis Rizzuto

flow of work. In cycle billing, every customer receives his bill monthly. But one group of customers may receive bills on the 15th of each month and another group may receive them on the 22nd. Each bill covers the period from the date shown on the bill, but not including that date, back to the same date in the preceding month. Thus, a bill dated May 21 would cover the period from April 21 through May 20.

Most large retailers issue a charge plate to customers whose standing has been found acceptable by the store. The charge plate is often made of metal or plastic and has the customer's name, address, and account number in embossed, or raised, letters and numbers. During a sales transaction, the charge plate is inserted into a special machine that prints the embossed information on a sales slip.

Installment Account. A customer who makes a large purchase is likely to use an installment account, because it permits him to buy an expensive item, take it home, and pay for it over a specified period of time. In an "installment account," the customer agrees to make a down payment on the item and to pay a specific amount at specific intervals until he has completely paid for the item. He also agrees to pay a service charge and to allow the seller to repossess the item if he, the customer, does not meet his financial obligations to the seller.

Automobiles, TV sets, and household appliances are some of the big-ticket items usually purchased on the installment account. Airline tickets and vacation package trips are also available on this form of credit.

Revolving Account. A "revolving account" is an account on which the retailer determines the maximum amount that the customer is allowed to charge and the period of time the customer can have to pay off that amount. A service charge is added to the balance each month. The customer decides on the amount of his monthly payment within the limits set by the retailer. As he makes a payment, the amount of that payment again becomes available to him as credit.

Although the revolving account involves an expensive service charge, it has an important advantage: It encourages sales without encouraging customers to assume more debt than they can afford.

Budget, or 90-Day, Account. The budget, or 90-day, account is becoming increasingly important among larger stores. In the budget account, the customer makes a purchase and agrees to pay one-third of the total amount of his charge every 30 days, so that he has paid in full at the end of a 90-day period. The budget, or 90-day, account does not require the customer to pay a carrying charge.

Credit-Card Companies

Most credit-card companies charge the holders of their credit cards a set annual fee. In addition, they require prompt monthly payment from users and may add a service charge if a bill becomes overdue. Some credit-card companies do not charge an annual fee but add a service charge to the card holder's balance each month.

Credit-card companies include the American Express Company, Carte Blanche, and the Diners Club. The credit supplied by these companies can be used on airlines and at hotels, motels, restaurants, stores, and other business establishments. The user of such credit need not carry much cash, an important consideration for anyone who travels often. Furthermore, the bills that the companies send the user are good, compact records of his various expenses.

Many traveling businessmen, such as this young executive, use credit cards to pay their hotel and travel expenses.

Bank Credit Cards

Bank credit cards have become very popular. In 1965 there were fewer than 5 million bank credit cards in circulation. Today, more than 80 million are in circulation, distributed by some 8,000 banks, with about a million more cards being issued each month. The holder of a bank credit card usually is not charged a fee. Instead, there is a service charge which is added to his balance every month.

MERCANTILE CREDIT

The form of credit used by a manufacturer to buy his raw materials and operating supplies is called *mercantile credit*. This form of credit is also used by a wholesaler to buy the stock he wants and by a retailer to buy the products his customers want. Mercantile credit is often obtained from the supplier of the materials, supplies, stock, or products.

Sources of Information About Businesses

Companies check business firms that are applicants for credit in the same way that marketers check consumers who apply for credit. Trade organizations are useful in furnishing information about business firms within a particular trade. Salesmen who visit the firm know what the firm is like from the inside. Local attorneys often know the firm personally from having been involved in business concerning it. Local banks are also a good source of credit information on businesses.

Perhaps the most important information will come from Dun & Bradstreet, Incorporated, an agency which collects credit information throughout the business world. Dun & Bradstreet gathers credit and financial information about every business firm in which its subscribers might be interested. It prepares a report about each company and keeps the report up to date. It gives each company a rating based on the company's financial standing. This rating, in turn, reflects the credit status of the company. All this information is available to Dun & Bradstreet's subscribers.

Types of Mercantile Credit

Unlike consumer credit, mercantile credit does not involve charge plates or credit cards. In most cases, a letter, draft, or credit memo is the only visible sign of credit. The result, however, is the same as with consumer credit: Money is lent, or goods and services are delivered, on an agreement to pay later.

The length of time for which mercantile credit is extended is known as the *credit period.* The credit period varies, with a usual range of from 30 to 120 days. Whatever the length of the credit period may be, a customer is expected to pay within that time for the goods or services he has received. Also, the credit terms usually mention a *cash discount,* which is a percent of the bill that the credit customer may deduct if he pays promptly.

COLLECTING ACCOUNTS

Once the creditor has billed his customers for the amounts owed him, he then waits to receive payment. Most accounts will pay quite promptly and in full. Some will pay slowly. Still others will never pay all of what they owe. Just when a creditor should become concerned about outstanding bills and try to collect them depends on many factors. For example, a business or customer with a good credit record may not be reminded of an overdue payment as quickly as one with a poor credit record. Also, regular-account customers are not likely to be watched as carefully as installment-account customers, because the amount of credit involved in an installment purchase is usually much larger than that involved in a regular account.

It matters, too, whether the creditor is a manufacturer, a wholesaler, or a retailer. Retailers allow their customers some leeway, allowing for the possibility that they may not have understood the obligations of credit. Manufacturers and wholesalers, however, expect retailers to pay promptly, on the theory that businesses should be businesslike.

Collection Procedure

Exactly how creditors collect what is owed to them varies according to the company. However, every company that gives credit has a definite, often complicated, collection system. The general procedure is as follows:

1. If no payment is received after a specific length of time, the creditor sends a second bill or statement. This is usually flagged with a polite "reminder" sticker.
2. If no payment is received, the creditor then sends a series of two, three, or four letters, each more insistent, at specific intervals. In addition, he may try to reach the debtor by telephone or may even visit him at his home or office.
3. If none of these attempts brings the required payment, the creditor turns the uncollected accounts over to collection attorneys or collection agencies. These lawyers and agencies, who are often paid a percentage of what they collect, make more visits and use even more forceful letters in their attempts to collect.
4. Should these means fail, the debtor may be sued in court for what he owes.

THE FUTURE OF CREDIT

Credit is a valuable tool in the American economy. Yet, like many valuable tools, it can be dangerous. As the use of it has increased, the number of business and personal bankruptcies has increased. Consequently, city, state, and federal laws have been passed to govern the use of credit. These laws attempt to make credit terms more understandable to credit users and to protect these users from dishonest and unethical credit grantors.

Marketers who grant credit have come to realize that some customers do not understand the terms of credit and consequently do not use it wisely. Because of this, the retailers and financial institutions in a community often join with their local credit bureau in a campaign to educate people in the proper use of credit. In some communities, students are taught the use of credit in high school. In addition, various communities offer similar courses evenings for interested adults.

In the future, credit will certainly be used more frequently. With the present interest in credit education and credit legislation, it may also be used more wisely.

YOUR MARKETING VOCABULARY

On a separate sheet of paper define each of the following marketing terms; then use each term in a sentence.

Cash discount
Credit
Credit bureau
Credit card
Credit period
Customer services
Cycle billing
Mercantile credit

FOR REVIEW AND DISCUSSION

1. According to many economists, what is the importance of credit?
2. What is the major advantage of credit?
3. List and explain two disadvantages of credit.
4. Give three sources of information that are important in checking an applicant for consumer credit.
5. Name four types of consumer-credit accounts.
6. Describe briefly how a revolving account works.
7. Explain the advantages of having a credit card from a credit-card company.
8. Give examples of the purposes for which a manufacturer, a wholesaler, and a retailer would use mercantile credit.
9. Briefly describe the procedure for collecting accounts.
10. What attempts have been made to safeguard businesses and individuals against bankruptcy resulting from improper use of credit?

ANALYZING MARKETING CONCEPTS

1. When an applicant for credit has been accepted as a good risk, he may have a choice of several credit plans. Prepare a form like the one below and list the following types of credit accounts in the left-hand column: (a) 30-day, (b) installment, (c) revolving, (d) 90-day. In the right-hand column, describe briefly how each type of account operates.

Type of Credit Account	Description of Operation

2. Mercantile credit information can be obtained from a number of sources. Prepare a form like the one below. In the left-hand column, list five possible sources of this credit information. In the right-hand column, indicate the information available from each source.

Sources of Mercantile Credit Information	Type of Credit Information Available

MARKETING PROJECT 37
Analyzing a Credit System

Project Goal: Given a store that offers credit as a customer service, analyze its credit system.

Action: Select a store that offers credit to its customers. By interviewing its management, collecting materials, and talking with customers, obtain data on the following aspects of the store's credit system: (a) credit information, (b) types of accounts, (c) credit cards, and (d) billing system.

Prepare a form like the one below. Write the name of the store at the top of the form. Then list each of the above aspects in the left-hand column. In the right-hand column, write the key points of your findings about each aspect.

Attach all materials you have collected to your form.

Aspect of Credit System	Findings
Example: Types of accounts	Regular, or 30-day, account; installment account; and revolving account.

part 38

Other Customer Services

YOUR GOALS

1. Given a consumer product, explain the details of several customer services offered with this product.
2. Given a written guarantee for a specific product, evaluate the contents of the guarantee.

In addition to extending credit, marketers must offer other customer services in order to meet competition. These services include quality and price guarantees, a policy permitting adjustments and returns, delivery service, installation and repair services, and consultation service. Often the number and type of customer services offered by competing companies will be the deciding factor in a customer's choice of where to buy.

GUARANTEES

A *guarantee* is an assurance of the specific quality and performance of a product, or a promise to maintain a certain price level for a specific period of time. Quality and performance guarantees and price guarantees are discussed in the following paragraphs.

Quality and Performance Guarantees

The guarantees concerning the quality and performance of a product usually originate with the manufacturer of the product. From the manufacturer they are passed along the marketing channel to the wholesaler, from the wholesaler they are passed to the industrial user or retailer, and from the retailer they are passed to the final user.

A guarantee may involve an industrial product. For example, a furniture producer who buys an expensive lathe for use in his factory will expect a guarantee from the lathe manufacturer. The furniture producer will want the guarantee to specify both the kind of service and the length of performance he can expect from the lathe. Such a guarantee might say that under normal conditions the lathe will operate for three years without need of repair. The guarantee would ensure that if the lathe did require repair within three years, it would be replaced or repaired free of charge by the manufacturer.

A guarantee may also involve a consumer product. A woman may buy a cotton dress with a guarantee that normal washing will not shrink or fade it. If washing does damage the dress, the customer is entitled to return it for

SINGER
GUARANTEE

WE GUARANTEE that each SINGER* sewing machine has been carefully manufactured and is in perfect operating condition on delivery. When subject to normal family use and care, any parts requiring replacement at any time owing to defects in material or workmanship will be replaced without charge.

THIS GUARANTEE does not apply to parts requiring replacement owing to natural wear or to abuse or negligence of the user or in the event the machine is serviced by other than a SINGER representative or Approved Dealer or with parts other than those supplied by The Singer Company.

IN ADDITION to the above guarantee of parts, each machine will be inspected and adjusted whenever necessary without charge for labor for a period of one year from date of purchase.

THIS GUARANTEE is effective only with respect to the person making the purchase from The Singer Company or one of its Approved Dealers. The original Sales Agreement, or Cash Receipt, must be presented to obtain the benefits of the guarantee.

AGREEMENTS inconsistent with the foregoing shall be void and of no effect.

THE SINGER COMPANY

This quality and performance guarantee sets no time limit on the manufacturer's promise to replace defective parts without charge.

Courtesy The Singer Co.

either a replacement or a refund. Such a guarantee usually originates with the garment manufacturer; therefore, a store that replaces a dress or gives a refund under that guarantee will be reimbursed by the manufacturer.

Price Guarantees

Price guarantees are usually promises that the manufacturer makes to wholesalers or retailers who buy his products. These price guarantees usually state that the market price for a specific product will remain the same for a certain length of time. Price guarantees are used mainly for seasonal goods that are apt to fluctuate in price. Some guarantees protect the price until an order is delivered. Others protect the price until a particular time in the selling season. If the price drops before the guarantee has expired, the manufacturer agrees to refund the difference to the wholesaler or retailer. For example, suppose that the manufacturer's price is $2 an item when the wholesaler or retailer buys his goods and that it drops to $1.80 before the specified guarantee date. In that case the wholesaler or retailer is given a credit or refund of 20 cents an item.

Price guarantees can be useful for the manufacturer because they encourage middlemen to place orders early and thus bring in a steady flow of cash. However, they are also financial risks for the manufacturer. If he has guaranteed a price and later his production costs rise, the manufacturer is forced to absorb these increased costs himself because he cannot raise the guaranteed price.

If price guarantees have become common in a particular field, it is likely that every marketer in the field offers them. Price guarantees are often available on high-priced items because they safeguard the middleman's investment until he can sell such items.

ADJUSTMENTS AND RETURNS

Willingness to make reasonable adjustments and permit the return of merchandise is an important part of today's marketing philosophy. An "adjustment" refers to the handling of a customer's complaint about merchandise or service in a manner that will satisfy the customer.

The customer may seek an adjustment or make a return for several reasons. He may find after taking the purchase home that the color is wrong or the design inappropriate. He may have bought the wrong size. Or, he may simply change his mind.

Sometimes an adjustment or return results from the marketer's mistake. The goods sold may have imperfections. They may have been damaged while being sent to the customer. They may not be the type, color, or size ordered

Adjustments and returns of merchandise may result from an error on the part of either the customer or the salesperson.

by the customer. The salesperson may have given misleading information that caused the customer to buy the wrong product. In all such cases, the marketer is obligated to correct the error.

Adjustments and returns that occur in the industrial market are usually the result of a marketing error. The customer may receive incorrect or incomplete shipments, defective merchandise, or damaged shipments. The manufacturer or wholesaler usually tries to correct such matters promptly, because he knows that the success of his business depends on how quickly and how well he handles customer complaints.

DELIVERY

Many stores provide free delivery service for customers living within a certain distance from the store. Other stores charge a fee for delivering merchandise. These are usually the stores that emphasize economy and low prices, and they maintain that they can keep the prices of their merchandise lower if they charge for delivery.

Some stores that offer delivery service have their own fleet of delivery vans and trucks. Others rent or lease the equipment. Most retailers, however, now handle delivery through independent delivery companies. The best-known and perhaps most widely used delivery company is United Parcel Service.

INSTALLATION AND REPAIR

It is simple enough to buy an electric mixer, take it home, plug it into an outlet, and flip the switch to put the mixer into operation. Plugging in the appliance is all the installation it needs. On the other hand, a giant turbine (a kind of engine) to be used in an industrial complex would require installation that is far more complicated. *Installation* is the process of setting up a product in position for use and making necessary mechanical, electrical, or drainage connections.

If the mixer needed repair, the consumer might know enough about electrical appliances to fix it. However, the chances are that an expert would be needed. Certainly an expert—perhaps many experts—would be needed to repair the turbine. A company that gains a reputation for competent installation and repair service has a tremendous advantage in the marketplace.

In the industrial field, installation and repair service are particularly important for large or complicated equipment, such as turbines and other engines, motors, furnaces, conveyors, cranes, and computers. The seller agrees to make sure that the equipment is set up correctly and working properly at its new site. He also agrees to make any repairs necessary during the course of the equipment's use. Often the cost of installation is part of the selling price. The selling price may also include the cost of training the buyer's staff to use the equipment.

Installation and repair service is also important in the consumer field, particularly for major appliances, such as automatic washers, TV sets, and stereo sets. The installation or repair may be a fairly simple procedure, but it is usually best to have the work done by a specialist who knows how to put the appliance in working order. An added advantage in having an employee of the seller install an appliance is that the consumer is protected if the appliance is damaged during installation; in that event, the seller must assume responsibility for damages.

In the consumer field the cost of installation may be included in the cost of the appliance sold, or installation may be handled as a separate service.

Many consumers and industrial users buy the service contracts offered by sellers. A *service contract* is an agreement between the buyer and seller in which the buyer agrees to pay a specified sum to have the seller furnish parts and service for a product for a certain period. The contract, however, does not cover damage resulting from misuse, abuse, or failure to follow instructions furnished with the product, or damage resulting from fire, flood, and lightning or from service by someone other than the company named in the contract.

The contract may specify that a repairman will be available on a customer's request or that a serviceman will make regular maintenance checks. Consumers usually choose the contract that provides for service on request. Business firms, however, prefer to have equipment checked periodically in order to avoid delays and losses caused by breakdowns.

CONSULTATION SERVICE

It is not always easy for a prospective purchaser to decide what to buy. A company seeking equipment to automate its bookkeeping activities may not know exactly what equipment is needed. Similarly, a woman interested in changing to a more personalized line of cosmetics may not be sure of the exact makeup that will improve her appearance. Consultation service, whether in the industrial or consumer field, can turn a prospect into a customer.

Industrial Assistance

Even after the customer has chosen and purchased the proper equipment for the job, the manufacturer's responsibility does not end. The technical department of the manufacturer usually stays in close touch with the customer, answering questions, making suggestions about changes in technique, sometimes suggesting new uses for the equipment or the training of employees.

It is this kind of technical consultation service that enables the industrial buyer to get the full value from the very expensive equipment he purchases. Without this service, the equipment very likely would not be worth its price to the buyer, because he could not use it properly. With the complexity of today's equipment, no company is ashamed to ask, "How does it work?"

Retailer Assistance

Both manufacturers and wholesalers frequently offer consultation services to retailers who are their customers. These services are designed to help the retailers sell more products. A retailer may carry hundreds of kinds of products while the manufacturer or wholesaler may specialize in one or two. Consequently, the manufacturer or wholesaler has expert knowledge about his own product that can be of use to the retailer.

Such knowledge may involve departmental layouts, displays, advertising, or training of salespeople. The wholesaler may point out the best sales pos-

This manufacturer's customer engineer is testing electronic equipment to locate a malfunction reported by the customer.

Courtesy IBM

sibilities by styles or types and suggest those styles or types that should get special emphasis. Because the wholesaler or manufacturer keeps track of how well his product is selling in retail stores, he is often in a better position than the retailer to judge customer tastes and trends in his particular field.

Customer Assistance

Many large retailers offer their customers a variety of consulting services. Retailers may employ fashion experts, hair stylists, interior decorators, makeup specialists, and bridal consultants to help customers with special buying problems. During a shopping trip, customers are likely to see any one of these specialists giving a free demonstration or consultation.

The advantage to the customer is obvious: He gets expert advice free. The advantage to the store is equally obvious: By offering free consultation and advisory service, the store can expect more-satisfied customers and additional sales.

◇ **YOUR MARKETING VOCABULARY**

On a separate sheet of paper define each of the following marketing terms; then use each term in a sentence.
> Guarantee
> Installation
> Service contract

◇ **FOR REVIEW AND DISCUSSION**

1. Why must marketers offer other customer services in addition to credit?
2. Where do the guarantees concerning the quality and performance of a product usually originate?
3. Why can price guarantees be considered a financial risk for the manufacturer?
4. Explain how the marketer may cause a request for an adjustment or return of a consumer product.
5. How do most retailers handle delivery service?
6. For what kinds of industrial equipment is installation service particularly important?
7. In the consumer-goods field, what appliances may require installation and repair service?
8. Name five things that a service contract does not cover.
9. Explain the value of consultation service to an industrial user.
10. By offering free consultation and advisory service, what advantage can a store enjoy?

◇ **ANALYZING MARKETING CONCEPTS**

1. Merchandise adjustments and returns are often caused by an employee's mistake. Prepare a form like the one below. In the left-hand column, list the following employee mistakes which might cause a customer to complain or to return merchandise: (a) correct style suit but wrong size sold, (b) wrong item delivered, (c) appliance installed incorrectly, (d) defective part sent, (e) incorrect bill. In the right-hand column, state how the employee could have avoided each mistake.

Employee Mistake	How Mistake Could Have Been Avoided
Example: Wrong film sold for customer's camera.	Before selling film, employee should study manufacturers' literature on types of film usable in specific cameras.

2. Consultation service can be an important factor in acquiring customers and keeping them satisfied. In a form like the one below, list the following types of businesses in the left-hand column: (a) food wholesaler, (b) hardware retailer, (c) carpet company, (d) construction company, (e) printing company. For each business, describe in the right-hand column one consultation service that it might offer to customers.

Business	Consultation Service
Example: Flower nursery	Nursery has trained specialists who go to the customer's home to advise him on the most attractive placement of shrubs and flowers.

◆ MARKETING PROJECT 38
Studying Customer Services

Project Goal: Given a consumer product, explain the details of several customer services offered with this product.

Action: Select a consumer product that is a major appliance; for example, a dishwasher, refrigerator, or electric range. By writing to the manufacturer and by visiting a store that sells the product, obtain detailed information on the following customer services with regard to the product: (a) delivery, (b) installation, (c) repairs, (d) adjustments.

Prepare a form like the one below. In the left-hand column, write the name of the product you have chosen. In the center column, list each of the customer services mentioned above. In the right-hand column, explain the details of each service with regard to the product.

Product	Customer Service	Details of Service
Example: TV set	Guarantee	Defective parts are replaced within 90 days. Picture tubes are guaranteed for one year. Warranty does not cover damage from misuse. Labor service charges are not covered. Dealer has a one-year free labor warranty. Written guarantee is attached.

Marketing Management

UNIT 11

part 39

Organization for Marketing

YOUR GOAL

Given a business that markets a specific product, develop a marketing plan for the business, specifying your goal, a program for achieving the goal, and a completion schedule.

Today many companies make similar products, and each product competes for the customer's dollar. In order to survive in this competitive atmosphere, a business cannot market its products in the same packages year after year or introduce new products unless the customer is willing to buy them. To do so would mean the eventual collapse of the business. To be successful, a company must first do research to determine what products its customers want and need, and then produce and market the products that meet those needs more efficiently than its competitors. In other words, a company must practice the marketing concept: It must strive to fulfill the needs of its customers.

To put the marketing concept into action, business organizations prepare a marketing plan that lists the activities of their marketing staff. A company's marketing plan and marketing staff are vital for the achievement of successful marketing.

THE MARKETING PLAN

A company's marketing activities—research, product planning, transportation and storage, financing, promotion, selling, and customer services—do not take place independently of each other. They are planned and coordinated by the company's management by means of a marketing plan. A *marketing plan* is a set of marketing guidelines prepared by the management of a business firm. It states the goals or objectives that the company wants to achieve within a certain period of time and the methods by which it intends to achieve those goals. It designates the length of time that each project should take and the amount of money each should cost. In short, a marketing plan states how much a company should grow within a certain period of time and how this growth should be accomplished.

Importance of a Marketing Plan

Today a company cannot hope to succeed by simply manufacturing its products and putting them on the market. A business firm must always seek new and better ways of marketing its goods or services. It must be able to convince customers that its products are the ones they should buy. It must seek out new markets for its products. It must develop new products and improve older products. It must keep informed of what customers want and of what competitors are offering. The best way a company can be sure that "all its bases" are covered—that it is doing all it can for successful marketing—is through the use of a marketing plan.

Elements of a Marketing Plan

A marketing plan consists of a statement of the company's goals, including a forecast of sales, market share, and profits and expenses; the programs for achieving these goals; and a schedule for completing the activities in the marketing plan.

A marketing plan must be a formal, written document. Every key executive in an organization, all members of the marketing department, and the key people in the company's advertising agency should be familiar with the company's marketing plan. Only when the marketing plan is a written one can everyone concerned with the successful marketing of the company's products be completely and correctly informed of the marketing strategy to be followed.

Statement of Goals. The marketing plan starts with the establishment of the goals to be attained. In large firms the boards of directors and chief executives usually set these goals or objectives. Their decisions are usually

A good marketing company covers all the bases.

based on the advice and suggestions of the members of the marketing staff.

The primary goal of every business organization is to increase profit. To accomplish this, a company usually sets specific goals to be reached in a certain period of time. For example, the following goals may be set by a manufacturer of small home appliances:

- A 5 percent increase of the total market share, from 25 percent to 30 percent.
- A 10 percent increase in dollar sales.
- A 5 percent increase in the number of all products sold.
- A 10 percent increase in the number of blenders sold.
- A 15 percent increase in the number of electric mixers sold.
- A $200,000 profit on first-year sales of a new waffle iron.

Programs. The second part of the marketing plan states the programs to be used in achieving the goals. It is the detailed part of the plan, the part that lists the responsibilities of each department involved in the marketing effort. It states how the jobs of each department will contribute to the company's goals.

Every department concerned must function according to the programs outlined in the plan. The product-planning department must develop the products required by the plan. Advertising and sales promotion campaigns must be done in accordance with the plan. Test marketing and marketing research must be done in accordance with the plan. The salesmen must center their selling efforts around the programs outlined in the plan.

The appliance manufacturer mentioned above might list the following programs for achieving his goals:

- Addition of 20 retail dealers: six in the Northeast, three in the South, five in the Midwest, three on the Pacific Coast, one in Alaska, one in Hawaii, and one in Mexico.
- Development of a new advertising campaign to introduce the company's new waffle iron.
- Demonstration of the company's blenders in stores throughout the nation.
- Development of a six-slice toaster.

Completion Schedule. The completion schedule specifies the period of time in which the marketing plan will be implemented and indicates when the activities in the plan will take place. Thus, the marketing plan provides a calendar by which a company can conduct its marketing activities and measure its progress. There are both short-range and long-range marketing plans. A short-range plan covers a company's activities for a relatively short period of time, usually one year. It is the basis of day-to-day operations and may contain considerable detail about the operations. A long-range plan, on the other hand, covers a long period of time, often from five to ten years. Although the long-range plan is not as detailed as the short-range plan, it is often more difficult to formulate. The reason is that predicting the relatively distant future is more difficult than predicting the near future, even when the long-range predictions are based on careful research.

A short-range marketing plan for a supermarket might include replacing the meat counter, finding a more satisfactory source for produce, and increasing the percent of nonfood items carried. A long-range plan might include installing automatic check-out counters, purchasing additional parking space, and building a new section to stock the increasing inventory of nonfoods.

The supermarket's marketing plan might state that a week-long survey of sales in the health and beauty-aids section should be completed by the end of April. On the basis of that April deadline, it might require that a revised list of health and beauty products to be ordered be ready by the end of May. Deadlines such as those give the departments concerned and top management an exact date on which each step should be completed and thus a means of checking the progress of a project.

THE MARKETING STAFF

Although job titles and responsibilities vary tremendously from company to company, a typical marketing staff, or department, in a large organization might be composed of a marketing manager, a sales manager, an advertising manager, a product manager, a marketing research manager, and a marketing services manager. Their relative positions in the department are shown in the following chart.

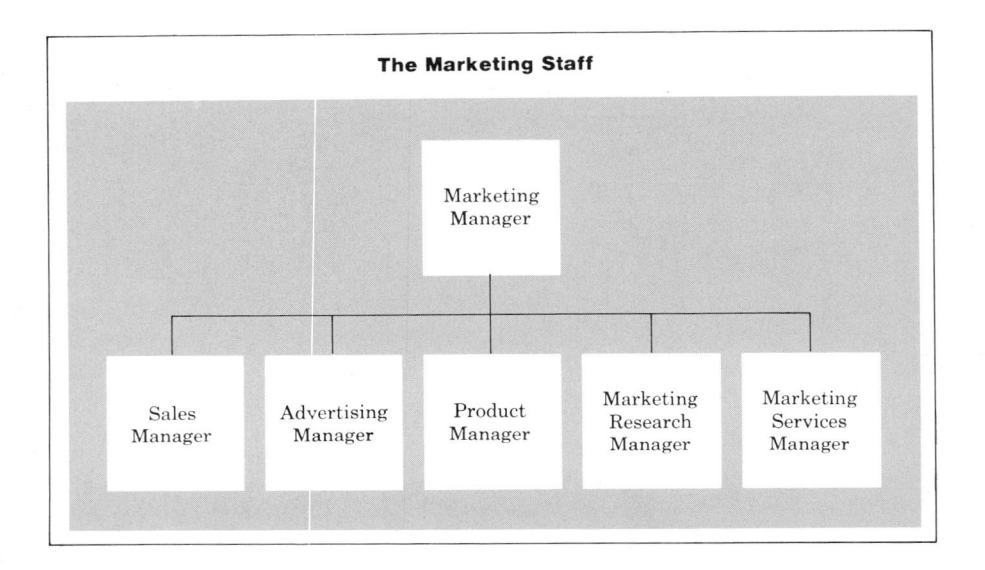

The Marketing Staff

```
                    Marketing
                     Manager
                        |
   ┌────────┬──────────┼──────────┬────────┐
 Sales  Advertising  Product   Marketing  Marketing
Manager   Manager   Manager   Research   Services
                               Manager    Manager
```

The Marketing Manager

The person responsible for the entire marketing organization of the company is called the *marketing manager*. He is in charge of the marketing department, and all other persons in the department report to him. The marketing manager himself usually reports to the chief executive. In some companies the title used for this position is "marketing director" or "vice president of marketing."

The marketing manager should have considerable marketing experience and a good knowledge of his company's products. Some of his major responsibilities are as follows:

- Works with top management to develop long-range marketing plans and policies.
- Plans, coordinates, and supervises the development of marketing programs for all products or services of the company.

464 / Unit 11 / Marketing Management

- Supervises and coordinates the activities of the sales manager, advertising manager, product manager, marketing research manager, and marketing services manager.
- Finds new markets for existing products and recognizes the need to develop new products.
- Studies the market for the company's products as well as general economic conditions that may affect the sale of the products.
- Selects the channels of distribution for getting the company's products to the final user.

The Sales Manager

The person responsible for selecting, hiring, training, supervising, and controlling the activities of the salesmen is called the *sales manager*. To do his job well, the sales manager must have experience in selling, so that he can understand the problems faced by his salesmen. He must strive to build and direct a sales organization that will achieve the selling goals of the company at the lowest cost.

The sales manager is expected to assist the marketing manager by providing him with recommendations on the following: sales policies, sales goals, selling prices, and channels of distribution.

The Advertising Manager

The functions of the advertising manager have been discussed in the unit on advertising. As part of the marketing staff, the *advertising manager* is the person responsible for creating advertising and sales promotion programs and for developing, with the aid of the advertising department, materials necessary for these programs.

The Product Manager

Although the final responsibility for product planning rests with the top management of a firm, some companies today have created the job of product manager. The *product manager* is the person responsible for the sales and profits of the product or product line assigned to him. His job is to study the market for his products; plan the variety that should be included in his product line; select packaging; and recommend pricing, distribution, and sales and advertising programs for his product or product line. The product manager deals with all phases of marketing. He must coordinate his activities with the sales, advertising, and marketing research departments, but he has no control over departments other than his own. The product manager is sometimes referred to as the "brand manager."

The Marketing Research Manager

An important member of the marketing staff is the *marketing research manager*, the person responsible for studying the markets for the company's products to determine customer needs. The marketing research manager makes his information available to the marketing manager for use in planning, developing, producing, and selling the company's products.

The Marketing Services Manager

The person responsible for the various services necessary in filling customers' orders is known as the *marketing services manager*. These services include order processing, customer services, shipping, warehousing, inventory control, and upkeep of sales records and reports.

THE RESPONSIBILITY OF MARKETING MANAGEMENT

The marketing success of any company depends largely on the people assigned to key marketing positions. These people must be highly capable of providing the imaginative planning needed for the company's continued profit and growth. They must be sure that the company explores and develops every marketing opportunity, that the products continue to satisfy customers, and that the company maintains a favorable standing among its competitors.

◻ YOUR MARKETING VOCABULARY

On a separate sheet of paper define each of the following marketing terms; then use each term in a sentence.

Advertising manager
Marketing manager
Marketing plan
Marketing research manager
Marketing services manager
Product manager
Sales manager

◻ FOR REVIEW AND DISCUSSION

1. In order to be successful, what must a company determine first?
2. How do business organizations put the marketing concept into action?
3. What does a marketing plan consist of?
4. In large firms, which people usually set the marketing goals? On what are their decisions based?
5. What is the detailed part of a marketing plan? Explain.

6. Why is the completion schedule an important component of a marketing plan?
7. Explain the difference between a short-range marketing plan and a long-range one.
8. List four functions of the marketing manager.
9. Who reports to the marketing manager?
10. What are the responsibilities of marketing management?

ANALYZING MARKETING CONCEPTS

1. A short-range marketing plan covers a company's activities for a short period of time. Prepare a form like the one below and list the following businesses in the left-hand column: (a) service station, (b) neighborhood grocery store, (c) women's specialty shop, (d) barbershop, (e) motel corporation, (f) bicycle manufacturer. In the right-hand column, write one possible goal of a short-range marketing plan for each of the businesses you listed.

Business	Short-Range Marketing Goal
Example: Clothing manufacturer	To develop a new promotion campaign for the youth market.

2. A long-range marketing plan covers a company's activities for a long period of time. On a form like the one below, list the following businesses in the left-hand column: (a) service station, (b) neighborhood grocery store, (c) women's specialty shop, (d) barbershop, (e) motel corporation, (f) bicycle manufacturer. In the right-hand column, write one possible goal of a long-range marketing plan for each business. Assume that the goal is expected to be achieved over a five-year period.

Business	Long-Range Marketing Goal
Example: Clothing manufacturer	To develop new markets in the South and build a new factory there.

MARKETING PROJECT 39
Organizing a Marketing Plan

Project Goal: Given a business that markets a specific product, develop a marketing plan for the business, specifying your goal, a program for achieving the goal, and a completion schedule.

Action: Assume that you own and manage a record shop. Your chief competition is the record departments in six department and discount stores. Your present share of the market is 25 percent. Marketing research has indicated that you need to aim your promotions at the teen-age market segment. There are about 10,000 teen-agers in your market area. Your present expenses and profit rate are satisfactory. Your major goal is to have 35 percent of the market one year from now.

Prepare a marketing plan for your record shop, including the following elements: (a) your goal, including expected share of the market and anticipated sales volume, expenses, and profit; (b) your marketing program for accomplishing this goal; and (c) a completion schedule.

part 40

Financing a Marketing Business

YOUR GOALS

1. Using the Yellow Pages of your local telephone directory, identify the sources of capital available to businesses in your area.
2. Given a firm that specializes in making capital available to businessmen, determine the qualifications the firm requires of the businessmen seeking the capital.

Suppose you decide to go into business for yourself. The first—and probably biggest—problem you will face is getting the necessary capital. *Capital* is money and other assets owned by a business organization. (An "asset" is anything of monetary value that a business owns.) After acquiring the necessary capital, you will need a building in which to operate your business. Then you will need equipment—manufacturing machinery if you have a manufacturing business, or display cases, office machines, and delivery trucks if you have a retail store. These assets, which may cost thousands of dollars, are called "fixed assets" because they are a fairly permanent part of the business and are expected to last a long time. The money used for purchasing assets expected to last a long time is called long-term capital.

Getting long-term capital for your business is only one financial problem you will face. After you obtain this capital and establish the business, you must have a steady flow of capital to operate the business. You must meet expenses such as salaries, advertising, insurance, telephone calls, electricity, and taxes. And if you plan to take on new lines or to expand your operations, you will need additional capital to finance these activities. Capital needed to finance current operations is called "short-term capital" or *working capital.* It consists of cash and other assets that can be quickly converted into cash.

It is easy to see why marketing could not take place without both long-term and short-term capital. Consider a new car, for example. The companies that supply the steel, upholstery, and accessories have invested money in buildings, equipment, tools, inventory, and labor. The manufacturer of the car has made a similar investment. Shippers, warehousing firms, and advertising agencies have also invested large sums to get the car to the consumer. Finally, the car dealer has invested capital in his building and inventory.

To carry on his business, a marketer often borrows the capital he needs. The borrowing of capital to operate a business is called *financing.* Financing is a vital marketing activity. It plays an important role in business operations by providing companies with the capital necessary to develop new products, expand their operations, reach new markets, and sell more aggressively.

CREDIT AS A SOURCE OF BUSINESS FINANCING

Many marketers obtain production machinery, operating equipment, or money through the use of credit. As defined in Part 37, credit is the power to obtain goods, services, or money in return for a promise to pay at a future date.

Some individuals feel that to borrow money or to ask for credit is an indication of poor management. Sometimes this is true. But businesses are expected to borrow, and often the use of credit is a sign of good management. For example, suppose the Wright Hardware Store has a chance to buy at great savings all the modern display fixtures of the General Appliance Center, whose owner is retiring. Wright Hardware can save money by borrowing enough to make the purchase, and it would be a poor manager indeed who let pride stand in his way of making a good business deal.

Even large corporations with assets worth millions of dollars borrow money. They need long-term capital to build warehouses, to retool for new models, or to establish branch distribution offices.

Credit is vital to marketing finance. A newspaper in need of a new printing press may buy it on credit from a manufacturer. The newspaper might possibly buy on the installment plan, which requires regular payments over a specified period of time. Likewise, the manufacturer of the printing press may buy on credit most of his fabricating materials and other equipment from various suppliers.

Most businesses are financed by credit.

Businesses need both short-term and long-term credit. "Short-term credit" is credit which is needed for a relatively short time, usually less than a year. It is used, for example, by a business owner who wants to buy a special shipment of goods that he expects to sell quickly. He obtains a loan from a bank or other source, agreeing to repay it within a brief period, for example, within 90 days.

"Long-term credit" is credit which is needed for more than a year. Some long-term loans may be for several years. Capital borrowed to purchase a building, to open a new branch store, and to buy expensive equipment are typical examples of long-term credit.

SOURCES OF CAPITAL

The financing needed to start a new business is often referred to as "venture capital." The businessman may seek venture capital from several sources. Some of the most important sources are business creditors, investors, banks, loan companies, factors, insurance companies, the Small Business Administration, and small-business investment companies.

Business Creditors

Any firm uses the capital of another firm when it buys on credit the equipment needed to operate its own business. A retailer may feel, for example, that he could improve his business if he redecorated his store with new wall-to-wall carpeting, colorful vinyl-covered chairs, fluorescent lighting, and new display cases. If his business is a thriving one, he will have little difficulty in obtaining credit from furniture manufacturers. The retailer will make an agreement with each of the manufacturers to pay for the various items over a specified period of time. By buying on credit in this way, he will be using the capital of other businesses to develop his own business.

Investors

Much of the capital needed to finance a business is supplied by investors. Corporations sell shares of their stock to investors. The investors therefore become stockholders and collect dividends on their stock from the corporation. Corporations also issue bonds. A bond is a promise to pay a given sum of money at a certain date. Investors purchase bonds because of the interest that the bonds earn. Money to finance a business may also come from friends, relatives, various investors, and other businesses.

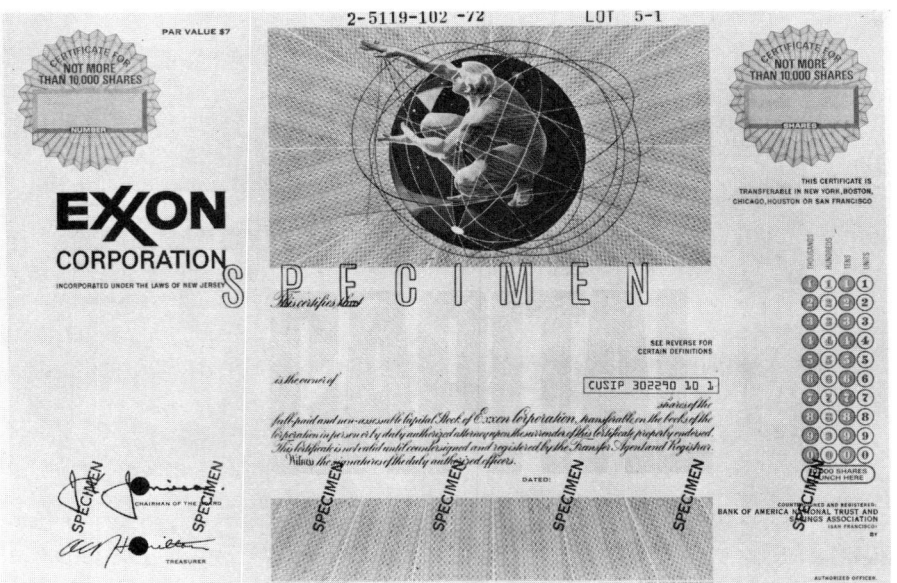

Courtesy Exxon Corp.

When you buy stock in a company, you are issued a certificate showing the number of shares you have purchased.

Banks

Perhaps the best-known source of capital for both short-term and long-term needs is banks. Businesses borrow money from banks to expand, modernize, relocate, or carry on current operations.

Bank loans may be secured or unsecured. An *unsecured loan* is one in which the borrower's reputation is the determining factor in granting a loan; that is, no security in the form of buildings or other assets is required. A secured loan is one in which some of the borrower's assets are pledged as a guarantee of repayment.

The assets that the borrower pledges to the bank as security are called *collateral*. Collateral may be in the form of stocks and bonds, buildings, or life insurance. Accounts receivable are often used as collateral. *Accounts receivable* are sums of money owed to a business by its customers. When a borrower who uses his accounts receivable as collateral does not repay his loan, the lending institution may claim the amounts which are collected from the customers. Sometimes collateral is merely the signature of an endorser or cosigner, who becomes liable if the loan is not repaid.

Loan Companies

A firm that needs money immediately for growth purposes or for purchasing merchandise may decide to obtain that capital from a loan company. Certain loan companies will advance cash against accounts receivable up to 90 percent of their face value. The firm repays the loan as it collects the customers' accounts in the usual way.

Factors

A company that is owed large amounts of money by customers may turn these accounts receivable into cash by means of a factor. A "factor" is a financing company that provides cash for a company's accounts receivable and may take over all details of collecting these accounts. The cost of such service to the firm is a percent of the value of the accounts receivable taken over by the factor. It may be as low as ½ of 1 percent or as high as 2 ¾ percent of that value.

Insurance Companies

Insurance companies are important sources of long-term capital for large marketing organizations. A chain organization expecting to open several branch outlets may seek a loan from an insurance company. Hotels and motels, office buildings, and other enterprises also borrow from insurance companies. Most insurance companies are not interested in lending less than

$500,000, and the loans they make usually run from 5 to 15 years. Larger insurance companies frequently make loans amounting to millions of dollars to large marketing organizations.

Small Business Administration

Many small businesses are unable to obtain long-term loans from private sources because of their size or their credit standing. To help such businesses, the Small Business Administration (SBA) lending program was initiated by the federal government in 1953 and was made permanent in 1958. The SBA either participates with banks in granting loans or provides direct loans itself. However, SBA policy encourages bank loans or other private loans.

The SBA assists small businesses in four important ways:

- Obtains for them a fair share of business generated by the needs of the government.
- Gives them access to capital and credit.
- Provides them with competent counsel on management.
- Gives licenses to the small-business investment companies.

In addition, the SBA offers financial advice on possible ways of obtaining credit on reasonable terms, on alternative ways of financing production, on various aspects of financial management, and on ways of increasing equity capital (capital that the owners or stockholders invest in a business).

Small-Business Investment Companies

Small-business investment companies are privately owned lending agencies regulated by the U.S. government through the Small Business Administration. These companies were organized to make both short-term and long-term loans to small businesses.

THE BUSINESS AS A CREDIT RISK

Obtaining credit is not difficult for the marketer who operates his business efficiently and shows a promising future. However, lending institutions must determine whether the firm is a good credit risk before granting a loan. Among other things, the lending agency wants to know the following:

- *The condition of the business.* Is the business in sound financial condition? Is it likely to grow and prosper?
- *The character of the borrower.* Is the borrower honest and dependable? Does he value his reputation?

- *The purpose of the loan.* How will the money be used? Does that use appear to be a sound move for the business?
- *The security of the loan.* Is there a good chance that the loan will be repaid? How will payment be assured?
- *The managerial ability of the borrower.* Is the borrower a good manager? Are his goal and his intended means of achieving the goal realistic?

Marketers who can supply satisfactory answers to questions such as the ones mentioned here are able to obtain credit with little difficulty from any of the sources that have been discussed.

ESTIMATING CAPITAL NEEDS

One of the most important jobs of the sales manager or director of marketing is to estimate his short-term and long-term capital needs. This is a crucial decision because intelligent planning for future marketing operations cannot take place until it is known how much capital will be needed to finance them. If a company does not estimate its financial needs accurately, it may be caught short of funds and thus fail to achieve its aim.

Forecasts of financial needs are always prepared in the form of a budget. Such a budget includes two basic elements: anticipated income from sales and anticipated expenses. Budgeting for the purpose of estimating capital needs is not solely a responsibility of marketing personnel. It is the concern

Sales records of current and previous years are helpful in forecasting sales and estimating capital needs for the coming year.

Courtesy Electrical Wholesaling

of all top management. However, the marketing department must supply much of the data needed. In estimating sales income, the marketing director must consider factors such as population trends, customer buying power, price increases, competition, and expansion of the product line. At the same time, he must estimate the costs of obtaining this sales income: possible increase in the sales staff, transportation and delivery expenses, advertising, losses from uncollected accounts, cost of services, and so forth.

For a business, forecasting the future is usually based on past experience; that is, the 1980 budget is likely to be based on what happened in 1975—and possibly earlier. Once the forecast is made, it must be continuously reviewed and adjusted for changes, both real and anticipated. No progressive marketing business can afford to be without sufficient working capital. And when a business turns to a lending institution for money, one of the first things required is an intelligent forecast of future operations—a budget.

EFFICIENT USE OF CAPITAL

Certain measurements aid the marketer in answering the important question "Is my capital working hard enough?" Three such measurements are stock turnover, accounts receivable turnover, and working capital ratio.

Stock Turnover

The frequency with which merchandise, or stock, is sold and replaced by new merchandise is called *stock turnover.* The rate of stock turnover (or stockturn, for short) may be figured for a season or on a yearly, monthly, or weekly basis. For example, a yearly stockturn of 12 means that the stock is sold and replaced by new stock 12 times a year, or that merchandise remains on the shelves an average of one month.

Obviously the more often stock is turned over, the more capital is available to the marketer and the less money is tied up in inventory. Stock turnover is an excellent measurement of the progress of a retail merchandising business.

Accounts Receivable Turnover

Businesses that sell on credit often have large amounts of working capital tied up in accounts receivable; thus, it is important that these accounts be turned over as many times as possible during the year. The rate of accounts receivable turnover is determined by dividing the total sales on account for the year by the total accounts receivable at the given date.

For example, suppose that during a given year a business has total sales of $900,000. On December 31, its accounts receivable total $90,000.

To determine his rate of accounts receivable turnover, the owner of the business divides $900,000 by $90,000. The result is 10, which is his turnover rate. To encourage accounts receivable turnover, many manufacturers, some wholesalers, and a few retailers offer a cash discount to those who pay their bills promptly or within a stated period.

Working Capital Ratio

"Current assets" include cash and other property owned that can be readily converted into cash. *Current liabilities* are debts owed by a business and due within a limited period of time, such as a year. The working capital ratio is the ratio of current assets to current liabilities. Obviously, the total current assets of a business should be much larger than its total current liabilities. Businessmen and their bankers watch this ratio very carefully, because it is an important indicator of the condition of a business.

◘ YOUR MARKETING VOCABULARY

On a separate sheet of paper define each of the following marketing terms; then use each term in a sentence.

Accounts receivable
Capital
Collateral
Current liabilities
Financing
Stock turnover
Unsecured loan
Working capital

◘ FOR REVIEW AND DISCUSSION

1. Suppose you decide to go into business for yourself. What is the first—and probably biggest—problem you will face?
2. What kind of capital is used to meet expenses such as salaries, advertising, insurance, telephone calls, electricity, and taxes? What does this capital consist of?
3. Could the marketing of goods, such as new cars, take place without both long-term and short-term capital? Explain.
4. Explain the difference between short-term and long-term credit. Give examples of how a business uses both types of credit.
5. Name five sources of capital for marketers.
6. Describe how one firm sometimes uses the capital of another firm when it buys on credit.
7. Explain the function of a factor.
8. What is the SBA and what are its functions?
9. Explain the function of small-business investment companies.
10. What facts does a lending agency want to know about a borrower?

11. How do marketers go about estimating, or forecasting, their financial needs?
12. Define "working capital ratio." To whom is it important and why?

ANALYZING MARKETING CONCEPTS

1. A marketer may seek capital from several sources. Prepare a form like the one below, list the following sources of capital in the left-hand column: (a) creditor, (b) investor, (c) bank, (d) factor, (e) loan company. For each source, think of a situation in which a marketer would seek capital from that source. Describe each situation in turn in the right-hand column.

Source of Capital	Situation
Example: Insurance company	A chain organization wanting to open several branch stores.

2. Assume that you are the manager of a department store and are responsible for the financial needs of your business. Prepare a form like the one below. In the left-hand column, list the following reasons for obtaining credit: (a) to buy merchandise for resale during the Easter season, (b) to open a small branch store, (c) to buy an electronic calculator, (d) to buy a delivery truck, (e) to add a new appliance line, (f) to meet current salary expenses.

   For each reason listed, place a check mark in the appropriate right-hand column to indicate whether you, as manager, would need to obtain long-term or short-term credit.

Reason for Obtaining Credit	Credit Term	
	Long	Short
Example: To make a special purchase of merchandise being promoted.		✔

MARKETING PROJECT 40
Studying Sources of Capital

Project Goal: Given a firm that specializes in making capital available to businessmen, determine the qualifications the firm requires of the businessmen seeking the capital.

Action: Using the Yellow Pages of your telephone directory, select a firm that specializes in making loans available to marketers in your area. If necessary, refer to page 471 of this part for suggestions on sources of loans. With your teacher's guidance, contact the firm and obtain answers to the following questions:

1. What types of loans can a marketer in your area obtain from the lending institution?
2. What does the firm require of the marketer seeking the loan? (Obtain sample loan application forms, if possible.)

Prepare a written report of your findings. Be prepared to discuss your findings in class.

CASE STUDY
Managing a Business for Profit

"Lush Times for the Pet-Food Producers"—that was the title of the *Fortune* article that had interested Spring Foods Company in the pet-food business. The company was a small and successful producer of several lines of regular foods distributed through the outlets of three supermarket chains. Recently it had added "Diamonds," a quality dog food, to its product line (see pages 96–97, 231–233, and 433–435). Now a Spring Foods management team was studying the financial results for the first six months of the dog-food operation. The following table shows the results.

	Sales Planned	Sales Actual	Expenses Planned	Expenses Actual
July	$ 8,000	$ 7,000	$16,000	$14,000
August	8,000	7,000	14,000	13,000
September	10,000	8,000	14,000	13,000
October	12,000	9,000	14,000	13,000
November	12,000	10,000	14,000	14,000
December	14,000	11,000	13,000	14,000
Total	$64,000	$52,000	$85,000	$81,000

"We didn't plan a profit for the first six months of the 'Diamonds' operation," said Leon Hamil, executive vice president of Spring Foods. "But the figures are not so good as we had hoped for. They're not below the limits we established, but we're going to have to do something about this operation anyway."

Mr. Hamil reviewed the background of the operation for the management team: Nationwide, the pet-food business was considered to be very profitable and to have an even better future. Research had showed that people were buying more pet food, and they seemed willing to pay any price for it. Thus there was a good market for quality pet food. Spring Foods had wanted to expand its product line and therefore decided to produce pet food. After some initial difficulty, the company had been able to distribute the new line easily through the three supermarket chains that carried the other Spring Foods lines. It was unfortunate that the operation had not met financial expectations.

"Any ideas?" Mr. Hamil asked his management staff.

One member of the staff thought that the company simply had been wrong to go into the pet-food business in the first place. "Yes, research made it seem like a good idea, but those figures don't look all that good. After all, look at Kellogg's experience. Several years ago they gave up trying to get a share of the pet-food business because it overtaxed their resources. Who are we to try to compete?"

Another staff member thought that the company might experiment with selling a less expensive dog food. "After all, people will buy anything more readily if it costs a little less. We could advertise that we offer a quality product at a budget price."

"How about trimming production costs instead," the production manager said. "We could cut the number of varieties we offer from the present six to three. That would bring our expense figures almost in line with our sales figures."

"Give me a little more money to spend in the next six months," the advertising manager said. "I know I'm prejudiced in favor of this dog-food line. But because of that newspaper strike last summer, we were a little low on promotion early in the game. Let me put some extra money into advertising and dealer aids. I think we can pull those sales up."

"Maybe we just need to go into the pet-food market on a larger scale," another member of the management staff said. "We could put out a cat-food line, too. That would get our brand more shelf space and make us more important as a pet-food name."

Questions

1. What are the advantages and disadvantages of each suggestion?
2. Taking all the information into consideration, what do you think the company should do?

part 41

Reducing Marketing Risks

YOUR GOAL

Given a local marketing business, identify four types of business risks it faces, and list specific ways in which management is minimizing these risks.

The marketer faces a number of risks, and these risks can increase the costs of getting goods from the producer to the consumer. The grocer, for example, risks having his fresh meats and vegetables spoil before he can sell them. To reduce this risk, he buys expensive refrigeration equipment for the goods and, in so doing, raises the cost of selling.

Like the grocer, many marketing businesses face the risk of product *obsolescence*. "Obsolescence" is the process in which a product deteriorates or becomes old and nonfunctional. The risk of deterioration in shipping perishables such as frozen foods makes it necessary for the shipper to use special refrigerated railroad cars and trucks. Obviously it costs more to maintain this special transportation equipment than ordinary kinds, and the added expense increases the cost of distribution.

When a retail store hires security guards to protect it against shoplifters, it reduces risk but increases the cost of marketing by having to pay the guards. When a business permits customers to buy on credit, it takes the risk that some of them will not pay their bills; and for any who do not, the business will have to stand the loss.

Because risks increase the costs of doing business, they are under constant study by modern marketers. Of course, no marketer expects to eliminate risks completely, but he can reduce them through careful planning and management.

TYPES OF BUSINESS RISKS

While there are many types of business risks, they can be broadly classified into three groups: economic risks, natural risks, and human risks.

Economic risks, sometimes called "market risks," are those caused by changes in the market. The changes usually force a marketer to accept a lower price for his goods, which in turn results in a setback for the marketing company. Economic risks can also be caused by shifts in consumer demand and by increased competition.

One of the best illustrations of a shift in consumer demand is a change in fashion. More than any other marketer, the fashion merchant faces the risk of his goods going out of style. If this happens and he has a supply of goods that customers no longer demand, he must reduce his prices drastically to sell the merchandise.

Competition is an ever-present economic risk. The owner of a flourishing small retail store may see his business destroyed by the appearance of a large competitor next door who offers a wider selection of merchandise at lower prices.

Another common kind of economic risk is that involved in selecting a business location. For example, suppose that an oil company chooses a site for a new service station along the proposed route of a new superhighway. However, an alternate route may unexpectedly be chosen for the superhighway. If so, the service station will not be in a well-traveled area and hence will get very little business.

Risks caused by natural phenomena are called *natural risks*. Natural phenomena include fires, floods, lightning, earthquakes, and hurricanes. Floods in North Dakota, hurricanes in Florida and Louisiana, and earthquakes in California and Alaska, for example, have done millions of dollars' worth of damage to businesses.

Perishability is also a natural risk. Vegetables that reach the market fresh command a good price; those that arrive in poor condition have to be sold at a reduced price or thrown away. Steaks that have been cut, packaged, and put in a supermarket display case have to be sold while they are still fresh; if they begin to spoil, they no longer have market value.

Businessmen must always face natural risks, such as fires. Insurance provides protection against such risks.

Editorial Photocolor Archives, Inc.

Those risks which are caused primarily by human frailty and unpredictability are called *human risks*. Human risks are caused mainly by employees and customers. Risks attributable to employees include dishonesty, incompetence, carelessness, sickness, and accidents. Those caused by customers include nonpayment of accounts, dishonesty, and unusually high returns or adjustments.

REDUCING RISKS THROUGH INSURANCE

Many of the risks faced by businesses can be protected against by insurance. Insurance does not remove or reduce the risks; it protects the businessman, by paying him for losses caused by the risks. For example, insurance may protect him against losses from fires, accidents, bad debts, and thefts.

Insurance is so important that the credit rating of a business is affected directly by the amount of insurance it carries. It is easy to see why a bank would not be likely to lend money to a business that carried little or no insurance. If the business were destroyed by fire, for example, the bank would have a difficult time collecting its money.

Types of Insurance

A business may buy insurance to cover almost any kind of risk. The most common types of insurance that a business may obtain are (1) property insurance, (2) transportation insurance, (3) robbery and theft insurance, (4) insurance covering personal accidents, and (5) insurance covering business interruptions or setbacks.

Property Insurance. Insurance against loss or destruction of property is called *property insurance*. Property insurance is one of the most common forms of business insurance. There are various forms of property insurance, the most important being fire insurance. Fire insurance covers more than the losses caused directly by a fire. It also covers losses from damage caused during a fire by water, heat, and smoke.

Additional forms of property insurance can be purchased (often in the same contract with fire insurance) to protect against losses due to windstorms, explosions, riots, strikes, falling aircraft, and colliding vehicles.

Transportation Insurance. A company that transports and stores goods assumes several risks. Goods may be damaged in transit due to highway accidents or improper packing and moving facilities. They may be damaged in storage due to fire, water, or improper storage facilities. Goods may be stolen while in storage or on loading platforms. To protect itself against such risks, a company can obtain *marine insurance*, which covers the transporting of goods. While the term "marine insurance" implies protection for water travel only, it actually covers all forms of transportation, including mail, truck, bus, and air.

Robbery and Theft Insurance. A business may obtain insurance to cover losses from robbery and theft. Such losses may consist of merchandise, equipment, cash, or other valuables. A business may choose only one of the several forms of such insurance. For example, a specific policy may cover only shoplifting or holdups. However, insurance against a combination of theft risks can often be obtained in a single policy.

Insurance Against Personal Injuries. Most companies carry liability insurance. *Liability insurance* is protection against losses due to claims by customers or employees for personal injuries they received on the company premises. Liability insurance covers bodily injuries caused by elevators, escalators, moving vehicles, and other possible hazards.

Insurance Against Business Setbacks. Insurance that covers losses due to a temporary halt in business operations is called *business-interruption insurance*. For example, such coverage may protect the owner of an apartment building against loss of rentals while his property is being rebuilt after a fire. Because fires or other casualties may cause temporary halts in business, fire and casualty policies sometimes also provide for business-interruption insurance.

Another form of protection against business setbacks is called weather insurance. It might compensate the promoter of a baseball game, for example,

What kind of insurance would cover these telephone linemen?

when gate receipts suffer because of rain. Resorts sometimes purchase weather insurance and offer it to their customers. In such cases, the vacationer is reimbursed when weather conditions keep him from engaging in a particular sport.

Another type of insurance that protects against loss of business earnings is known as *credit insurance.* Credit insurance compensates a business for losses it suffers because of nonpayment of bills by customers.

Cost of Insurance

When a firm applies for insurance, the insurance company's agent determines the amount of risk involved. The cost to the firm is based on the insurance company's estimate of that amount.

Insurance costs are hard to determine because every case is slightly different. For example, two applicants—the ABC Company and the XYZ Company— may have identical store buildings with identical appraisal values. After investigation, however, the insurance company may charge the ABC Company a slightly higher rate than the XYZ Company, because the XYZ

Company has a better sprinkler system. The sprinkler system makes the risk involved in insuring the XYZ Company slightly less than the risk for the ABC Company.

The following are some of the factors considered in determining the costs of various types of insurance:

- *Fire insurance.* In arriving at the cost of fire insurance to a firm, the insurance company considers whether the building has a wood frame, is made of brick and fire-resistant materials, or is of mixed construction. It is also interested in the types of materials used in the interior, the age and condition of the electrical wiring, the fire-protection equipment on the premises, and the kinds of goods kept in the building.
- *Workmen's compensation.* There are 900 classifications of workmen's compensation insurance. This insurance provides that an employee may collect payment from his employer for injuries suffered during the course of his employment. The minimum cost at which this insurance may be offered to employees is usually a matter of state law.
- *Premise liability.* The number of customers that a retail store attracts directly affects the cost of its liability insurance. For that reason, larger stores are required to pay higher rates than smaller stores, since they draw a greater number of customers.
- *Burglary coverage.* Burglary insurance is costly today, but rates may be reduced if the insured employs guards and uses burglary protection devices such as television surveillance, special cylinders on locks, tear-gas devices on safes, and night lights.

Insurance companies also offer contracts which include all the major kinds of insurance that a marketer might want. The cost of coverage is very high, and such contracts are usually of interest only to large businesses.

The modern marketer looks to his insurance agent for information and advice and is in constant touch with him. Only an informed agent can give wise counsel on the various types of insurance available to and suitable for a particular business.

REDUCING RISKS THROUGH GOOD MANAGEMENT

The best way to reduce losses from risks is to do everything possible to prevent trouble. Because the main job of insurance companies is to pay off the insured when something goes wrong, they put strong emphasis on prevention. For example, an insurance agent examining a building whose owner wants fire insurance might point out what could be done to reduce the risk of fire. If the owner follows the suggestions, the insurance company might offer him a lower rate.

Good management within the company is most important in reducing risks. While it is impossible to eliminate risks, careful planning and quick action on management's part can avoid some kinds of trouble and can reduce the impact of others.

Reducing Economic Risks

Economic risks are the hardest of all to minimize, because a great many of them are beyond the businessman's control. He cannot help it if there is a national depression or if costs skyrocket.

The best that a marketer can do is to anticipate his risks as wisely as possible and be prepared for them. This means that he must study market conditions and general economic trends. He must keep up to date on local conditions — political events, population shifts, traffic patterns, new real estate developments, and competition. The marketer who does not keep up to date on marketing trends and conditions multiplies his risks.

Reducing Natural Risks

Losses from natural risks often can be reduced by careful preventive measures. For example, the citrus grower in Florida knows that frost is a hazard to his crops. Therefore, he watches the weather closely to see whether smudge pots will be needed to heat the orchards. The farmer provides irrigation systems against the possibility of a drought. The owner of a business guards against possible fire hazards by making sure that defective electrical equipment and wiring are repaired, by having the premises inspected at regular intervals, by discouraging careless use of lighted cigarettes, and by providing special storage for flammable liquids. Because fires are frequently due to the carelessness of people, one of the best forms of insurance against this risk is careful and reliable employees.

Reducing Human Risks

Theft is a major risk in any business that deals in merchandise or keeps cash on the premises. Businesses lose millions of dollars a year from pilferage and theft. Managers can reduce this risk in a number of ways. One way is to safeguard all valuables. Another way is to place under bond employees who handle cash and other valuables. *Bonding* is a method of insuring whereby the employer buys insurance on his employees to protect himself against possible thefts by them. In the event that such a theft is discovered, the employer can claim compensation from the insurance company for any loss.

Another way to reduce losses from pilferage and theft is to hire guards (either on the company's payroll or from an agency) to watch for shoplifters and dishonest employees.

Most companies require workers to wear safety masks when operating certain kinds of equipment. This man is applying polyurethane foam insulation to the side of a new house.

Courtesy United States Steel

Some losses result from people issuing bad checks, forged (altered) checks, and counterfeit money. These losses can be reduced by setting definite policies as to who can accept checks and by instructing those who handle cash on how to detect counterfeit money.

Accidents can be very costly to a business. However, accident risks can be reduced by removing as many hazards as possible. Vehicles, elevators, escalators, high-speed machines, and other equipment should be inspected often. Employees engaged in dangerous work should be provided with necessary safety equipment, such as goggles, or special clothing, such as shoes and gloves. In cold weather, stores and other businesses should keep walks and outdoor passageways free from ice and snow. Many firms employ safety directors who keep a constant watch to prevent and eliminate accident hazards, and set up training programs to teach safety to employees.

Credit risks may be reduced by carefully screening those who apply for credit and by following up regularly on accounts that are past due.

◨ YOUR MARKETING VOCABULARY

On a separate sheet of paper define each of the following marketing terms; then use each term in a sentence.

Bonding
Business-interruption insurance
Credit insurance
Economic risks
Human risks
Liability insurance
Marine insurance
Natural risks
Property insurance

FOR REVIEW AND DISCUSSION

1. What are three types of risks?
2. Give three examples of risks that increase the cost of marketing.
3. How does the amount of insurance carried by a business affect its credit rating?
4. Name four types of insurance coverage for a business. State the losses which each type protects the business against.
5. Since risks cannot be eliminated, through what two ways can they be reduced?
6. Name some factors that can influence the cost of fire insurance.
7. How can management reduce economic risk?
8. Name two types of natural risks and discuss ways in which those risks can be reduced.
9. What safeguards can businesses use against the risk of theft?
10. What action can businesses take to reduce human risks other than theft?

ANALYZING MARKETING CONCEPTS

1. The businessman can reduce marketing risks by taking preventive measures. Prepare a form like the one below and list the following types of businesses in the left-hand column: (a) department store, (b) jewelry store, (c) drugstore, (d) steel-products manufacturer. In the center column, describe for each business a preventive measure that it might take to reduce marketing risks. In the appropriate column at the right, place a check mark to indicate whether the risk involved is economic, natural, or human.

Type of Business	Preventive Measure	Economic	Natural	Human
Example: Supermarket	A uniformed guard is placed on duty to help prevent shoplifting.			✔

2. Many of the risks faced by a company can be covered by insurance. Prepare a form like the following one, listing these types of businesses in the left-hand column: (a) supermarket, (b) restaurant, (c) TV dealer, (d) service station, (e) automobile dealer, (f) clothing store, (g) self-service laundry. In the center column, describe for each business one risk that could be covered by insurance. In the right-hand column, name the type of insurance that would be used to cover the risk.

Type of Business	Insurable Risk	Type of Insurance
Example: Furniture store	Customers who do not pay accounts.	Credit insurance

◊ MARKETING PROJECT 41
Identifying Marketing Risks

Project Goal: Given a local marketing business, identify four types of business risks it faces, and list specific ways in which management is minimizing these risks.

Action: With your teacher's guidance, arrange to interview the manager of a business in your community. Ask the manager to identify four major risks that his business faces. Ask him also to explain what steps are taken to minimize these risks.

Prepare a form like the one below. Write the name of the business and the manager at the top of the form. Then record your findings in the proper columns.

Major Risks	Ways of Reducing Risks

part 42

Financial Management

YOUR GOAL

Given financial statements or financial information for a particular business and some key business ratios, analyze the financial strength of the business according to the ratios.

Money enables people to buy things they want and need, and they get more value for their money when they use it carefully. If you get an allowance or earn a salary to pay some of your expenses, you know the importance of using money carefully. You probably practice some form of financial management, although you may not think of it as that. Either in your head or on paper, you figure the amount of money you will receive next week or next month, and you decide how you are going to use that money. Then, if you are wise, you keep a written record of how you actually spend your money, just to make sure that you are spending your money in the ways you had planned to spend it.

This simple kind of financial management helps you make sure that you have enough money to cover all your essential expenses. It helps you determine what you can afford to spend on nonessentials. It helps you save money for the future.

Thus, *financial management* is the process of planning and measuring the flow of money. The financial management that marketers practice is a complicated version of what you do, and it helps them in the same ways that it helps you.

Financial management in marketing depends upon a good recordkeeping system. Records enable the marketer to measure all the money that comes in and goes out of the company. They help him to measure the company's financial status at any particular time. The marketer uses records and other information to do his financial planning.

FINANCIAL STATEMENTS

Financial information is generated in many places. Information about how money was earned is found on cash register tapes and in sales books. Information about how money was spent is found on orders placed by company buyers and on bills sent in by other companies. In a good recordkeeping system all these useful financial data are collected by the company and arranged in an organized form so that reports and statements can be prepared at regular intervals.

The basic financial information of interest to the marketer is summarized in two financial statements: the income statement and the balance sheet.

Income Statement

A summary of the revenue and expenses of a company over a period of time is known as an *income statement*. It is also called an "operating statement" or a "profit and loss statement." In some companies an income statement is prepared every three months or perhaps only at the end of a year. In other companies it is prepared at the end of each month. The illustration on page 493 shows an income statement of the Home Wholesale Company for the month of June, 19--.

The data in the income statement may be expressed by the following arithmetic equation:

$$\text{Sales} - \text{Cost of Goods Sold}$$
$$= \text{Gross Profit on Sales}$$
$$- \text{Operating Expenses} = \text{Net Income}$$

In addition to being given in dollars, certain figures may also be shown as an operating ratio. An *operating ratio* is a percentage relationship between the dollar amount of net sales and some other dollar amount such as net income or gross profit on sales. For example, if in a given year a wholesaler

Home Wholesale Company
Income Statement
For the Month Ended June 30, 19--

Revenue From Sales:		
Gross Sales	$458,335	
Less: Refunds and Allowances	4,000	
Net Sales		$454,335
Cost of Goods Sold:		
Merchandise Inventory, June 1, 19--	$332,000	
Purchases	400,000	
Cost of Goods Available for Sale	$732,000	
Less: Merchandise Inventory, June 30, 19--	385,000	
Cost of Goods Sold		347,000
Gross Profit on Sales (Gross Margin)		$107,335
Operating Expenses:		
Advertising Expense	$ 28,800	
Bad Debts Expense	3,900	
Delivery Expense	10,750	
Depreciation Expense—Building	800	
Depreciation Expense—Equipment	700	
Depreciation Expense—Fixtures	550	
Payroll Taxes Expense	1,850	
Salaries Expense	31,500	
Supplies Expense	850	
Utilities Expense	4,300	
Total Operating Expenses		84,000
Net Income (Net Profit)		$ 23,335

has net sales of $1 million ($1,000,000) and a net income of $25,000, his net income is 2.5 percent of his net sales. The 2.5 percent is an operating ratio. In the case of the Home Wholesale Company, the operating ratio of net income to net sales for June, 19--, is 5.1 percent ($23,335 net income divided by $454,335 net sales). This ratio represents a good net income for the month.

The operating ratio is useful in helping the marketer determine how well he has used his money. It tells him much more than the plain dollar figures does. For example, suppose that a marketer has a $25,000 net income one year and a $30,000 net income the next year but his net sales are $1 million ($1,000,000) the first year and $1.35 million ($1,350,000) the second year. This means that his net income would amount to 2.5 percent of net sales the first year but only to 2.2 percent of net sales the second year. Actually, he would have less net income the second year in relation to his net sales.

Good financial management means having money when you need it.

Revenue From Sales. During the course of any selling period, every marketer has some customers who return what they have bought and are given either a full refund or a partial allowance. To determine the net sales, therefore, the marketer lists the dollar amount of gross sales (total sales before refunds and allowances); from that figure he subtracts the dollar amount of refunds and allowances to arrive at the amount of net sales. For June, 19--, the Home Wholesale Company has net sales of $454,335 (gross sales of $458,335 minus refunds and allowances of $4,000). If a company grants sales discounts, the amount of those discounts is also subtracted from gross sales to obtain net sales.

Cost of Goods Sold. The major outlay of money for wholesalers and retailers is the cost of the goods they buy for resale. Determining the cost of goods sold during a particular period is done as follows:

The marketer starts by recording the cost of his merchandise inventory at the beginning of the period. "Merchandise inventory" consists of the goods the marketer has on hand. Then he adds the cost of the merchandise he purchased during that period (less the dollar amounts of refunds, allowances, and discounts, if any). The sum of the beginning inventory and the purchases is the cost of goods available for sale. Next the marketer subtracts the cost of the merchandise inventory on hand at the end of the period to get the cost of goods sold for the period. The income statement of the Home Wholesale Company for June, 19--, shows a cost of goods sold of $347,000 ($332,000 plus $400,000 equals $732,000 minus $385,000).

Gross Profit on Sales. By subtracting the cost of goods sold from the net sales, the marketer arrives at the *gross profit on sales*, or, as it is often called, the "gross margin." The gross profit on sales for the Home Wholesale Company is $107,335 (net sales of $454,335 minus cost of goods sold of $347,000).

Operating Expenses. On the income statement all expenses of doing business are grouped together as operating expenses. Some typical operating expenses are the costs of advertising and promotion, delivery, depreciation, rent, utilities, and insurance. All such costs are added together on the income statement to determine the total operating expenses. As shown in the illustration, the Home Wholesale Company has total operating expenses of $84,000.

Net Income. The amount that a company earned from its operations during the period of time covered by an income statement is called its *net income* or "net profit." Net income equals gross profit on sales minus total operating expenses. The Home Wholesale Company has a gross profit on sales of $107,335 and total operating expenses of $84,000. Subtracting $84,000 from $107,335 results in a net income of $23,335.

Balance Sheet

In contrast to the income statement, which shows a company's financial activities over a period of time, the *balance sheet* shows the financial position of a company at a particular time. The data in the balance sheet may be expressed by the following arithmetic equation:

$$\text{Assets} = \text{Liabilities} + \text{Owner's Equity}$$

The balance sheet is of particular importance to the owners of a company because it shows their financial interest in the business. Every executive of a company will also be interested in the figures on the balance sheet, because they show the financial health of the company. The following illustration is a balance sheet for the Home Wholesale Company as of June 30, 19--.

Home Wholesale Company
Balance Sheet
June 30, 19--

Assets

Cash		$ 75,500
Accounts Receivable	$195,000	
Less: Allowance for Bad Debts	3,900	191,100
Merchandise Inventory		385,000
Supplies on Hand		1,700
Building	$250,000	
Less: Accumulated Depreciation	154,000	96,000
Equipment	$ 69,500	
Less: Accumulated Depreciation	34,500	35,000
Fixtures	$ 41,700	
Less: Accumulated Depreciation	21,000	20,700
Total Assets		$805,000

Liabilities

Notes Payable		$ 23,000
Accounts Payable		62,600
Accrued Expenses and Taxes		25,700
Total Liabilities		$111,300

Owner's Equity

Robert Reed, Capital, June 1, 19--	$670,365	
Net Income for June 19--	23,335	
Robert Reed, Capital, June 30, 19--		693,700
Total Liabilities and Owner's Equity		$805,000

Assets. As mentioned in Part 40, assets are anything of monetary value that a company owns. Cash, accounts receivable, merchandise inventory, equipment, fixtures, and supplies on hand are among the assets of a typical merchandising company. In addition, a company might own a building and land. Note the assets shown on the balance sheet for the Home Wholesale Company. The assets total $805,000.

"Accounts receivable" are the amounts that customers owe the company for sales it made on credit. Many retailers do as much as 70 to 75 percent of their business on a credit basis, which means that most of their sales revenue is initially received in the form of accounts receivable. As mentioned earlier, "merchandise inventory" consists of the goods the marketer has on hand.

Liabilities. The amounts owed by a company are called *liabilities*. Accounts payable, notes payable, and loans payable are common liabilities. "Accounts payable" are the amounts a company owes to other companies for goods and services it purchased on credit. "Notes payable" are the amounts a company owes on promissory notes it issued. "Loans payable" are the amounts a company owes to a bank or other lending institution for loans it has taken out. Any expenses and taxes owed are called "accrued expenses and taxes." As shown on the balance sheet, the Home Wholesale Company has a total of $111,300 in liabilities as of June 30, 19--.

Owner's Equity. The financial interest that an owner has in a business is called *owner's equity*. Other terms, such as "capital," "proprietorship," or "net worth," are also used to refer to the financial interest of the owner or owners.

As expressed by the equation above, assets are the sum of the liabilities and owner's equity of a business. Owner's equity is therefore the difference between the assets and liabilities of the business. In the case of the Home Wholesale Company the assets are $805,000 and the liabilities are $111,300. Thus the owner's equity is $693,700 ($805,000 minus $111,300).

FINANCIAL PLANNING

A marketer collects a variety of data before making his financial plans. He studies the operating results of his own company and of his part of the marketing industry in general. He examines the economic forecasts both for the country in general and for his marketing area. He examines the trends in consumer demand that will affect his particular market. After he has examined all of the data, he plans what he believes to be logical, reasonable financial goals for his company.

Marketing plans are prepared for specific periods of time. A small marketer may set up quarterly, seasonal, and annual plans. Larger marketers may have monthly or weekly plans.

Financial planning is in the form of budgets. "Budgets" are plans which show the sales, expenses, and capital needs of a company for a future period. A marketer prepares two basic kinds of budgets, a sales budget and an expense budget. Together, these contain all the financial data that should be included in the income statement.

Sales Budget

A "sales budget" is a forecast of sales for a specific period of time. The forecast may be for a week, a month, a few months, or a year. The sales budget is usually the first budget to be prepared, and the other budgets are based on it.

In preparing the sales budget, the marketer takes into account all the factors that could influence his sales: He considers population trends, consumer buying power, consumer buying trends, prices, competition, and the state of his own operations.

Using the sales figures of the previous year as a base, he estimates his sales for the forthcoming period in dollars and in percentages of increase or decrease compared to the same period of the previous year.

The following is a simplified version of a sales budget for a small dress shop covering six consecutive months.

Sales Budget

Month	Dollars	Percentage change from previous year
January	$ 12,000	+5%
February	16,000	+5%
March	20,000	−3%
April	25,000	+8%
May	18,000	+5%
June	20,000	+5%
Total	$111,000	

Note that the marketer expects a 5 percent increase in sales for four of the six months. A change in the timing of holidays caused variations in his expectations for March and April. During the previous year, Easter was in late March, and the store did most of its Easter business in that month. However, during the present year Easter will be in April, and the store is expected to do most of its Easter business in that month. Other circumstances that can affect sales are unusual weather conditions, unexpected delivery problems, and special promotions. If any of these circumstances influenced sales during a particular month in the previous year, the marketer must take this into account in forecasting his sales for the forthcoming period.

Expense Budget

Once the marketer has prepared his sales budget and has a reasonable idea of the income he expects to earn, he is ready to prepare his expense budget. An "expense budget" is an estimate of the expenses to be incurred during a particular period of time. The expense budget is always prepared to cover the same period of time as the sales budget.

Wholesalers and retailers prepare two kinds of expense budgets, called the dollar merchandise budget and the operating expenses budget. The dollar merchandise budget is a plan showing the amount of money to be spent in buying goods for resale during the period. The operating expenses budget is a plan showing the amount of money to be spent on operating expenses during the period.

In preparing the dollar merchandise budget, the marketer must determine the amount of goods he will need to have on hand to generate the expected sales. He must also know when the goods should be on hand. The manager of the small dress shop, for example, must know when goods needed to generate Easter sales in April should be on hand. He probably should order them for delivery to the dress shop by mid-March. In addition, a marketer should buy only the amount of goods needed to generate the sales, because every dollar that the marketer ties up in inventory is a dollar less that he can spend elsewhere.

In preparing the operating expenses budget, the marketer must consider those expenses that are directly affected by sales and those that are the same regardless of sales. Expenses that are directly affected by sales may include selling expenses, advertising and promotion expenses, and delivery expenses. Expenses that stay the same regardless of sales may include administrative expenses, occupancy expenses, and the expenses for supplies.

Suppose the dress-shop manager planned to spend 60 percent of his expected sales in buying goods. The expected sales total of the dress shop is $111,000, and 60 percent of that equals $66,600. The following table represents a simplified version of how the shop manager might prepare a dollar merchandise budget.

Dollar Merchandise Budget

Month	Dollars
January	$ 8,000
February	12,000
March	16,600
April	11,000
May	10,000
June	9,000
Total	$66,600

YOUR MARKETING VOCABULARY

On a separate sheet of paper define each of the following marketing terms; then use each term in a sentence.

Balance sheet
Financial management
Gross profit on sales
Income statement
Liabilities
Net income
Operating ratio
Owner's equity

FOR REVIEW AND DISCUSSION

1. What does financial management in marketing depend upon? Explain your answer.
2. How does financial management help the marketer?
3. Where are financial data generated?
4. What two financial statements summarize the basic financial information of interest to the marketer?
5. How often is the income statement prepared?
6. How is the operating ratio useful to the marketer?
7. Explain how the cost of goods sold is determined.
8. How does a marketer go about making his financial plans?
9. What is a sales budget? an expense budget?
10. What must the marketer determine in order to prepare the dollar merchandise budget?

ANALYZING MARKETING CONCEPTS

1. The five major sections of an income statement must be thoroughly understood by a marketer. Prepare a form like the one below and list the following income statement sections in the left-hand column: (a) revenue from sales, (b) cost of goods sold, (c) gross profit on sales, (d) operating expenses, (e) net income. In the center column, write the key points that a marketer should know about each section. In the right-hand column, enter a dollar figure for each section of the income statement. The dollar amounts should be correctly related to each other so that they represent the income statement of a profit-making firm.

Income Statement Section	Key Points for Marketers	Dollar Amount

2. Study the following table, which represents the income statements of a retail store for three different periods.

Income Statements

Income Statement Section	March	April	May
Gross sales	$108,000	$90,000	$120,000
Refunds and allowances	8,000	5,000	10,000
Net sales	100,000	85,000	110,000
Cost of goods sold	60,000	50,000	65,000
Gross profit on sales	40,000	35,000	45,000
Total operating expenses	32,000	29,000	35,000
Net income	8,000	6,000	10,000

On a form like the one below, list the following income statement items in the left-hand column: (a) gross sales, (b) net sales, (c) cost of goods sold, (d) gross profit on sales, (e) total operating expenses, (f) net income. In the right-hand column, analyze the three statements of the retail store by writing comments about trends and possible marketing causes.

Income Statement Items	Financial Management Analysis

◊ MARKETING PROJECT 42
Analyzing Financial Strength

Project Goal: Given financial statements or financial information for a particular business and some key business ratios, analyze the financial strength of the business according to the ratios.

Action: With your teacher's permission, decide where you can gather financial information from a marketing business of your own choosing, such as a grocery store, a hardware store, or a variety store. Or, use the financial statements for the Home Wholesale Company given earlier in this part.

If you choose an actual business from which to gather data, talk with the owner or manager and ask him the following questions.

1. What is the company's ratio of net income to net sales?
2. What is the relationship of net sales to the capital of the business?
3. How many times larger than inventory is net sales?
4. What is the ratio of current liabilities to inventory?

Compare the answers you obtained from the marketer to the upper, median, and lower figures provided by the following table. You might guess why there are differences and discuss the matter with your teacher and other students.

If you choose to use the financial statements for the Home Wholesale Company, compute the answers to the questions above. Estimate why there are differences between your answers and the figures provided by Dun & Bradstreet. Discuss these differences with your teacher and other students.

Some Key Business Ratios

Line of Business	Net Income to Net Sales (Percent)	Net Sales to Capital (Times)[1]	Net Sales to Inventory (Times)	Current Liabilities to Inventory (Percent)
Wholesale furniture	2.80	6.06	7.7	65.0 (upper)
	1.43	4.23	6.3	101.4 (median)
	0.63	2.90	4.6	136.8 (lower)
Department stores	2.92	4.69	7.1	44.1
	1.55	3.13	5.6	69.8
	0.52	2.37	4.3	101.9
Furniture stores	4.74	4.28	5.2	57.9
	2.11	2.67	11.4	87.5
	0.76	1.71	26.1	145.4
Gasoline service stations	4.96	6.14	31.6	78.3
	2.97	4.07	51.2	163.4
	1.19	2.53	84.2	215.2
Grocery stores	1.80	14.37	39.6	65.5
	1.00	10.26	66.5	93.0
	0.54	7.48	96.5	128.9
Hardware stores	4.64	4.18	4.9	28.7
	2.64	2.51	3.9	50.0
	1.05	1.79	3.2	73.2
Variety stores	3.40	5.04	5.1	30.2
	2.31	3.84	4.1	42.9
	0.84	2.68	3.1	58.2

Source: *Key Business Ratios,* Dun & Bradstreet, Inc., 1971.

[1] For example, the ratio of net sales to capital is 6.06 to 1.

part 43

Systems and Uses of Data Processing

YOUR GOAL

Given a local marketing business, identify the principal methods it uses to process data. Specify how the output is used by the owners in managing the business.

Marketers receive and generate tremendous amounts of data every day. They receive orders from customers and information from suppliers by mail and by telephone. Stock clerks prepare new inventory records. Salespeople record sales transactions. Store buyers make out purchase orders. Receiving clerks record details about incoming shipments. All these functions are a part of data processing. Simply stated, *data processing* is the handling of information to obtain significant results.

The pace of marketing has increased, and with it has increased the need for data processing systems that can handle more data more quickly and more accurately. At one time, data processing was a tedious job, done by hand or adding machines. Today, this work is done much faster and more easily by automatic equipment, ranging from calculators to sophisticated electronic computers.

Marketers now realize that a good data processing system is one of a company's most valuable tools. Successful marketing management is based on facts, and a good data processing system produces these facts at the time they are needed.

FUNDAMENTALS OF PROCESSING DATA

Suppose that your school has organized an ecology fair and you are asked to sell tickets at 50 cents each for students and $1 each for adults. At the end of each week, you are expected to turn in a record of sales and the money you have collected. To keep track of your selling activities, you write down how many of each kind of ticket you sell and the amount of money you collect.

In making your notations and figuring your sales results, you are processing data. Although your amount of data is small compared to that of a company, you handle the data in the same way as the company. You go through the same stages of the data processing cycle, and you perform the same data processing operations.

The Data Processing Cycle

The four stages of processing data—origination, input, manipulation, and output—are called the *data processing cycle*. Any data processing job always consists of these four stages.

The first stage in the cycle is *origination*, the stage during which data are received or generated. A salesperson writing out a sales slip is originating data. When you wrote down the details about each ticket sale you made in your imaginary role as a ticket seller, you were originating data.

The second stage in the cycle is *input*, the stage during which data are placed into the processing system. At the end of each week of selling tickets, you had a stack of notations about sales you had made. Perhaps you made each notation on a separate slip, like a sales slip. Those slips were *input media*, which is the form in which data are prepared for entry into the processing system.

The third stage is *manipulation*, the stage during which the actual processing takes place. Data are arranged in groups, added together, and summarized. When you added the quantity of each kind of ticket sold and the money collected at the end of each week, you were manipulating the data.

The final stage in the data processing cycle is *output*, the result obtained by manipulating data. The total number of tickets you sold and the total sum of dollars you collected each week were the output data. Perhaps you prepared a memo for the person in charge of ticket sales, showing the output of your efforts.

The Data Processing Operations

Seven operations may occur in the processing of data. They are as follows:

- Recording— writing or printing data.
- Classifying— identifying the common characteristics of data so that they can be grouped.
- Sorting— arranging data into the desired groups.
- Computing— applying arithmetic to data.
- Summarizing— condensing data so that the main points are emphasized.
- Communicating— transmitting data from one place to another or from one person to another.
- Storing— filing data.

When you made notations about the kinds and amounts of tickets you sold, you were recording data. When you separated the student-ticket sales from the adult-ticket sales, you were sorting data. When you added the number of tickets sold and the amount of money collected, you were computing data. When you wrote down the total number of tickets sold and the total amount of money collected, you were summarizing data. When you reported this information to the person in charge of ticket sales, you were communicating data.

A data processing job does not necessarily involve all seven of the operations. For example, you did not store your information. Nor do the operations necessarily follow the same sequence. One job may require that data be recorded and stored before any other operation takes place, while another may require that data be classified and sorted immediately after they have been recorded.

METHODS OF PROCESSING DATA

Data may be processed manually, mechanically, by punched card, or electronically. The mechanical, punched card, and electronic methods are called automatic data processing (ADP) methods, because at least part of the job is done automatically.

The method used by any company to process data depends on the size of the job to be done, the speed with which results are needed, and the amount of money available to do the job.

Some data processing systems are simple.

Manual Data Processing

The processing of data by hand is called manual data processing. This is the oldest method of processing data. When you use a pencil or pen to prepare your homework, you are processing data manually. The student shown in the cartoon above is also doing manual processing.

Every data processing operation can be done by hand. Data can be manually recorded, classified, sorted, computed, summarized, communicated, and stored. Items such as paper clips, rubber bands, folders, and printed business forms make manual processing faster and easier.

Mechanical Data Processing

The processing of data by the use of office machines is called *mechanical data processing*. The typewriter is the most familiar machine used to record data. Other office machines, such as mimeograph, Multilith, and photocopy machines, reproduce data. Adding machines, calculators, cash registers, and accounting machines compute and summarize data.

Other data processing systems are complicated.

Courtesy IBM

In many situations the volume and complexity of the data are not great enough to require processing by punched-card or computer equipment. On the other hand, that data's volume and complexity may be great enough to require a method that is more economical, more accurate, and faster than manual data processing. Under such conditions, mechanical data processing would probably be used.

Punched-Card Data Processing

The system that involves putting information on cards in the form of patterns of punched holes and then processing that information by mechanical means is called *punched-card data processing.* You or members of your family may have received bills or checks in the mail which are printed on punched cards. The cards always carry the following warning: "Do not fold, spindle, or mutilate this card."

Punched-card processing is much faster and more accurate than manual or mechanical processing. However, it still involves considerable manual work. Sometimes, only one processing operation requires that the cards be

Part 43 / Systems and Uses of Data Processing / **507**

In punched-card processing, the same stack of cards may be run through several machines.

Courtesy IBM

run through the machine a number of times, and each time someone has to remove the cards from the finishing point and insert them in the machine again. In addition, most of the operations are performed on different machines, and the cards have to be taken from one machine to another.

In spite of these limitations, punched-card processing is very important in data handling. It is ideal for jobs that involve using the same data over and over, such as the job of preparing a payroll or updating an inventory list. Punched cards are also widely used to insert information into electronic computer systems.

Electronic Data Processing

As defined in Part 17, "electronic data processing" (EDP) is the processing of data by electronic equipment. The heart of an EDP system is a digital computer.

An EDP system can handle all the data processing operations and can be set up so that these operations are carried out automatically by the computer. The data are put into the computer system—for example, by punched cards prepared by human operators—and a program then takes over. In EDP a "program" is a set of instructions that outlines the work to be done by the computer step by step. A program tells the computer:

- When to start.
- Where to get data.
- What data to get.
- When to get the data.
- What to do with the data.
- When to process the data.
- What sequence of operations to follow.
- When to stop.

Once the program has been worked out and fed into the computer, jobs that might take years to do manually or with mechanical aids can be processed by the computer in minutes.

The equipment available for EDP systems makes EDP a versatile way of handling data. In addition to punched cards, there are a number of other means by which data can be put into a system: by punched paper tape, by electronic tape, by special typewriter, or by telephone signals. Data can be stored on magnetic tapes, magnetic disks, magnetic cores (tiny bits of metal strung on wires), or microfilm.

Computers are highly expensive pieces of equipment, and only large companies can afford to buy them. Even large companies often find it more practical to rent computers. Small companies can either rent computers or buy computer time, a service that is making EDP a possibility for all marketers.

USES OF DATA PROCESSING

Today, some of the most interesting uses of data processing in marketing management involve electronic computer systems. When a company decides to use EDP, it usually starts by converting the processing of one of its most basic jobs, such as determining payroll or accounts payable. Once a system has been developed to handle this job successfully, the system is enlarged to take on a more complicated job, such as handling accounts receivable. Only when the system is thoroughly established and accepted in all parts of the organization can it be used as an aid in one of the most crucial jobs of marketing management—that of merchandise management.

Payroll and Accounts Payable

"Payroll" is the money paid to employees for their work. "Accounts payable" is the money owed to other companies from which purchases have been made. Both are jobs that involve handling the same data in the same way

Courtesy American Telephone & Telegraph Co.
Magnetic tape on which data are stored can be filed so that the tapes are easily accessible when needed.

over and over. Because of their repetitive nature, both are easy to automate. Smaller companies often handle these jobs by punched-card processing; larger companies may choose them as the first jobs to be handled electronically.

Payroll. Payroll involves salaries, bonuses, commissions, the deductions (such as taxes) from these earnings, and the dates on which the net earnings are to be paid to employees. An electronic system can determine these earnings and print all the data required for each employee's payroll statement and check form.

An electronic payroll system can be set up to indicate new employees hired as well as employees who have left the company during any given period of time. This information can be classified according to job level, salary, age, and other categories that management thinks would be useful. By examining employee-turnover patterns, company management may be able to pinpoint areas within the organization where recruiting or training programs should be improved.

At one time, it was necessary for a large marketing organization to have a department whose main function was to update payroll records and prepare payroll checks manually. Today, the necessary basic information can be stored in an electronic system and updated when necessary. At specified intervals, the computer will do the necessary calculations, update its stored data, produce a tape that can be used to print checks automatically, and produce a report on whatever employee patterns management wishes to study—all on the command of the program that tells the computer exactly how to perform each required task.

Accounts Payable. A good accounts payable system assures that payments are sent out at the proper time. If a company pays its bills late, it may lose a discount granted only for prompt payment or even damage its credit rating. On the other hand, if a company pays its bills too early, it may be giving up money that could be invested profitably during that period.

Input for accounts payable comes from three major sources: purchase orders (legal contracts between the buyer and seller), receiving reports (records of the goods received), and invoices (bills for the goods being shipped). In an electronic system the information from these sources is usually punched into cards and then read into the computer. The computer is programmed to determine the amount owed to each company and the date on which the amount should be paid.

Accounts Receivable

In companies where sales volume is large, there are electronic systems to handle accounts receivable. "Accounts receivable" is the money owed to a company. Some retailers do 70 or 80 percent of their business on a credit basis and collect payment through their accounts receivable system.

Data to be handled by this system originate when someone applies for credit, makes a purchase on credit, or pays a bill. Output of data includes the billing of customers; the updating of lists used for credit authorization; and the updating of credit-sales figures by amount, department, and merchandise classification.

An accounts receivable system can be completely automatic. There are cash registers that produce the customer's receipt and a punched tape of the sales transaction. This tape can be fed into a computer, and the computer will sort and compute the data, store the data until needed, and then print out the customer's bill on the proper billing date.

Even a credit purchase can be authorized automatically. Some stores now use small authorizing machines, usually located near cash registers. When a purchase requires authorization, the salesperson simply punches the customer's credit number on the authorizing machine, which transmits the number to the computer. The computer scans a list of customers who are considered bad risks; if the present customer's number is not on the list, a green light flashes on the authorizer. That signal informs the salesperson that the purchase is authorized. This entire process takes only a few seconds and thus saves the salesperson and the customer precious time.

Data processing systems may seem very complex and mysterious, and computers may seem like individual minds. Yet these systems and their computers are simply machinery that man has set up to get his work done faster and more accurately. This speed and accuracy enables businesses to do a more effective job in marketing their products.

◻ YOUR MARKETING VOCABULARY

On a separate sheet of paper define each of the following marketing terms; then use each term in a sentence.

Data processing
Data processing cycle
Input
Input media
Manipulation
Mechanical data processing
Origination
Output
Punched-card data processing

◻ FOR REVIEW AND DISCUSSION

1. Name and explain the seven operations that may occur in processing data.
2. Do the data processing operations necessarily follow in the same sequence? Explain.
3. The method chosen by a company to process data will depend on certain factors. Name them.
4. What is the oldest method of processing data?
5. When is mechanical data processing used most often?
6. What are the advantages and limitations of punched-card processing?
7. In electronic data processing, what does the term "program" mean?
8. How does a company usually start when it decides to use EDP?
9. Name the three major sources of input for an accounts payable system.
10. Explain how an electronic accounts receivable system operates.

◻ ANALYZING MARKETING CONCEPTS

1. The data processing cycle consists of four stages that always occur in a data processing job and in the same order. Prepare a form like the one below and list the following information in the left-hand column: (a) total sales for one salesperson, (b) amount of one sales slip, (c) amount of several sales slips, (d) summarization of the sales for one department, (e) total dollar amount of inventory for the store, (f) statement from a creditor, (g) number of boxes received in one shipment.

For each item of information you listed, place a check mark in the appropriate right-hand column to indicate the stage of the data processing cycle involved.

	Stage of Data Processing Cycle			
Information	Origination	Input	Manipulation	Output
Example: Sales slip	✓			

2. Seven operations are involved in processing data, although one data processing job may not necessarily use all seven operations. On a form like the one below, list the seven data processing operations in the left-hand column: (a) recording, (b) classifying, (c) sorting, (d) computing, (e) summarizing, (f) communicating, (g) storing. In the right-hand column, describe for each operation a marketing activity which illustrates that operation.

Data Processing Operation	Marketing Activity
Example: Recording	Writing a sales slip for a suit.

▸ MARKETING PROJECT 43
Identifying Data Processing Methods

Project Goal: Given a local marketing business, identify the principal methods it uses to process data. Specify how the output is used by the owners in managing the business.

Action: With your teacher's permission, visit the data processing installations of a marketing business and identify the principal methods the business uses to process data. Find out what the data processed by each method is used for.

Prepare a form like the one below. Write the name of the business you visited at the top of the form. Then enter the information you gathered during your visit in the appropriate columns.

Data Processing Method Used by the Business	Use Made of Data Processed by This Method

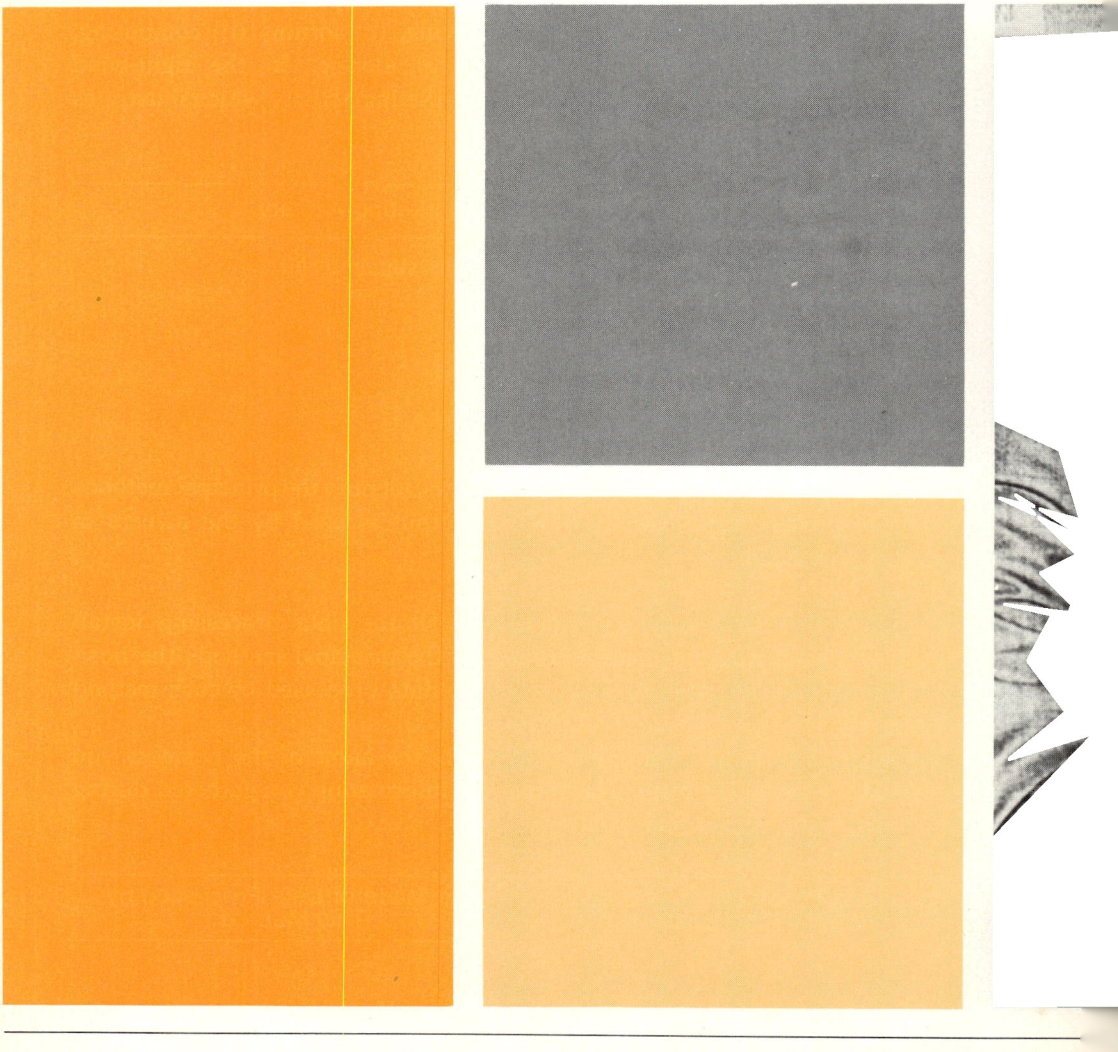

Your Career in Marketing

UNIT 12

part 44

Getting a Job

YOUR GOALS

1. Given a career field of your choice, locate several sources of information about jobs in it.
2. Given a career field of your choice, identify places where jobs are available. Then apply for one of these jobs in a real or simulated (classroom) interview, as determined by your teacher.

A job in marketing can be an exciting experience, one that can bring many lasting rewards as well as many hours of job satisfaction. Since you will spend many hours on your job, it is important that you find one that suits your interests and abilities. To do this, you cannot simply take any job. Instead, you must plan a job campaign aimed at finding the best possible job in line with your interests, experience, and capabilities. A successful job campaign consists of four steps: determining the type of job you want, exploring the opportunities, finding job sources, and applying for the job.

DETERMINING THE JOB YOU WANT

To select a job that you think is both interesting and challenging, you must first determine your interests and abilities. You can do this by answering several questions: What kinds of work do you do well? Are you good at mathematics? Do you express yourself well? Are you especially good at dealing with people? What special skills do you have? Can you drive a car? Can you operate a business machine? Are you systematic in your work habits?

What special interests do you have? Do you like swimming, baseball, or tennis? Possibly, you might be interested in the amusement business or the sporting-goods industry. Do you like to cook, give parties, or do interior decorating? If so, you may want to try the hospitality industry. Do you like to read, draw, or write? The field of advertising may appeal to you.

After you have thought about your interests and abilities, make a complete list of them. Use the following four questions as guidelines:

1. What kinds of work can I do well?
2. What special skills do I have?
3. What are my interests?
4. What is my career goal?

Your answers to these questions will help you to rate yourself more accurately. You may discover that you have interests and abilities that will open up job possibilities which you had never considered. Talk with your parents, close relatives, and friends. They may suggest possibilities to add to your list. Guidance counselors and teachers can also be helpful. They can give you useful information about your interests and abilities and provide you with sources of additional career information. Your guidance counselor is likely to have a record of tests that you have taken to help determine your strengths and capabilities.

STUDYING MARKETING CAREERS

After you have determined your interests and abilities, your next step is to learn how they can be applied to a job in marketing. This book has already introduced you to various jobs in marketing. You can learn more about these jobs by using some of the data-collecting techniques discussed in Part 21.

Start at your school. Your guidance counselor probably has information on jobs in marketing. Most counselors have copies of three valuable references: the *Dictionary of Occupational Titles*, the *Occupational Outlook Handbook*, and *The Encyclopedia of Careers and Vocational Guidance.* These books give thousands of job descriptions as well as more sources of information about your job interest.

Many libraries maintain a special reference shelf of pamphlets that describe various jobs and list sources to contact for more information. Look through the card catalog for books in your area of special interest. Also, check with the librarian, who may be able to give you information about areas of opportunity.

Courtesy DECA-Distributive Education Clubs of America
An interview with your guidance counselor will help you in launching a career.

If you know people who work in your specific area of interest, arrange to talk with them about their jobs. Find out the type of work they do, how they prepared for the field, what they like and dislike about the job, and what the long-range opportunities for the job are. If you do not know anyone who works in your specific area of interest, your marketing teacher or distributive education coordinator might be able to arrange for you to meet with such an individual.

INVESTIGATING SOURCES OF MARKETING JOBS

When you have decided on the areas of marketing you want to investigate, you will be ready to seek out the jobs available in your community.

Many schools have people who are very well informed about job opportunities in marketing. One of the best informed is the distributive education coordinator. The marketing teacher and the director of vocational education also may have suggestions on jobs in marketing. Some schools maintain job placement offices, where companies send notices about current openings. The placement office acts as the middleman between the employer and the student seeking a job. In other schools the vocational counselor or the guidance counselor can provide information on job openings.

You may also want to investigate the newspaper ads and employment agencies. Trade journals and trade associations can also be of assistance, and friends and relatives can often provide leads. Sometimes you can spot a job possibility yourself by being alert when in your local business district.

Newspaper Ads

The classified "help-wanted" ads in the newspaper are an important source of job information. Some of these ask job seekers to apply directly to the business, while others are blind ads. *Blind ads* are those that do not identify the advertiser. Instead, the applicant is asked to send a letter of application to a post-office box number.

Many ads now include the phrase "an equal opportunity employer." Since it is now illegal to practice employment discrimination based on race, creed, color, national origin, or sex, this phrase may seem meaningless. However, its use means that the employer is making a special effort to assure that no form of prejudice influences the hiring of employees.

Employment Agencies

An employment agency operated without charge to job applicants and supported by the state's taxpayers is called a *state employment service*. A state employment service provides applicants with job leads and helps arrange interviews with prospective employers. It also interviews and tests job seekers to find out what jobs they are qualified for.

A *private employment agency* is one which provides employment services for both job seekers and employers with job openings, and which charges a fee for its service. The fee may be a flat amount, such as $100, or it may be a percent of the salary to be earned by the person being placed by the agency. Some private employment agencies accept only job listings for which employers agree to pay the fee; other agencies list such jobs as well as jobs for which the employee pays the fee. Employers who agree to pay the agency fee do so to attract competent applicants.

Trade Associations

Trade associations can provide a wealth of job information for people seeking jobs in marketing. Sales and Marketing Executives International and the American Marketing Association have helped to arrange job interviews for many distributive education and college marketing students. For DECA members, local, state, and national association meetings bring marketing students in contact with business people who are in a position to offer career opportunities in marketing.

Friends and Relatives

It is a good idea to let your friends and relatives know that you are in the job market and to tell them the kind of job you are seeking. The possibility of finding the job you want increases with the number of people who know that you are job hunting. When your friends or relatives hear of a possible job, they will undoubtedly be glad to tell you about the opening.

Often there may be a job opening in the company where one of your friends works. Getting a job on the recommendation of a friend is a good career beginning. Companies are usually eager to consider job applicants recommended by their employees. In fact, some companies pay a bonus to an employee if he recommends an applicant whom the company eventually hires.

The Community

Frequent trips through the business district in your community can also help you to get your first job. Some large businesses maintain signs out front indicating the kinds of jobs available; others, usually small firms, put signs in their windows when a job opening occurs. Thus, a trip downtown on any day might reveal that the local supermarket needs a carry-out clerk, the coffee shop needs a full-time cashier, or the gasoline service station needs a part-time attendant.

APPLYING FOR THE JOB

When you have found the job opening that you are interested in, you are ready to apply for the job. Applying for a job is similar to a salesman's making a presentation, only in this case you are trying to sell your services. From the moment you first contact the employer until the time you have the actual interview, you are attempting to convince him that he should hire you. Unless you are recommended for a job by a friend, your prospective employer will know nothing about your skills, experience, or attitudes and habits. If you think you are really qualified for a job, you must be able to prove it by conducting yourself properly while applying for the job. You must present a clear and concise summary of your skills, education, and experience, and provide references with whom the employer can check regarding your character and work experience, if you have had any. Applying for a job can be divided into three steps: arranging for the job interview, preparing for the interview, and being interviewed.

Arranging for the Interview

The way in which you arrange for a job interview depends to a large extent on how you learned of the job. Suppose that you have seen the following help-wanted ad:

> **HELP WANTED**
>
> High school student for sales and cashier work in bookstore. Part time. Apply in person to Mrs. Ann Scott, Scott's Book Supplies, 1822 Chestnut, Oakdale.

Of course, in this case there would be no need to make an appointment for the interview. You would simply go to the bookstore and talk with Mrs. Scott about your qualifications for the job. In other cases, however, the applicant must telephone the prospective employer to make an appointment for an interview. This is true when a friend has recommended you for a job or when you answer a newspaper ad like the following:

> **NATIONALLY KNOWN STEEL COMPANY HAS OPENINGS FOR**
>
> Sales Trainees
> Inside Sales Personnel
> Outside Sales Personnel
>
> Good starting salary with employee benefits; opportunity for advancement.
>
> **AN EQUAL OPPORTUNITY EMPLOYER**
>
> Contact Mr. Eugene Melvin VP, Sales DI 8-2000

No company address has been given in the ad, and you therefore have no choice but to contact Mr. Melvin by phone.

Sometimes an ad will list both a telephone number and a company address. Although you know the firm's address, it is usually best to telephone for an appointment before visiting the company. Large organizations will sometimes mention in their classified ad the hours that their personnel departments are open. In such cases, it is perfectly all right to visit the personnel department without telephoning for an appointment. Personnel departments are generally prepared to give-employment tests and have-screening interviews with job applicants who come in without appointments. However, any visit after the first one is apt to be on an appointment basis, because you will then be interviewed by the department in which there is a job opening. The department must set aside a time in its workday schedule to interview you.

Sometimes an employer uses a blind newspaper ad, such as the following:

> Sales clerk wanted for large department store. Must be alert and quick with figures. Liberal employee discounts. Box X9432 Morning Clarion.

This type of ad means that the employer does not want telephone calls or personal visits from interested applicants. He therefore makes it possible for applicants to reach him only by writing a letter to the box number in care of the newspaper. From the replies that he receives, the employer will choose the applicants who appear to be most promising and contact each one to come in for an interview.

Preparing for the Interview

To prepare for an interview, you must make sure that you are properly dressed and groomed and that you have the necessary information about yourself and the business.

Dress and Grooming. Dress is a matter of individual taste, and applicants have a great deal of freedom in dressing for an interview. Choose a style of dress that would be appropriate for the job.

It is important that you abide by the accepted rules of good grooming: neat hair, clean nails, and a clean (bathed or showered) body. For girls, makeup should be moderate. Clothing should be clean and well pressed. It should also be in good condition, with buttons sewn on and snaps in place. Shoes should be polished, with heels in good condition.

Necessary Information. Having the necessary personal information available helps you and the job interviewer save time. Information that you will always

Personal appearance is important to any job applicant.

need in applying for a job are your social security number and—if you are under eighteen—a work permit. A "work permit" is written legal authorization permitting a person to work part time or full time. The interviewer will also ask you for the names of your previous employers, if any, and for references. Be sure to write out the full names and addresses in advance and to have that information with you.

If you have not submitted a personal data sheet before the interview, you should bring one with you. A *personal data sheet*, also called a "résumé," is a summary of information about you that would be of interest to a prospective employer—your experience, education, skills, and career goal. A sample personal data sheet is shown on the next page.

In preparing your personal data sheet, keep in mind that it may be the first impression you will make on a prospective employer. You therefore want it to be neat and well organized to reflect the impression you would hope to make at a personal interview. A personal data sheet must be typed and without errors. If you present your data sheet at a personal interview, you will give the interviewer a chance to get a quick picture of your background. You will also show him that you are alert and efficient enough to

<pre>
                    Eleanor R. Wells
                    1216 Pond View Road
                Durham, North Carolina 27706
                       (919) 682-4790
</pre>

PERSONAL INFORMATION

Birth Date: April 15, 19--
Social Security Number: 987-65-4321
Health: Excellent

POSITION DESIRED

Retail salesperson

EDUCATION

Graduate of Central Piedmont High School, June, 19--
Business subjects studied: Marketing, salesmanship, retailing, business law, business mathematics, typewriting

WORK EXPERIENCE

What's New Dress Shop. Salesperson-trainee during my senior year through the distributive education cooperative program.

Shopwise Supermarket. Part-time check-out clerk during my junior year.

ACTIVITIES AND INTERESTS

Member of DECA
Treasurer of Ecology Club
Hobbies: Painting, photography
Sports: Swimming, tennis

REFERENCES

Mrs. Mae Olin, Manager, What's New Dress Shop, 1450 Forbes Road, Durham, North Carolina 27706

Mr. William Dixon, Manager, Shopwise Supermarket, 429 Elm Road, Durham, North Carolina 27706

Mr. Eric Andrews, Distributive Education Teacher-Coordinator, Central Piedmont High School, Durham, North Carolina 27706

The personal data sheet introduces the applicant to the interviewer.

have gone to the trouble of preparing for the interview and that you want to proceed in a businesslike manner.

Another part of preparing for the job interview involves thinking of questions that you intend to ask the interviewer or finding out the answers ahead of time. You may want to think about questions such as the following:

1. What product or service does the company sell?
2. What and where is the market for the product or service?
3. To what type of customer does the product or service appeal?
4. How large is the company?
5. Is the company growing?
6. Does the company have a training program?
7. What are the company's relations with its employees?

With answers to such questions, you will have a basis to decide whether the company is for you.

Attending the Interview

You will find that you can face the job interview with confidence if you know that you have properly arranged for it, that you are appropriately dressed and groomed, and that you have the necessary information.

If you have an appointment for an interview, you should arrive early. You may first be asked to fill out a job application. A *job application* is a printed form on which the job applicant records information about his personal history, job experience, education, and references. Fill out this form neatly and completely because its appearance and accuracy will reflect much about your work habits and attitudes. Much of the information that you fill in on the job application form will be the same as that included on your personal data sheet. Although this may seem repetitious, the two documents serve different purposes. The personal data sheet is your written introduction to your prospective employer. The job application is the employer's method of recording information on all prospective employees.

The actual interview should run smoothly if you have prepared for it carefully. Try to avoid being nervous during the interview. The interviewer is likely to give you every opportunity to prove that you are qualified to fill the job opening.

Let the interviewer begin the conversation. Be pleasant and friendly but businesslike. Try to give answers that are complete without being long-winded and complicated. The interviewer will be trying to find out what your qualifications for the job are, and he will ask you to expand on the information you have related on your personal data sheet and application form. He will also be interested in your manner of speaking and responding to questions because this is often an indication of one's general self-confidence and personality.

Before a hiring decision can be reached, you may be asked to take some tests. Many businesses require tests as a condition of employment. Usually, these tests try to measure intelligence or aptitudes. Follow the test directions closely and work as efficiently as you can.

Recognize when the interview is over. The interviewer may say something like, "We will be getting in touch with you soon." Thank him for his time, and if you have not been offered the job, ask when you might call to learn his decision. Leave promptly.

Getting a job is not always easy, and hunting for a job can be frightening. But remember that millions of people have had to go through similar procedures. If you do not get the job, do not be discouraged. Review the interview in your mind to see where you can do a better job next time. Each job interview gives you an opportunity to improve your self-confidence and poise.

◇ YOUR MARKETING VOCABULARY

On a separate sheet of paper define each of the following marketing terms; then use each term in a sentence.

Blind ads
Job application
Personal data sheet
Private employment agency
State employment service

◇ FOR REVIEW AND DISCUSSION

1. Through what sources can you learn about the opportunities available in marketing?
2. Give the names of three books that contain job descriptions.
3. What sources are available to help you find a job?
4. What is meant by the term "an equal opportunity employer"?
5. What services do state employment services offer?
6. How do private employment agencies operate?
7. What are the three steps involved in applying for a job?
8. What personal information does a prospective employer expect from an applicant?
9. What will the interviewer mainly be trying to find out during your job interview?
10. What important points should you remember when attending the personal interview? What document should you bring with you?

ANALYZING MARKETING CONCEPTS

1. To help determine the type of marketing job that is best for you, prepare an extensive list of your interests and abilities on a form like the one below. You can do this by thinking about what you have done, the courses you have taken, the type of work you can do, and your specific skills, habits, and special interests. Interests and abilities do not have to be related to each other. The ideas discussed in this part will be helpful in developing your personal list.

Interest	Ability
Example: I enjoy being with my friends.	I express myself well and listen to others.

2. Seeking a marketing job involves investigation of many sources. On a form like the one below, list the following sources in the left-hand column: (a) classified ads, (b) schoolteachers, (c) school counselors, (d) state employment service, (e) private employment agencies, (f) the business community, (g) trade associations, (h) former employers, (i) friends and relatives, (j) school placement bureau. In the right-hand column, describe the type of information and assistance you would expect from each source.

Source	Information and Help Provided
Example: Help-wanted ads	Listings of job openings and information on where to apply.

MARKETING PROJECT 44
Applying for a Job

Project Goal: Given a career field of your choice, identify places where jobs are available. Then apply for one of these jobs in a real or simulated (classroom) interview, as determined by your teacher.

Action: Locate four possible job openings for which you believe you are qualified. For help in locating sources of information on job openings, you may refer back to pages 518-520. Prepare a form similar to the one below. In the left-hand column, write the name of each source through which you located a suitable job opening. In the center column, write the name and address of each prospective employer. State the job title and the special requirements or skills needed for each of the four job openings in the right-hand column.

Obtain a job application from your prospective employer or your teacher. Complete it and proceed through a real job interview or a simulated one in your classroom.

Source	Name and Address of Prospective Employer	Job Title and Special Requirements or Skills
Example: Classified ad	Treasure-Value Supermart, 10 Coster Avenue, Fairview, New Jersey	Cashier; must be adept at handling money and totaling customer purchases on cash register.

part 45

Working at Your Job

YOUR GOALS

1. Given a marketing business, obtain its handbook for new employees. Use the handbook to prepare an outline that includes information on salary and fringe benefits and on what is expected of employees.
2. Given a list of jobs in your career field, determine to what degree the five job competencies are required to perform each job.

Your job will involve a great part of your time. You will come to know your business surroundings better than any place except your home. You will probably see your fellow employees more often than you will see your personal friends. Your job will be more than a way of making a living—it will be a major factor in your life-style.

When you are offered a job and accept it, you will essentially be making an agreement with your employer. Both of you will agree to take on certain responsibilities with respect to each other. Your employer's responsibilities to you and your responsibilities to your employer are discussed in the following paragraphs.

YOUR PAY AND BENEFITS

The first responsibility of your employer will be to pay you a salary based on your duties and responsibilities. You will also be entitled to a number of fringe benefits, which are advantages that a company offers its employees in addition to a regular salary. Fringe benefits form part of the pay in every job. A few examples are life insurance and retirement plans, savings plans, and free medical service. Other fringe benefits are opportunities to increase the skills and abilities you need to perform your job. By taking advantage of these opportunities, you may also increase your chances for advancement.

Almost all large companies and many smaller ones publish a company brochure or handbook giving details about all employee fringe benefits. If your new employer has such a handbook, study it carefully. It will tell you just what you can expect from your employer and just what your employer expects from you.

Deductions From Your Paycheck

Your paycheck statement will probably show the full amount of salary agreed upon as well as the amount you receive after deductions. Deductions are withheld for income tax payments, social security payments, and, in many states, unemployment and disability insurance payments. By law, an employer is required to withhold these amounts and pay them to the proper authority. In the case of social security and some state insurance plans, the employer is also required to contribute toward each employee's account.

Insurance and Retirement Plans

Anyone who thinks ahead realizes that he is working to pay today's expenses and to save for tomorrow's needs. The assurance that one can meet current expenses and still provide for future needs is called *economic security*. The government makes certain that every worker has some economic security by requiring him to make regular social security contributions. To aid employees in increasing their economic security, many business organizations offer insurance plans and retirement plans.

Health and life insurance plans are available through almost all companies, and employees are encouraged to participate in them. These plans usually cost less than they would outside the company, because a business organization is able to get group rates for its employees. Group rates are lower in cost than individual rates. Some companies share the cost of such insurance, and some now shoulder all the costs themselves. A number of companies give each employee a free life insurance policy, the amount of which is based on his annual salary.

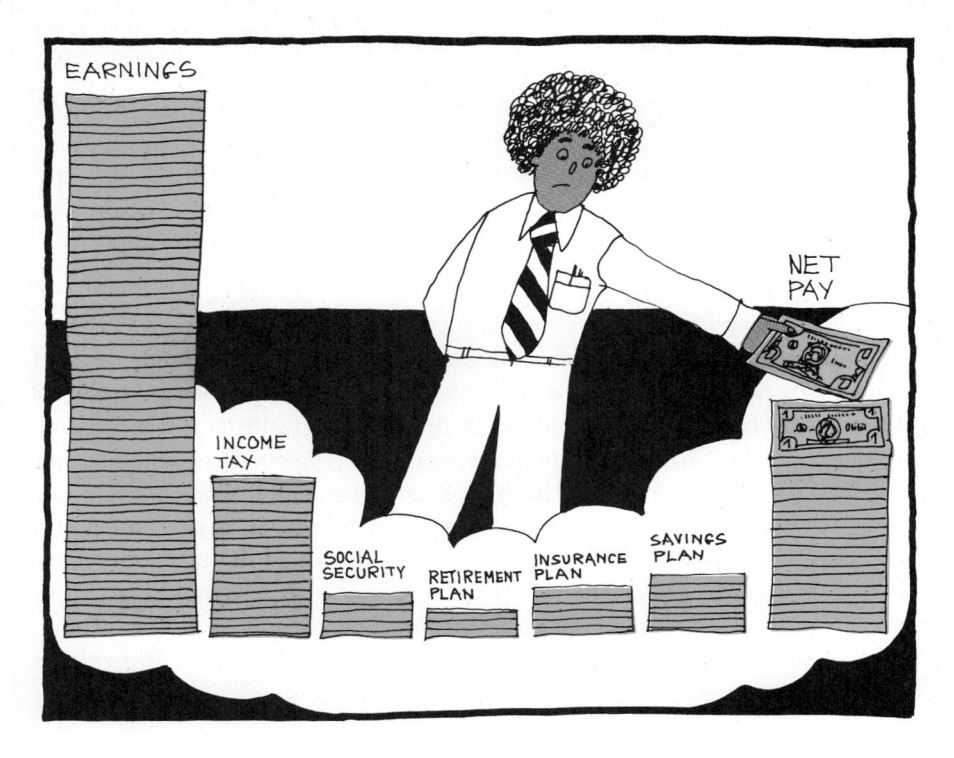

Deductions for taxes and economic security will make a difference between your earnings and your net pay.

Nearly every company offers one or more retirement plans. The most common plan is one that agrees to pay a retiring employee a specific amount regularly, based on his length of service with the company and his average salary during that period of service. Another type of retirement plan is the contributory plan, which provides a larger retirement income. Through the contributory plan, an employee contributes a certain percent of his regular salary to the retirement plan and the employer also makes a predetermined contribution.

Savings Plans

Two important services that many companies offer their employees are a payroll savings plan and an employee discount. A *payroll savings plan* is a plan in which an employee authorizes the company to withhold a specific amount from each paycheck and to put that amount in his savings account or use it to purchase bonds or shares of the company's stock. Some companies have credit unions through which employees can save money at good interest rates or take loans at lower interest rates than those available at banks or finance companies.

An *employee discount* is a reduction in the purchase price of any company product that the employee wishes to buy. Employees in department stores, for example, can buy almost any product in the store at a discount price.

Medical Service

In addition to health insurance plans, many companies offer employees the services of a doctor or medical department. The most important purpose for having such services is to provide immediate medical aid in the case of an emergency on the job. A small company, with few employees, is likely to have an arrangement with a nearby doctor. A large company may have its own medical department. Because it has many employees, a large company is likely to have a good number of medical problems. In addition to emergency diagnosis and treatment, the medical department of a large company may give physical checkups to employees on a regular basis. Employees may also go there to obtain medicine for minor ills. A good medical department increases both company productivity and employee morale.

Opportunities for Advancement and Training

Most companies have a schedule for evaluating the performance of an employee. Every six months or every year, depending on company policy, his record is checked to see whether he should receive an increase in job responsibility or an increase in salary. Businesses recognize that the cost of living goes up, and most businesses try to keep their salaries in line with those costs. In addition, an employee's value to a company usually increases as his length of service with the company increases.

To help employees improve their job performance, some companies offer training courses without charge and on company time. Employees may also take courses offered by outside organizations and schools. If such courses are job-related in that they provide a person with knowledge and skills that will enable him to perform his job more efficiently, a company will often pay part or all of the tuition.

YOUR JOB RESPONSIBILITIES

Your primary responsibility on the job will be to perform the duties required of you to the best of your ability. Taking a job means that you agree to work. It also means that you should be at your work station on time and ready to

Courtesy National Petroleum News

Training courses generally help the employee to perform his job more effectively.

start work immediately. It means that you should stay for the full amount of time you have agreed to work. It means that you should concentrate on the job you are doing. It is up to you to honor your agreement. In doing so, you will not only satisfy your obligation but will find that the day is a more interesting one.

When you begin a job, listen carefully to all instructions given you, ask questions when you do not understand, and try to put everything you have learned into the work. Once you have learned how to handle the immediate job, do not be afraid to learn more and more about it and what surrounds it. Try to learn how your particular job fits into the work of the company. The more you learn, the more valuable you will be to your employer and the higher your paycheck will be—and the more satisfaction you will get from your job.

The man who pumps gasoline in a service station can learn what the differences are in grades of gasoline, which cars use which grades, where the gasoline comes from, what affects its price, what kind of extra service customers want, how often certain types of cars need oil or battery checks, and where customers go for repairs. Knowing the answers to these questions and others can mean the difference between continuing to pump gas or being considered by the oil company for your own station.

Part 45 / **Working at Your Job** / **533**

COMPETENCY ON THE JOB

Success in marketing requires knowledge, skills, and the right personal attitudes. When considered in terms of achieving success on the job, these are called "job competencies." A competency is an ability to perform a task well. Five kinds of competencies are needed to succeed in a marketing job. They are (1) social competency, (2) marketing competency, (3) technological competency, (4) basic skills competency, and (5) economic competency. The degree of skill a person must develop in each area depends on his interests and abilities and on the requirements of his job.

The competency that most people develop first is *social competency*, which is the ability of a person to create a favorable impression and to work well with others. A person uses social competency when he applies for a job, when he deals with customers, and when he works with fellow employees. How do you develop social competency? Along with maintaining a good personal appearance, you must build the right attitude by completing your work correctly and on time and by learning to respect the rights of your fellow workers and your supervisors.

A person in any occupation must have a knowledge of that occupation. A general understanding of marketing practices and processes is called *marketing competency*. A person employed in marketing must understand what marketing is, what activities compose marketing, and how these activities are performed. His knowledge of marketing will continue to grow as he gains experience on the job.

Every person employed in marketing deals with a particular product, product line, service, or specialized selling method. And he must know his product or service well. A car salesman must have detailed information about the automobiles he sells. A restaurant franchisee must have a broad knowledge of the particular type of service he offers. This specialization in the marketing of a product or service is called *technological competency*.

The ability to communicate, or to give and receive information, is called *basic skills competency*. The tools of communication are language and mathematics. Through the use of words and numbers, sales transactions are made, advertising is presented, stock controls are maintained, orders are taken, sales adjustments are made, and credit is made available. As you progress on the job, your skills in these areas will improve.

An understanding of the purpose and goals of businesses in the United States and of the modified free-enterprise system under which they operate is called *economic competency*. The purpose and goals of businesses in the United States has been discussed throughout this book. Mainly, businesses operate to make a profit by producing or distributing products and services

Courtesy DECA-Distributive Education Clubs of America
Which competencies is this girl likely to be using in the performance of her job?

that consumers need or want. You have acquired an economic competency when you understand that as an employee, you are part of the team that will enable the company to make a profit. Moreover, it is important for you to remember that your job exists to serve society and to help your firm earn the profit it needs to keep serving. How successful a company is in terms of profits and serving its customers depends on how efficiently each person in the company does his job.

The importance of knowing a job well and how to perform it effectively cannot be overemphasized, for the best jobs go to those who have the necessary competencies.

UNIONS AND PROFESSIONAL ORGANIZATIONS

As a person employed in marketing, you may be asked to join a union or a professional organization. Membership in unions and professional organizations is usually helpful.

Unions were formed to give workers a way to bargain collectively with

Courtesy Today's Secretary

Happiness in your job will be an important asset to your way of life. Good luck!

employers. "Collective bargaining," in which a union spokesman speaks for all of the members of his union, gives workers much more strength than if each individual worker were to do his own bargaining. As long as unions and management can work together well, both find collective bargaining convenient.

The largest unions for marketing employees are part of the American Federation of Labor–Congress of Industrial Organizations (AFL-CIO). Among these unions are the Retail Clerks International Association (RCIA), with a half million members; the Hotel and Restaurant Employees and Bartenders International Union, with 450,000 members; the Building Service Employees'

International Union, with about 350,000 members; and the Retail, Wholesale, and Department Store Union (RWDSU), with about 200,000 members.

As you continue in your career, you may become eligible to belong to one of the professional groups for people in marketing. One of these is the Sales and Marketing Executives International (SMEI), an organization for marketing executives, salesmen, and sales managers. Another is the American Marketing Association (AMA), an organization made up of businessmen and educators who want to keep up to date on new marketing concepts.

You may be able to join a professional marketing organization while you are still in school. The AMA has chapters for college students. The SMEI often holds special meetings for students, and local advertising clubs may admit student members. Local chapters of DECA are part of many high school, post-high school, and college distributive education programs. These local chapters provide members with an opportunity to learn about careers in marketing and to practice marketing skills.

SUCCESS ON THE JOB

You will be a valuable employee to your company if you are able to perform your job efficiently and if you are willing to work. Having the right attitude, proper work habits, and an eagerness to learn will help bring you advancement and the substantial earnings that accompany success. But it all depends on you.

Best wishes for a satisfying career in the dynamic field of marketing!

◻ YOUR MARKETING VOCABULARY

On a separate sheet of paper define each of the following marketing terms; then use each term in a sentence.

Basic skills competency
Economic competency
Economic security
Employee discount
Marketing competency
Payroll savings plan
Social competency
Technological competency

◻ FOR REVIEW AND DISCUSSION

1. What are fringe benefits?
2. What deductions is an employer required by law to withhold from your pay?
3. Name two fringe benefits that increase economic security.
4. Discuss briefly health insurance plans that a company may offer.
5. What services may be offered to employees by the medical department in a large company?

6. What are the opportunities for advancement offered by most companies?
7. Name three situations in which social competency is used.
8. Explain the importance of technological competency.
9. Name the four largest unions and two professional organizations for people in marketing.
10. List five qualities that will help bring you success on the job.

◊ ANALYZING MARKETING CONCEPTS

1. When you are offered a job and accept it, you are essentially making an agreement with your employer. Each of you will agree to take on certain responsibilities with respect to the other. Prepare a form like the one below. In the left-hand column, list five of your employer's responsibilities. In the right-hand column, list five of your responsibilities.

Employer's Responsibilities	Your Responsibilities
Example: A fair and competitive salary	To perform the duties of the job to the best of my ability.

2. A competency is an ability to perform a task well. Prepare a form like the one below. In the left-hand column, list the following characteristics of competencies: (a) knowledge of occupation, (b) specialization in a product, (c) good personal attitude, (d) ability to give and receive information, (e) respect for the rights of fellow workers, (f) understanding of the purpose and goals of business.

   Place a check mark in the appropriate right-hand column to indicate the competency to which each characteristic applies.

Characteristic of Competency	Competency				
	Social	Marketing	Technological	Basic Skills	Economic
Example: Proper personal appearance	✓				

◊ MARKETING PROJECT 45
Determining Job Competencies

Project Goal: Given a list of jobs in your career field, determine to what degree the five job competencies are required to perform each job.

Action: Prepare a form like the one below. From the *Dictionary of Occupational Titles* or *The Encyclopedia of Careers and Vocational Guidance,* select five job titles in your career field. In the left-hand column of your form, list the job titles you have selected. Read the description of each job in the dictionary or encyclopedia. Using that information, determine the competencies required to perform each job. Identify those competencies by placing check marks in the appropriate columns.

	Required Competencies				
Job Title	Social	Marketing	Technological	Basic Skills	Economic
Example: Window-display decorator		✔	✔		

Glossary

Accessory equipment Equipment that is needed to operate a business but is not used in manufacturing a product or providing a service.

Accounts receivable Money owed to a business by its customers.

Advertising A nonpersonal sales message which is paid for by an identified company.

Advertising manager The person responsible for creating advertising and sales promotion programs and for developing materials necessary for these programs.

Advertising media Channels of communication used by advertisers to send their messages to potential customers.

Advertising research A study conducted to determine the effectiveness of a company's advertising.

Aerosol dispenser The form of packaging which is a can that releases its contents in spray or foam when a valve is pressed.

Agent middlemen Middlemen who perform buying and selling services for manufacturers or other middlemen.

Approach The process by which the salesman tries to gain the favorable attention of the prospect.

Automatic vending The marketing of goods through the use of a machine operated by the customer.

Balance of trade The difference in value between the goods a nation exports and the goods it imports.

Balance sheet Shows the financial position of a company at a particular time.

Basic skills competency The ability to communicate, or to give and receive information.

Blind ads Job advertisements that do not identify the advertiser and ask the applicant to send a letter of application to a post-office box.

Blister packaging The form of packaging in which a plastic bubble is placed over a product mounted on a card.

Bonded warehouse A particular type of warehouse used to store products requiring a federal tax.

Bonding A method of insuring whereby the employer buys insurance on his employees to protect himself against possible thefts by them.

Brand A name symbol, design, or any combination of these that identifies the goods or services of a seller and sets them apart from those of his competitors.

Brand mark The distinctive symbol that is used along with a brand name on a product.

Brand name That part of a brand that can be spoken.

Break-even point The point at which the money from the sales of a product equals the total costs involved to produce and market it.

Broker An agent wholesaler who represents either buyers or sellers in arranging purchases by business firms or sales by producers.

Bulk breaking The process of dividing large quantities into smaller quantities for the purpose of selling in small units.

Business-interruption insurance Insurance that covers losses due to a temporary halt in business operations.

Buyers Individuals who purchase goods for resale in retail stores.

Buying behavior The way a person acts and reacts in the marketplace.

Buying motive An urge that prompts a person to buy something.

Capital Money and other assets owned by a business organization.

Carload lot A shipment that completely fills a freight car.

Carrier A company that transports goods between the producer and the consumer or industrial user.

Cash discount A percent of the bill that the credit customer may deduct if he pays promptly.

Channel of distribution The transfer of ownership or control of the goods as they pass from the manufacturer to the final user.

Classified advertisements Advertisements that are grouped in special pages of newspapers or magazines by the product or service advertised and generally only contain copy.

Clients The companies that use advertising agencies.

Close The completion of the sale.

Closed displays Displays in which merchandise is housed inside a display case.

Cognitive activities The mental processes of perceiving, remembering, thinking, and judging involved in making a buying decision.

Collateral The assets that the borrower pledges to the bank as security.

Commodity exchange A center where buyers and sellers of agricultural goods transact business.

Common carrier A transportation company that provides equipment and services to any shipper for a fee and takes full responsibility for the safe arrival of the goods.

Community relations The activities a company engages in to gain the respect of the community.

Competition The struggle of each business to obtain a share of the market.

Consumer Anyone who uses products or services.

Consumer advisory boards Panels of consumers who determine what customers want and do not want in the way of merchandise and services.

Glossary / 541

Consumer farm products Products that reach the consumer without undergoing major changes in form.

Consumer goods Products intended to satisfy the needs and wants of the individual consumer.

Consumer market All the potential customers for goods and services sold for personal use.

Containerization The transportation of goods in specially built shipping containers.

Contract carrier A transportation company that owns transportation equipment and rents it to other companies for special lengths of time.

Convenience goods Goods that the customer buys often and without shopping around for the best buy.

Cooperative A business that is owned and operated by its customers.

Copy The message that appears in an ad.

Corporate chain A number of similar stores owned and managed by a central corporate organization.

Corporation A business organization that has many owners, called stockholders, and operates under a charter granted by a state or the federal government.

Cost-profit squeeze A condition in which costs rise more rapidly than sales and thereby decrease profits.

Creative Marketing Projects Activities conducted by a local group or chapter of DECA members in cooperation with Sales and Marketing Executives International (SMEI), an organization of sales executives.

Credit The power to obtain goods or services (or money) in exchange for a promise to pay later.

Credit bureau An organization that specializes in collecting and interpreting credit information.

Credit card A card that entitles the holder to enjoy credit privileges with a variety of businesses.

Credit insurance Insurance that protects against loss of business earnings.

Credit period The length of time for which mercantile credit is extended.

Crops Products obtained from the soil.

Cue A stimulus that, in certain situations, leads the individual to respond to a need.

Current liabilities Debts owed by a business and due within a limited period of time, such as a year.

Customer Anyone who buys products or services.

Customer services Extra aids, conveniences, or facilities offered to the customer to make him more willing to buy.

Cycle billing A system which spreads the preparation of customers' bills throughout the month, so that the billing department always has an even flow of work.

Data processing The handling of information to obtain significant results.

Data processing cycle The four stages of processing data—origination, input, manipulation, output.

Demand The amount of a product that consumers are willing to purchase at different prices.

Department store A large retail establishment that is organized into individual departments according to the type of merchandise sold.

Derived demand The demand for industrial goods which depends on the demand for consumer goods produced by using the industrial goods.

Direct channel of distribution The channel of distribution used when a manufacturer markets his goods direct to the final user.

Direct mail advertising A form of advertising that is sent to prospective buyers by mail.

Discount store A retail store that makes a policy of selling merchandise at reduced prices.

Discretionary income The money a person has left to spend after he has paid for the basic living costs.

Dispensing closure A cap, lid, or seal through which the contents of the container can be dispensed.

Display advertisements Advertisements that appear throughout a newspaper and use pictures, art, or different styles of type, or print.

Disposable income The amount of money that a person has for spending and saving.

Distribution The total process of moving, handling, and storing goods on the way from the producer to the consumer.

Distribution center The link between the supplier and the customer; the place where products are received, stored, and processed, and from which products are shipped.

Distributor An independent middleman who stocks the industrial products of various manufacturers and sells them to industrial users.

Domestic goods Products produced within the country in which they are sold.

Drop shipper A wholesaler who takes orders from retailers and arranges for delivery of goods directly from the producer.

Economic competency An understanding of the purpose and goals of businesses in the United States and of the modified free-enterprise system under which they operate.

Economic goods Goods that have utility and require human effort to bring them to market and are said to have economic value.

Economic risks Risks caused by changes in the market; sometimes called "market risks."

Economic security The assurance that one can meet current expenses and still provide for future needs.

Electronic data processing (EDP) The handling of information by electronic machines.

Employee discount A reduction in the purchase price of any company product that the employee buys.

Ethnic group All the people who have certain characteristics in common, such as language, social customs, or physical traits.

Exclusive distribution The form of distribution in which a manufacturer selects only one middleman within an area to handle his product.

Expenditure patterns The different ways in which groups of people spend their money.

Experimentation A form of research involving a scale model or representation of a real marketing situation.

Exporting Marketing the products of one's own country in other countries.

External data Data collected from sources outside the company.

Fabricating materials Goods that have already been changed from their natural state or form.

Family brand A brand name used for all products of a company.

Farm bloc A group of legislators who frequently vote the same way on agricultural issues.

Farm cooperative An association of farmers organized to process and market their products.

Fashion The style preferred by the majority at any given time.

Fighting brand A low-priced brand used to compete aggressively with other companies that use low-price strategies.

Financial management The process of planning and measuring the flow of money.

Financing The borrowing of capital to operate a business.

Flexible pouch A package formed from plastic film or paper that is filled with the product and sealed by a heat process.

Form utility The increased usefulness of a product to a consumer because of a change in the basic material of the product.

Formal opening Usually a brief but impressive public ceremony to open the business officially.

Formal research The process of collecting and analyzing information about a problem.

Franchise chain A group of independently owned stores which are run under an agreement with a sponsoring manufacturer.

Freight forwarders Independent companies that collect the small shipments of various businesses, combine them into truckload or carload lots, and ship them.

Grades The letters, numbers, or words used to indicate that a product has met certain standards.

Gross national product The total value of the production of goods and services over a specified period; often referred to as "GNP."

Gross profit on sales Arrived at by subtracting the cost of goods sold from the net sales; often called the "gross margin."

General-merchandise store A retail establishment that offers a large variety of goods for sale.

General-merchandise warehouse A warehouse that stores any kind of product that needs only protection from the weather.

Grading The act of sorting goods into established categories.

Guarantee An assurance of the specific quality and performance of a product, or a promise to maintain a certain price level for a specific period of time.

Horizontal expansion The process by which a retailer increases the number of his retail units.

Human risks Those risks which are caused primarily by human frailty and unpredictability.

Importing Buying the products of other countries for resale.

Impulse buying Buying with little or no advance planning.

Impulse goods Items that a customer wants when he sees them although he had not set out to buy them.

Income The money received or earned that a person has to spend.

Income statement A summary of the revenue and expenses of a company over a period of time.

Independent stores Stores operated and managed by the owner.

Indirect channel of distribution The channel of distribution used when the manufacturer does not deal directly with the final user of his product but uses a middleman.

Industrial distributor A wholesaler who sells equipment, accessories, standard parts, and supplies to industrial and business firms.

Industrial farm products Products that reach the consumer after having undergone a major change in form during a manufacturing process.

Industrial goods Products intended to satisfy the needs and wants of businesses.

Industrial market All the potential customers for industrial products.

Industrial salesmen Individuals who specialize in selling products or services to industry.

Industrial services Services intended to satisfy the needs and wants of businesses.

Input The stage in the data processing cycle during which data are placed into the processing system.

Input media The form in which data are prepared for entry into the processing system.

Installation The process of setting up a product in position for use and making necessary mechanical, electrical, or drainage connections.

Installations Machines used to process raw materials or manufacture products from fabricating materials, and equipment used to conduct a service business.

Institutional advertising The type of advertising that builds an image for the business organization without mentioning a specific product.

In-store salesmen Individuals who engage in selling inside a store.

Insurance Protection against losses resulting from property damage, theft, accidents, sickness, and even death.

Integrated distribution The form of distribution in which the manufacturer handles the functions of retailer or wholesaler.

Intensive distribution The form of distribution in which a manufacturer distributes his product to any middleman who agrees to stock and sell it.

Internal data Data collected from sources within the company itself.

International marketing The buying and selling of goods among companies in different countries.

Job application A printed form on which the job applicant records information about his personal history, job experience, education, and references.

Label An informative tag, wrapper, or seal attached to the product or the product's package.

Leased dealership A business that is owned by one company but is leased to another to operate.

Less-than-carload lot A shipment that does not fill a freight car.

Liabilities The amounts owed by a company.

Liability insurance Protection against losses due to claims by customers or employees for personal injuries they received on the company premises.

Limited-line store A retail establishment that sells only one kind of merchandise or several closely related lines of merchandise.

Livestock products Items obtained from animals.

Local chain A corporate chain that has outlets within a very small area, usually a city.

Mailing list A list of the names and addresses of potential buyers for the goods or services of a firm.

Manipulation The stage of the data processing cycle during which the actual processing takes place.

Manufacturer-owned stores Stores that are owned by the manufacturer of a particular product.

Manufacturer's agent An independent salesman who handles part of the output of one or more manufacturers within a particular territory.

Manufacturers' salesmen The salesmen who represent the manufacturers in selling to customers.

Marine insurance Protection against damage or loss of goods while they are being transported. The term applies to all forms of transportation.

Market All the potential customers for a product or service, or group of products or services.

Market position A company's competitive standing based on its sales volume compared with that of the other companies in the same industry.

Market research The study of the nature and characteristics of a market.

Market segmentation The division of a total market into groups according to customer characteristics.

Marketing The sum total of the planning, pricing, promotion, and distribution activities that take place in order to get goods or services from the producer to the consumer.

Marketing competency A general understanding of marketing practices and processes.

Marketing concept The viewpoint that the purpose of business is to fulfill the needs of consumers.

Marketing manager The person responsible for the entire marketing organization of the company.

Marketing plan A set of marketing guidelines prepared by the management of a business firm.

Marketing research Defined by the American Marketing Association as "the gathering, recording, and analyzing of all facts about problems relating to the transfer and sale of goods and services from the producer to the consumer."

Marketing research manager The person responsible for studying the markets for the company's products.

Marketing services manager The person responsible for the various services necessary in filling customers' orders.

Materials handling The process of assembling, packing, weighing, and moving products from a producer to a warehouse, from a warehouse to a carrier, or from carrier to carrier.

Mechanical data processing The processing of data by the use of office machines.

Mercantile credit Credit used by a manufacturer to buy his raw materials and operating supplies.

Merchandise manual A notebook of facts about a product, prepared by the manufacturer for his salesmen and customers.

Merchant middlemen Middlemen who assume ownership of goods.

Middlemen Business organizations that perform buying and selling services which aid the flow of goods from the producer to the consumer.

Model displays Displays used to show merchandise as it would look in actual use with related items.

Modified free enterprise An economic system in which the people make most of the decisions, but some decisions are controlled or modified by the government.

Monopoly The control by one company of the supply of one kind of economic goods.

Motivation research A form of market research that studies factors influencing buying behavior.

Multipack A special package design that groups two or more packaged products into a unit.

National advertiser A manufacturer of consumer goods who advertises his product by its brand name.

National brand The branded product of a manufacturer; also referred to as name brand, brand-name product, producer's brand, and manufacturer's brand.

National chain A corporate chain that has outlets in every state.

National income The money measurement of the annual flow of goods and services in a nation.

Natural risks Risks caused by natural phenomena.

Net income The amount that a company earned during the period of time covered by an income statement; also called "net profit."

Observation The process of collecting information about customers, product acceptance, and sales effectiveness by watching the actions of people without interviewing them.

Obsolescence The process in which a product deteriorates or becomes old and nonfunctional.

Open displays Displays in which the merchandise shown is not enclosed in a display case.

Operating ratio A percentage relationship between the dollar amount of net sales and some other dollar amount such as net income or gross profit on sales.

Operating supplies Low-cost items necessary to business operations.

Origination The stage in the data processing cycle during which data are received or generated.

Outdoor advertising A form of modern traffic media that includes signs and posters displayed on billboards, building walls, and other rented outdoor spaces.

Output The result obtained by manipulating data, the final stage in the data processing cycle.

Owner's equity The financial interest that an owner has in a business.

Packaging Use of containers and wrapping materials to protect, contain, identify, promote, and facilitate the use of the product.

Panel A group of people selected as subjects of a continuing survey.

Partnership A business owned by two or more people.

Patronage motives The sum of all the reasons why a person decides to buy from a certain retailer.

Payroll savings plan A plan in which an employee authorizes the company to withhold a specific amount from each paycheck and to put that amount in his savings account or use it to purchase bonds or shares of the company's stock.

Personal care services Those services that help a person to be well groomed.

Personal data sheet A summary of information about you that would be of interest to a prospective employer; also called a "résumé."

Personal income The amount of money that a person earns or receives before any taxes are deducted.

Personal selling The direct effort made by a salesperson to convince a customer to make a purchase.

Physical distribution The total process of moving, handling, and storing goods on the way from the producer to the final user.

Place utility The increased usefulness of goods that results because they have been located where it is convenient to buy them.

Planned economy An economic system in which the government makes all the decisions; also called a "controlled economy."

Point-of-purchase advertising The use of advertising or display material in and around a retail store.

Possession utility The increased usefulness of goods to a customer that results from helping him to obtain them.

Posttesting The process of measuring the actual effectiveness of advertising after it has appeared.

Preapproach The part of the selling process that consists of gathering information about the prospect and preparing the sales presentation.

Preliminary research The process of identifying a problem and devising a plan for solving the problem.

Premium Something given free with the purchase of a product.

Pretesting The process of measuring the probable effectiveness of advertising before it appears.

Price The amount of money a customer needs at a particular time to acquire a product or service.

Price-oriented promotion Promotion that offers a special price reduction to the buyer.

Primary data Data gathered by the researcher for current use.

Private brand A product that carries the label of the middleman (wholesaler or retailer) who sells it.

Private carrier A transportation facility owned and used by a firm to transport its products.

Private employment agency An employment agency which provides, for a fee, employment services for both job seekers and employers.

Private warehouse A storage and handling facility owned by the company that uses it.

Product All the physical features and psychological satisfactions received by the customer.

Product advertising The type of advertising that stresses specific products or services.

Product item A specific product.

Product life cycle The period from the introduction of a product to the market until it is withdrawn.

Product line A group of similar types of product items that are closely related because they satisfy a class of customer needs, are used together, or are sold to the same customer groups.

Product manager The person responsible for the sales and profits of the product assigned to him.

Product mix The total of all product items and product lines offered for sale by a company.

Product planning The direction and control of all stages in the life of a product—from the time of its creation to the time of its removal from the company's line of products.

Product research The study of consumer reactions to a product.

Product sample A small sample of an advertiser's product that is given away free.

Production The process of creating or improving goods or services.

Profit The amount left from sales income after deducting all expenses.

Promotion Those activities that are designed to bring a company's goods or services to the favorable attention of potential customers.

Promotional mix The combination of different forms of promotion.

Property insurance Insurance against loss or damage of property.

Prototype A model of the new product, the first form of the product that the company makes.

Public relations The total process of building goodwill toward a business organization.

Public utility A business organization performing a public service and subject to government regulation.

Public warehouse An independent business that provides the service of storing and handling goods for other businesses.

Publicity Unpaid advertising for a company or its products.

Punched-card data processing The system that involves putting information on cards in the form of patterns of punched holes and then processing that information by mechanical means.

Purchasing agents Individuals who buy for business use; sometimes called "industrial buyers."

Rack jobber A service wholesaler who sells specialized lines of merchandise to certain types of stores.

Raw materials Goods that are more or less in their original form.

Reinforcement An action that tends to confirm a previous response and lead the customer to make the same response again.

Regional chain A corporate chain that has outlets in a geographic area covering a few states.

Research findings The results of research.

Research plan A step-by-step outline of everything that is to be done during a research project.

Research report A document that contains the results of research and is the basis for action.

Response An action that the person takes after being exposed to cues.

Retail advertiser A store or service organization whose advertising message encourages consumers to shop at its place of business.

Route salesmen Individuals who travel a regular route; sometimes called "driver salesmen."

Sales manager The person responsible for hiring, training, and supervising activities of the salesmen.

Sales presentation The part of the selling process in which the salesman explains his product and attempts to build a desire for ownership within the customer.

Sales promotion Any sales activity that supplements or coordinates advertising and personal selling.

Sales prospects Potential customers for a product or service.

Sales research The study of sales data.

Scrambled merchandising The stocking and selling of untraditional lines of goods by a store.

Secondary data Data that have already been collected by someone else for another purpose but which may be of use for the task at hand.

Selective distribution The form of distribution in which a manufacturer carefully chooses a number of middlemen to market his product within a geographic area.

Selling agent An independent specialist who sells the entire output of a line of goods for one or more manufacturers.

Service contract An agreement between the buyer and seller in which the buyer agrees to pay a specified sum to have the seller furnish parts and service for a product for a certain period.

Service wholesaler The merchant wholesaler who performs all wholesaling functions for his customers; also called a "regular wholesaler."

Services Benefits or satisfactions offered for sale, or provided in connection with the sale of goods.

Shoplifting The theft of merchandise from a store.

Shopping goods Items that the customer usually compares with other similar items before deciding to buy.

Shrink pack A package made by placing clear film around the product itself.

Skin packaging The form of packaging in which plastic film is molded over a product mounted on a card.

Social competency The ability of a person to create a favorable impression and to work well with others.

Sole proprietorship A business owned by one person.

Special events Activities sponsored by a business in order to build good community relations.

Specialty advertising Advertising that consists of providing a useful item to a potential customer and placing an advertising message on it.

Specialty goods Definite brands of products that the customer will go out of his way to obtain.

Specialty salesmen Individuals who sell a particular product or line of products to the customer in his home or place of business.

Specialty shop An apparel and accessory store that sells only women's wear.

Sponsor The company that pays for the advertising.

Standards Measurements of the quality of manufactured goods and natural and agricultural goods.

State employment service An employment agency operated without charge to job applicants and supported by the state's taxpayers.

Stock turnover The frequency with which merchandise, or stock, is sold and replaced by new merchandise.

Stockkeeping The job of keeping goods on the shelves in the right quantity and variety.

Store layout The interior arrangement of a store for both selling and nonselling activities.

Studies in Marketing Individual research activities for DECA members.

Suggestion selling The selling of related items along with items the customer has already purchased.

Supermarket A large, departmentized self-service food store.

Supply The amount of a product that a supplier decides to sell at a specified price.

Survey A method of collecting opinions by questioning a limited number of people chosen from a larger group.

Target return A method of pricing that involves setting prices according to the rate of profit that a company wants to earn from its sales.

Tariff The tax that an international marketer pays to a foreign country for the privilege of selling his product there.

Technological competency The specialized knowledge and information about the marketing of the particular product or service with which a person deals.

Test marketing The marketing of goods to consumers in several carefully selected areas before the goods are released on a wide scale.

Time utility The increased usefulness a marketer gives to a product by making it available to the customer when the customer wants it.

Trade mission A group of businessmen who volunteer to go abroad to promote the foreign commerce of the United States.

Trademark That part of a brand that has been legally registered with the U.S. Patent Office.

Transportation advertising Advertising that is used in buses, subways, and taxis, and in railroad, bus, and airline terminals.

Twig A limited-line store that is owned by a department store.

Unsecured loan A bank loan in which the borrower's reputation is the determining factor in granting a loan; that is, no security in the form of buildings or other assets is required.

Utility Usefulness to consumers. The production processes add one utility to products: *form utility*. The marketing processes add three other utilities: *time utility, place utility,* and *possession utility*.

Vertical expansion The process by which a retailer branches out into other kinds of businesses, such as wholesaling or manufacturing.

Visual merchandising The display of a product at or near the point of purchase.

Voluntary chain A group of independently owned stores that share some or all of their buying.

Warehouse A storage and handling facility.

Warehouse receipt A statement given by the warehouse management indicating the value of the goods placed in the warehouse for storage.

Warehousing The process of handling and storing goods in one place.

Wholesale salesmen Individuals who sell the products of a manufacturer to retailers, business firms, and organizations.

Wholesaler A person or firm that buys merchandise from the manufacturer and sells it either to retailers for subsequent resale to the consumer or to business firms for industrial or business use.

Working capital Capital needed to finance current operations; sometimes called "short-term capital."

Index

A

Accounts (*see* Credit; Consumer credit)
Accounts payable, 496-497
Accounts receivable, 473, 496
Accounts receivable turnover, 476-477
Adjustments and returns, 451-452
Advertisements, classified and display, 366
Advertisers, types of, 354-358
Advertising, 352-362
    business-directed, 356
    costs, 361-362
    direct mail, 370-371
    by directories, 374-375
    farm, 358
    institutional, 353, 354
    outdoor, 371-372
    point-of-purchase (POP), 384-385
    product, 353-354
    professional, 356
    program, 374-375
    in promotion campaigns, 428-429
    radio, 368
    specialty, 374
    television, 368-369
    trade, 356, 429
    transportation, 373-374
Advertising agencies, 359-360
Advertising departments, 358-359
Advertising media, 365-375
    defined, 343
    selecting, 360-362
Advertising and promotion services to industry, 156
Age groups, market segmentation by, 51, 62-67

Agent middlemen, 166-167
Agent wholesaler, 212-214
Agriculture, U.S. Department of, 281
American Marketing Association (AMA), 149, 237, 519, 537
American National Standards Institute, 280
Apparel and accessory stores, 183-184
Approach, sales, 412
Assets, 496
    current, 477
    defined, 469
    fixed, 469
Automatic vending, 190-191
Automotive dealers, 185

B

Balance sheet, 495-497
Balance of trade, defined, 137
Bank credit cards, 444
Basic skills competency, 534
Behavior patterns, customer, 79-82
Benefits and pay, employee, 530-532
Blind ads, 519
Blister packaging, 303
Bonded warehouses, 334
Bonding, 487
Bonds, defined, 472
Brand mark, defined, 285
Brand-name products, 286
Brand names
    characteristics of, 291-292
    defined, 285
    family brands, 289
    fighting brand, 291
    middleman's (private), 286-287
    national, 286
    reasons for using, 287-289

Brand names (*continued*)
    strategies in using, 289–291
    types of, 285–287
Break-even point, 309
Brokers, 212–213
Budget (90-day) accounts, 443
Budgets
    defined, 497
    expense, 498–499
    marketing business, 475–476
    operating expenses, 499
    sales, 497–498
    typical, 56 (*table*)
Bulk breaking, 208–209
Business-directed advertising, 356
Business-interruption insurance, 484–485
Business ownership, forms of, 31–34
Business risks, 482–483
Buyers, 88–89
    defined, 16
    industrial (*see* Industrial buyer)
Buying, 16–17
    customer motives in (*see* Customer buying motives)
    impulse, 86–87
    industrial, 115–117
    by wholesaler, 207
Buying decision, 92–93

C

Capital, 27, 497
    defined, 469
    efficient use of, 476–477
    estimating needs, 475–476
    long-term, 469
    sources of, 471–474
    venture, 471
    working (short-term), 470
Carload lots (CL), 323
Carriers, 321
Cash discount, defined, 445
Catalog retailing, 186–188
Census, U.S. Bureau of the, 252
Chains, types of, 173–175

Chamber of Commerce, U.S., 138
Channels of distribution, 162–167
    for consumer goods, 218–219
    defined, 163
    direct, 164–166
    exclusive, 227
    indirect, 166–167
    for industrial goods, 219–221
    integrated, 228–229
    intensive, 226–227
    length of, 211–225
    middleman, 224–225
    selective, 228
    width of, 225–229
Classified advertisements, 366
Clayton Act, 311
Close, sales, 416
Collateral, 473
Collective bargaining, 535–536
Commerce, U.S. Department of, 253, 306
Commodity exchange (central market) for farm products, 127
Common carriers, 321
Common Market (European Economic Community; EEC), 142
Community relations, 394–395
Competency, on the job, 534–535
Competition
    in modified free-enterprise, 30
    and pricing, 310–311, 315–316
    and product planning, 273
Computers, 202 (*see also* Data processing)
Consulting firms, 252
Consulting services, 105, 454–455
Consumer advisory boards, 392
Consumer credit, 440–444
    bank credit cards, 444
    credit-card companies, 443
    information about consumers, 441

555

Consumer credit (*continued*)
    types of accounts (credit plans), 441–443
Consumer farm products, 122
Consumer goods, 48
    channels of distribution for, 218–219
    types of, 93–94
Consumer market (*see also* Income; Population)
    defined, 48–49
    expenditure patterns, 55–58
    product planning and, 273
Consumers' Research, 280
Consumers Union, 280
Consumption, defined, 26–27
Containerization, 336
Contests, 379
Contract carriers, 321
Controlled (planned) economy, 27
Convenience, customer buying patterns and, 87–88
Convenience goods, 93
Cooperatives, 33–34
    consumers', 34
    farm, 131–132
Copywriters, 358
Corporate chains, 173–174
Corporations, 33
Cost of goods sold, 494–495
Cost-profit squeeze, 195–196
Costs
    advertising, 361–362
    of marketing, 41–42
    pricing and, 309
Coupons, 378
Credit, 17–18, 438
    advantages and disadvantages of, 439–440
    collecting accounts, 445–446
    consumer (*see* Consumer credit)
    convenience and, 88
    as customer service, 438–446

Credit (*continued*)
    extended by wholesalers, 209
    in financing marketing business, 470–471
    mercantile, 444–445
    users of, 439
Credit bureaus, 441
Credit-card companies, 443
Credit cards, 440
    bank, 444
Credit insurance, 485
Credit period, defined, 445
Credit plans, types of, 441–443
Creditors, business, 472
Crops, 123–125
Current assets, 477
Current liabilities, 477
Customer buying behavior, 72–82
    behavior patterns, 79–82
    cues, 77–78
    defined, 73
    people and surroundings and, 78–79
    stimulus and response in, 73–74, 76
Customer buying motives, 75–77
    customer awareness of, 79–80
    defined, 73
    industrial buyer, 112–115
    motivation groups, 81–82
    patronage motives, 76–77, 89–90
    physical and psychological motives, 75
    product motives, 76–77
    rational and emotional motives, 75–76
Customer buying patterns, 85–94 (*see also* Consumer goods)
    buyers, 88–89
    buying decision, 92–93
    choice of store, 89–90
    convenience and, 87–88
    impulse buying, 86–87

Customer buying patterns (*continued*)
   placing value on time, 87
   timing and, 91–92
Customer consultants, 392
Customer relations, 392–393
Customer services, 449–455 (*see also* Credit; Guarantees)
   adjustments and returns, 451–452
   consultation, 105
   defined, 438
   delivery, 452–453
   installation and repair, 453–454
   in marketing industrial goods, 114–115
Cycle billing, 441

D

Data, marketing research, 245–256
   analyzing, 254
   classification of, 253–254
   collecting, 245–253
   defined, 245
   external, 246
   internal, 246
   preparing, 253–254
   primary, 246–250
   secondary, 250–253
Data processing, 503–512
Dealerships, leased, 175
DECA (Distributive Education Clubs of America), 261–264
Demand, defined, 312 (*see also* Supply, and demand)
Department stores, 180–181
Derived demand, 112
Direct mail advertising, 370–371
Direct selling, 162 (*see also* Channels of distribution)
   door to door, 166
   in international marketing, 144–145

Direct selling (*continued*)
   through the mail, 166
   at point of production, 164–165
   at producer's retail store, 165–166
Directories, advertising in, 374–375
Discount department stores, 181–182
Discount stores, 199–200
Discretionary income, 52
Displays, types of, 383
Disposable income, 52
Distribution (*see also* Channels of distribution)
   defined, 6
Distribution centers, 335 (*see also* Warehouses)
Distributors
   industrial buying from, 117
   as middlemen, 145
Domestic goods, defined, 142
Drop shipper, 211–212

E

Ecology, defined, 24
Economic competency, 534–535
Economic (market) risks, 482, 487
Economic security, 530
Economic system (economy)
   defined, 27–29
   planned (controlled), 27
Emotional and rational buying motives, 75–76
Employee benefits, 530–532
Employee discounts, 532
Employee relations, 395
Employment agencies, 519
European Economic Community (EEC), 142
European Free Trade Association (EFTA), 143
Exchange activities, 39

Exhibits, sales promotion, 380
Expenditure patterns, 55-58
Expense budget, 498-499
Export-Import Bank (Eximbank) of the United States, 138
Exporters, 138-139, 145
Exports, U.S., 136, 138 (*table*)

F

Fabricating materials, 103
Facilitating activities, 40
Factors, defined, 472
Factory packs, 379
Fair Packaging and Labeling Act, 306
Fair-trade laws, 311
Family brands, 289
Farm advertising, 358
Farm bloc, 129
Farm cooperatives, 131-132
Farm products
    central market (commodity exchange), 127
    classification of, 123-125
    consumer, 122
    crops (soil products), 123-125
    grading, 126, 128
    industrial, 122-123
    livestock, 123, 125
    local markets, 126
    marketing, 122-133
    marketing services for, 127-128
        grading, 128
        storage, 127-128
        transportation, 127
    prices of, 128-129
    supply and demand, 128-129
Farmers, government programs for, 129-131
Fashion
    pricing and, 310
    product life cycle and, 277-278
Federal Power Commission, 253
Federal Trade Commission, 281, 306

Fighting brand, 291
Financial planning, 497-499 (*see also* Budgets; Financial statements)
Financial statements, 492-497
    balance sheet, 495-497
    income statement (operating or profit and loss statement), 492-495
Financing
    business (*see* Marketing business)
    defined, 470
Fishyback railroad service, 323
Flexible pouch, 303
Food and Drug Administration, U.S., 281
Food stores, 185-186
Foreign markets (*see* International marketing)
Form utility, 36
Franchise chains, 175
Free enterprise, defined, 27
Free-enterprise system, modified (*see* Modified free-enterprise system)
Freight forwarders, 328
Fringe benefits, 530

G

General Agreement on Tariffs and Trade (GATT), 142
General-merchandise stores, 180-182
General-merchandise warehouse, 333
General stores, 182
Geographical location of consumer market, 67-68
Goods
    consumer (*see* Consumer goods)
    domestic, 142
    impulse, 86
    industrial (*see* Industrial goods)

Government
    assistance to farmers, 129–131
    price regulation by, 311
    standards set by, 280–281
Grade label, 298
Grades
    defined, 279–280
    and standards, 279–281
Gross national product (GNP), 24
Gross profit on sales, 495
Guarantees, 449–451
    defined, 449
    price, 451
    quality and performance, 450–451

H

Health, Education, and Welfare, U.S. Department of, 306
Home-furnishings stores, 184

I

Importers, 145
Imports, U.S., 136, 139 (*table*)
Impulse buying, 86–87
    motivation for, 82
Impulse goods, 86
Income, 52–54
    available, 52–54
    discretionary, 52
    disposable, 52
    expenditure patterns and, 55–56
    geographical location of, 54
    national, 52
    net, 495
    personal, 52
    population distribution and, 54
Income statement, 492–495
Independent stores, 172–173
Industrial buyer, 111
    buying motives of, 112–115
    supplier reputation and, 113–114
Industrial buying, 115–117
Industrial distributors, 210–211
Industrial farm products, 122–123
Industrial goods, 102–104
    accessory equipment, 104
    buying motives, 112–115
    channels of distribution for, 219–221
    customer service, 114–115
    defined, 100
    derived demand, 112
    installations, 104
    marketing, 109–119
    materials, 103
    operating supplies, 104
    price, 115
    promoting and selling, 109–112
    quality, 112–113
Industrial market, 101–102
    defined, 100
    size of, 110
Industrial Revolution, 26, 171
Industrial salesmen, 110
Industrial selling, 15
Industrial services, 105–106, 156–157
    consulting, 105
    defined, 100
    maintenance, 105, 106
    protection, 105, 106
In-store salesmen, 12–13
Installation and repair services, 453–454
Installations as industrial goods, 104
Installment accounts, 442–443
Institutional advertising, 353, 354
Insurance, 155–156
    bonding, 487
    cost of, 485–486
    defined, 155–156
    marketing jobs in, 19
    reducing risks through, 483–486
    types of, 483–485
    workmen's compensation, 486
Integrated distribution, 228–229

Intensive distribution, 226–227
International market, 136–139
    analyzing, 139–141
    differences in buying habits,
        140–141
    differences in customs and
        traditions, 140
International marketing, 135–147
    defined, 135
    joint ventures, 147
    licensing, 147
    middlemen in, 145–146
    problems in, 142–144
        communications, 144
        risks, 144
        shipping, 143
        tariffs, 142–143
    selling and distributing,
        144–147
    wholly owned subsidiaries,
        146–147
Interviews
    job, 521–526
    personal, 248
    telephone, 248
Inventory, merchandise, 494
Investors, 472

J

Job (see also Marketing jobs;
    Selling jobs)
    competency on the, 534–535
    pay and benefits, 530–532
    responsibilities, 532–533
    working at, 529–539
Job application, 525
Joint ventures, 147

L

Labeling
    laws on, 305–306
    and packaging, 297–307
Labels
    brand, 298
    descriptive, 298
    grade, 298

Labor Statistics, U.S. Bureau of,
    252–253
Less-than-carload lots (LCL), 323
Less-than-truckload lots (LTL), 324
Liabilities, 496–497
    current, 477
Limited-function wholesalers,
    210–212
Limited-line stores, 183–186
    defined, 183
    types of, 183–186
Livestock products, 123, 125
    sales of, 125 (table)
Loan companies as source of
    capital, 473
Local (retail) advertiser, 354, 356

M

Magazine advertising, 367–368
Mail
    advertising by, 370–371
    direct selling through, 166
Mail-order houses, 187
Mail questionnaires, 248
Mailing lists, 371
Manufacturers
    industrial buying from,
        115–116
    selling for, 402–403
Manufacturers' agents, 214
Manufacturer's brand, 286
Manufacturers' salesmen, 402–403
Market
    central (commodity exchange),
        for farm products, 127
    consumer (see Consumer
        market)
    defined, 48
    industrial (see Industrial
        market)
    international (see International
        market)
Market position, 314
Market segmentation, 60–69
    defined, 61

Market segmentation (*continued*)
    education, 67
    ethnic group, 68–69
    geographical location, 67–68
    limitations of, 69
Marketing
    activities of 39–40
    benefits of, 36–45
    cost of, 41–42
    defined, 6
    economic climate of, 23–25
    organization for, 460–466
    test, 249
    value added by, 42–43
Marketing business, financing, 469–477
Marketing competency, 534
Marketing concept, defined, 26
Marketing jobs, 10–22, 516–526
    applying for, 520–526
    in retail promotion, 15–16
    in retail stores, 16–18
    in selling (*see* Selling jobs)
    in service enterprises, 18–20
    sources of, 518–520
Marketing management, responsibility of, 466
Marketing manager, 464–465
Marketing plan, 461–463
Marketing research, 236–243 (*see also* Data, marketing research; Research report)
    advertising research, 240
    bias, 254
    kinds of, 237–240
    market research, 238
    problem-solving process, 241–243
    product research, 239
    in promotion campaigns, 427–428
    research plan, 242–243
    sales research, 239
Marketing risks (*see* Risks)

Marketing services for farm products (*see* Farm products, marketing services for)
Marketing staff, 464–466
Marketing techniques
    of farm cooperatives, 131–132
    for farm products, 125–127
Marshall Plan, 136
Mass production, 26
Materials handling, 335
Media research in promotion campaigns, 427–428
Mercantile credit, 444–445
Merchandise displays, 383
Merchandise inventory, 494
Merchandise manual, 405
Merchandising
    pipe-rack, 200
    scrambled, 201
    self-service, 199–200
    visual (*see* Visual merchandising)
Merchant middlemen, 167
Merchant wholesaler, 210–212
Middlemen, 126, 162 (*see also* Channels of distribution)
    agent, 166–167
    distributors, 145
    exporters and importers as, 145
    in international marketing, 145–146
    manufacturers' agents, 145–146
    merchant, 167
Modified free-enterprise system, 29–31
    defined, 27
Monopoly, defined, 311
Motives, buying (*see* Customer buying motives)
Multipack packaging, 303

N

National advertisers, 354
National brands, 286

National income, 52
Natural resources, U.S., 24–25
Net income, 495
Net worth, 497
Newspaper advertising, 365–366, 519
90-day (budget) accounts, 443
Nonstore retailing, 187–188
Notes payable, 497

O

Obsolescence, 481
Operating expenses, 495
Operating ratio, 492–493
Operating (income) statement, 492–495
Operating supplies, 104
Outdoor advertising, 371–372
Owner's equity, 497

P

Packaging
    defined, 297–298
    design of, 300, 304–305
    forms, 302–304
    functions of, 298–300
    labeling and, 297–306
    laws on, 305–306
    materials for, 301–302
    producers of, 300–301
Panels, marketing research, 248–249
Partnerships, 32–33
Party-plan selling, 189, 190
Patronage motives, 76–77, 89–90
Pay and benefits, employee, 530–532
Payroll savings plans, 531–532
Peoples Involvement Corporation (PIC), 26
Performance and quality guarantees, 450–451
Personal care services, 153–154
Personal data sheet (résumé), 523–524
Personal income, 52

Personal selling, 399–406 (*see also* Salesmen; Selling jobs)
    defined, 344, 399
    qualities of salesmen, 404–406
Physical distribution activities, 40 (*see also* Transportation; Warehousing)
Physical and psychological buying motives, 75
Place utility, 37
Planned (controlled) economy, defined, 27
Point-of-purchase (POP) advertising, 384–385
Population (U.S.), 49–52
    age groups, consumer, 51, 62–67
    diversified, 25–26
    farm, 123
    geographic distribution, 51–52
    households, 50–51
Possession utility, 38
Posttesting, defined, 428
Preapproach in selling, 410–412
Premiums, 377–379
Pretesting, defined, 428
Price, 308
    in marketing industrial goods, 115
Price guarantees, 451
Pricing, 308–316
    break-even point, 309
    causes of changes, 311–313
    competition and, 310–311, 315–316
    costs of expenses and, 309
    fashion and seasonal appeal and, 310
    goals of, 313–316
    government regulations on, 311
    market position and, 314
    supply and demand and, 312–313
    target return and, 314–315

Primary data, 246–250
Private (middleman's) brand, 286–287
Private carriers, 321
Producers' brands, 286
Product (*see also* Packaging; Utility)
    convenience in, 87
    defined, 271
    developing, 273–276
    nature of, in selecting channels of distribution, 222–223
Product life cycle, 277–278
Product line, defined, 271
Product mix, defined, 271
Product and patronage buying motives, 76–77
Product planning, 270–281
    competition and, 273
    defined, 270
    objectives, 271–273
    production capabilities and, 273
Product research, 239
Production, defined, 24
Production rate, U.S., 24–26
    diversified population and, 25–26
    national resources and, 24–25
    technical expertise and, 26
Productive resources, 27
Professional advertising, 356
Profit and loss (income) statement, 492–495
Promotion, 342
    elements of, 343–344
Promotion campaign, 423–431 (*see also* Sales promotion)
    advertising, 428–429
    dealer aids in, 430
    market and media research in, 427–428
    publicity and special promotions, 430

Promotional mix, 344–345
    case history, 345–349
Prospecting in selling, 409–410
Psychological and physical buying motives, 75
Public relations, 391–395, 396
    defined, 344, 391
Public utilities, defined, 155
Publicity, 388–391, 396
    defined, 344, 388
    in promotion campaigns, 430
Purchasing agents, defined, 16

Q

Quality and performance guarantees, 450–451
Questionnaires, mail, 248

R

Rack jobber, 211
Radio advertising, 368
Railroad transportation (*see* Transportation, railroad)
Rational and emotional buying motives, 75–76
Raw materials, 103
Receiving departments, 17
Rentals and service sales by retailers, 201–202
Repair and installation services, 453–454
Research (*see* Marketing research; Student research)
Research plan, 242–243
Research report
    elements in, 258
    oral presentation, 259–260
    research findings, 258
    written, 257–258
Resources, 27
Response
    defined, 77
    and stimulus in customer buying behavior, 73–74, 76
Résumé (personal data sheet), 523–524

Retail selling, 12–14, 417–419
Retail stores, 170
    chains, 173–175
    department stores, 180–181
    discount, 199–200
    exterior and interior of, 381–383
    general, 182
    general-merchandise, 180–182
    independent, 172–173
    layout of, 88–89
    leased dealerships, 175
    limited-line stores (*see* Limited-line stores)
    manufacturer-owned, 176
    marketing jobs in, 16–18
    ownership of, 172–176
    producer's, direct selling at, 165–166
    variety stores, 182
Retailers
    opportunities for, 198–203
    problems for, 195–198
    services offered by, 152–153
Retailing, 170–176 (*see also* Selling)
    development of, 171
    importance of, 170–171
    nonstore, 186–191
        automatic vending, 190–191
        through catalogs, 186–188
        by department stores, 187–188
        direct-to-consumer, 188–189
        mail-order houses, 187
        telephone-order, 188
Returns and adjustments, 451–452
Revolving accounts, 443
Risks (*see also* Insurance)
    business, 482–483
    economic (market), 482, 487
    human, 483, 487
    in international marketing, 144
    in modified free-enterprise system, 31
    natural, 482, 487

Robinson-Patman Act, 311
Route salesmen, 13
Route-selling, 190

S

Sales and Marketing Executives International (SMEI), 262, 519, 537
Sales presentation, 413–415
Sales promotion, 343–344, 377–385
    (*see also* Visual merchandising)
    combination offers, 380–381
    contests and sweepstakes, 379
    exhibits, 380
    price-oriented, 380–381
    product samples and container promotion, 380
    special price reduction, 380–381
Sales research, 239
Salesmen, 400–402, 404–405
    industrial, 110
    in-store, 12–13
    manufacturers', 402–403
    route, 13
    service, 15
    specialty, 13
Scrambled merchandising, 201
Secondary data, 250–253
Selective distribution, 228
Self-service merchandising, 199–200
Selling
    approach, 412
    close, 416
    departure and follow-up, 416–417
    direct (*see* Direct selling)
    and distributing in international marketing, 144–147
    handling objections, 415
    industrial, 15
    on-the-street, 189
    party-plan, 189, 190
    personal (*see* Personal selling)

Selling (continued)
    preapproach, 410–412
    and promoting of industrial
        goods, 109–112
    prospecting, 409–410
    retail, 12–14, 417–419
    sales presentation, 413–415
    suggestion, 418–419
    telephone in, 419
    wholesale, 14, 206–216
Selling jobs, 12–15
    for manufacturers, 402–403
    for retailers, 404
    for wholesalers, 403–404
Service contract, 453–454
Service salesmen, 15
Service wholesaler, 210–211
Services
    automotive, 154
    classification of, 153–157
    communication, 155
    to consumers, 153–156
    customer (see Customer
        services)
    defined, 149
    entertainment, 154–155
    food, 153
    growth of, 151–153
    industrial (see Industrial
        services)
    insurance (see Insurance)
    lodging, 155
    marketing as, 4–5
    personal care, 153–154
    transportation, 155
Sherman Antitrust Act, 311
Shipping, 325
Shoplifting, 196–197
Shopping centers, 198
Shopping goods, 93–94
Shrink pack, 303
Skin packaging, 302
Small Business Administration,
    138, 474

Social competency, 534
Sole proprietorship, 32
Specialty goods, 94
Specialty salesmen, 13
Specialty shops, 183
Standard of living, defined, 24
Standards
    defined, 279
    and grades, 279–281
Stock turnover, 476
Stockholder relations, 395
Stockholders, 33
Stockkeeping, 17
Stores (see Retail stores)
Student research, 260–264
    Creative Marketing Projects,
        262–263
    Studies in Marketing, 264
Subsidiaries, wholly owned,
    146–147
Suggestion selling, 418–419
Supermarkets, 185
Supply
    defined, 312
    and demand, 312–313
        of farm products, 128–129
Surveys, marketing research,
    247–248

T

Tariffs, 142-143
Technological competency, 534
Telephone-order retailing, 188
Television advertising, 368–369
Test marketing, 249
30-day (regular) accounts, 441–442
Time utility, 36
Trade, balance of, 137
Trade advertising, 356, 429
Trade mission, defined, 137
Trade restrictions, U.S., 137
Trademarks
    and brand names, 284–294
    defined, 285–286
    registration of, 293–294

565

Trading stamps, 378
Training, employee, 532
Transportation, 155
    air, 326–327
    carriers, 321
    of farm products, 127
    freight forwarders, 328
    motor (trucks), 323–324
    parcel post, 327–328
    pipeline, 326
    railroad, 321–323
        carload lots (CL) and less-than-carload lots (LCL), 323
        fishyback, 323
        piggyback (TOFC), 322–323
    Railway Express Agency (REA), 327
    water, 325
Transportation advertising, 373–374
Twig (limited-line store), 184

U

Unions, 535–537
Unit value, 223n.
Utility
    defined, 36
    form, 36
    place, 37
    possession, 38
    time, 36

V

Value-added approach to marketing, 42–43
Variety stores, 182
Visual merchandising, 344, 381–385
Voluntary chains, 174–175

W

Warehouse receipts, 333
Warehouses
    materials handling, 335
    operations within, 334–338
    purposes of, 331–333
    types of, 333–334
Warehousing, 331–339
    defined, 208
    by wholesalers, 208
Wholesalers
    agent, 212–214
    brokers, 212–213
    cash-and-carry, 211–212
    defined, 206
    drop shipper, 211–212
    functions of, 207–210
        bulk breaking, 208–209
        buying, 207
        credit, 209
        market information, 209–210
        promotional assistance, 209
        selling, 207
        transporting, 209
        warehousing, 208
    industrial distributors, 210–211
    limited-function, 210–212
    manufacturers' agents, 214
    merchant, 210–212
    rack jobber, 211
    selling for, 403–404
    selling agents, 214
    service, 210–211
    truck jobber, 211–212
Wholesaling, 14, 206–214
Wholly owned subsidiaries, 146–147
Work permits, 523
Working capital ratio, 477
Workmen's compensation, 486

5726